BEYOND EQUILIBRIUM THEORY

Theories of Social Action and Social Change Applied to a Study of Power Sharing in Transition

M. Ross DeWitt

University Press of America, ® Inc.
Lanham • New York • Oxford

Copyright © 2000 by
4720 Boston Way
Lanham, Maryland 20706

12 Hid's Copse Rd.
Cumnor Hill, Oxford OX2 9JJ

All rights reserved
Printed in the United States of America
British Library Cataloging in Publication Information Available

Library of Congress Cataloging-in-Publication Data

DeWitt, M. Ross
Beyond equilibrium theory : theories of social action and social change applied to a study of power sharing in transition / M. Ross DeWitt.
p. cm.
Includes index.
1. Power (Social sciences) 2. Human behavior. 3. Social change.
4. Rural families—Wisconsin. I. Title.
HM1256.D48 2000 303.3—dc21 00-032526 CIP

ISBN 0-7618-1738-7 (cloth: alk. ppr.)
ISBN 0-7618-1739-5 (pbk: alk. ppr.)

∞™ The paper used in this publication meets the minimum
requirements of American National Standard for Information
Sciences—Permanence of Paper for Printed Library Materials,
ANSI Z39.48—1984

DEDICATION

To Professor Burton R. Fisher, a person of flawless intellectual integrity, who inspired students to stretch their minds and abilities to capacity, in confidence that what they attempted could be achieved, and with conviction that what they achieved could be worthwhile.

Contents

List of Figures xi

List of Tables xiii

List of Abbreviations xv

Foreword xvii

Preface xix

Acknowledgments xxi

Part One: Theories of Social Action and Social Change

Chapter 1	CREATING A RESEARCH-FRIENDLY THEORETICAL FRAMEWORK	3
	Preview of the Model	4
	Review of Similar Approaches	6
	The Social Context of Action	8
	Understanding the Dynamics of Social Order; Predicting Directions of Social Change . .	10
	Problem-solving as the Impetus for Goal Formation	10
	Rejecting the Normative Assumption in Social Theory Development	11

        Designing a New Approach
           A Dialectical Perspective of Change   12
           The Requirements of Theory   14
           Techniques of Theory Construction   15
           Cognitive Dissonance and Balance Theories .   15
           The Relevance of Subjective Theory to
               Sociological Theory   17
        Concluding Remarks   17

Chapter 2   SUBJECTIVE THEORIES OF SOCIAL ACTION AND SOCIAL CHANGE
        A Cognitive Contingency Theory of Social Action
           Constructing a Theoretical Framework   19
           Basic Premises   22
           The Cognitive Orientation of Social Action .   24
           Cognitive Orientations Within the Context of
               Social Experience   26
        A Cognitive Inconsistency Theory of Social Change
           Cognitive Progressions: Some Further
               Considerations   29
           Cognitive Sequence Interruption and
               Reorientation   30
           Processes of Cognitive Reorientation   31
           Incomplete Reorientation and System Change   34
           Transformation Through Phases of System
               Reorientation   36
        Summary   40

Chapter 3   SUBJECTIVE THEORIES AND SOCIAL RESEARCH
        Falsifying the Theories; Empirical Tests
           Testing the Theory of Social Action   43
           Testing the Theory of Social Change   46
        Implications for Research
           Subjective Theory as a General Framework
               for Analyzing Action Systems   49
           Subjective Theory, Social Context, and the
               Analysis of Social Movements   50

Chapter 4	SUGGESTED RESEARCH APPLICATIONS	
	The Theory of Social Action and Ideal Types	
	Subjective Cognition, Social Context, and Constructed Typology	53
	The Theories of Social Action and Social Change Applied to an Analysis of Deviance	
	Acute and Chronic Tension States and Resulting Modes of Alienation	54
	The Theory of Social Action as a Framework for the Analysis of Production Systems	
	Class Analysis and the Formation of Class Consciousness; Implications for System Change	55

Notes for Part One	67
General Glossary	77
Glossary of Special Terms	83
Index for Part One	87

Part Two: **Theories Applied to a Study of Power Sharing in Transition**

Chapter 5	SOCIAL ORDER, SOCIAL CHANGE, AND POWER SHARING IN U.S. FARM FAMILIES	
	General Considerations	93
	Debates on the nature of society and on the nature of the social	95
	Debate on the nature of links between different aspects of society	96
	Debate on the nature of changes in society (the dynamic nature of social relations) . .	97
	Relevance for U.S. Farm Families	99
	Key Concepts	104
	Purpose of the Study	107

	Theory of Power Sharing	
	Rationale for a Theory of Power Sharing . .	107
	Theory of Gender Power Sharing in Transition	108
	Theories of Social Action and Social Change	109
	Goal of the Study	112
	Focus of the Study	113
	Statement of the Problem	116
Chapter 6	REVIEW OF THE LITERATURE	
	Innovation and Agriculture	119
	Power Sharing	
	Power Sharing in Gender Relations	123
	Husband-Wife Power Sharing	124
	Power Sharing in Farm Families	124
	Theoretical Support for an Interactive Analysis of Social Structure and Social Process . . .	125
Chapter 7	RESEARCH DESIGN	
	Preview of the Study	129
	Selection of the Sample	130
	Profile of Wisconsin Farms	132
	Profile of Wisconsin Farm Couples	132
	Latent Causal Chain and Selection of Variables	135
	Measurement of the Study Variables	136
	Deriving Hypotheses of Higher-Order Interactive Effects	140
Chapter 8	BACKGROUND ANALYSIS	
	Introduction	143
	Farm Development and the Family Life Cycle	144
	The Wife's Farm Roles	146
	Progress, Productivity, and Farm Continuity .	147
	Progress, Productivity and Husband-Wife Decision-Sharing	149

		Direct Effects of Contextual Variables on Recent Adoption	149
Chapter 9		METHOD OF ANALYSIS	
		Introduction to the Method	151
		The Model of Interactive Effects	152
		Application of the Model of Interactive Effects	154
		Introduction to the Model of Multiple Effects	157
		A Logic of Causal Analysis of Social Change	160
		Summary of the Logic of Causal Analysis of Social Change	163
		Rationale for a Logic of Multiple Causal Analysis of Social Change	163
		The Model of Multiple Effects	166
		A Logic of Multiple Causal Analysis of Social Change	171
		Dimensions of Power as Initiators of Social Change; Implications of 'Power-Shift' for Social Transformation	176
		Criteria for Using Multiple Models of Interactive Effect	180
		A Logic of Causal Analysis of Social and Personal Change	180
		Building a Predictive Model	181
		Applying the Predictive Model to the Analysis	184
		Falsifying the Models of Interactive and Multiple Effects	189
Chapter 10		DESIGN OF THE ANALYSIS	
		Preview of the Analysis	191
		Criteria for Variable Selection	193
		Selection and Use of Statistical Tests and Techniques	193
		Formulas for Predicting Higher-Order Interactive Effects	195
		Fitting the Analysis to the Theories	201
		Hypotheses for Predicting Two Patterns of Wife Influence	203

Chapter 11   TESTS OF HYPOTHESES
Introduction 209
Findings..................... 210
    Direct effects, two-way interactions, and
      alternative explanations of findings 212
    Three-way Interactions 216
Discussion of the Findings........... 216
Interpretation of the Findings 219

Chapter 12   SUMMARY AND CONCLUSIONS
Summary..................... 223
Conclusions 225
Suggestions for Future Research 226

Appendix A. **Survey of Wisconsin Farm Families** 229

Appendix B. **Graphs and Path Diagrams** 237

Appendix C. **Reference Tables** 251

Notes for Part Two...................... 257

Bibliography 267

Index of Authors 335

Index of Topics 339

About the Author...................... 345

List of Figures

Figure A	The progression of cognitive interpretation of social experience (an example)	05
Figure B	Cognitive differentiation and mediation of social experience (an illustration)	06
Figure C	A cognitive progression, as affected by the controls, conditions, and constraints of its context of social experience	21
Figure D	An illustration of the cognitive contingency progression model, contrasting folk and normless societies	56
Figure E	Application of the theories to an analysis of deviance: tension states, states of action directives, modes of alienation, and target groups	63
Figure F-1	Application of the theories to interpretations of social experience in production systems: opportunity, satisfaction, and allegiance relative to equity, ownership, and efficacy	64

Figure F-2	Cultural interpretation/reinterpretation of social experience in production systems: potential for generating new insights, system changes, and system transformations	65
Figure G	Structured propensity for social change, as basis for type of goal-directed social action, by mode of resolving disparities to achieve, maintain or restore social order	98
Figure H	Points of entry into response sequences of six phases of structural disintegration, transformation, and reintegration	170
Figure I-1	Profile of expected high recent adopters among Traditional farm couples	174
Figure I-2	Profile of expected high recent adopters among Nontraditional farm couples	175
Figure J	Power-shifts associated with each structural change phase	177
Figure K-1	Hypotheses for predicting pattern of wife influence on recent adoption for Traditional couples	206
Figure K-2	Hypotheses for predicting pattern of wife influence on recent adoption for Nontraditional couples	207

List of Tables

TABLE 1	Characteristics of 616 Wisconsin farm families, 1977	133
TABLE 2	Characteristics of 176 Wisconsin farm couples, 1979	134
TABLE 3a	Family context for new adoption I: The wife's farm roles, role changes, and role context, and the husband's farm role context	145
TABLE 3b	Family context for new adoption II: Past farm progress, present roles and role contexts of husband and wife, and future farm plan	148
TABLE 4	Analysis of wife influence on recent farm practice adoption, 1974-1979 (ANOVA)	211
TABLE 5	Tests of hypotheses of predicted highest average recent adoption of farm practices, within family type, by phase of family transition, by contextual variables, by dimensions of the wife's farm role	217

List of Abreviations

The following abbreviations are used in the Notes and Bibliograpy:

Admn.	Administrative
AES	Agricultural Experiment Station
Ag.	Agricultural
Ag. Econ.	Agricultural Economics
Ag. Ext.	Agricultural Extension
AJS	*American Journal of Sociology*
ASA	American Sociological Association
ASR	*American Sociological Review*
Assn.	Association
Bull.	Bulletin
Coll.	College
Ctr.	Center
Econ. Res. Serv.	Economic Research Service
Ed(s).	Editor(s)
Ext.	Extension
Info.	Information
Inst.	Institute
Int'l	International
JASA	*Journal of the American Statistical Association*
JMF	*Journal of Marriage and the Family*
Jn.	Journal
Mtg.	Meeting

List of Abbreviations (cont.)

NCFR	National Council on Family Relations
NIH	National Institutes of Health
NIMH	National Institutes of Mental Health
NYC	New York City
Psych.	Psychological
Res.	Research
Res. Ctr.	Research Center
RSS	Rural Sociological Society
Rur. Soc.	*Rural Sociology*
Tran(s).	Translator(s)
UK	United Kingdom
U. or Univ.	University
USDA	United States Department of Agriculture
Wash.	Washington
Wis.	Wisconsin

Foreword

DeWitt, a recent University of Wisconsin graduate, is an original thinker who bridges the gap between social theory and social research in an interesting and thought-provoking way. Accompanying fresh theories of social action and social change, suitable for micro-, meta-, and macro- analysis of social systems, DeWitt offers suggestions for a wide-range of research applications in areas of interest to sociologists, social psychologists, psychologists, economists, and political scientists.

DeWitt's abstractions are followed by a detailed application of the theories to innovative responses of farm families in Midwestern United States in the 1970s to the impact of far-reaching technological changes in agriculture. Using uniform data obtained from questionnaires and interviews, DeWitt gives structural and process variables equal weight in the analysis.

In a departure from Parsonian theory, pattern variables are defined as shifts in each of six power bases, to predict as well as explain systemic changes. Both the complexity of the analysis, and the comprehensiveness of the theories upon which the analysis is based, require a degree of concentration that may be hard to maintain on first reading. Overall, however, the presentation demonstrates a logical consistency that lends credence to both the theories and the research.

Joseph W. Elder
Madison, Wisconsin

Preface

Two theories are proposed in Part One. The first is a theory about the subjective origins of social action, an interpretive theory in the tradition of Max Weber. Unlike Weberian Sociology, the theory has a deterministic aspect, reflected in a fixed-process model. A method of testing the theory is suggested that permits falsification.

The second theory, related to the first, describes stages in the formation, disintegration and reintegration of action systems, an evolutionary but also a transformational theory that combines a structural-functional interest in system integration, a Marxist interest in contradiction and dialectical change, and the social psychological theories of cognitive dissonance (Festinger) and balance (Heider). This is a probabilistic theory, more difficult to research, less predictively efficient, and not as easily falsified as the contingency theory of social action, but perhaps more intuitively useful in addressing matters of public concern.

These theories provide the theoretical framework for an analysis of power sharing in transition, in Part Two, in which an interactive methodology is formulated, and applied to a study of family structural changes associated with recent adoption of innovative farm technology.

In a multifactor analysis of direct and interactive effects, the theory of power sharing in transition is assessed using data obtained from structured interviews with 176 farm couples. The theory of power sharing states that, as the wife's role in farming increases, her influence on recent adoption is expressed first as a silent but working partner, and then as a direct participant in decision-making. Effects of four dimensions of the wife's farm role on recent adoption appear to be determined by type of husband/wife role sharing and phase of transition, within a context of financial risk and occupational commitment.

Theories of social action and social change, adapted from modified functionalist and symbolic interactionist perspectives, are used to identify types of husband/wife role sharing as well as changing phases of role sharing. The theories were developed while studying adaptations by young farm families to the changing requirements and challenges of labor-intensive family farming after W. W. II. Early analyses were guided by ideas for a theory of power sharing, inspired by the leadership-in-small-groups studies of Lewin, Lippitt, and White.

The central question during data analysis, theory construction, planning for further data collection, and subsequent hypotheses testing was: under what circumstances is decision sharing beneficial in advancing shared goals? Insights gained during early interviews with young farm couples were directly responsible for a "two patterns of influence" thesis that guided theory construction and the selection of variables for further research.

Applying a *logic of causal analysis of social change,* constructed as a methodology for the theories of social action and social change, hypotheses are tested to demonstrate the utility of models of interactive and multiple effects. Findings support the thesis of two patterns of wife influence on the adoption of new technology, by family-managed farm enterprises in Wisconsin, during the five year period 1974-1979.

Acknowledgments

This work is dedicated to the memory of Professors H. P. Becker, B. R. Fisher, F. C. Fliegel, H. K. Geiger, C. W. Mills, S. S. Stouffer and E. A. Wilkening, each of whom contributed in some way to the formulation of theories or methods applied herein.

The theories developed for this work draw upon many traditions of past conceptualization, interpreted through personal insights and experiences, and applied in the hope of contributing to a growing synthesis of shared understandings. Within the limitations of their day, all people express their ideas about what life means, and thereby contribute to the consciousness of the whole, but only as their expressions touch the lives of others. For helping to make this presentation possible, I am deeply indebted to Professors W. H. Sewell and J. W. Elder for their confidence in me over the years.

I am also indebted to Professors O. G. Brim, D. G. Marshall, A. O. Haller, R. A. Schoenherr, C. P. Cell, C. B. Marrett, R. P. Hawkins, and B. N. Adams for their help and encouragement at crucial times, and to Professors J. D. DeLamater, P. J. Nowak, and J. A. Logan for helpful comments and suggestions on aspects of this work in its later stages. I am especially indebted to Professor H. A. Michener, for guiding me through the maze of options encountered while restructuring variables for the summary regression analysis presented in Part Two, and to Professor B. S. Yandell for advice and assistance in the final stage of preparing this analysis for academic review.

The editorial "we" is sometimes used in the pages that follow, to acknowledge the fact that few research efforts are accomplished alone, but depend on the skills and insights of many individuals, and on the cooperative efforts of a team of investigators and their subjects. Most of all, I am indebted to the farm couples, themselves, who gave of their time and interest to provide information that was sometimes rather personal, on a subject, farming, that deeply affects their lives.

Finally, I greatly appreciate the sacrifices made by my children, family of origin, and friends; the unfailing support, encouragement, and assistance of my partner; and the examples of dedication and accomplishment provided by my mother, a Missouri farm girl who became an educator, a scientist, a businesswoman, an environmentalist, a feminist, and a continuing source of inspiration to her 32 children, grandchildren, and great grandchildren.

Part One

Theories of Social Action and Social Change

Chapter 1

Creating a Research-friendly Theoretical Framework

The impetus for generating the ideas presented in this work began as an effort to resolve discrepancies between expectations and actual experience in applying existing sociological theory to practical situations and problems. The motive for translating such ideas into a schema for others to understand and use lies entirely in a more specific need, that of acquiring professional recognition, professional status, and thereby a means of making a living. This illustrates a key differentiation of motivation into two component parts, *cause* and *reason*, essential to understanding the theory of social action that is to follow. The first component of motivation represents a response to a generalized, universal need to acquire understanding of one's surroundings, whereas the second is specific to a given situation of individualized, personal need. "Motivation," as defined below, refers to the second component exclusively, so that a motive-force ascribed to a specific need will not be confused with the more generalized motive-force of tension reduction analyzed as a universal. The implication of this differentiation and redefinition of motivation for action theory will be discussed further below. Briefly, it achieves the purpose of "unmotivating" thoughts and feelings that precede goal formation, eliminating a general assumption that thoughts and feelings necessarily occur in relation to either an experienced or an anticipated need state. "Attention" is a way of visualizing such "unmotivated" mental activity. The impetus for "attention" may be unrelated to any specific need, from the time of object definition, through the formation of ideas, beliefs, attitudes and interests regarding the object, to the point in time when the object is recognized as a potential object of a specific need. Even then, motive-force in the sense of a "drive" toward object attainment may be delayed until the specific need is sufficiently differentiated and specified to permit the identification of appropriate means for object acquisition and an assessment of other situational factors conditioning and controlling the act of attainment. Motive, in this sense of a drive, is consequently limited in its causal significance. It is an important variant nevertheless, and will be analyzed further in relation to other variants as part of a causal sequence, process model.

Preview of the Model

In the history of social thought, several recurring themes and problems have been addressed and debated without resolution. One of these is the nature of human consciousness in relation to society (cf. Hughes, 1958). Is consciousness a social product, or does it transcend society? Is "truth" an absolute, and the search for truth an increasingly exact and accurate approximation? Or is one's perception of "truth" so bound by culturally defined, socially validated values, so "rationalized" to meet what one believes to be one's needs, and so constrained by the commitments somehow made to oneself and others, that, collectively, we are incapable of discerning absolutes?

In the theories presented in this work, consciousness is viewed both as a socially derived product of society and as an interpreter and mediator of social experience. The processes of interpretation and mediation are viewed as coherently separate. The first is theorized as a developmental progression of cognitive states potentially culminating in social action, proposed as a cognitive contingency theory of social action. The second is theorized as a process of cognitive differentiation of contradictions and competing requirements of social experience culminating in choices among ways to resolve these inconsistencies, proposed as a cognitive inconsistency theory of social change.

The process of cognitive interpretation of social reality is analyzed as a fixed, deterministic, exact sequence or progression of cognitive states, but nevertheless fluid in content. (The product is variable even though the process is not.) The actual interpretation of social reality, although it conforms to an exact, predetermined sequence, is potentially quite flexible, sensitive to reinterpretation of social experience at any point in the progression. But these changes may be anticipated, observed or inferred, and analyzed as to content. The theory is able to predict their occurrence. Given a specified type of change in the context of an experience, the interpretation sequence of that experience is altered in a predictable way. (See Figure A.)

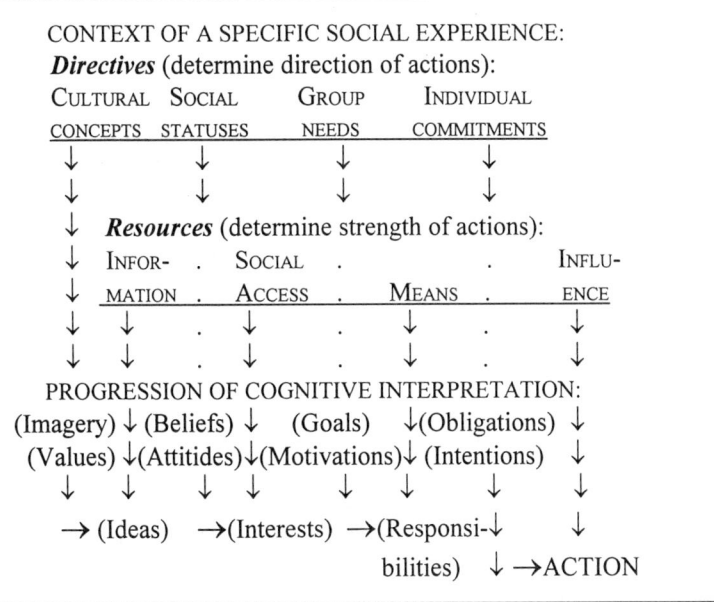

Figure A. The progression of cognitive interpretation of social experience (an example).

The process of cognitive differentiation and mediation is probabilistic rather than deterministic, subject to influences observed or inferred by the actor and/or the researcher from the context of social experiences examined, but which nevertheless compete with influences that *might not* be observed or inferred. However, analysis of this process over time, examining specific types of indicators of change and mechanisms employed to deal with it, can increase the efficiency of prediction. (See Figure B.)

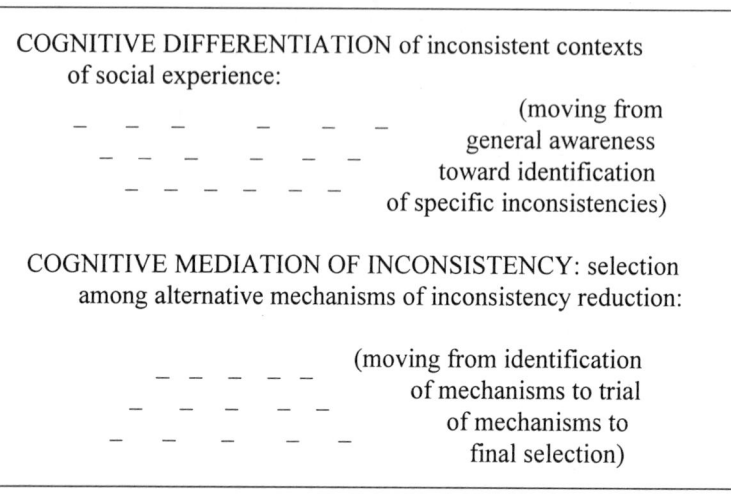

Figure B. Cognitive differentiation and mediation of social experience (an illustration).

REVIEW OF SIMILAR APPROACHES

In considering such a model, one might begin by analyzing three tension states of individuals, groups, and larger social entities that result in conscious planning to reduce or extinguish these tension states. This approach to a theory of social action originated at the same time as and is almost identical to the approach of Overington & Zollschan (1976). The convergences are discussed below. A difference is that Overington and Zollschan restrict their focus to the individual as the unit of analysis. Separate traditions guided the two formulations, but each is a conscious departure from the work of Parsons (1948) while also indebted to Parsons. Zollschan was additionally influenced at the London School of Economics by the work of Popper, exposure to Freudian psychology, a Weberian fascination with the nature of meaning, and the excitement of Neo-Marxist discussion (cf. Overington, 1976). (Jewish mysticism and compulsive wry wit add to this uneasy mix an aura of almost comic satire.) In contrast, the work presented, here, was influenced by Lewin, Mead, Tönnies through H. P. Becker, and Diffusion Theory beginning with studies on the acceptance of hybrid-corn technology in American agriculture. (The style is WASPish Middle American, dry, bland, unfootnoted, but more directly to the point.)

A common root, therefore, was Parsons and the Parsonian synthesis of the European tradition (1948, 1951). Basic components of the tension states of each analysis are explicitly defined by Parsons as thought, feeling and evaluative "learning" processes, which he thereafter makes little use of. From here the paths diverge. Overington and Zollschan provide a loose, two phase theoretical framework from which to examine problem-solving empirically at the institutional and organizational levels, still insisting on the primacy of the individual actor. The work presented, here, concentrates instead on abstracting a detailed process model, to analyze step by step the translation of tension states into objectives, actions to attain objectives, and subsequent tension reduction. The unit of analysis is not exclusively the individual. Following Parsons, it is assumed that the actor may be a more complex social entity: a family, a small group, an organization, a community, a nation-state. In Lewinian fashion, it is assumed that such entities may be characterized as thinking, feeling, purposive, and reactive beings for the purposes of empirical investigation, as observed in communicative acts as well as other interactive physical and symbolic expressions.

These responses are separated into two phases: an object orientation phase of goal formation (including what Overington and Zollschan define as articulations of thoughts, feelings and evaluations in response to exigencies [1976]), and an action orientation phase of goal attainment (including what they define as assessments of priorities, abilities and willingness [1976]). The three "learning" processes analyzed by Overington and Zollschan in the first phase (which Parsons identified but failed to utilize to give his theory predictive momentum) correspond to Freud's conceptualization of two mental processes (1911, 1959tr.): *thought,* as represented by the reality principle, and *feeling,* as represented by the pleasure principle, adding a third mental process: *evaluation,* analyzed in recent decades as a principle of cognitive consistency (see Heider, 1958; Festinger, 1957; Cartwright & Harary, 1956; Osgood & Tannenbaum, 1955). Parsons (1951:68) recognized that thought and feeling are not entirely separable, i.e., that the processes are interrelated. Evaluation, similarly, he defines as an extension of the other two processes rather than as a distinctly separate phenomenon (1951:70). In the process model that follows, the exact interconnectedness of these three mental processes is examined, as well as the implications of each for tension states affecting social action formation and social structural change.

The fact that Parsons minimized the causal significance of mental processes and overlooked their critical function in resolving discrepancies may be accounted for by his over reliance on motivation as a primary determinant of thought, feeling and evaluation. He refers to these processes, in fact, as "modes of motivational orientation," implying the actors awareness of their relevance to specific needs. But Freud's more comprehensive analysis of mental processes (1911, 1959tr.) appears to make no such assumption of motivational primacy. In discussing the reality principle, he states: "A special function was instituted which had periodically to search the outer world, in order that its data might be already familiar *if an urgent inner need should arise* [emphasis added]; this function was *attention.* Its activity meets the sense-impressions halfway, instead of awaiting their appearance" (1959:15). The implication is that thought may be unmotivated, that is, unrelated to specific needs, wishes, drives, or even to Parson's "undifferentiated" "urge to gratification," which he believed provides the initial impetus for goal-orientation specification (Parsons, Bales, & Shils, 1953: 208-210).

The Social Context of Action

In addition to analyzing tension states and mental processes, it is important to consider the social context of action, including critical elements of the cultural, social, economic and political spheres identified by Parsons (1951) in his systems analysis of the "environment of society." Initially these were represented as functions of action systems (his famous AGIL analysis of adaptation, goal attainment, integration, and latency or pattern maintenance). Parsons later abstracted these influences to their systemic origins. Compatible with this approach, the current analysis *sequences* these influences in a *process model of cognitive responses* oriented toward objects, actions, and potential reduction of tension states. The key organizing principle is the consciousness of the actor: 1) in cognitive awareness of tension states, 2) in perception of external resources or conditions (cultural, social, economic and political), and 3) in recognition of directives or controls (*also* cultural, social, economic and political). The initial means-ends *adaptive* schema of Parsons' social action theory (1948) is expanded to include an influence to carry out obligations (a *goal attainment* schema), an information to reinforce past imagery (a *pattern maintenance* schema), and a socially positioned access to promote beliefs (an *integrative* schema). The four action system *"functions"* identified by Parsons (1951) have thereby been (sequentially) incorporated into a process model. In addition, the "conditions" of the initial formulation have been specified as resources supplied by the four environmental systems. The fourth term, "norms," is discarded in favor of four structural control elements: conceptualizations, social interactions, needs, and commitments (normative to a degree, as defined by social expectations within each specific social context). This expansion of Parsonian social action theory, which is fairly consistent with his reformulations over forty years (1937-1977), was an unintended consequence of the process model rather than a derivation.

In developing a social action process model, a primary consideration was to ensure that any action or action sequence might be broken down into its basic component parts to determine at what point it has been (or might be) stalled, diverted, re-channeled or altered in any way, and how this may have (or might) occur. The basic anatomy of social action is described without reference to specific content, with a view toward diagnostic potential and the development of intervention strategies. The use of such a model requires a storehouse of practical knowledge of specific content in specialized areas, and is therefore not a shortcut to diagnosis or intervention. It is, nevertheless, an instrument of precision for the trained practitioner. Briefly, the practitioner must ask: what are the options open to and perceived by the actor (individual or larger entity) and how are these being translated into action? The model is a detailed guide to the translation process.

The proof of such a model is not easily acquired, but requires a methodology that is seldom utilized by the social sciences: *analysis of data over time*. Recent sophisticated variations of correlational analysis are as useless as the techniques they have replaced in researching such a model. Current empirical findings are therefore of little value in assessing the accuracy of this model of interrelationships. Case study and aggregate data methods are available, however, for studying such relationships over time. It is anticipated that validation procedures may be lengthy and costly, and may require extensive justification on the basis of intuitive merit.

Understanding the Dynamics of Social Order; Predicting Directions of Social Change

The ultimate test of a social action theory must be its usefulness in advancing an understanding of the dynamics of social order and in predicting the possible directions of social change. Parsonian theory has been hampered in this effort by the normative assumption underlying equilibrium theory and the functionalist assumption underlying both equilibrium and social evolution theory. A more or less static social order is implied in these theories, stabilized by a unidimensional motivational energy directed toward needs that are primarily socially determined (or structured) within an integrated system. But Parson's static answer to "the Hobbesian problem of order" has not been that convincing (Burger, 1977). Moodie (1976) has derived a dynamic reply to the Hobbesian question of social order from Zollschan's theory of institutionalization. Zollschan's theory proposes three types of "exigencies" to which individual actors respond by cognitively "articulating" goals (phase one) which then provide the motive-force for action within a context of need priority, ability to act, and willingness to act (phase two) (1976:120-121). The theory is a reconceptualization of "the unit act" of Parsons theory of social action (means-ends-norms-conditions) to permit a more voluntaristic conceptualization of the actor's subjective reaction to personal and public experience. Social order is consequently seen by Moodie as a *manifestation* of social change, as represented by Zollschan's dynamic, historically specific "institutionalization" of responses to exigencies, rather than as a *counterpoint* to change, as represented by the Parsonian, functionalist view of social order as a structured pattern of positions and performances, controlled by objectively defined and relatively unchanging values, norms, and roles, and conditioned by relatively stable situational constraints. Social order, according to Moodie, is responsive to *changing* articulations (cognitive reinterpretations) of a constantly *changing* social reality, and is constructed from the social change process itself (1976). (See Wexler, 1977, for a somewhat parallel analysis of the dynamic articulation of social control.)

Problem-Solving as the Impetus for Goal Formation

This view of social order *as* social change *rejects the functionalist assumption* that goal formation is determined primarily by the social system in response to generalized needs, and focuses instead on the subjective awareness of actors individually and collectively (through their leaders and representatives) of discrepancies in their social experience. This shift of focus not only introduces a greater degree of flexibility and voluntarism into social action theory, but changes the meaning and implications, for action theory, of the concept of "motivation" (discussed briefly above). In the Overington and Zollschan formulation, the impetus for goal formation is problem-solving, to reduce discrepancies of thought, feeling and evaluation. The motive-force toward action is derived from goals only *after* goal formation. (For a detailed analysis of both types of "purpose" see Zollschan and Overington, 1976: 308 ff.). But Parsons has assumed that motivation precedes value selection, implying that needs are anticipated (if not by the individual at least by the social system) and thereby supply the primary impetus for goal formation.

Rejecting the Normative Assumption in Social Theory Development

The theory of social action described below makes no necessary assumption of prior motivation or anticipated need, but recognizes its *potential* occurrence; and thought, feeling, and evaluation are analyzed as cognitive processes that not only precede goal formation but follow completed action, in an interpretive review preceding goal *re*formation. The direct effects of motivation on social action are analyzed, as in the Zollschan and Overington analysis, in relation to need priority *following* goal formation. Discrepancies in thought, feeling and evaluation, defined in special terms by Overington and Zollschan as the three types of exigencies resulting in goal formation, are conceptualized in very similar terms, below, as tension states of uncertainty, discomfort, and inconsistency (characterizing the tension state rather than the actor's response to it). Reduction of uncertainty and discomfort are analyzed as consecutive processes in the cognitive contingency theory of social action, while reduction of inconsistency is analyzed as a separate, mediating process in the cognitive inconsistency theory of social change. The normative assumption of Parsons is disregarded in these theories in favor of a more emergent view of values, norms and roles, amenable to repatterning and restructuring as goals are reformulated, consistent with Moodie's view of social order as a social change dynamic. *The functionalist assumption is similarly disregarded*, as unnecessary to an explanation of social action. Though it may be true that normative patterns develop and persist at least in part because they fulfill needs, the *process* of their development and persistence is not elucidated by this fact, any more than the motive-force of needs can account for specific patternings of need response. With these assumptions dismissed, the equilibrium and social evolution theories are stripped of their explanatory power. A stable social order cannot be inferred from an examination of norms, and the direction of social change cannot be projected by examining needs.

Having rejected the normative and functionalist assumptions as the basis for social theory development, a theory of social change is derived from the cognitive contingency theory of social action, and describes the formation and transformation of social entities in an entirely abstract and non-historical way, such that any social entity at any time period might be examined to determine its location, direction, speed and acceleration with regard to change (assuming a multidimensional, multidirectional space). This theory, like the theory of social action, is intended as a diagnostic instrument, without regard for the specific content of what is diagnosed. For example, the specific (cultural) symbolic constructions, (social) interactions, (economic) needs and (political) commitments that control the behavioral options of a social entity are of interest only in relation to the tension states of discomfort, uncertainty, and inconsistency experienced by the entity in its efforts to consciously interpret these options and reduce its tension states, utilizing the resources available from the same spheres (cultural, social, economic and political). Briefly, the observer must ask: what discrepancies are perceived by the social entity and what options are available for resolving them? The theory then abstracts a set of potential consequences in relation to the various possibilities for social change.

DESIGNING A NEW APPROACH

A Dialectical Perspective of Change

After identifying a *non*-normative, *non*-value-deterministic framework of analysis, it seems essential to select a theoretical perspective that regards behavioral inconsistency as more than just a "special case." Without debating essential logic, here, the positivist, rationalist, functionalist perspectives have been rejected as too restrictive. The dialectical view of social entities advanced by Marx seems more compatible, with its central insistence on the relevance of normative contradiction.

Benson (1977) has summarized the Marxist perspective with reference to the analysis of organizational phenomena. Benson states: "Dialectical analysis involves a search for fundamental principles which account for the emergence and dissolution of specific social orders." He identifies four such principles. The first is *social construction,* in which he would agree with Parsons and Shils (1951) as to the importance of situational effects, but then he defines the situation to include not only the effects of the existing social structure (and its tendencies toward self-reproduction) but also the efforts of various social entities to "transcend the limits" of the social structure (a variation that functionalists might regard as only a variation in degree of emphasis). A second principle is *totality,* the multiple interconnections, or "relationality," of social phenomena. The functionalists also recognize this principle. It accounts for the development of a systems perspective and the importance of an integration concept in the work of Parsons and other functionalist theorists. For the Marxist scholar, however, the recognition of "relationality" occasions "a search for dominant forces" and evidence of the "relations of dominance" between sectors or layers of a social organization. As a consequence (of this differentiation) social structures develop "major breaks or divisions" with "divergent, incompatible productions." The third principle, not surprisingly, is *contradiction,* which, in the dialectical view, is built into the fabric of social life. Some contradictions are maintained and reproduced within the social order (e.g., the class conflict of owners and workers), while others may destroy the system (e.g., expanding forces of capitalist production "must," in this view, eventually destroy the economic system). Contradictions arise in the production of new and differentiated social forms, effecting "search" behavior, facilitating or thwarting social mobilization, and creating at least temporary system constraints. In the equilibrium models associated with the functionalist perspective, these contradictions are seen as system strains, to be dealt with and corrected, rather than as potential beginnings of system transformation. A fourth principle of central interest to the Marxist perspective is *praxis,* a commitment to intervene, rationally and purposefully, in the formation and transformation of social arrangements. Although a less interventionist position is usually claimed by the functionalists, they are charged with a "reactionist" political position by the Marxists.

With exceptions, the dialectical perspective is the more compatible of the two approaches with the basic assumptions of this analysis. But forces of integration are regarded with as much interest as forces of disintegration, and "forces of dominance" are seen as quantifiers rather than as qualifiers of human actions and social constructions. The Marxist's goal of rational intervention is a compelling one, but rational criteria have yet to be established, and the search for such criteria may prove to be difficult. Moreover, a shared belief of the Marxists and functionalists in an "absolute" value of rationality is not shared by the perspective developed here. Rather, the *premise of social relationality* suggests that intervention should be relevant to the social experience of the social entity undergoing change.

The Requirements of Theory

In discussing the place of empirical generalization in relation to theory, Merton (1968) has identified several requirements of theory. The first requirement is that uniformities of relationship be "conceptualized in abstractions of higher order," extending the scope of empirical findings, to perhaps discover interrelationships of seemingly disparate empirical findings. The second is that it systematically accumulate a set of propositions, confirmed by the empirical research that it generates. A third requirement is that its generalizations have relevance to other "quite remote" areas of inquiry, as a result of successive exploration of its implications. A fourth is that it provides a "rationale" from which to introduce "a ground for prediction which is more secure than mere empirical extrapolation from previously observed trends." To these requirements, derived from an analysis of Durkheim's (1897, 1966) formulations regarding suicide, Merton adds two more desirable attributes of theory. These are: *precision* and *internal coherence*. "If theory is to be productive, it must be sufficiently precise to be determinate." Precision of a theory is evidenced in its improved prediction over competing hypotheses. Similarly, an integrated, logically coherent theory is (potentially) more highly predictive, as well as more capable of accumulating a "weight of evidence," than are single hypotheses.

Merton (1968) warns the theorist that premature insistence on precision "may sterilize imaginative hypotheses." He cautions against reformulating scientific problems to permit measurement, only to lose sight of an initial, significant problem. Similarly, he warns that the pressure of logical consistency may result in sterile theorizing, too far removed from empirical referents or too highly abstract to permit empirical inquiry. But even though both pressures "can lead to unproductive activity," he adds, "the warrant for these criteria of inquiry is not vitiated by such abuses" (1968: 151f).

Techniques of Theory Construction

Hage (1972) has suggested that "a theory should contain not only concepts and statements but definitions - both theoretical and operational - and linkages, again both theoretical and operational. The concepts and definitions should be ordered into primitive and derived terms and the statements and linkages should be ordered into premises and equations" (l972: 172f). He summarizes the contribution of each of these elements as follows:

Theory Part	Contributions
1. Concept names	Description, classification
2. Verbal statements	Analysis
3. Theoretical definitions	Meaning
Operational definitions	Measurement
4. Theoretical linkages	Plausibility
Operational linkages	Testability
5. Order into primitive & derived terms (elements, dimensions, modes and operatives)	Eliminates tautology
6. Order into premises and equations (explains why and how)	Eliminates inconsistency

The theories presented here appear to explicitly or implicitly contain each of these elements. Substantive theories derived from these general formulations might benefit greatly in specifically identifying and explicating linkages and orderings as suggested by Hage.

Cognitive Dissonance and Balance Theories

Cognitions have been defined by Jones and Gerard (1967: 708) as "knowledge, interpretations, understandings, [and] thoughts that an individual has about himself and the environment. A cognition is a discrete bit of knowledge," they add, "an element of understanding". The idea that cognitions (beliefs, attitudes, values, etc.) will tend to be logically or psychologically consistent with one another is basic to a number of theories of attitude structure and change. Perhaps the best known in social psychology is Festinger's Theory of Cognitive Dissonance (1957). The term cognitive dissonance refers to a *state of tension* generated when a person holds two cognitions that are inconsistent with one another. According to the theory, dissonance does not occur unless the inconsistency holds contradictory implications for behavior, by generating "mutually incompatible behavior dispositions, such as approach and avoidance tendencies toward the same object or the desire to be in two distinct places at once" (Jones & Gerard, 1967: 191). Basic to the theory is that the tension produced by dissonance is unpleasant and tends to "drive" the person to engage in some activity to reduce the tension, to transform dissonant relations into consonant or relevant ones. The theory states, further, that dissonance increases as the number and "importance" of cognitions involved in the relationship increases. A basic premise of the cognitive dissonance theory is that, during a period prior to decision and action, a person takes an *objective point of view* regarding decision alternatives and is *open to information* regarding the (consequences of) alternatives. Subsequent to decision and action, outcomes are reviewed and an effort is made to minimize any dissonance created by inconsistencies between choices and values.

Another view of cognitive consistency is presented in Heider's Theory of Cognitive Balance (1944, 1958). Heider distinguished between unit relations and sentiment relations (approximately equivalent to beliefs and values, Jones & Gerard, 1967: 165). In his theory, sentiment relations and unit relations are "in balance" (i.e., consistent) when sentiments attached to the "members" of a unit "are in the same affective direction." When these relations are not in balance, "the individual suffers feelings of strain and there are tendencies to change one or more cognitions in the direction of greater balance" (Jones & Gerard, 1967: 166). Osgood and Tannenbaum (1955) similarly differentiate beliefs and attitudes (concepts and evaluations), introducing a "congruity" principle, and predicting a reevaluation of objects whose relationship is seen as incongruous. (In The Cognitive Contingency Theory of Social Action, a distinction is made between reconceptualization and reevaluation, with the latter considered to be more resistant to change.)

The Relevance of Subjective Theory to Sociological Theory

Not all social scientists have concerned themselves with subjective phenomena. B. F. Skinner (1953) and other "behaviorists" are notable examples of those who have not. Marx (1859, 1964tr.; 1867 to 1895, 1976tr.), especially in his later work but even in his early analysis of alienation, insisted on the primacy of objective states. Blau (1964) and other "structuralist" organizational theorists have confined their analyses to "idealizations and formalizations of the social world" independent of *any* observation or measurement of individual conduct. The subjective point of view has long fascinated most social theorists, however, sometimes to the exclusion of the objective point of view. Schutz (1965:53-67), a phenomenologist, discussing the meaning for sociologists of each point of view, cautioned that fallacies arise "in the process of transgressing from one level to the other in the continuation of... scientific work," and urged that "for a theory of social action the subjective point of view must be retained in its fullest strength." He concluded: "I cannot understand a social thing without reducing it to the human activity which has created it and, beyond it, without referring this human activity to the motives out of which it springs."

Having thus established the relevance of a subjective social action theory to an understanding of social phenomena, he then pointed out the advantage of using constructed typologies (a technique of analysis developed by Weber, Durkheim and others). He stated that "[because] the type is constructed in such a way that it performs exclusively typical acts, the objective and subjective elements in the formulation of unit-acts coincide." Further, he stated that the conceptual terms of the typology "can be discussed objectively and... are open to criticism and verification." Four postulates are given to test the relevance, adequacy, logical consistency and compatibility of an ideal type construction, to guarantee "that social sciences do in fact deal with the real social world".

Concluding Remarks

A *causal sequence, process model*, designed to explain and predict the formation of social action in the "real social world," has been previewed. Derivations and departures of this model from key assumptions of earlier approaches have been reviewed. Finally, criteria have been summarized for assessing the adequacy, relevance, and logical consistency of this model, which is part of a larger theoretical framework, to be presented in Chapter 2, and applied to a study of power sharing in transition, in Part Two.

Chapter 2

Subjective Theories of Social Action and Social Change

A COGNITIVE CONTINGENCY THEORY OF SOCIAL ACTION

Constructing a Theoretical Framework

Social action might refer to any action that occurs within a social context, including some actions that might otherwise be considered nonsocial. All behavior might therefore be considered as the focus of study. Understanding human behavior with a view toward prediction is the overall aim of this theoretical analysis. A conceptual framework relevant to all human action must therefore be developed.

Parsons and Shils, (1951: 4f), in developing a framework of analysis for a general theory of action, refer to behavior as "action" if it can be analyzed "in terms of the anticipated states of affairs toward which it is directed, the situation in which it occurs, (its) normative regulation ...and the expenditure of energy or 'motivation' involved."

Departing from the Parsons-Shils analysis, the normative regulation of behavior will here be regarded as a variable element of the situation rather than as a "given" orientation of action. This is a significant departure, in that "action" in the present analysis is not automatically assumed to be "normative" (in the sense of being prescribed by a well defined, well understood set of role expectations).

The anticipated states of affairs toward which behaviors are directed in the Parsons-Shils analysis might be referred to as goals or objectives. "Value-orientations," in their framework, help to account for the selection of such goals or objectives. In the present analysis, the term "object-orientations" is substituted as an equivalent term. (The term "value" refers, here, to one of six object orientations, a conceptual awareness of the existence of something prior to idea formation about its specific use or purpose, and will be omitted from most of the discussion because of the variety of theoretical and common sense meanings attached to it.) The situation or social context in which behavior occurs is comprised, in the framework developed for the present analysis, of eight types of structural variables (See Columns 1 and 2, Figure C), each of which might contain "normative" elements that are not necessarily consistent within or between structures. Four of these types are viewed as "control" variables (needs, commitments, symbolic constructs, and social interactions) that determine the direction of social actions. The other four types are regarded as "conditions" (means, influence, information, and social position) that determine the "strength" of an action rather than its direction.

Motivation, a key orientation in the Parsons-Shils framework, is viewed as only one of a series of "contingent" variables in the present analysis. (See Column 4, Figure C.) It is still a critical variable, however, in that it quantifies the awareness within the organism of a state of need-discomfort, or unsatisfied need. This state of discomfort supplies the "motor force" for each cognitive progression. It is reinforced, at intervals, by an awareness of a state of uncertainty, adding the more focused energy of "intention" to the less focused energy of "motivation." Potentially, each energy is extinguished while interpreting the completed action. Uncertainty is alleviated through "object definition or value identification," which provides a rationale for the action. Discomfort is alleviated through a primarily socially determined "attitude" toward (or feeling about) the object or value, an implication being that "attitude" is formed within a context of present, remembered, or anticipated approval or disapproval, by the social entity in association with (select) other social entities (sometimes referred to as a reference group, cf. Merton, 1968).

Beyond Equilibrium Theory   21

CONTROLS	CONDITIONS	CONSTRAINTS	COGNITIVE
(Directives)	(Resources)	(Physio-chemical Sensitivities)	PROGRESSION (Orientations)

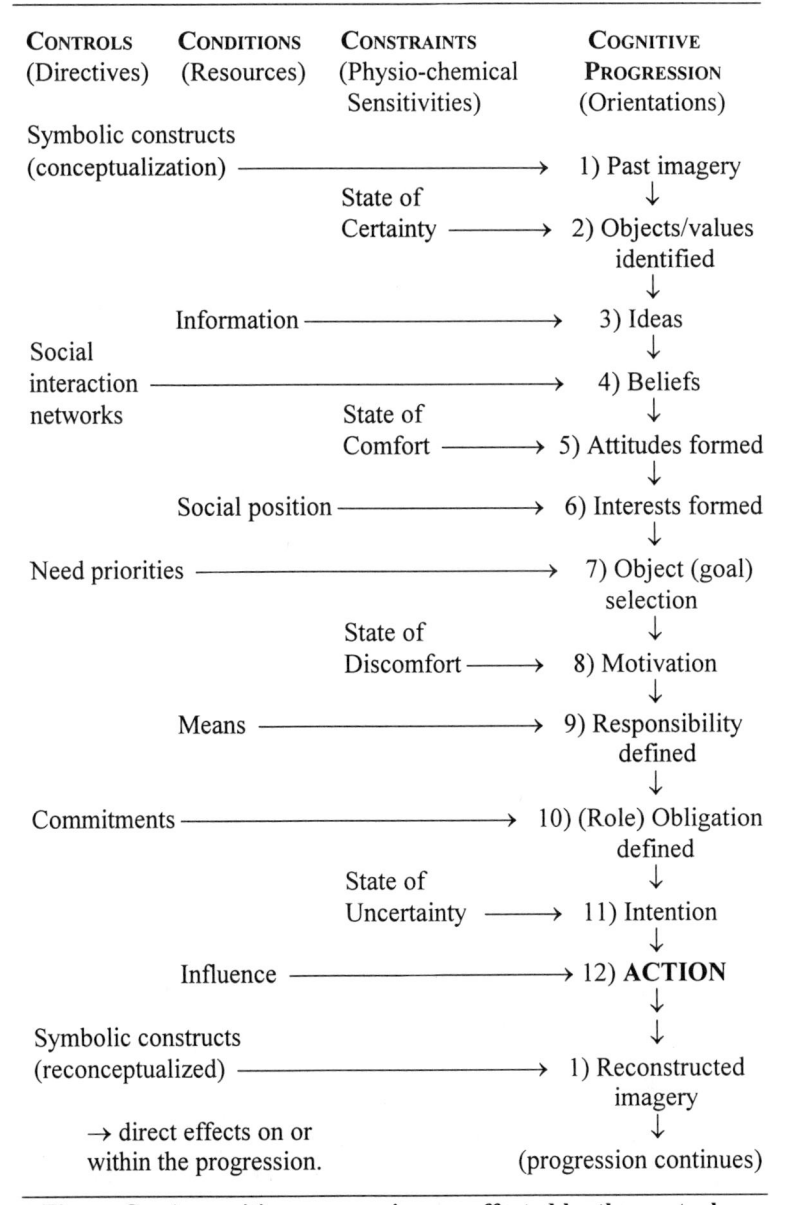

Symbolic constructs
(conceptualization) ──────────────→ 1) Past imagery
                        State of   ↓
                        Certainty ────→ 2) Objects/values identified
                                              ↓
        Information ──────────────→ 3) Ideas
Social   ↓
interaction ──────────────────→ 4) Beliefs
networks   State of   ↓
                        Comfort ────→ 5) Attitudes formed
                                               ↓
             Social position ──────────→ 6) Interests formed
                                             ↓
Need priorities ──────────────→ 7) Object (goal) selection
                        State of   ↓
                        Discomfort ────→ 8) Motivation
                                            ↓
             Means ──────────────────→ 9) Responsibility defined
                                            ↓
Commitments ──────────────────→ 10) (Role) Obligation defined
                        State of   ↓
                        Uncertainty ────→ 11) Intention
                                              ↓
             Influence ──────────────→ 12) **ACTION**
                                                ↓
Symbolic constructs   ↓
(reconceptualized) ──────────────→ 1) Reconstructed imagery
   → direct effects on or   ↓
     within the progression.   (progression continues)

Figure C. A cognitive progression, as affected by the controls, conditions, and constraints of its context of social experience.

Four of a set of twelve sequentially related orientations in the cognitive contingency progression have been identified: *motivation, intention, object (value) identification,* and *attitude.* This progression is cyclical, in that object identification and object disposition (elements of object orientation) have preceded as well as followed the translation of motivation and intention (action orientation) into social action.

Another dimension of the context for social action, defined as the dimension of "constraints" (see Figure C, Column 3), limits action variability according to various physio-chemical thresholds. These include basic energy levels, intelligence capacities, tolerance quotients, and other sensitivities that may increase, or reduce, or even modify in unanticipated ways the degree, or direction, or timing of a social response. Of little interest to sociologists, perhaps, under ordinary circumstances, it is a dimension that increases in significance during times of intensively experienced social stress (as, for example, in concern during the 1960's regarding the effects of the drug culture on the social functioning of youth).

This brief introduction of conceptual considerations, and preview of the theory, is suggestive of the type of analysis offered. The Parsons-Shils framework has been a point of departure, with several modifications necessitated by a slight restatement of the problem, resulting in a new approach, with implications for a very different kind of theory of social system development and transformation.

Basic Premises

One of the distinguishing characteristics of this new approach to general theorizing is that a framework is being presented for analyzing processes and relationships, to determine the effects of structures rather than to describe their characteristics; and to explain and predict the construction and reconstruction of behavior rather than to describe its modes and functional consequences. These distinctions are reflected in the basic premises of the theory:

The first major premise is a premise of social relativity: i.e., *that social reality is necessarily altered by the social experience that seeks to define it.* Consequently, the "real truth" of social existence is not assumed to be progressively approximated, but rather to be indeterminate. Images of social reality are constructed and tested and revised within the context of social experience. Such images are treated as representations or estimates or approximations of reality, subject to symbolic verification, social validation, and planned or chance comparison for consistency with other images of reality. But the reality, itself, is ever changing, ever inaccessible to precise definition.

A second major premise, however, *is that the process of image construction is fixed, a fixed sequence of interpretation that must occur in a given, logically derived order, and culminate in a performed* (or symbolically performed) *SOCIAL ACT,* an experiencing of the image that has provided the basis for image testing, revision, and reconstruction.

A third major premise is that images are communicated and shared, becoming collective representations that may assume an independent importance to a larger social entity, with the process of their further interpretation, reconstruction and combination with other images "taken over" by the larger entity, to be differentiated, specialized, and elaborated beyond the ability of any one individual to alter, comprehend, or even experience. Durkheim (1915) refers to such a phenomenon as a synthesis of consciousnesses (in his example of religious sentiments, ideas and images) that, once born, obey laws all their own. Scientific disciplines, language systems and worldwide industrial complexes would seem to provide examples of image constructions that have achieved such autonomy. Even at these macro-levels, however, the premises of social relativity and fixed process just described are assumed, as universals, to apply.

Durkheim and also Mead (1934:19) appear to equate the concept of "consciousness" with the completed construction of imagery. (Mead states that consciousness must follow the social act, not precede it.) But a more emergent view of consciousness is needed to elaborate the process of image construction now being described. Mead speaks of the "organization of the act" prior to the act "in terms of attitudes. "Consistent with this view, *a fourth major premise is that cognitive states are activated prior to social action and sequentially interpret the context of its related social experience* (see Premise 2). Parsons (1951) has referred to these cognitive interpretations of context as "orientations." An ordered sequence of such orientations has been identified in the Cognitive Contingency Theory of Social Action (Column 4, Figure C). These orientations are viewed as progressive states of consciousness, culminating in action, and completed in image construction (the "consciousness" of Mead and Durkheim).

The Cognitive Orientation of Social Action

From basic premises two and four, then, a progression of cognitive states is hypothesized that bears an exact relationship to social action and to its context of social experience. Four of these states have been identified and interrelated above. They are: *object (value) identifications, attitudes, motivations,* and *intentions.* This progression of cognitive states is posited as a circular sequence; e.g., attitudes develop toward identified objects, motivations are rationalized in ways that are usually consistent with already justified feelings or attitudes, and intentions, best understood, perhaps, within the context of role expectations, are directed toward goal achievements that are consistent with already established motivations.

This sequence can be analyzed further (see Figure C, Column 4). A sequence suggests a series of logical possibilities. A first step toward narrowing the range of possibility is to elaborate the intervening links in the sequence. For example, identified objects (material and ideational) determine the range of new *ideas* that may be understood and subsequently accepted (or rejected), since those ideas that are inconsistent with already identified objectifications cannot be readily interpreted. Ideas may come to be regarded as *beliefs* when they have been clearly formulated and have received social acceptance or corroboration. Ideas and beliefs directly affect the formation of *attitudes,* since an attitude is a response to a state of mind. By reduction, the scope of attitude formation is dependent on the extent of mental conceptualization.

Following this elaboration further, attitudes predispose a social entity to be *interested* in the objects toward which attitudes have been formed. Interests of sub-entities (e.g., subgroups) may not become interests of the social entity itself until such attitudinal direction has been established within the overall social entity (e.g., through social interaction), and objects toward which attitudes have not been formed, either collectively or individually, may not become objects of interest at all. Interests that have been formally stated and agreed on are then recognized as *object selections.* Subsequently, the *motivations* of an entity are a function of the organized priorities of these objectives (which are related to the structural directive of needs, to be discussed further in the next section).

The intervening cognitive states between motivation and social action require an analysis of *role expectations* in terms of three additional orientations. These are: *responsibilities, obligations,* and *intentions.* A predisposition toward action, implied in motivation, requires that a social entity as a whole or one or more of its parts respond in such a way as to obtain an already determined goal. The recurrent nature of this required response and the consequent efficiency of its relegation to selected sub-entities (role differentiation), has been documented in Bales' *Interaction Process Analysis* (1950) of goal oriented, problem solving groups. The implied necessity of motivation is that *responsibilities* (necessary responses) must exist. The observable consequence of motivation and recognized responsibility is the acceptance, by sub-entities, of *obligations.*

Obligations might be accepted according to assignment, or possibly follow from competition. Regardless of the process of role differentiation, however, the key determinant of fulfilled expectation is the degree of *intention* as evidenced by the adequacy of an implementive plan. The actual fulfillment of a role, then, requires recognition of a responsibility consistent with group motivation, acceptance of the responsibility as an obligation, *and* intent to carry out the obligation, as evidenced by a plan of action that results in goal attainment for the social entity. The evidences of intent may be analyzed in terms of the principles used in a plan of approach, or the plan as it is carried out in theory, but should not be analyzed by observing actual techniques or other physical means of completing an action, since these may be subject to other conditions or constraints. Under special conditions, then, intent may be inferred from certain observed symbolic acts but should not be inferred from other observed overt acts.

(Because of this requirement of inference rather than direct observation, in a research situation intent should be analyzed at several levels of abstraction, supported logically at each level. Such a procedure suggests that intention requires consideration as a major concept, comparable in significance to the concepts of motivation, attitude, and object or value identification. To avoid extensive digression at this point, perhaps it is sufficient to partially interpret the concept of intention by stating its relationship to the concept of norms. The norms of a group include those manifestations of intent that the group has already accepted. Because a norm is a product of group acceptance of orientation and actions, it is not appropriate to use the concept of norms in a conceptual scheme that is designed to study processes of change. Such inclusion would exclude non systematized response alternatives that describe the orientation of an entity prior to response alternatives that describe the orientation of an entity prior to collective acceptance of the orientation. Social entities frequently do not follow consistently logical sequences, as the conceptual scheme suggests, but deviate [often repetitively] in various ways. To conceptualize only in terms of normative orientation and behavior would be to discount consistent directions and degrees of deviation, and thereby lose the indications of change as they are developing.)

The observable behavior of action (in contrast to the interpretive response, *action orientations* considered above) should not be analyzed as a further cognitive state. Although an act is a consequence of one or more cognitive sequences of the "self," "other," group, institution, etc., the act must be abstracted from all such interpretations of context in order to be accurately reported and subsequently analyzed in relation to each context without subjective bias. The perception of the observer must be trained to separate, in order to consciously recombine, the act events from the conditions, controls, constraints and contingents for act occurrence.

A progression has been outlined of cognitive states that precede social action. Familiar concepts have been used in this analysis, organized according to relationships that are intuitively logical. Social action has been differentiated from intent, intent existing as a cognitive orientation, represented only symbolically in the principles and processes of action, whereas actions are independently analyzed as observed outcomes of intent.

Cognitive Orientations within the Context of Social Experience

An evolving or changing social entity incorporates the characteristics of various structures existing in its ideational and behavioristic environment. Some of these are resource structures; others impinge as directives. Resource structures determine the range of *logically* "possible," *status* "appropriate," *economically* "feasible" and *influentially* "permissible" responses to impinging directives. Directives include *conceptual* structures, structures of *social interaction*, structures of *need*, and structures of *individual commitment*. The characteristics of these various constellations of structures determine the characteristics of cognitive orientations and ultimately the characteristics of the social entities or systems that they combine to form or transform. These structures thereby comprise a "context" of social experience and will be considered in order of their relevance for the cognitive progression, beginning with the effects of the conceptual structure of symbolic constructs. (See Figure C, Lines 1 to 3.)

The conceptual structure belongs to the symbolic system, and affirms through definition the *past imagery* (consciousness) of past social experience, and thereby determines the range of *identifiable objects* (values) that may be used to interpret present experience. Conceptual structures, in other words, define past experience and control the interpretation of present experience. A subsequent effect of conceptualization, *conditioned by the added "logic" of information as a resource,* is in the formulation of *ideas* about, for example, an object's purpose. Within the symbolic structural context, an entity in its formative stages may be most perceptive of the *utilitarian* purposes of objects, whereas a more developed entity may become increasingly more perceptive of the *sociative* purposes of objects. In this illustration, then, the first differentiating characteristic of the social entity, controlled by its conceptualizations and conditioned by its access to and utilization of information, is its relative perception of the *direct utility* of objects as against their more *sociatively defined* purposes.

Subsequent to the (symbolic) identification of object purpose, differentiating characteristics are further determined by the structure of social interaction. (See Figure C, Lines 4 to 6.) The first differentiating effect is in relation to determining the direction and extent of an object's purpose. In the course of interacting with valued objects (or objects situationally related to them), both the *direction* of utility (and/or social access) and also the *extent* of use (and/or social contact) are learned and confirmed within the context of social interaction. These *beliefs* about the nature (or limits) of an object's purpose are learned either imitatively from the observed cognitive orientations of those interacted with or observed, or conditionally in the course of self-other controlled responses. (The structure of social interaction decides not only who *initiates* but also who *dominates* this interaction.)

The second differentiating effect of social interaction is on *attitude* formation. A social entity's (or sub-entity's) subjective sensitivity to interaction experience detects either a decrease and/or an increase in individual *discomfort*. This sensitivity is attitudinally translated as "like" or "dislike" for the object and/or object related situation (to the extent that comfort is most relevant to individuals in the situation, as defined conceptually, and also depending on the consistency of conditions producing comfort/discomfort). Formations of consistent attitudes of object like and dislike confirm the existence of a cognitive orientation at this point in the cognitive progression, and the extent to which these attitudes are sociatively linked further differentiates the "type" of social entity.

Following attitude formation *interests* develop, *conditioned by social access* and subject to the third differentiating effect of the structure of social interaction. An interest consists of an inclination toward contact with the object, or toward involvement in object related situations. A disposition either of approach or of avoidance may then occur. (The "emotional" content of characteristics of differentiated types of social entities are a *composite* of attitude and interest.)

The need structure of a social entity initiates the most critical step in the cognitive progression. (See Figure C, Lines 7 to 9.) Whereas conceptual and interaction structures have determined object orientation, need structure determines *object selection* and initial action orientation. Although the decision to attain an object's purpose is controlled by the directive of needs (situationally focused and ordered according to functionally or sociatively determined priorities), this decision is nevertheless contingent upon emotional feelings and dispositions (i.e., attitudes and interests) appropriate to the choice.

The cumulative effect of conceptual, interaction, and need structures on differentiating social entities is further evidenced in subjective sensitivity to need situations and priorities following object-selection. Entities or their sub-units, evaluatively aware of an object's existence and attitudinally aware of its associative relevance to individual states of comfort/discomfort, at this point become *motivationally* aware of the degree of importance of individually or collectively attaining (or perhaps negating) the object's purpose. Type of social entity is differentiated by the need structure according to the relative emphasis of functional as against sociative definitions of need priorities.

Need structure further determines the characteristics of the cognitive sequence (and ultimately differentiates social entities) by influencing the perception of *responsibilities*. Responsibilities are defined as the perceived degree, duration and timing of goal attainments, as these fulfill need requirements. This effect of the need structure on the perception of responsibility is *conditioned*, not surprisingly, *by already acquired economic means and by anticipated means acquisition.*

The structure of individual commitments completes the list of "directives" controlling the formation of a cognitive sequence. (See Figure C, Lines 10 to 12.) This structure determines the assignment and acceptance of responsibilities as *obligations* (demonstrated, for example, in organizational "role differentiation") and the internalization of obligations as *intentions*. These intentions, demonstrated in the development of principles and plans of action, are the final evidence, preceding action, that a cognitive sequence has formed. Intentions confirm that a subjective sensitivity to personal accountability for the results of action has occurred. These various effects of personal commitment are, of course, *contingent* on the series of effects of previously considered directives, or on evidence of their cumulative effect.

A COGNITIVE INCONSISTENCY THEORY OF SOCIAL CHANGE

Cognitive Progressions: Some Further Considerations

The origin of interpretive responses in social entities prior to observable behavior has been described as a fixed, progressive sequence of cognitive orientations. *Actuation* and *institution* describe the continuation of this sequence beyond the level of subjective orientation. Described as completed sequences, these progressions are generated by need, instrumented as *action* (in accord with entity commitments), instituted as conscious *imagery* (in accord with preexisting symbolic interpretations of meaning), and reinforced during social interaction to become integrated into *systems* of cognitive response.

These completed sequences are derivatives of the intersection of numerous contexts of social experience with three basic levels of consciousness: *awareness, perception* and *recognition*. Awareness is defined as the very basic sensitivity of a social entity to increases and decreases in its states of comfort, discomfort, certainty and uncertainty (i.e., internally experienced constraints). Perception refers to a more advanced, *quantitative* sensitivity to the presence of various resources (conditions). Recognition refers to a *qualitative* sensitivity regarding the requirements of directives (controls). In the cognitive progression, these sensitivities add "layers" to the development of a full state of consciousness represented by image construction.

In addition to the need initiated, commitment activated, conceptually interpreted, socially reinforced cognitive progressions described, there are sets of mechanisms that define the linking of each pair of consecutive cognitive orientations, and there are sets of forces that define the association of each cognitive orientation with its paired context variable. These mechanisms and forces are variable. They may be formed in reaction to current events or they may continue in existence as "remembered" formations of prior events. They may initiate cognitive orientations or they may be necessary to their continuation. In complex social systems, these mechanisms and forces are usually formalized and often become institutionalized, providing much of the subject matter for social inquiry.

Cognitive Sequence Interruption and Reorientation

In the histories of social entities and entity systems, two kinds of situational change occur that affect the initiation and continuity of cognitive orientation sequences:
1) A change in needs and/or in the interpretation of need requirements results in the discontinuation of these sequences and initiation of new sequences, a developmental kind of change characterized by redirection of cognitive orientations, beginning either with new object definition or with new object choice.
2) A change in the conditions for need satisfaction also results in sequence interruption, introducing a readjustive kind of change characterized by disintegration of the sequence (beginning at any point where a formerly appropriate orientation is either no longer adequate or no longer possible) and reintegration of the sequence to the extent that *new conditions* for need satisfaction are defined and verified.

Developmental change occurs, then, whenever *needs* or *need requirements* change. Ideally, for any social entity, a succession of anticipated needs might exist corresponding to cycles of events that have occurred predictably in the past. Such a predetermined succession of needs might generate a successive series of learned or reasoned reorientations, which might then develop in an orderly way through cognitive sequence redirection. Where such events have not been experienced and/or anticipated, the reorientation is more experimental in nature, developing gradually or erratically in the course of many trial sequences.

Readjustive change occurs, on the other hand, whenever the *conditions* for need satisfaction change. These conditions consist of access to information about and approach toward valued objects, and access to the means and power of attaining those objects chosen as objectives. (If changes in the conditions for need satisfaction reduce the satisfaction of a majority of the needs of actors in a social system, a readjustment of the total system may occur, possibly extending to transformation of the system as well, during which time the major characteristics of system orientation may change from one type to another, e.g., from mechanistic to organic or traditional to modern.) Reintegration of sequences occurs in relation to the perception of new conditions for need satisfaction.

As noted, developmental change occurs through sequence discontinuation and redirection; readjustive change occurs through sequence disintegration and reintegration. These changes may occur independently of each other, or they may result from situational changes that have been caused by the same external events, occurring therefore about the same time and in interdependent association.

Processes of Cognitive Reorientation

Reorientation of cognitive sequences may occur under varying circumstances: *During sequence redirection* 1) *object* orientations are redirected when reevaluation of needs and need requirements results in new object identification, and social consensus results in object confirmation; 2) *action* orientations are redirected when new objects are then selected as objectives and commitments made to attain them. *During sequence readjustment* 1) *object* orientations are reintegrated when a) new channels of communication are discovered for obaining information about familiar objects; or b) new statuses are acquired from which to approach these objects; and 2) *action* orientations are reintegrated when a) new means are acquired that make object attainment feasible; or when b) new authority is obtained for control over the uses of these means.

When needs are cyclical and/or anticipated and conditions for need satisfaction are stable, a social entity's "memory" of each completed cognitive orientation sequence is reinforced by repetition, as need arousing events are interpreted, tension reducing thoughts, emotions and objectives are selected, and appropriately related acts are performed.

When unanticipated needs are in the process of being defined, or when conditions for need satisfaction are unstable, tension may not be reduced by selection of learned and remembered mental, emotional, motivational and action alternatives. If needs are not satisfied and discomfort continues, further contact with objects associated with the need arousing event produces uncertainty due to anticipated tension. Slight degrees of uncertainty result in selection of slightly different alternatives. Such alternatives may be learned imitatively from present or remembered observations, or may be chance selections, or may be uniquely reasoned by combining observations from past experience, extending the ability of the unit to react to more varied events without contradicting previously selected alternatives.

Cognitive orientation sequences, then, are either reinforced through repetition or adjust to new experience through selection of known alternatives or experimentation with new alternatives. In cases of cyclical change (e.g., seasonal), previously learned sequences are likely to be repeated. In cases of advancing change (e.g., aging), familiar orientation sequences (observed in similar entities) are frequently duplicated imitatively. Innovative or random alternatives may be chosen if observation or imitation are not possible. As long as these do not conflict with other of its orientation sequences, the social entity remains stable within the context of its social experience.

A process of cognitive reorientation may begin at any point in the orientation sequence, starting with the selection of an expedient or conveniently accessible alternative in place of a previously habitual or trial orientation. If the sequence of which this alternative is a part appears to result in need satisfaction, the sequence is reinforced. The process of reorientation then continues into a period of action review and verification.

Review begins with the construction of an *imagery* of the object-attaining (need-satisfying) act. This consists of a symbolic interpretation of the act by conceptually identifying the action with reference to past imageries of "like" actions. The imagery of the act is then translated into object identification, and the object identified evaluated as to its effect on the entity's state of certainty or uncertainty. If it is felt to decrease uncertainty, the imagery of the action is reinforced and the object identified is accepted by the social entity as one toward which further cognitive response may be oriented. This instituting of the act (of object attainment) *as* an object further reinforces the sequence of reorientation that preceded "successful" (need satisfying) object attainment.

Review is followed by verification. Verification occurs within the context of social agreement (and disagreement) during social interaction. Symbolic interpretations may be altered or reversed during interaction. Opinions may be expressed directly, or be communicated indirectly through seemingly irrelevant messages that contain implications of affect, or be implied through actions. Opinion consensus either reinforces cognitive reorientation through the sanctioning of the resulting object identifications, or impedes the reorientation process by rejecting the identified objects. If the objects are collectively or mutually rejected (i.e., by a consensus), either the act must be reinterpreted and new object meanings identified, or the act and the orientation sequence preceding it must be regarded as unverified and non-sanctioned. *(Lack* of opinion consensus has variable effects, for further interaction as well as for further orientation.)

Following a period of favorable review and positive verification of action, the final reinforcement of reorientation takes place during a period of response validation. In the "arena" of simultaneous competition (and possible conflict) among orientation sequences, contradictions eventually show up that were not obvious during response reorientation. Actions that have successfully decreased mental uncertainty and emotional discomfort in one situation may have produced circumstances that change the context of social experience with reference to other events. Sometimes, however, these actions are so far removed from their consequences that conscious analysis of the contradictions cannot be made. Therefore, validation of a reoriented cognitive sequence may appear to be complete before its orientations (and accompanying action initiating mechanisms) are sufficiently compared with those of other sequences, both within and between social entities. (Major factors are time, contact, and communication.)

If contradictions do not exist to any great extent and validation is completed, the process of reorientation results in tension reduction. Tension is due to an expectation that a need cannot be satisfied. When reorientation is complete, the social entity expects that object attainment will continue to occur and will continue to satisfy the need.

When selection of conveniently accessible or expediently necessary orientations (in place of previous thoughts, feelings and actions) does not resolve discrepancies that arise between situational factors and either 1) the recognition of what is required or 2) the perception of what is available, and if external events causing the discrepancies between situation and orientation appear to be permanent or of continuing reoccurrence, further sequences may be characterized either by more extreme efforts to redirect or reintegrate orientations, or by omission of further response to the need in question, and reorientation toward substitute needs. Discrepancies between situation and orientation may seem unresolvable EITHER because the social entity is unable to satisfy a need, by 1) redirecting response sequences to adjust to new need definition and/or new need requirements or 2) reintegrating response sequences to adjust to new conditions for satisfying a need, OR because response reorientation is incomplete, due to 1) failure of redirected sequences to adequately interpret a need or 2) failure of reintegrated sequences to adequately interpret conditions.

The more extreme reorientations become, the more complex becomes the symbolic interpretation of resulting actions. Tension produced by the difficulties involved in complex symbolic interpretation may be system disruptive if reorientation is prolonged; however, the process of reorientation might continue indefinitely without becoming system disruptive if the failure to achieve completion of reorientation does not interfere with the satisfaction of other needs.

The omission of further response to a need has a different effect on the social entity. It must reevaluate all objects associated with events that have previously stimulated response to the need, rejecting those directly identified with the need. This alternative may seem less disruptive to the system than prolonged reorientation, but its long-range effect is to limit the ability of the social entity to vary its orientations toward objects identified with future uncertain situations, i.e., when future ambiguity requires cognitive reorientations, adjustive object identifications are restricted from the area of objects associated with the latent, unsatisfied need.

If reorientation is successful, review is favorable, and verification is positive, but validation does not occur (i.e., if redirected sequences conflict or reintegrated sequences are inconsistent with other orientation sequences of the system) tension is not reduced and tends to disrupt the system. If system stability cannot be maintained, the *system (as well* as each individual sequence) is subject to developmental or readjustive change or a combination of the two.

Incomplete Reorientation and System Change

When it becomes apparent that system stability cannot be maintained: 1) needs may be reinterpreted so as to block the initiation of sequences that conflict with other sequences or that contain inconsistent orientations; or 2) sequence reorientation may progress without further attempts to compare orientations associated with other needs, and techniques may develop to prevent contradiction awareness.

In the first case, *convenience* is employed by the social entity in the form of initiation of only those sequences that result in tension reduction. Tension exciting orientation sequences are either omitted, by suppressing the recognition of needs, or postponed, by suppressing the awareness of need importance. If the environment permits omission or postponement of needs, this convenient solution results in the restructuring of needs, but of a type antithetical to that which occurred during developmental formation of the system.

In the second case, *expediency* is employed by the social entity in the form of compartmentalization of each need related area of orientation, action initiation, and resulting activity. In this way, the social entity prevents disintegration of sequences that adequately satisfy needs but conflict with or are inconsistent with other sequences of the system. This expedient solution is a characteristic of the first transitional phase of system change.

In this first phase of system transition, need-related areas continue as separate parts of the system and the social entity is no longer a consistently reacting entity. Newly developing sequences are characterized as dissociative, that is, they are unrelated to a larger network of orientation sequences except as directly affected by the structure of needs (the operative structure that continues to control the priority of action initiation through control of choices of objectives). Each part of the system continues or is reoriented or is newly formed as though it were independent of the other parts; its orientation sequences changing without system validation. There is still friction, however, due to conflict with other social entities in various stages and phases of sequence and system reorientation.

In this phase of system transition, with sequences originating without regard for validation or system maintenance, reorientation is affected primarily by events (operating through the need structure) and very little by socially instituted controls (operating through the structure of interaction). Verification is less significant than in prior phases of system reorientation, mostly because the structure of social interaction is uncertain and changing. The structure of individual commitments is reduced to a minimum number of commitments without major reference to continuing social interaction, and determined primarily by the need structure. Reinterpretation of and reorientation to need stimulating events, aided by the fact that this does not have to be consistent with orientations to other needs, is to some extent impeded by the unpredictability of social objects, whose situational presence neither assures nor consistently prohibits the satisfaction of needs.

Following these reactions to incomplete reorientation that has disrupted the system, 1) the formation of a new system depends on expanding the structure of symbolic constructs, whereas 2) the emergence of a transformed system depends on reinterpreting the structure of symbolic constructs. These changes are accomplished by the intellect in the case of the individual, or by influential leaders and their advisors in the case of collectivities. (The equivalent of leader in the case of the individual is the developed, self directing "consciousness of internal existence," i.e., the identification by the self of the self as an object, the formation of attitudes toward the self, and the motivation and actuation of the self as a self by the self.)

This restructuring of the symbolic system, consisting of either a reinterpretation and/or an expansion of conceptualizations of the external environment, requires a reexamination and reevaluation of already constructed images and identified objects plus an attempt to construct new images and discover new objects (i.e., new meanings). This restructuring takes place independently relevant to the review of each orientation sequence. (The overall structure is therefore a synthesis of overlapping, separately constructed images.) The relationship of the symbolic structure to a system that is both emerging (transitionally) and being formed (developmentally) is particularly interesting. During system reorientation, reexamination and reevaluation of objects frequently results in such sharp contrasts between new interpretation and prior interpretation of *familiar* objects that compromise between opposite viewpoints seems impossible. The destructive force of such oppositions is eventually moderated, however, by the discovery of *new* objects (or new interpretations of *additional* objects not previously associated with the area of uncertainty) that explain what seemed to be unexplainable contradictions. The destructive effects of apparent differences are in this way resolved through conceptual expansion.

Transformation Through Phases of System Reorientation

When changes in some of the situational contexts of a social entity are anticipated, variations of orientation can be considered in advance and satisfactory alternatives chosen that will be consistent with continuing sequences. When changes occur that have not been anticipated, however, it may not be possible to maintain sequence and system consistency while satisfying needs. If these inconsistencies create too much uncertainty, a period of conceptual interpretation and social interaction will follow during which new orientations might be alternately accepted and rejected. Sequence and system consistent selections are integrative. Inconsistent selections are disintegrative, unless their differences are resolved through conceptual redefinitions that become socially sanctioned.

The period during which a social entity is able to maintain sequence and system consistency sufficiently to satisfy the requirements of most of its needs might be referred to as an *established phase* of the system. A period of reintegration or redirection of most of the sequences of a system might be referred to as a *vacillating phase*, since new orientations tend to disrupt the established equilibrium. This phase is *transitory*, for eventually new orientations result either in a reduction of uncertainty (following success in satisfying needs), and in resolved differences with the system, or in an increase of uncertainty, and in unresolved differences.

The first alternative is likely to occur when the pressure of unpredictable events is only occasional and/or their consequences become predictable. *The reason:* new orientations are realistic, conceptual comprehension of outcomes becomes possible, uncertainty is reduced, and social acceptance is assured. *The result:* a return to the *established phase*, with a system of reintegrated orientation sequences.

The second alternative is likely to occur under constant pressure from conflicting events whose consequences are unpredictable. *The reason:* realistic orientations are almost undeterminable, conceptual comprehension of outcomes is vague and possibly ambiguous, and the uncertainties produced by conflicting events are further complicated by social controversy regarding new orientations, making consistent social acceptance impossible. *The result:* a new period begins, characterized by conflict of and controversy over many and varying orientations, old as well as new. The system of orientation sequences becomes fragmented, and the composition of social entities tends to become reduced to the smallest activationally cohesive, socially intra-active, intra-communicative intellect; the nuclear, small group. This period might be thought of as a *disrupted phase*. New orientations are selected with much confusion and contradiction and without consistent conceptual identification or social sanction. To compensate for the fact that objects of utility value are not consistently attainable, a degree of certainty and system maintenance is obtained through increased valuation of sociatively defined objects. A *disrupted phase* is *transitional* since the earlier system is no longer in effect and a new system has not taken form. If during this phase, however, predictability of events begins to occur, making the selection of realistic orientations possible, inconsistency and uncertainty are reduced, accompanied by a return to a period of reintegration and reformation of the orientation sequences of the earlier system.

Under the pressure of unpredictable events that appear to continue indefinitely through the *disrupted phase*, even the attainment of sociatively valued objects eventually fails to provide minimum certainty, and the sociatively defined situations in which they are attained fail to provide minimum comfort. A point is reached where reduction of uncertainty can occur *only* through reinterpretation of the utility value of objects, together with direct satisfaction of needs, disregarding the sociative value of objects.

At this point all aspects of the earlier system are non-operative and the possibility of orientation consistency depends on the emergence of a new system. This second transitional phase, similar to the *disrupted phase* but directed toward the formation of a new system rather than the discontinuation of the earlier system, might be called an *emerging phase*. An atmosphere of "anything is possible, nothing is certain" prevails. The most efficient unit or reorientation becomes the individual. The most practical orientations are those learned by trial and error in the course of direct attempts to satisfy needs. Identification and selection of objects for their sociative value becomes problematic during this phase because the relationship between social situations and the requirements for need satisfaction are difficult to interpret (occurring briefly, and changing frequently).

In the course of determining which orientation sequences result in circumstances favorable to specific need satisfactions, a degree of predictability is obtained regarding the consequences of various repetitive events. Although this process progresses independently relevant to each need, inconsistency awareness necessarily occurs when one orientation sequence conflicts with another or others. Satisfactory sequences, to the extent that they do not conflict with or contradict others, reduce uncertainty and inconsistency and contribute toward system formation by approximating a tentative framework for a new system during what might be referred to as a *fluctuating phase* (a second transitory phase, like the **vacillating phase** in that it is highly unstable).

If these sequences reduce uncertainty for the majority of a class of social entities, i.e., increase predictability of event outcomes when resulting methods of action are adopted, and if these solutions facilitate further orientation selections that clarify other inconsistencies, a *stabilized phase* occurs. During this phase, emphasis is on identifying utility values and on selecting orientations that attain the utility value of objects necessary for need satisfaction. This phase of stabilization guarantees the formation of a new system of sequences. The redirection and reintegration of each of these sequences has been based on information about and approach toward only those objects that are directly necessary to basic need satisfaction, and on the means and power of attaining only these objects.

After a new system has been formed (that is, non-contradictory orientation sequences developed that result in the satisfaction of needs) it remains to be conceptually rationalized and socially verified. Utility values identified during system formation have already been rationalized by necessity and might be regarded as the *material basis* for new cultural definition. The orientations selected for attaining utility value have been rationalized by expediency, but at least partly within the context of fragments of previous cultural learning and social approval. Conceptual reevaluation of orientations now takes place, modifying those that appear, with reference to continuing symbolic constructs, to be overly extreme for stabilized conditions. Modifications are considered through social interaction until consensus is reached, perhaps through legal sanction as well as social approval. These sanctions regarding conceptual redefinition verify the institution of a new system, initiated and formed during the phases of emergence, fluctuation and stabilization. What remains to be determined are the sociative values of the system. This occurs in the final phase, which has been referred to previously as the *established phase* (with regard to the earlier system of orientation sequences).

In the *established phase*, with a new system having been formed, instituted, and sanctioned regarding the appropriate, guaranteed methods of obtaining satisfaction of needs, attention is turned to institutionalizing these methods and defining the situations in which the success of these methods tends to be assured. In this phase, utility values eventually lose their primary significance because the situations by which or in which they are attained become sociatively defined and various situational objects become identified as objects of sociative value, the attainment of which appears to assure need satisfaction. (To the extent that these situations involve social interaction, and also because social interaction, itself, is valued as a way to verify a state of certainty, social objects now obtain sociative value apart from any utility value they may have.) Following the identification of objects of *sociative value,* social verification of their value completes the establishment of a new system.

SUMMARY

In the theories just presented, social reality is fluid, and images of man are selected or rejected, not on the basis of an abstract logic, but according to their effect on current states of certainty and uncertainty, conditioned and controlled by the context of current social experience. The first theory describes levels of consciousness that precede the outward expression of consciousness as behavior, and the subsequent interpretation of that behavior as having social meaning. Levels of consciousness are assumed to progress from thought and feeling, without any necessary reference to needs, though purpose and volition, which are need related, to the social act. At each level, changes may impinge that have consequences for subsequent levels, and ultimately for action and its social interpretation. These changes might be analyzed, empirically, as having direct effects at any level, (e.g. attitude changes that appear to result in the modification of behavior). A path model, therefore, might deviate considerably from the general model (assuming that a covariance analysis can be justified). But the researcher should be aware that such effects may be mediated by other changes impinging at the intermediate levels. What has been presented here, as a fixed process model of consciousness formation, includes all the essential elements of interpretive response, whether or not these happen to be invariant in any given situation.

One might ask, if this is the anatomy of consciousness, then what is "unconscious" mental activity? Is it an incomplete process? a separate, perhaps parallel process? or a process at all? The key to an answer may lie at the consciousness level of object selection. The actor, experiencing a need, presumably has multiple possible object choices for which thought and feeling (the pre-selection responses) have already been developed. Some if not most of these are associated with remembered or anticipated action consequences that are known or expected to either increase or decrease various tension states. The expected effect on discomfort (consistent with the primacy of Freud's "pleasure principle") may be the more important determinant of object choice, but two other tension states may subsequently modify object choice. One is an awareness of uncertainty, the other of inconsistency. Discomfort and uncertainty directly affect purposive and volitional responses, respectively, prior to the expression of consciousness as action, whereas awareness of inconsistency may affect consciousness at any level. Although distortion of response may occur at all levels of consciousness because of actual or anticipated difficulty in reducing tension states, it is at the level of response to a need through object selection that consciousness is "aborted", that is, cut off by denial (of the need). Purposive and volitional responses may subsequently develop to satisfy that need without consciously being associated with the need. An "unconscious" response sequence might therefore refer to a dissociated sequence of motivated consciousness formation, that is, one in which the actor is unaware of the nature of the need being satisfied (by the subsequent activity). In this view, "unconscious"ness is an associative problem (a self-protective unawareness of association) that does not imply a separate process or an incomplete process but a system stabilizing reaction to an aborted process.

Changes initiated in the levels of consciousness that precede action are explained by changes in systemic sensitivities and/or changes in the social environment. Four structures of the social environment are examined: the symbolic or cultural, the social, the economic, and the personal/political. These four structures control and condition the cognitive progression through levels of consciousness, and through action and its social interpretation. Additionally, this progression is constrained by tension states resulting from imbalances of sensitivity to and intolerance of discomfort, uncertainty, and inconsistency. These tension states are individually and collectively variable. The excitation of tension states are instrumental in energizing purpose and volition. The reduction of tension states are instrumental in securing the formation of thought and feeling. (Purpose and feeling conform to the mental activity described by Freud in his discussion of the pleasure principle; volition and thought conform to the activity described in his discussion of the reality principle.) Finally, each level in this cyclical progression of consciousness is contingent on the development of responses at the previous level(s).

The second theory is derived from the first. It is the first theory "set in motion." It describes the dynamics of social change when entire systems of action and interaction are undergoing changes initiated at the various levels of consciousness by changes in the social environment. Six phases of system reaction are described. Each has characteristics that may change in the direction of either an adjacent "earlier" phase or an adjacent "later" phase with reference to a cyclical (rather than temporal) order of change. No progression is implied, however, and the cyclical order is not predictive of what will occur, only of what immediate changes may occur. A completed cycle of six phases would be considered an exception rather than the rule.

The utility of these theories was described in Chapter 1. Their limitations are the boundaries of practical knowledge and experience in recognizing the processes as they are occurring. A caution is that ethical standards should be developed to prevent the use of these theories as instruments of social engineering. As scientific discoveries, they are as potentially harmful as they are creatively useful. They make it possible to analyze and purposefully change our ways of interacting with one another in almost any social setting. Whether this knowledge is put to egalitarian use or applied to enhance techniques of tyranny is a critical choice. It is a resource to expand resources. "Whose ?" is a vital question.

Chapter 3

Subjective Theories and Social Research

FALSIFYING THE THEORIES; EMPIRICAL TESTS

Testing the Theory of Social Action

According to the cognitive contingency theory, action varies qualitatively with "directives," and quantitatively with access to "resources," contingent on an ordered sequence of cognitive interpretations. Empirical testing of the theory requires, first, the verification or falsification of the cognitive contingency progression, and second, a corroboration that the categories of interpretation are meaningful. What must be determined is whether the social context variables are, in fact, subjectively interpreted, at what time this is done with reference to action, and whether this occurs in the designated sequence (or in any other predictable sequence).

Outline of a research design: The purpose of the research is to examine the effects of "directives" (symbolic constructs, expectations experienced during social interaction, need requirements, and personal commitments) on audience descriptions of filmed segments of behavior. Levels of experience are taken into account. The intensities of awareness of the four dimensions of social experience are varied during the experiment.

In the first part of the study, filmed segments of various types of active, aggressive behavior are shown to small audiences (not more than 20 subjects, in a somewhat informal setting). One third of the episodes shown portray confrontation, one third portray conciliation, and one third portray coercion. Half of the episodes portray interaction between persons of unequal status. The other half exclude status differences. Macro-level, micro-level and organizational level activity are each portrayed. After viewing each filmed segment, the subjects (individually) answer the following:

>What is occurring in this film? Why is it happening? What will happen next? Under what circumstances? If you were in this situation, what would you be doing? Why? What or who night prevent you from doing this? For what reason? How familiar are you with the kind of situation or activity shown in this film? (check any that apply)
>   (_____) Have been in such a situation.
>   (_____) Have directly witnessed such activity.
>   (_____) Have discussed this kind of situation with family or friends.
>   (_____) Have read about this kind of activity or seen it on T.V.
>   (_____) Have not thought about this until now.

Each filmed segment is then described by the subject with reference to the four dimensions of directives defined in the theory. These descriptions are structured. *Conceptualizations* are presented in a series of polar opposite word images. The subject is asked to select between each pair of opposites on a seven point scale, with the number four indicating a neutral interpretation. *Social expectations* are gauged in a series of evaluations of various aspects of the behavior shown, also on seven point scales with the "four" as a neutral position. *Needs* are assessed by asking the subject to first identify the "need" or "desire" being served by each behavior and then rate its estimated importance, on a four point scale. *Commitments* are similarly identified and evaluated as to strength on a four point scale, indicating to whom or to what the commitment may be.

In the second part of the study (subsections of which may alternately precede the first part just described), subjects are asked to analyze the four "directive" dimensions of their own social context of behavior. Familiar *word images* are selected from a long list, and rated on a scale of four as to degree of familiarity and usage. *Social relationships* are inventoried, indicating frequency or intensity of contact as well as positive, negative valence, type of relationship, and "setting." Associations are ranked according to importance, and valence and intensity are rated on a seven point scale. *Needs and desires* are listed and ranked according to their importance to the subject in several different contexts, including family, work or school and community. *Commitments* are identified: personal, group (including kinship), organizational and national. These are ranked and rated as to importance to the subject.

By then varying the "sensitization" of the subjects, with a personal analysis of one or more of these subsections prior to viewing the filmed segments, the researcher may answer a series of questions regarding "differentiation" of the (structured) film interpretations. (Differentiation occurs to the extent that interpretations deviate from the neutral scores.) Basically, two questions are of interest in corroborating the meaningfulness of the categories: is differentiation associated with the familiarity of the subject with the kind of situation or activity shown (see questions on previous pages)? and is it intensified by "sensitization?" These questions can be answered by averaging the scores. (Criteria for evaluating the results are suggested in the next section.) Assuming an affirmative answer to the question of corroboration, the next question is whether there is sufficient evidence of an ordered progression of cognitive interpretation. A natural ordering is implied in the structured responses to the question of "familiarity with the kind of situation or activity shown." Each level of this familiarity roughly corresponds to one of the four "directive" dimensions: the highest level to commitments, the next to aspects of need arousal, the third to social interaction, and the fourth to conceptualization or image formation. If differentiation is progressively associated with these experience levels (and the logical ordering of these levels is empirically confirmed), this key aspect of the theory of action would appear to be supported (or at least not contradicted).

Evaluating the results: The proposed research has been designed so that a falsification test of key aspects of the theory can be made with each subject (cf. Camilleri, 1970:78). It isn't essential that a random sample be drawn, since the results are not generalizable; each negative result contradicts the theory, whereas positive results are merely consistent with the theory. In testing a deterministic theory, however, one looks for ways to explain the exceptions, e.g., additional factors that might complement the theory or circumstances beyond the scope of the theory that might expand the theory. With this in mind, the following interpretations of results are suggested:

1) Positive results: experience and interpretation "match," i.e., the level of experience appears to determine the extent of interpretation in 19 out of 20 observations for the same individual, that is, interpretations are more differentiated at the levels of experience.

2) Indeterminate results: experience and interpretation "match" in less than 19 but more than 14 observations. (Check for effects of the testing situation, e.g., is subject over-responding or over interpreting the expectations of the interviewer?) Are there "carry over" effects: i.e., is this "like" a situation with which the subject feels greater familiarity? Look for "patterns" of deviation. (Revise the theory?)

3) Negative results: experience and interpretation match in more than five but less than 15 observations. (Any pattern of deviance? or are responses more or less random?)

4) Reverse results: experience and interpretation match in less than six observations: look for evidence of psychological "blocking" - or unblocking, i.e., response to "forgotten" experience.

5) "Confounded" results: evidence of contradiction of directives (see suggestions for testing the theory of change). Question: does "sensitization" (reviewing dimensions of subject's social context before viewing film segments) confound the results? What implications for the theory?

Testing the Theory of Social Change

In the first study, the emphasis is focused on interpreting behavior in situations of relative uncertainty, primarily involving active, "aggressive" behavior: confrontation, coercion and conciliation (as opposed to passive, "defensive" responses: avoidance, compliance and acceptance). Assuming that the theory is supported for this type of action predisposition, what empirical evidence might verify, or support, or falsify a cognitive inconsistency theory of social change?

In the cognitive contingency theory of action, an ordered progression is theorized. Because this progression is deterministic, it can be examined at any point in time and its potential impact on choice of action alternatives predicted without having to examine formation of the progression over time. But in studying social change, a probabilistic process rather than a deterministic progression is theorized. Such a process must be examined at intervals, to determine its points and angles of new direction, rather than assessed at its endpoint of formation. This requires time series or other longitudinal study.

The probabilistic assumption of this theory is that cognitive inconsistencies within or between the cultural, social, economic and political contexts of situations or events affecting a social entity will activate one or more consistency producing mechanisms, any of which might interrupt and significantly redirect a number of cognitive progressions and their determinant social actions. Such a process of change may very well zig-zag, reversing direction at seemingly unpredictable intervals. The analysis of such a process might first examine evidence of contradictions of "directives" (see *"Evaluating the results"* in the previous section). It might then proceed by experimentally simulating "experience" within the deviating context, looking for evidence of a change in the corresponding cognitive progression (i.e., artificially expanding the deviating state of consciousness and noting the effect). The risk of this approach is that the "experience" may reinforce the contradiction (e.g., increase cognition of a need that is in conflict with personal commitments, cultural traditions, and social expectations). Before assessing this as a "negative effect," experiences should then be simulated in the non-deviating contexts to see if convergences follow in the direction of the deviating context (e.g., do cognitions of commitment, concept, and affiliation *preferences* begin to converge with newly defined need requirements?). [This multiple possibility is what makes the theory probabilistic rather than deterministic.]

In this analysis, what is assumed to be a high activator of consistency producing mechanisms (that is, exposure to contradiction) has been artificially introduced to determine whether it, in fact, produces an effect. The actual mechanisms are not identified, and if such mechanisms are not activated at all, this may be interpreted as a negative result when, in fact, the testing situation is at fault.

Ideally an investigation of the validity of a cognitive inconsistency theory of social change should identify the actual mechanisms employed to produce cognitive consistency; these should be identified within natural settings over time, and, since this is a probabilistic theory, a well defined universe should be randomly sampled for this purpose. In addition, situations and events that tend to increase cognitive inconsistency should be analyzed and mechanisms identified that might be employed to produce inconsistent or non-consistent cognitive responses (including, for example, dissociation).

Preliminary to such an investigation, sets of alternative or alternating mechanisms might be identified intuitively at each level of analysis: e.g., invasion, embargo and negotiation at the international level; wage-price stabilization, minimum wage, and farm subsidies at the national level; public information, inter-organizational networks and personnel relations at the institutional and organizational levels. As diverse as these "problem solving" techniques or policies might seem, each set represents an effort to resolve a contradiction of directives. In the first example the contradiction is between culturally defined ideology and economically defined "national purpose"; in the second between social requirements of "the good life" and economic difficulties in meeting income needs; in the third between organizationally defined objectives and individually defined loyalties or commitments. Although most problems (at each level) may not necessitate the resolution of a contradiction of directives at all, but may be concerned primarily with the acquisition and perhaps monopoly of assets required by each directive, all problem solving mechanisms utilized to reduce uncertainty are potentially linked to such contradictions of directives, as rationalizations, and might therefore effectively produce cognitive consistency.

At the macro-level, historical analysis and analysis of current events are possible from archives, biographies and published records. At the organizational level, observation, interviews and analyses of documents are possible. At the micro level, observation, interview and biography are one set of alternatives, experimentation in a natural or simulated setting is another.

This theory assumes that "rational choice" may be incidental to human deliberations, even when rationality is a stated objective, but that logics of action may always be discerned (cf. Karpik, 1972), and although these compete, dominant courses of action are directed toward inconsistency reduction. Falsification of this contention would seem to require the simultaneous study of subjective and objective manifestations of the same phenomena, with a view toward proving the latter to be better predictors of behavior.

IMPLICATIONS FOR RESEARCH

Subjective Theory as a General Framework for Analyzing Action Systems

Two general theories have been presented for analyzing social phenomena. One is a theory of the origins of individual and collective behavior. The other is a theory of social behavior change. From these, "ideal types" might be constructed to examine the structural characteristics of behavior systems. (See Chapter 4.)

Other general formulations might be constructed, compatible with these, to focus on, for example, symbolic systems, or stratification systems. A comprehensive framework would thereby be provided from which each social theorist might choose a segment for detailed analysis, aware of its contribution to the whole, and able to move into adjacent segments to examine wider implications or trace the roots of unexpected results.

From this approach one might address the issues of holism, reductionism, collective representations at the macro-level vs. individual representations at the micro-level, and the virtues or shortcomings of the various theoretical perspectives. Integration and differentiation, conflict and consensus, communication and coercion are viewed in this approach as alternative mechanisms for inconsistency reduction rather than as either functionalist or dialectical explanations for stability, growth, or transformation. The emphasis therefore shifts from which mechanisms are seen as predominant to what variations in the context of social experience account for each. Interactionist concerns with socialization processes, exchange relations, leadership effectiveness, and reciprocity are similarly refocused, emphasizing the situational context of interaction rather than a categorization of its modes or the generalization of its consequences. Social manipulation, negotiation, persuasion, and bargaining are viewed as mechanisms for inconsistency reduction rather than as determinant processes, and are seen in relation to the variable forces that control and condition their outcomes far more decisively than the manner in which they are performed.

On the other issues: macro-level and micro-level phenomena are viewed as different in content but parallel in process, possibly defusing the reductionist debate, and holism is seen as a legitimate, practical analytical concern for anyone whose imagination and resources are unlimited.

Central to the approach outlined in these theories is a volitional view of the nature of man, and his formal and informal associations, subject to the context of social experience. Rationality is neither assumed nor denied. Social reality is theorized as fluid, ever changing, ever escaping precise definition. And the question of whether one is master of one's fate is therefore a relative question: in what directions? within what limits? subject to what constraints?

One of the characteristics and consequences of structuring thought about the nature of man and his social institutions is that what they are thought to be is often a reflection of what it is felt that they have been or should be, and such views, in turn, become a part of the fluid social reality of what they now are or will become. Images of man, therefore, are selected or rejected, not on the basis of an abstract logic, but according to their effect on current states of certainty and uncertainty, conditioned and controlled by the context of current social experience.

Subjective Theory, Social Context, and the Analysis of Social Movements

An analysis of social movements using this perspective might conclude that a primary concern with the problems of redistribution of resources (wealth, income, social status, technological advantages, political influence) will result in reforms rather than revolution. Such reforms will benefit primarily a coalition of those striving for change and those in power who respond to the reform effort, but not necessarily those on whose behalf the reforms were sought (the poor, the landless, etc.). In this type of social change: conceptual structures, structures of social interaction, need priorities, and structures of personal commitment, regardless of the intensity of conflict in the competition for resources, are basically shared by the competing factions. This consensus is reaffirmed after the problems of redistribution are resolved, as reflected in legal and other ritualized customs, in the general stability of these four types of operative structures, and in the overall social integration of the system.

Revolution, in the light of this theoretical perspective, would not begin with a challenge to the distributive mechanisms of society, but rather with a challenge to the functional prerequisites of the system: the institutionalized needs (as reflected in goals). If these are successfully challenged, individual commitments become the next target. These are more immediately translated into social action than are challenges to embedded traditions and status hierarchies. Social actions then become the means of challenging the conceptual structure, which in turn becomes the basis for challenging the social structure. The initial thrust of a revolutionary effort must be either to create intolerable inconsistencies in the context of social experience and/or to increase awareness of such inconsistencies. Ultimately the work of the revolution must be to recreate all four of the operative structures that direct the activities of society: need priorities, individual commitments, symbolic conceptualizations, and social expectations. The eventual success or failure of this effort will be determined, not by how "good" or "true" or "beneficent" its aims, but by an ability to decisively reverse the original thrust, that is, to reduce either the inconsistencies of social experience or the cognitive awareness of such inconsistencies.

Chapter 4

Suggested Research Applications

THE THEORY OF SOCIAL ACTION AND IDEAL TYPES

Subjective Cognition, Social Context, and Constructed Typology

The differentiating effects of social context on the cognitive progression can most efficiently be analyzed by identifying social context "constellations." This might be done by specifying the spatial arrangements and physical mobility of primary interactive social entities. For the purposes of this analysis, social entities are classified as either stationary and sparsely located or mobile and densely congregated. (Other possibilities are here excluded.) Further, the stationary entities are assumed to be in an "established" phase of social system formation and the mobile units are assumed to be in an "emerging" phase of system formation. This conforms the classification to an already well defined typology of "folk" and "normless" society (Becker's sacred-secular extremes, 1950: 254 ff.).

In the analysis to follow, the structural (context) components of this typology are shown in the left column, as controls (directives) and conditions (resources); the orientational components are shown in the right column as contingents (each orientation being contingent upon the immediately preceding orientation) and their effects. The "constructed typology" comprises the entire set of differentiating and differentiated characteristics. The translation of this typology into a fixed-sequence progression marks a transition from the generation of a classificatory system to the specification of a predictive theory.

(See Figure D. An Illustration of the Cognitive Contingency Progression Model, Contrasting Folk and Normless Societies.)

This illustrates the way in which the characteristics of an already well developed typology of social entities may be systematically reconstructed using the contingency progression model of orientation formation. Other typologies may be similarly constructed, beginning with selected structural differentiations of the social context.

The practical applications of this specific constructed typology might include community studies concerned with problems of "mixed" neighborhoods, school integration, crime prevention in areas of cultural transition, social programs for economically depressed areas, and economic effects of rapid industrialization on socially isolated areas. Studies of organizations might utilize this typology in determining the significance of "job" for different segments of its occupational structure or in further assessing bureaucratic structure with reference to changing organizational environment. Individual applications are also feasible, using variations of this specific typology. Other applications may be suggested by other typologies.

THE THEORIES OF SOCIAL ACTION AND SOCIAL CHANGE APPLIED TO AN ANALYSIS OF DEVIANCE

Acute and Chronic Tension States and Resulting Modes of Alienation

(see Figure E. An application of the theories to an analysis of deviance: tension states, states of action directives, modes of alienation, and target groups)

NOTE: Some Freudian terms for defense mechanisms are included as "specific responses" and "specific consequences" in Figure E.

THE THEORY OF ACTION AS A FRAMEWORK FOR THE ANALYSIS OF PRODUCTION SYSTEMS

Class Analysis and the Formation of Class Consciousness

(see Figure F-1. An Application of the theories to interpretations of social experience in production systems: opportunity, satisfaction, and allegiance relative to equity, ownership, and efficacy)

Implications for System Change

(see Figure F-2. Cultural interpretation/reinterpretation of social experience in production systems: potential for generating new insights, system changes, and system transformations)

NOTE: Marxian terminology is used where appropriate in Figures F-1 and F-2.

FIGURE D. AN ILLUSTRATION OF THE COGNITIVE CONTINGENCY PROGRESSION MODEL, CONTRASTING FOLK AND NORMLESS SOCIETIES

SOCIETY:	(1) (PAST) IMAGERY:	⇑	(2) OBJECT (VALUE) IDENTIFICATION:
Folk	Symbolic definition of an *unchanging* situation.		Awareness of those objects which are essential to a *stable* life situation.
	(A state of equilibrium reduces personal uncertainty.)		
Normless	Symbolic definition of an *unstable* situation.		Awareness of those objects which are essential to an *improving* life situation.
	(A state of change, with the possibility of improvement, reduces personal uncertainty.)		⇓
SOCIETY:	INFORMATION:	⇑	(3) IDEAS:
Folk	Sources of information concern *sociational* objects related to the conceptually defined life situation.		Perception of the *sociative* purpose of objects, (of interaction with family, relatives, neighbors, and friends).
Normless	Sources of information concern *useful* objects related to the conceptually defined life situation.		Perception of the *utility* purpose of objects, (e.g., of a better job, higher salary, better investment opportunity).
			⇓

Beyond Equilibrium Theory 57

FIGURE D. (continued)

SOCIETY:	INTERACTION:	⇒	(4) BELIEFS:
Folk	*Limited* variety of social contacts.		Recognition of *few* differences between social situations.
	Undifferentiated sociational initiation.		Recognition that sociation with any object may be *initiated by either* self or other (or mutually).
	Well defined sociational context for utility objects.		Recognition of *specified* types and amounts of uses of utility objects. (*Finite* utility.)
Normless	*Unlimited* variety of social contacts.		Recognition of a *variety* of highly different social situations.
	Differentiated sociational contact initiation.		Recognition of *differences* between objects in their prerogatives for initiating sociation.
	Undefined sociational context of utility objects.		Recognition that types and amounts of uses for utility objects are *unlimited*. (*Infinite* utility.)

FIGURE D. (continued)

SOCIETY:	(INTERACTION):	⇒	(5) ATTITUDES:
Folk	(*Social* situations reduce discomfort.)		Awareness of likes and dislikes for *sociative* objects.
Normless	(*Utility* relevant situations reduce discomfort.)		Awareness of likes and dislikes for *utility* objects.
		⇒	
SOCIETY:	SOCIAL POSITIONS:	⇑	(6) INTERESTS:
Folk	*Unrestricted* accessibility to social objects.		Perception that *social* objects are to be approached or avoided so as to maximize maintenance of a stable life situation.
	Defined limits of object use.		*Utility* objects are to be approached to the extent that their uses have been previously defined.
Normless	*Restricted* accessibility to social objects.		Perception that *social* objects are to be approached to the degree that they are observed to be accessible.
	Undefined limits of object use.		*Utility* objects are to be approached or avoided so as to maximize the process of improving the life situation.
			⇒

FIGURE D. (continued)

SOCIETY:	NEEDS:	(7) OBJECT SELECTION:
Folk	*Social* objects necessary to the satisfaction of each basic need have been culturally identified and socially verified. *Utility* objects are assumed to be available, given attainment of the social situation.	Recognition of the need for attaining *social* objects toward which (mental and emotional) predispositions have been directed. *Established phase*: Object choice is based on recognition of "like" sensation and "approach" disposition. The primary emotion is love. *Disrupted phase*: Object choices may also be based on "dislike" and "avoidance." Emotions may therefore also include hate, as well as sorrow, loneliness, fear and resentment of persons, and jealousy.
Normless	*Social* objects necessary to the satisfaction of basic needs are in the process of being culturally identified and socially verified. *Utility* objects are identified directly as objects of need.	Recognition of the need for attaining *utility* objects toward which (mental and emotional) predispositions have been directed. *Emergent phase*: Object choice is based on recognition of both "like" and "dislike" sensations, and both "approach" and "avoidance" dispositions. Emotions include anger, unhappiness as well as happiness, fear and resentment of situations, and envy. *Stabilized phase*: "Like" and "approach" are the primary basis for object choice. The primary emotion is happiness.

60   Beyond Equilibrium Theory

FIGURE D. (continued)

SOCIETY:	(NEEDS):	⇒	(8) MOTIVATIONS:
Folk	(Need relevant situations increase discomfort, and create an urgency for attaining the *sociative* value of objects.)		Awareness of the relative importance of *sociative* objects according to mental and emotional recognition of their *situational* relevance to the alleviation of need discomfort.
Normless	(Need relevant situations increase discomfort, and create an urgency for attaining the *utility* value of objects.)		Awareness of the relative importance of *utility* objects according to mental and emotional recognition of their *direct* relevance to the alleviation of need discomfort.

SOCIETY:	MEANS:	⇒	(9) RESPONSIBILITIES:
Folk	The degree, duration, and repetitiveness of object attainment required for need satisfaction have been *determined by past experience* to be practicable.		Perception of the minimum degree and duration of object use required for comfort. Perception of the maximum conditions for assuring repetition of the instrumental social situation.
Normless	The degree, duration, and repetitiveness of object attainment required for need satisfaction *are being defined*, and have not yet been proven as practicable.		Perception of the maximum degree and duration of object use required for comfort. Perception of an uncertain relationship of the social situation to need satisfaction ⇒

Beyond Equilibrium Theory 61

FIGURE D. (concluded)

SOCIETY:	COMMITMENTS:	⇒	(10) OBLIGATIONS:
Folk	Primary commitment concerns maintaining the *"status quo"*.		Recognition of a personal responsibility for attaining sufficient need satisfaction is *secondary* to providing continuing assurance of a predetermined need related situation.
	Commitments, whether by ascription or by competition, tend to be *permanent*.		Recognition of a *long term* responsibility.
Normless	Primary commitment concerns bringing about an improvement with *change*.		Recognition of personal responsibility for attaining a permanent need related situation is *secondary* to providing sufficient need satisfaction.
	Commitments are *not permanent*, due to changing circumstances and unpredictable events.		Recognition of *short term* responsibility.

SOCIETY:	(COMMITMENTS):	⇑	(11) INTENTIONS:
Folk	(Sensitivity to personal accountability for discharging obligations increases uncertainty, and creates an urgency for *establishing the situation* defined as necessary for satisfaction of group needs.)		Awareness of methods of recreating and maintaining the *social situations* relevant to fulfillment of obligations.
Normless	(Sensitivity to personal accountability for discharging obligations increases uncertainty, and creates an urgency for *achieving direct satisfaction* of group needs.)		Awareness of methods for attaining the *utility* of objects relevant to fulfillment of obligations.

| INFLUENCE | | ⇑ | (12) ACTIONS |

FIGURE E. APPLICATION OF THE THEORIES TO AN ANALYSIS OF DEVIANCE: TENSION STATES, STATES OF ACTION DIRECTIVES, MODES OF ALIENATION, AND TARGET GROUPS

Tension State	State of Action Directives	General Response	General Consequence	Specific Responses	Specific Consequences	Target Groups
DISCOMFORT (problems of the Id, i.e. of the organism)	Needs unstructured (and/or goals undefined)	FRUSTRA-TION	Emotional detachment. (Motivational energy unchanneled and/or under-challenged)	Indiscriminate goal substitution → (boredom) (restlessness) ⇒	Fetishism (passive reaction to discomfort; implications for self-expression)	Young; Unskilled, and Semi-skilled work force; Lower social strata; Social substrata
			Aggression (and aggression displacement)	⇒ Violence: against others, against self		
UNCERTAINTY (problems of the Ego, i.e. of the personality or polity)	Needs structured; Commitments unstructured.	ANXIETY (as well as frustration)	Emotional attachment; Mental detachment: reasoning ability disrupted or impaired (Motivational energy over-challenged; Intentional energy unchanneled and/or under-challenged)	Feelings of helplessness ⇓ (loss or loneliness) ⇓ (despair) ⇓ Feelings of depression	⇒ Situational personality disorder (possibility of Fixation) ⇒ Neurosis (possibility of Regression)	Elderly; Administrative, and Entrepreneurial work force; Middle social strata
INCONSISTENCY (problems of the Superego, i.e. of the acting system)	Competing Needs and/or Contradictory Commitments and/or Needs and Commitments are incompatible	AMBIVA-LENCE (as well as anxiety and frustration)	Emotional and Mental confusion. (Motivational energy over-challenged; Intentional energy over-challenged)	Inhibition ⇓ (fear, guilt) ⇓ Reaction-formation; or Repression	⇒ Inadequate personality (passivity) ⇒ Split personality; or Personality disintegration	Middle aged; Professional, CEO, and Highly skilled work force; Upper social strata

64   Beyond Equilibrium Theory

FIGURE F-1. APPLICATION OF THE THEORIES TO INTERPRETATIONS OF SOCIAL EXPERIENCE IN PRODUCTION SYSTEMS: OPPORTUNITY, SATISFACTION, AND ALLEGIANCE RELATIVE TO EQUITY, OWNERSHIP, AND EFFICACY

Production System	Directives	Resources	Structured Social Experience	Relational Social Experience	Cognitive Interpretation of Social Experience
Social Relations of Production	Networks of Social Interaction	Social Access	Horizontal Division of Labor vs. Vertical Division of Labor	Equity vs Superior or Subordinate	Possibilities for Lateral Mobility vs. Potential for Upward Mobility Reciprocity (2-way access) vs. Dominance-Submission (1-way access)
Modes of Production	Hierarchy of Needs	Distribution of Means	Ratio of 2ndary to Primary (subsistence) Needs	Ownership vs. Non-ownership of means of production	Emphasis on Relative Need Satisfaction vs. Relative Deprivation Relationship to means of production vs. Separation from the means of production
Modes of Exchange	Individual Commitments	Influence	Unit of allegiance (for purposes of sustenance): family; tribe, clan, caste vs. work group, production unit, or organization	Direct exchange in markets of choice vs. Contract purchasing	Commitments to personalized social units vs. Commitments to abstract, impersonalized bargaining units Involvement in bargaining vs. Separation from economic and political aspects of exchange decisions

FIGURE F-2. CULTURAL INTERPRETATION/REINTERPRETATION OF SOCIAL EXPERIENCE IN PRODUCTION SYSTEMS: POTENTIAL FOR GENERATING NEW INSIGHTS, SYSTEM CHANGES, AND SYSTEM TRANSFORMATIONS

Production System	Directive	Resource	Cognitive Interpretation of Social Experience and the Generation of New Insights
Institution of Production System	Symbolic Constructs		*Generation of value premises* (through an integrative process of reinterpretation of "old" reality tested meanings): *"equality vs. inequality" in social relations of production* (task differentiation and social access), *in modes of production* (rights & privileges in relation to needs,... duties & legal obligations in relation to means of production), *and in modes of exchange* (internal structure within bargaining units, external relations between bargaining units).
Introduction of System Change		Information	Acquisition (through a process of differentiation) of *"new" reality testing data and data techniques* (methods of collection analysis, and interpretation) *resulting in the generation of new insights*
Initiation of System Transformation	Symbolic Constructs		*Contradiction is "constructed" in the generation of competing value premises* (an internally, structurally generated process of system disintegration which might also be influenced by the interpretation of social experience with an external system, but only if that experience has either precipitated the internal contradiction or focused attention on the manifestations of it).
		Information	*Contradictions are mediated* (and/or reinforced) *in the generation of new imagery* (a relational process of analytic differentiation of system parts and reexamination of system "facts," i. e., of the basic elements of objectified meaning; "relational" between or among subsystems, but including the possibility of occurring between the system and an external system). *New imagery is rationalized, justified and legitimated in successive cognitive progressions.*

Notes for Part One
(Arranged by author, see Bibliography for full citation)

Adams, B. N. (1966). Coercion and consensus theories: Some unresolved issues.
Adams suggests a coercion theory of social integration, in preference to consensus theory. He argues that consensus is derived from coercion, and conflict is a rebellion against coercion: "it is coercion which maintains society and its subdivisions, and it is conflict which changes them."
This is a more determinist position than that taken in cognitive consistency theory (which is usually applied to micro-level phenomena rather than to society as a whole).

_____. (1967). Interaction theory and the social network.
Adams differentiates consensus and positive concern as bases for friendship and kinship relations, adding "feelings of obligation" and "mutual aid" experience to the more usual indicators of attraction: value consensus, affectional closeness, and shared activities.
This research identifies "obligation" as an important, separate dimension of behavior predisposition.

Becker, H. P. (1950). *Through values to social interpretation*, p. 254 ff.
Folk-Urban 'constructed typology' of sacred-secular societal extremes.

Benson, J. K. (1977). Organizations: A dialectical view.

Blumer, H. (1966). Sociological implications of the thought of G. H. Mead.
Blumer suggests a voluntaristic view of social action formation, in contrast to the more determinist views of other behaviorists, as an implication of Mead's emphasis on human beings as organisms having

selves. In a rejoinder, Bales feels that Blumer has overreached. However, the two agree on Blumer's interpretation of Mead's social act as "joint action," implying a fitting together or alignment of acts (in an ongoing process) that "need not involve, or spring from, the sharing of common values." Further, "meaning, common meaning, and also values" are seen by Bales as a product of social interaction (in the thinking of Mead), as well as a basis for unity.

_____. (1970). An essay on the nature of social theory, pp. 84-95.
Blumer defends development of "naturalistic" theory, developing concepts, models and images from the real world, relevant to natural happenings. He supports sensitizing approaches in research.

Burger, T. (1977). Talcott Parsons, The problem of order in society, and the program of an analytical sociology. (Followed by Parsons, Comment on Burger's Critique, and Burger's Reply to Parsons.)
(See also: Ellis, Moodie.)

Camilleri, S. F. (1970). An essay on the nature of social theory.
Distinguishes between deterministic theory and probabilistic theory, the former requiring analytical induction to explain all cases.
Discusses rules and procedures for empirical tests and theory verification.

Cartwright, D. & Harary, F. (1956). Structural balance: A generalization of Heider's theory.

Chaliand, G. (1977). *Revolution in the third world, Myths and prospects.*
An impressionistic but realistic appraisal of recent revolutions, analyzing the cultural and historical reasons why some revolutions are "better" than others. An interesting conclusion: "Aggression and destruction, domination and submission are a much greater part of the historic heritage of the species than once it seemed. Sole responsibility should not perhaps be attributed to leaders and systems" p.193. A sympathetic warning and theme of the book.
In a foreword, I. Wallerstein summarizes the three problems addressed: 1) Revolutions that do not reform (oppression continues), 2) Revolutions that bureaucratize (creating a "new class" of elites), and 3) Revolutions that fail to politically mobilize the most oppressed segments of society - for the long term.

Coleman, J. S. (1970). Properties of collectivities.
Methodological problems and considerations.

Coser, L. A. (1977). *Masters of sociological thought, Ideas in historical and social context*
    C. H. Cooley: The organic view of society, p. 307;
    K. Mannheim: The sociology of knowledge, pp. 429-437;
    Recent trends in American sociological theory, pp. 561-585;
    Functional analysis: A new course in sociology, p. 562 ff.;
    Exchange theories: G. Homans & P. Blau, p. 572 ff.;
    Parsons new directions, p. 569 ff. (Functionalism adapted to the evolutionist model).

Crozier, M. (1971). The relationship between micro and macrosociology.
    Crozier proposes a "strategic analysis" of power relations, at the organizational level, ignoring types of organizations (looking for what is generic to all of them), studying processes rather than structures, emphasizing the *how* rather than the *why* of these processes, and thus "freeing organizational analysis from historical and functional determinism.

    Crozier is interested in how the means of controlling human resources are organized. He assumes that the strategies accomplishing this are rational, although "the elements brought into the game by the players are not necessarily so." Ultimately he takes into account the interplay between organizational mechanisms and individual emotions, subject to the "constraints of technology, law, formal organizational structure and other more general elements of the environment."

Curtis, J. E., & Petras, J. W., (Eds.). (1970). *The sociology of knowledge*.
    (See also: Adams, Mannheim, Marx & Engels, Parsons, Wolff.)

Davis, J. A. (1963). Structural balance, mechanical solidarity, and interpersonal relations.
    Heider's Balance Theory, as formalized by Cartwright & Harary, is used to organize a wide variety of ideas about social relations from the work of Gestalt social psychologists (cognitive consistency theory), Homans (distributive justice), community and opinion theorists (clique formation), Durkheim (collective consciousness, mechanical solidarity) and S. Stouffer, et al.. (relative deprivation). (See also Heider)
    The resulting "theory of similarity" is not advanced "as a general theory of interpersonal relations but as a theory of one major component." Additional components include "mutual benefit" and other aspects of the exchange process (Homans) and "the effects of competition for scarce values" (resources).
    The theory of similarity, by limiting its formulations to considerations of cognition of "sameness" or "liking," excludes considerations of social action and joint action based on mutual benefit, shared obligations and

reciprocity (the "fitting together" of social acts described by Blumer in discussing the implications of Mead). A theory of compatibility would seem to complement the theory of similarity, the former with reference to action orientations, the latter with reference to object or value orientations.

Durkheim, E. (1915). *The elementary forms of the religious life.*

In the conclusion, Durkheim defines collective consciousness as a synthesis of individual consciousnesses, and states: "Now this synthesis has the effect of disengaging a whole world of sentiments, ideas and images which once born, obey laws all their own" p. 471. Further, he states that: "It is by common action that (society) takes *consciousness* of itself and realizes its position" p. 465. He then interprets religious beliefs *as* collective representations of society, stating: "religion, far from ignoring the real society and making abstractions of it, is in its image."

Ellis, D. (1971). The Hobbesian problem of order. (See also: Burger, Moodie)

Etzioni, A. (1970). Toward a macrosociology.

A theory aimed at mobilization of societal resources for change. The problem: toward what goals?

Fishbein, M. & Ajzen, I. (1975). *Belief, attitude, intention and behavior, An introduction to theory and research.*

Four coherently separate variables are distinguished in an effort to objectively assess what an attitude is, how it is formed or changed, and what role, if any, it plays in influencing or determining behavior. Relations among these variables are viewed as "a causal chain linking beliefs, formed on the basis of available information, to the person's attitudes; beliefs and attitudes to intentions; and intentions to behavior. Since the performance of behavior may provide the person with new information that again influences his or her behavior, the causal chain starts all over again" p. vi, Preface.

In Ch. 2 they review theories of cognitive consistency. Empirical evidence is reviewed throughout.

Gibbs, J. (1972). *Sociological theory construction.*

In Criteria for assessing sociological theory, he discusses the lack of agreement among sociologists re: criteria, but states that predictive power is the primary one.

He reviews three schools of "sociological subjectivism": phenomenology, ethnomethodology, and Weberian sociology, and states: an assertion about motives, perception, values, or meaning is not testable unless additional assertions are made about behavioral manifestations, and those additional assertions cannot be divorced from the theory" p. 74.

Hage, J. (1972). *Techniques and problems in theory construction.*

Specifying theoretical orientations, he discusses structural-functionalism, value orientations, and the systems approach. Three types of system "feedback" are discussed: 1) integration: the regulation of conflict and deviance; 2) adjustment: changes in outputs (values or goals) and inputs (resources); and 3) adaptiveness: changes in performances and structures (Ch. 8).

Rank inconsistency and rising expectations are mentioned as alternative explanations of revolution, p.180-181. Balance theory and exchange theory are mentioned as alternative theories of interaction, p.178.

Homans, G. (1961). *Social behavior: Its elementary forms.*

Exchange Theory, a theory of interpersonal interaction: maximizing gains, minimizing losses. Implications for coalition theory: power as a potential gain. Interaction as the dependent variable: the concept of commitment.

_____. (1970). An essay on the nature of social theory, pp. 51-69.

Points out the need to develop propositions of interrelations between social events.

Hughes, H. S. (1958). *Consciousness and society: The reorientation of European social thought, 1890-1930.*

The question: "how the human mind can arrive at knowledge of society at all" p. 24. *Sorel:* non-logical motivation and "the fluid character of reality"... which combine to form the myth, a "complex of pictures," reflecting reality at more than one point, p. 175. *Durkheim:* the scientific reality of religious experience is a *social* reality. "The practice of religion produced a sense of solidarity, of personal reinforcement through the group - in short, a sense of society itself" p. 285. *Mannheim's* "relationism": "all of the elements of meaning in a given situation have reference to one another and derive their significance from this reciprocal interrelationship"... of shifting relationships in uneasy balance... with contradictory and conflicting currents, p. 419, cf. *Ideology and utopia* (1936) preface by L. Wirth, p. xxv. *Weber:* "*both* reason and illogic (are) essential to the comprehension of the human world." The sphere of logic and the sphere of value must be combined and held together in the same formulations, p. 431.

Jones, E. E. & Gerard, H. E. (1967) *Foundations of social psychology.*

Discussion of cognitive dissonance (Festinger) and balance (Heider) theories.

(See also: Osgood & Tannenbaum)

Karpik, L. (1972). "Les politiques de les logiques d'action de la grande entreprise industrielle."
Supports a holistic approach to the study of organizational phenomena but strongly cautions against efforts to develop universal laws. Each object of study is unique: systems must be studied within their larger environments.

Kockelmans, J. J. (1966). *Phenomenology and physical science*.
Nature as the intentional correlate of physical science, viewed from the theory of relativity: being and becoming, Ch. 9.

_____, (Ed.). (1967). *Phenomenology, The philosophy of Edmund Husserl and its interpretation*.
Hegel's definition of phenomenology: knowledge as it appears to consciousness, not a knowledge of the Absolute, but only an approach toward absolute knowing. Philosophy is distinguished by Husserl from "the natural attitude." *Intentionality* is defined as a characteristic of consciousness "to form a meaning and consequently to constitute its own objects." "Intentionality... is essentially an act that gives meaning" p. 34, (and)... "consciousness appears to be not pure interiority, but should be understood as a going-out-of-itself, as ek-sistence" p. 36.

Lewin, K. (1951). *Field theory in social science*.
Conceptualized the group as a single organism, comprised of interdependent parts (a "dynamic field" of coexisting facts), within a finitely structured space (geometrically analyzable), with *goals, intentions,* and *will* "directed" within the present time-space continuum (i.e., neither the future nor the past is the "cause" of behavior), and with needs, aspirations, and value substitutes, p. 24-29. Lewin disdained teleological and associational explanations of causality, and ignored alarm over assigning individual attributes to groups.

Mannheim, K. (1936). *Ideology and utopia*.
(See also: Coser, Curtis & Petras, Hughes.)

Marx, K. & Engels, F. (1970). Concerning the production of consciousness.
The real process of production "explains the formation of ideas from material practice" and "revolution is the driving force of history... of religion, of philosophy and all other types of theory" p. 98.

Mead, G. H. (1934). *Mind, self and society*.
Consciousness is defined as "emergent" *from* behavior, and the social act "in its more elementary stages or forms, is possible without, or apart from, some form of consciousness" pp. 17-18. But Mead also describes the

social act as constructed by the actor *conscious of the social milieu through an interpretive process* (cf. Blumer, 1966, p. 542).

_____. (1938). *The philosophy of the act.*

_____. (1964). The genesis of the self and social control. In A. Reck,' ed., *Selected writings*, pp 267-293.

Merton, R. K. (1968). *Social theory and social structure.*
Requirements of Theory, p. 151 f.
Contributions to the theory of reference group behavior (with A. Rossi), implications for social context and social mobility. Related concepts: in-group, out-group (Sumner); the social self (James, Cooley, Mead); attitudes, perceptions, and judgments (Hyman, Sherif, Newcomb). Also see The theory of relative deprivation, S. A. Stouffer, et al. In *The American soldier* (1949), Princeton University Press.
Continuities in the theory of reference groups and social structure. Basic concepts: group properties, pp. 364-330; role-sets, pp. 422-438.

Moodie, T. D. (1976). Social order as social change.
(See also: Burger, Ellis)

Nagel, E. (1961). *The structure of science.*
Patterns of scientific explanation (four types). The cognitive status of theories. The reduction of theories.

Osgood, C. E. & Tannenbaum, P. H. (1955). The principle of congruity in the prediction of attitude change.

Overington, M. A. & Zollschan, G. K. (1976). Goal formation.

Parsons, T. (1961). *The structure of social action.*
Discussion of Weber's contributions to the theory of social action; e.g. the role of ideas: "non-scientific ideas form a cognitive element in the value complex" p. 537; "what one believes has much to do with what one does" p. 538. Four types of social action (including attitudes and subjective meanings in the definition of action). Three modes of orientation of social action (all normative).
Tentative methodological implications. The structural elements of action theory: ends, means, conditions and norms. A tension exists between conditions and norms; if either aspect is eliminated, the concept of action is eliminated. Means and effort provide connecting links between conditions, ends, and normative rules of action.

_____. (1970). An approach to the sociology of knowledge.

Parsons, T., Bales, R. F. & Shils, E. A. (1953). *Working papers in the theory of social action.*
Motivation is defined "originally" as an "undifferentiated" "flow of energy," an *"urge to gratification"*... to "level the existing state of motivational tension" p. 208.

Parsons, T. & Shils, E. A. (1951). *Toward a general theory of action,* p. 4 ff.

Popper, K. R. (1959). *The logic of scientific discovery.*
A survey of some fundamental problems. Theories. Falsifiability.

_____. (1962). *Conjectures and refutations: The growth of scientific knowledge.*
Three views concerning human knowledge. Conclusion: "all universals are dispositional" p. 118.
Truth, rationality and the growth of human knowledge, Ch. 10. (Three requirements of new theory: simplicity, testability, empirical success.)

Rotter, J. B. (1967). Beliefs, social attitudes, and behavior.
A psychological model of relationships between beliefs, expectancies for "behavior-reinforcement sequences," and behavioral choice. Sources of variance are discussed. The model is elaborated to include internal versus external control of reinforcement.

Schutz, A. (1965). An essay on social action theory, pp. 53-67.

_____. (1967a). Phenomenology and the social sciences, pp. 450-472.

_____. (1973). *Collected papers, Vol. I: The problem of social reality.*
(See also: P. Berger & T. Luckman, *The social construction of reality,* 1966, for a discussion of many of Schutz's ideas.)

Skocpol, T. (1976). Explaining revolutions: in quest of a social-structural approach, pp. 155-175.
A critique of current theories of revolution, including systems and value consensus theories as well as the political conflict perspective. Suggests a structural and comparative-historical approach, and explains why the Marxist approach is inadequate.

Tönnies, F. (1963). *Community and society (Gemeinschaft und Gesellschaft).*
The basis for H. P. Becker's Folk-Urban constructed typology.

Van Den Berghe, P. L. (1963). Dialectic and functionalism: Toward a theoretical synthesis.

Four basic postulates or elements of structural-functionalism: 1) Societies as systems (holistic view), 2) Causation is multiple and reciprocal, 3) Consensus (stable value systems), and 4) Integration (dynamic equilibrium).

Hegelian-Marxian dialectic has two basic elements re: change: 1) change is ubiquitous and is generated within the system, 2) change arises from contradiction: in values, ideologies (Hegel), institutions, or groups: i.e., in roles and statuses (Marx). These consist of cultural contradictions (Hegel) and structural tensions or conflicts of interest (Marx).

Warner, R. S. (1978). Toward a redefinition of action theory: Paying the cognitive element its due. (Followed by commentaries from Parsons and from Pope & Cohen.)

Weber, M. (1949). *The methodology of the social sciences.*

Reportedly, Weber believed that it is "impossible to arrive at laws - or causal explanations - that would in any sense give a satisfactory or exhaustive explanation of even the simplest human action." "In the social and cultural world (he had found) a fixed reality was undiscoverable." As a compromise however, between scientific objectivity and value judgment he suggested "hypothetical causal explanation" (the construction of ideal types), p. 306 and p. 310, cit. H. S. Hughes (1958).

On the other hand, Weber saw man as having become "almost totally governed, managed, dealt with", and subject to "structured constraints", and yet having a "variety of alternatives of action" and a growing "liberation from contexts... of tyranny, from values.. that were suffocating life and creativeness." Between these two views, he began to develop insight into the actor's subjective interpretation of the action situation, a position that anticipated the later development of "Psycho-Social Dynamics" (as a set of intervening variables between structural forces and individual actions), p.295, cits. W. Buckley (1967) *Sociology and modern systems theory*, and R. A. Nisbet (1966) *The sociological tradition*, New York: Basic Books. (See also p. 473f in Nisbet re: Weber's view of the interactive aspect of social action).

(See also: Hughes, Parsons.)

Wexler, P. (1977). Comment on R. Turner's 'The real self: from institution to impulse.'

See p. 178ff for discussion of social control parallel to Moodie's 1976 analysis of social order (e.g., on p. 181, Wexler states that the impulsive self, compared to the institutional self, expresses "a different mode" of social control, rather than no social control).

Wilson, T. P. (1970a). Conceptions of interaction and forms of sociological explanation.

Interaction is an essentially interpretive process in which meanings evolve and change over the course of interaction, p.700, such that, what the situation "really was" and what the actors "really did" on a particular occasion are continually open to redefinition, p.701.

To study this process, the researcher must examine the manner in which the participants sense of an objectively existing social reality is produced and sustained through given occasions of verbalized interpretation of interaction, p.707, assuming that "action is forged by the actor out of what he perceives, interprets, and judges" p.701.

Wolff, K. H. (1970). The Sociology of knowledge and sociological theory.

Zollschan, G. K. & Overington, M. A. (1976). Motivational ascription.

General Glossary
(See also: *Glossary of Special Terms*)

Access: (see Social access.)

Action orientation: cognitive orientation that begins with object selection (i.e., goal formation) and ends with symbolic interpretation (of the meaning) of the completed action directed toward object attainment.

Actor: (see Social entity.)

Actuation: the instrumentation of a cognitive progression sequence (of consciousness formation) as action.

Certainty: (see State of certainty, *Glossary of Special Terms*.)

Cognition: any type of "knowing", at whatever level of consciousness, including "reasoned" and "felt" knowledge concerning the characteristics and uses of objects, as well as (attributional) knowledge of the "purposes" and "volitions" preceding one's own or another's actions, and "comparative" (evaluative or relational) knowledge of action outcomes and consequences. Includes *awareness* of tension states, *perception* of resources, and *recognition* of directives.

Beyond Equilibrium Theory

Cognitive consistency: a state of tension balance in which the tolerance of contradiction is greater than the sensing of it.

Cognitive inconsistency: a state of cognitive consistency imbalance (intolerance of contradiction exceeds the sensing of it).

Cognitive orientation: a conscious objectification of and reaction to some aspect of social experience (i.e., of the structured social environment).

Cognitive progression sequence: (see Consciousness.)

Comfort: (see State of comfort, *Glossary of Special Terms*.)

Conceptual structure: the organized structure of symbolic constructs (conceptualizations: see *Glossary of Special Terms*.)

Conditions: resource structures in the social environment: information, social access, means and influence. (See also Resources)

Consciousness: three levels of cognition: awareness, perception, and recognition; twelve levels of progressively structured and conditioned *cognitive response to social experience*. (See Cognition; see also Social experience.)

Constraints: states of comfort/discomfort and certainty/uncertainty (in action formation).

Constructed typology: Weber's "ideal type," renamed by H. P. Becker for conceptual clarity.

Context: (see Social experience.)

Contingents: prior cognitive orientations in the cognitive progression sequence.

Controls: determine the formation of goals and the direction of action. (See also Directives.)

Directives: structures in the social environment: conceptual, social interaction, need, and internalized commitment that control the direction of action formation and determine goal selection.

Discomfort reduction: may occur in any of three ways: 1) discomfort reduced through a process of (social) justification of its "value," i.e., as having favorable consequences in relation to the satisfaction of a need (e.g. fraternal initiation); 2) tolerance of discomfort is increased through process of (social) justification of "suffering" as something to be endured in the given circumstances (e.g., the pain of childbirth); or 3) sensing of pain is reduced by sedation, distraction, or dissociation. (See also State of discomfort, *Glossary of Special Terms*.)

Entity: (see Social entity.)

Goals: (see Objectives.)

Goal formation: (see Object selection, *Glossary of Special Terms*.)

Inconsistency reduction: May occur in any of three ways: 1) inconsistency (dissonance) reduced through a process of (selective) legitimation, e.g., legal decision or arbitration, narrowing the possibilities of interpretation; 2) tolerance of inconsistency is increased through a process of (selective) legitimation, e.g., court ordered delay, postponing the necessity of interpretation; or 3) sensing of inconsistency reduced by sedation, distraction, or dissociation. (See Cognitive inconsistency.)

Institution of a completed cognitive orientation progression: symbolic codification (in the cultural domain) of the social meaning of action, subsequently reinforced during social interaction (in the social domain).

Interpretation: (see Cognitive orientation.)

Interpretive response: cognitive orientation toward some aspect of the social environment.

Mental process: a cognitive (conscious) discrimination of thought, feeling or evaluative response in the reduction (respectively) of a state of uncertainty, discomfort, or inconsistency. (See Cognition.)

Need priority: the salience of a need relative to other needs.

Need structure: the hierarchy of need priorities.

Object: any focus of attention for the purpose of interpretation of meaning and possible identification as a focus of orientation of thought, feeling, and interest. Also: an element of objectified meaning (See also Imagery, *Glossary of Special Terms*).

Objectives: objects (and object states) selected as objects of need (sometimes referred to as "values", cf. H. P. Becker).

Object orientation: cognitive orientation that begins with object identification and proceeds (through thought, feeling, and evaluation processes) to object selection.

Orientation: the organization of cognitive responses to the internal as well as external context of social experience (i.e., to states of discomfort, uncertainty, and inconsistency as well as to the symbolic and stratification systems comprising the cultural, social, economic, and political structures of the social environment).

Resources: structures of the symbolic and stratification systems: information, social access, economic means, and political influence that are necessary conditions for action formation, and determine the degree of goal attainment.

Sensitivity (or sensing): cognitive awareness of discomfort, uncertainty, or inconsistency in response to requirements of the social environment and the possibilities for meeting those requirements.

Social access: a resource (condition) in the social domain, complement of social position (see *Glossary of Special Terms*). Implies maneuverability in relation to objects and object states.

Social entity: any acting unit: individual, group, organization, community, institution, or nation-state.

Social environment: the directives, resources, and tension states that, respectively, control, condition, and constrain social action. (See also Social experience.)

Social experience: the context of ideational (symbolic system) and behavioristic (stratification system) structures and tension states in the external and internal social environment that control, condition, and constrain cognitive orientations, their actuation and their institution.

Sociative purpose: the purpose of an object or object state in providing the "social context" within which needs tend to be satisfied.

Sociative value: the relevance for an actor that an object or object state has acquired because of its sociative link to objects of need (i.e., as part of the "social context" within which needs tend to be satisfied by objects of utility value).

State of consistency: (see Cognitive consistency.)

State of inconsistency: (see Cognitive inconsistency.)

Tension reduction: may occur *either* through rationalizations, social justifications, and/or selective legitimations that interpret the source of tension in ways that reduce it or cause its acceptance, *or* through desensitization to avoid the source of tension. (See also: Discomfort reduction, Uncertainty reduction, and Inconsistency reduction).

Tension state: state of balance between sensing and tolerance of discomfort, uncertainty, or inconsistency.

Tolerance: acceptance of discomfort, uncertainty, or inconsistency.

Uncertainty reduction: may occur in any of three ways: 1) ambiguity is reduced through processes of rationalization (reasoning) that increase comprehension; 2) tolerance of ambiguity is increased through processes of rationalization that increase acceptance (e.g., applying faith, trust, or confidence in lieu of comprehension); or 3) sensing of ambiguity is reduced through sedation, diversion of attention, or dissociation.

Utilitarian purpose: the purpose of an object to directly satisfy a need.

Utility value: awarenness of an object's association with the direct satisfaction of a need, apart from any sociative value it may have in connection with attaining other objects or object states.

Value: a conceptual awareness of the existence of something that reduces uncertainty for the actor (e.g. 'the flag, motherhood, and apple pie'), which may or may not lead to the formation of ideas about how it is relevant as a need object (e.g., having sociative or utility value).

Defined (in contrast) by Parsons as "a conception... of the desirable which influences the selection from available modes, means, and ends of action" (in *Toward a general theory of action*, 1951: 395), containing, as essential elements, what Parsons has defined as motivational orientations: thought, feeling, and evaluation (in equivalent terms), that are defined, here, as six sequentially related "non-motivated" object orientations, of which value is the second, associated only with thought.

Glossary of Special Terms
(See Figure C, page 21)

Action: the outward, presumably observable, expression of subjective consciousness as deliberate, purposive, volitional acts, presumably intended to satisfy a need and generally reflecting thought and feeling (in the selection of object or objective of action).

Attitudes formed: the formation of positive and negative affective responses (feelings) concerning ideas that have been verified as beliefs in the course of social interaction. (Nonverification may result in the distortion of affect or in its suspension, but affect is assumed to be a derivative of social reinforcement resulting in discomfort reduction or in discomfort increase, depending on the nature of the reinforcement).

Beliefs: shared objectified meanings (cf. Imagery) that have been abstracted from experience as "objects" for further consideration, conceptualized as ideas, and verified during social interaction.

Commitments: directives internalized by the actor as part of a more or less integrated system of "personality" or "polity" that recognizes "parts" or "roles" that should be performed regardless of social reinforcement.

Conceptualization (with reference to symbolic constructs): patterns of constructed imagery that have acquired cultural (symbolic) as well as social meaning (i.e., are culturally transmitted).

Constructed imagery: the interpretation of new experience according to symbolic constructs (culturally shared meanings, cf. Imagery.)

Ideas: conceptualizations of objectifications of meaning (cf. Imagery) that have been abstracted from (shared) experience, identified as objects of investigation, and combined with new information following "search," "retrieval," and "evaluation."

Imagery (constructed, past): tangible objectifications of action, such as traditions, folk ways, and customs, that are descriptive representations of actions that have, at some time, occurred and been interpreted as having occurred, and as having social meaning (i.e., as objects of further social action).

Fantasies, myths, and folklore are special cases of imagery, in that they are representations of "possibilities" of past, present or future action (in the form of imagined situations or events and their projected outcomes). They are constructions of a "social reality" that is unobserved and presumably unobservable, but is, nevertheless, assumed to have objectifiable cultural and social "meaning" (i.e., as projections of unresolved fears, longings, anxieties, etc., common to those in the society or culture).

In between these two categories of (collective) imagery, that is, of the codified "real" and the codified "nonreal" (the validated and the unvalidated) there is a range of "approximated" (individual and collective) representations of social reality, as actions that are "thought" to have occurred, but about which there is not an absolute consensus as to occurrence *or* as to interpretation of social meaning (i.e., relevance for future action).

Influence: a manifestation of volitional power, as a resource in the personal/political domain of social action formation, when expressed directly to determine outcomes through the actions of self and/or others using persuasion or coercion.

Influence is expressed indirectly in the cultural, social, and economic domains, as manifestations of legitimate, informational, referent, reward, and expert power (cf. French & Raven, 1959, for definitions). See Part Two, theories applied to a study of power sharing in transition, for a multi-dimensional analysis of influence.

Information: any and all sense data that has been sorted, categorized, and codified as to relevance and meaning for purposes of rational analysis. (See also Resources, *General Glossary*)

Interests formed: the formation of an "approach" or "avoidance" predisposition (cf. K. Lewin) toward objects of affect (i.e., toward which attitudes have formed), consistent with social positions (locations in social networks, determining access).

Intention: the energizing of a volitional response toward completion of an obligation, as a result of an increase in a state of uncertainty relative to fulfillment of a commitment.

Means: tangible resources available to facilitate the accomplishment or acquisition of objects or object states necessary to satisfaction of needs, including instruments, techniques, objects of exchange, and supplies of credit, as well as more direct means.

Motivation: the energizing of a purposive response toward acquisition or accomplishment of an objective, as a result of an increase in a state of discomfort relative to the unsatisfied need.

Needs: include socially structured and conditioned needs as well as the biological requirements and physiologically triggered systemic needs of individual organisms and the more complex social entities that they combine to form.

Object identification: selection of, as foci of reasoning responses (thoughts), specific aspects of objectified meaning (cf. Imagery) that either reduce uncertainty (through direct comprehension of the social environment) or increase the actor's tolerance of uncertainty (through mediated assurances of future comprehension).

Object selection: selection of, as objectives, objects (or object states) interpreted as necessary to satisfaction of a need, and toward which thought, feeling, and an "approach" predisposition have (generally) already been formed.

Obligations defined: actions defined as responsibilities are matched with internalized commitments to more generalized "roles" (objectified constellations of integrity). Responsibilities that are consistent with commitments are selected as obligations.

Past imagery: the interpretation of past experience according to symbolic constructs (culturally shared meanings, cf. Imagery.)

Responsibility defined: means are matched to ends and a more or less tentative "role" is defined specifying typical actions known or expected to assure satisfactory goal outcomes, cf. Role Theory.

Social interaction: networks of social relationship, in which actors "test" the sharing of meanings acquired in new conceptualization (object identification and idea formation).

Social position: location within social networks that determines social access (see *General Glossary*) to objects toward which attitudes have been formed.

State of certainty: a state of tension balance in which the tolerance of ambiguity regarding an object, event, or situation is greater than the sensing of it.

State of comfort: a state of tension balance in which the tolerance of pain regarding an object, event or situation is greater than the sensing of it.

State of discomfort: a state of comfort imbalance (intolerance of *pain* exceeds the sensing of it).

State of uncertainty: a state of certainty imbalance (intolerance of *ambiguity* exceeds the sensing of it).

Symbolic constructs: culturally shared meanings, transmitted verbally, visually and audially to new initiates of the cultural system. A residue of many constructed images, and also a primary determinant of the character and complexity of new image construction.

Index for Part One
(Authors are cross referenced to Index of Authors for Part Two)
(Topics are referenced to Notes and to Glossaries of General & Special Terms)

Adams, B. N., 67n
Action, *See* Social action
Actor(s), 5, 7-11, 40-41, 73n (Mead), 76n (Wilson), 77, *83-84, 86*
   See also Social entity
Actuation, 29, 36, 77, 81
Attitude(s), 4-5, 15-16, 21-25, 70n (Fishbein), 73n (Merton, Osgood, Parsons), 74n (Rotter), *83, 85-86*
   formation of, 23-24, 27-28, 36
Ajzen, I., 70n, 261n, *335*
Awareness, 6, 8, 11
   as a cognition, 77
   first level of consciousness, 29
   of inconsistencies, 38, 44
   and social change, 51
   as a sensitivity, 80
   suppression of, 34-35
   types of, 20, 41
Bales, R. F., 8, 25, 67n-68n, 74n, 262n, *335*
Becker, H. P., 7, 53, 67n, 74n, 78
Benson, J. K., 13
Beliefs, 4-5, 9, 16, 21, 70n (Durkheim, Fishbein), 74n (Rotter), *83*
   formation of, 24, 27
Blau, P., 17, 69n, *335*
Blumer, H., 67n-70n, 72n-73n, *335*
Buckley, W., 75n, *335*
Burger, T., 10
Camilleri, S. F., 45, 68n
Cartwright, D., 7, 69n
Certainty, 29, 38, 40
   state of, 32, 40, 50, *86*
Chaliand, G., 68n
Cognition(s), 15-16, 47, 53, 69n (Davis), *77, 78*

Cognitive consistency, 7, 16, 67n (Adams), 70n (Fishbein), *78*
   production of, 47-48
Cognitive inconsistency, *78*
   production of, 48
   and social change, 7, 11, 29, 46-47
Cognitive orientation, 24-30, *77-81*
   sequences, 30-39
Cognitive progression, 4-5, 20-22, 24, 26-29, 41, 43, 45-47, *77-78*
   and constructed typology, 53-54
   See also Consciousness, levels of
Cognitive sequence, 28-38, 41, 43
   See also Cognitive progression; Cognitive orientation, *sequences*
Cohen, J., 75n
Coleman, J. S., 68n, *335*
Comfort, 27, 38
   state of, 28-29, *78, 86*
Commitment(s), 5, 71n (Homans), *83*
   as controls of action formation, 9, 12, 20-21, 26, 28-29, *79, 85-86*
   measurement of, 44-45, 47
   and social change, 31, 35, 50
Conceptualization(s) 7, 10, 16, 24, 27, *84, 86*
   as image formation, 21, 36, 44-45
Conceptual structure, 26-27, *78*
Conditions, 25-27, 39, 73n (Parsons)
   for need satisfaction, 30-31, 33
   as resources, 8, 21, 54, *78, 80*
Consciousness, 4, 8, 23, 47, 55, 69n (Davis), 70n (Durkheim), 71n (Hughes), 72n (Kockelmans, Marx, Mead)
   and action, 83
   levels of, 29, 40-42, *77-78*

Consistency, 15, 17-18, 23, 27
  system, 37-38, 69n (Davis)
  (*See also* Cognitive consistency)
Constraints, 19, 13, 21, 25-26, 50, *78*
Constructed imagery, *See* Imagery,
  See also Symbolic constructs,
  See also Conceptualization
Constructed images, 36, 86
Constructed typology, 53-54,
  67n (Becker), 74n (Tönnies), *78*
Context(s), 10, 24, 27, 30, 36, 39
  social, 8, 19-20, 43, 45-47, 50, 53-54, 69n (Coser), 73n (Merton)
  of social experience, 5-6, 21-24, 26-27, 29, 32, 40, *80, 81*
  ...and social change, 33, 49-51
Contingent, 20, 28-29, 41, 43, 54
Contingents, 26, 54, *78*
Contingency theory, 4, 11-12, 16, 19, 21, 23
  testing the theory, 43, 46
Contingency progression, 22, 43, 54
  See also Cognitive progression
Control, 9, 12, 41, 74n (Rotter), *81*
  over use of means, 31
  of object (value) identification, 27
  of object(ive) selection(choice), 35
  of outcomes, 49
  social, 10, 73n (Mead), 75n (Wexler)
Controls, 26, 35, *78*
  as directives, 8-9, 21, 53, *79*
Cooley, C. H., 69n, 73n
Coser, L. A., 69n
Crozier, M., 69n
Davis, J. A., 69n-70n
Discomfort, 11-12, 27, 31, 41, *80*
  state of, 20-21, 28-29, *78, 85-86*
Discomfort reduction, 11-12, 33, *79, 81, 83*
Durkheim, E., 14, 17, 23, 69n-71n, *335*
Engels, F., 72n
Entity, *See* Social entity

Etzioni, A., 70n
Festinger, L., xix, 7, 16, *336*
Fishbein, M., 70n, 261n, *336*
Freud, S., 6-8, 54
French, J. R. P., Jr., 84, *336*
Gerard, H. E., 16
Gibbs, J., 70n
Goals, *See* Objectives
Goal formation, 3, 7, 10-11,
  73n (Overington), *79*
  See also Object selection
Hage, J., 15, 71n, *336*
Harary, F., 7, 69n
Hegel, G. W. F., 72n, 75n
Heider, F., xix, 7, 68n-69n, *336*
Hobbes, T., 10, 70n, 260n, 266n, *336*
Homans, G., 69n, 71n, *336*
Hughes, H. S., 4, 71n, 75n
Hyman, H. H., 73n
Husserl, E., 72n
Ideas, 3-4, 21, 23-24, 27,
  70n (Durkheim), 72n (Marx),
  73n (Parsons), *83-84, 86*
Image construction, 23, 29, *86*
Imagery, 9, 21, *84, 86*
  as consciousness, 23, 27, 29
  and object identification, 80
  and reveiw of action, 32
Inconsistency, 6, 12, 15-16,
  71n (Hage), *82*
  awareness & tension, 38, 41, *80*
  state of, 11-12, *80*
  (*See also* Cognitive inconsistency)
Inconsistency reduction, 6, 11, 38, *80*
  mechanisms for, 48-49, *79, 81*
Inconsistency theory, 4, 11, 29, 46-47, 69n (Davis)
Influence, to carry out obligations, 9
  as a resource, 20-21, *78, 80, 84*
  wife's, two patterns of, xx
Information, 9, 16, 48, 70n (Fishbein)
  and cognitive reorientation, 31, 39
  as a resource, 20-21, 27, 31, *78, 80 , 84-85*

Institution, 26, 75n (Wexler), *81*
 *of a cognitive orientation sequence
  or progression*, 29, *79, 81*
 of a new system, 39
Interest(s), *80*
 formation of, 4, 21, 24, 28, *85*
Intention(s), 21-22, 24-25, 29,
 70n (Fishbein), 72n (Lewin), *85*
Interpretation, 4-5, 23, 30, *79, 80*
 cits., 67n (Becker), 72n (Kockelmans), 73n (Mead), 75n (Weber), 76n (Wilson)
 of social meaning, 40-41, *84*
 as symbolic constructs, 27, 32, 34, 36-37, *77, 86*
 and theory testing, 43-46
 See also Cognitive orientation
Interpretive response, 26, 29, 40, *79*
James, W., 73n, *336*
Jones, E. E., 16
Karpik, L., 48, 72n
Kockelmans, J. J., 72n
Lewin, K., xx, 7, 72n, 85, 261n, 263n, *336*
Lippitt, R., xx, *336*
Mannheim, K., 69n, 71n-72n
Marx, K., xix, 12-14, 17, 55, 72n, 75n, *336*
Mead, G. H., 7, 23, 67n-70n, 72n-73n, *337*
Means, 3-5, 25, 69n (Crozier), 73n (Parsons), *82, 86*
 as resources, 21, 28, 30-31, 39, *78, 80, 85*
 and social change, 50-51
Mental process(es), 7-8, 24, 40-41, *80*
Merton, R. K., 14-15, 73n, *337*
Moodie, T. D., 10-11, 75n
Motivation(s), 3, 8, 11, 22, 24
 71n (Hughes), 74n (Parsons), *85*
 and role expectations, 24-25
 and self-actualization, 36
 and state of discomfort, 20-21
Nagel, E., 73n

Need(s), 3-5, 8-12, 20-21, 26, 28-29, 43-45, 72n(Lewin), *79-81, 83, 85*
 & social change, 30-42, 47-48, 50
Newcomb, T. M., 73n
Nisbet, R. A., 75n
Object, 4, 7, 16, 27-28, *80-83, 85-86*
 (goal) attainment, 4, 7-9, 25, 32-33, 38, 40, *77, 80*
 identification, 20, 22, 24-25, 30-34, 36, *80, 85*
 selection, 21, 24, 28, 30, 40-41, *77, 80, 85*
Objectives (goals), 7, 20, 24, 30-31, 48, *80, 85*
Obligation(s), 9, 21, 25, 28-29, 69n (Davis), *85-86*
Orientation(s), 8, 20, 22-24, 29-31, 54, 73n (Parsons), *80*
 action, 7, 20, 26, 28, 31, *70, 77*
 object, 7, 22, 28, 31, *70, 80, 82*
 See also Cognitive orientation
Osgood, C. E., 7, 16
Overington, M. A, 6-7, 10-11
Parsons, T., 6-11, 13, 19-20, 22-23, 68n-69n, 73n-75n, 82, 258n-259n, 263n, *337*
Perception(s), 4, 26, 70n (Gibbs), 73n (Merton)
 of resources, 8, 27-29, 31, 33, *77-78*
Popper, K. R., 6, 74n, 263n, *337*
Raven, B. H., 84, *337*
Reck, A., 73n
Resource(s), 5, 12, 26-27, *77, 85*
 as conditions, 8-9, 29, *80-81*
 and social change, 42, 50, 69 (Crozier), 70 (Etzioni)
Responsibility(ies), 21, 25, 28, *86*
Recognition, 25, 33, *78*
 of directives, 8, 29, *77*
 suppression of, 35
Role expectations, 20, 24-25, *86*
Rossi, A., 73n
Rotter, J. B., 74n

Schutz, A., 17
Sensitivity, 22, 27-29, 41, *80*
Sherif, M., 73
Shils, E. A., 8, 13, 19-20, 22, 74n
Skinner, B. F., 17
Skocpol, T., 74n
Social access, *as a resource for social action formation*, 5, 9, 28, 30, *78, 80-81, 86*
Social action, 19, 50
  cits., 67n (Blumer), 69n (Davis), 73n-74n (Parsons), 74n (Schutz)
  formation of, 8, 17, 21-26, *81, 84*
  theory, 3-6, 9-12, 16-17, 43, 53-56
Social change, *& balance theory*, 16
  and normative assumption, 25-26
  and Hobbesian Q of social order, 10-12, 70n (Ellis), 73n (Moodie)
  theory, 4, 8, 11-12, 14, 29-35, 42, 46-47, 49-50, 54-55, 70n (Etzioni), 75n (Van Den Berghe)
Social context, *See* Context, *social*
(Social) entity(ies), 6-7, 12-14, 23-37, 39, 47, 53-54, *81, 85*
  See also Actor(s)
(Social) environment(s), 15, 26, 35-36, 41-42, 54, 69n (Crozier), 72n (Karpik), *78-81*
  See also Context, *social*
(Social) experience(s), cognition of, definitions, *78, 81, 83-84, 86*
  in theory development, 4-6, 10-11, 14, 22-23, 27, 32
  in theory applications, 43-47, 55
  See also Context, *of social experience*
Social interaction, 49, 67n (Adams), 68n (Blumer), 71n (Hage, Homans), 76n (Wilson), *86*
  as control of action formation, 9, 21, 26-29, 32-33, 43-45, *79, 83*,
  and social change, 35, 37, 39-40
Social position(s), 21, *81, 85, 86*
Sociative purpose(s), 27-28, *81*
Sociative value(s), 38-40, *81, 86*

Sorel, G., 71n
State of inconsistency,
  See Inconsistency, *state of*
Stouffer, S. A., 69n, 73n
Sumner, W. G., 73n
Symbolic constructs, *78, 84, 86*
  as controls (directives) of social action formation, 20-21, 27
  and social change, 36, 39
Tannenbaum, P. H., 7, 16
Tension reduction, 3, 7, 31, 33, 35, *81*
Tension state(s), 6-8, 11-12, 16, 41, 54, 73n (Parsons), *77-78, 81, 86*
  production of, 33-34
Tönnies, F., 7, 74n
Tolerance, *of pain (discomfort), ambiguity (uncertainty), contradiction (inconsistency)*, 22, 41
  78-79, 81-82, 85-86
Uncertainty, 32, 37, 41, 46, *80-82, 85*
  state of, 11-12, 20-21, 29, 32, 40, 50, *80, 85-86*
Uncertainty reduction, 11, 32-33, 37-39, 48, *81-82, 85*
Utilitarian purpose(s), 27, *82*
Utility value(s), 27, 37-40, *81-82*
Value(s), contrasting views, 10-11, 14-16, 20-21, 25, *81-82*
  cits., 67n (Adams, Becker), 68n (Blumer), 70n (Davis, Gibbs), 71n (Hage, Hughes), 72n (Lewin), 73n (Parsons), 74n (Skocpol), 75n (Van Den Berghe, Weber)
  See also Sociative value, Utility value
Van Den Berghe, P. L., 75n
Wallerstein, I., 68n
Warner, R. S., 75n
Weber, M., xix, 6, 17, 70n-71n, 73n, 75n, 78, *338*
Wexler, P., 10, 75n
White, R. K., xx, *338*
Wilson, T. P., 76n, *338*
Wirth, L., 71n
Zollschan, G. K., 6-7, 11

Part Two

Theories Applied to a Study of Power Sharing in Transition

Chapter 5

Social Order, Social Change, and Power Sharing in U.S. Farm Families

General Considerations:

In the historical development of the study of social reality, theorists have tended to explain social phenomena by focusing either on the structure of social acts and social order (Marx, 1844, 1867; Weber, 1904, 1914, 1920; Parsons, 1937, 1951) or on the processes whereby individuals and societies evolve and change (Durkheim, 1893, 1895, 1897, 1912; Simmel, 1900, 1908, 1917; Mead, 1934). Although many sociological theorists have dealt with both social order and social change, differences in emphasis have often resulted in long-standing debates and seemingly irreconcilable differences, with attendant problems in generating all-encompassing theories from the abstractions of either (Sperber, 1990; Hage, 1994; Anthias & Kelly, 1995; Mouzelis, 1995; Scott, 1995; Campbell, 1996).

In recent decades, critiques of grand theory (Mills, 1959; Merton, 1968) discouraged use of the structural functional approach that culminated in Parsons' equilibrium theory of social systems (1951). General systems theory offered a more manageable structural framework for descriptive if not predictive analysis (Buckley, 1967). The process-oriented approach of symbolic interactionism (Mead, 1934) gave way to more limited assumptions about processes of social discourse (Heider, 1944, 1958; Festinger, 1957; Goffman, 1959). Social psychologists and sociologists were advised to pursue middle range theories, in the belief that a researchable, all-encompassing general theory of social reality was as yet unattainable (Merton, Broom & Cottrell, 1959; Merton, 1968).

Precipitating this shift in emphasis, societal changes were occurring in post-World War II Western civilization that could not easily be accounted for by Parsons' equilibrium model or by Mead's symbolic interactions. Both schools of thought embodied normative assumptions. Neither was adequate to the task of comprehending a full range of challenges to the social order and accelerating demands for social change. Moreover, the phenomena of social order and social change were often seen as opposing forces, rather than as analytically separate continua, one of social structure the other of social process.

Failed attempts at drafting ahistorical, acultural theories of social and societal development, transformed by generalized processes of social and societal change, discouraged theorists from continuing this effort. Research needs and methodologies outdistanced the ability of theorists to reconcile the diverse traditions of abstract thought that had challenged the imaginations of generations of scholars.

About this time, researchers in Iowa and Wisconsin were studying the impact of technological changes in agriculture on farmers and their families, specifically: how farmers went about adopting innovative farm practices (Beal, 1957; Beal & Bohlen, 1957; Bohlen, 1964). One focus of these studies dealt with the social-psychological concept of innovativeness, seen as an attribute on which individuals could score on a continuum ranging from low to high (Wilkening, 1950, 1953, 1958b; Rodgers, 1958, 1962).

In a study of young farm families in Wisconsin, the possibility of a two-directional association of couple shared decision-making with overall level of adoption was noticed by the writer. During follow-up interviews, two types of husband/wife partnership were observed, one in which the wife was involved in farm work but not in farm management, another in which she was involved in all aspects of farming. With new data, positive associations of both high and low decision-sharing with level of farm practice adoption were detected using a series of structural and process variants as controls. From the results, concepts were developed by the writer to explain these variations as "two patterns of wife influence." From these concepts, and consistent with theoretical constructs in sociology and related fields at the time, two general theories were formulated to differentiate the causal contexts of these parallel effects: one a theory of social action formation, the other a theory of social and societal change.

The theory of social action proposes an ordered sequence of internally and externally guided and supported steps that must precede any new act, such as adoption of an innovative farm practice. The theory of social change proposes an evolving progression of actor transitions, in which the boundaries of the acting unit may change, e.g., as when the wife's role in farming shifts from subordinate to full partner, as happened for many young farm families following World War II. Both theories incorporate elements of structure and process. Neither relies on a normative assumption. These theories were submitted and accepted in partial fulfillment of doctoral degree requirements at the University of Wisconsin-Madison in 1977-78.

In 1978-79, a study of Wisconsin farm couples of all ages provided data to apply these interlocking theories to a new study of decision-sharing in farm families. Within the broad, general framework provided by these theories, hypotheses are generated from a theory of power sharing, to test the ability of this dual framework to predict and explain innovative behavior of farm families in transition. It is hoped that this will be the first of many applications in the social sciences. To facilitate this, it might be helpful, as a first step, to address the dilemmas and debates that have challenged social theorists and discouraged the development of an overarching framework for analysis of social events (cf. Anthias & Kelly, 1995: p. xv):

Debates on the nature of society and on the nature of the social.

First, the approach taken here is a cognitive approach that assumes that social acts originate as conscious and deliberate attempts to satisfy high priority needs, whether or not the acts or the needs are viewed as rational by other actors. Second, these social acts are assumed to have consequences for other actors, as evidenced by cultural interpretation and social assessment (cf. Campbell, 1996: p.140 for an opposing critique). Third, these consequences may then affect how other actors see and attempt to satisfy their own need priorities. Fourth, society is viewed as an interconnected network of social acts and their residues, i.e., those acts that are codified and continue to affect subsequent social activity. Fifth, society is also viewed as an interconnected network of actors attempting to negotiate their social settings to maximize gains and minimize losses while satisfying priority needs. These actors are variously constituted, such that a social act may be performed by one or more individuals on their own or others' behalf, representing an individual, group, organization, association or larger social entity.

Analysis of society thus requires consideration of both the act and the actor, singly and in combination with other acts and actors. Their interactions occur within broader cultural, economic, political and social domains, each of which provides options and opportunities as well as limitations and restrictions. The organizing foci of actors' actions are need priorities. As these are identified for self and others, it becomes possible to predict and strategize. To the extent that need priorities are hidden from self or others, there are likely to be miscalculations. The researcher has recourse to many sources of information about the need priorities of the various social entities that dominate a given society. Theoretically it should be possible to infer the existence and even the agendas of those social entities that determine need priorities of the society as a whole. However, such entities are capable of going to great lengths to conceal or misrepresent their priorities. The phenomenon of unintended consequences increases the difficulties of identifying need priorities, especially of those social entities that determine priorities of the society as a whole.

Debate on the nature of links between different aspects of society.

Just as social act formation is viewed, in the approach taken here, as a conscious and deliberate attempt to satisfy a priority need, social interactions are viewed as conscious and deliberate attempts to negotiate the settings in which priority needs are addressed (viewing social interactions as a subset of social acts, to the extent that they are culturally interpreted as well as socially assessed). Links among various aspects of society may be categorized as consensual, cooperative, coordinated, competitive, or conflicted, depending on how each actor seeks to reconcile the incompatibilities of his/her/their goal priorities with those of others. Such attempts may be incongruous at times, in that one actor may ascertain compatibility while another sees an actual or possible conflict of interests.

Links of interdependence (consensual, cooperative, or coordinated) may be formalized or even institutionalized, adding to their predictability in determining social action directed toward goal attainment. Of course, there may be complications due to greater compatibility of some goals than others. As need priorities shift, complications may surface. Links of interdependence are also affected by unequal power relations, such that dominance may create barriers to adequate need satisfaction, usually for the less powerful. This is especially true of established links between disadvantaged persons or groups and larger, more advantaged sectors of society.

Debate on the nature of changes in society (the dynamic nature of social relations).

Change is viewed, in the approach taken here, as ongoing and inevitable. What leads to change is changing resources (in this view), including novelty and abundance as well as scarcity and depletion. But change is also guided or driven by directives, which often precede and anticipate the real or perceived changes in resources. This interactive process may start in any of the domains: cultural, social, economic or political.

Disparities occur between social entities that seek to monopolize resources and those that seek to redistribute them as information, social access, means or influence. At one end of the continuum, restrictive societies seek to monopolize resources (not just maintain the status quo) and put tight restrictions on directives. At the other end of the continuum, liberating societies seek to redistribute resources and redefine or recreate directives, i.e., create contextual patterns that will best utilize new or altered resources to enhance the society as a whole, not just the dominant sectors.

This dimension of a society's social organization (restrictive - normative - liberative) defines a structured propensity for change, with implications for social stability along a different dimension: mode of resolving disparities to restore "order" within and between organizations, groups, societies, etc. Accompanying the society's structured propensity for change are types of goal-directed social action, with restrictive societies providing a setting for coerced social action, normative societies providing a setting for guided social action, and liberative societies providing a setting for self-initiated social action (see Figure G).

Modes of resolving disparities between and among social entities vary from consensus-building to cooperative to coordinated to competitive to conflicted. At one extreme is the dynamic of self-or-other-imposed *conformance*, self-imposed in "liberating" societies, rule

98   Beyond Equilibrium Theory

		TYPE OF GOAL DIRECTED SOCIAL ACTION:		
		Self-initiated	Guided	Coerced
MODE OF RESOLVING DISPARITIES TO ACHIEVE, MAINTAIN, OR RESTORE SOCIAL ORDER:	Consensus	Common needs, goals provide motivation to achieve group consensus. *Voluntarily accepted rules shape consensual interaction.*	Common values, ideas provide the rationale for group consensus. *Group formulated norms reinforce consensual interaction.*	Autocratically dictated processes require group consensus. *Leader imposed rules regulate consensual interaction.*
	Cooperation	Interdependence provides motivation to obtain cooperation. *Mutually acceptable rules shape cooperative interaction.*	Social and religious organizations provide the rationale for cooperation. *Community norms reinforce cooperative interaction.*	Tribal chieftains, clan elders enforce social customs that require cooperation. *Leader imposed mores regulate cooperative interaction.*
	Coordination	Compatible needs provide motivation to coordinate efforts. *Mutual accommodation shapes coordinated interaction.*	Government and civic organizations provide the rationale for coordination. *Societal norms reinforce coordinated interaction.*	Rulers or heads of state enforce traditions that require coordination. *Leader imposed legislation regulates coordinated interaction.*
	Competition	Competing needs motivate seeking of opportunities for competition. *Negotiated rules shape competitive interaction.*	Commercial and educational organizations provide the rationale for competition. *Media promoted fads reinforce competitive interaction.*	Administrative edicts or decrees encourage competitive struggles. *Leader sponsored propaganda regulates competitive interaction.*
	Conflict	Thwarted needs provide motivation for conflict. *Opponents and proponents strategize to invent rules to shape the conflict.*	Institutionalized values of dominant elite rationalize conflict. *Political advisers establish norms of engagement that reinforce conflict.*	Ruler-justified processes set the stage for conflict. *Leader pronouncements dictate rules of engagement to regulate the conflict.*
STRUCTURED PROPENSITY FOR SOCIAL CHANGE:	Liberative			
	Normative			
	Restrictive	Social order in equilibrium	"Alliances" stabilize social order	Evolving, adaptive social order	"Balance of Power" stabilizes social order	Social order subject to abrupt changes

Figure G. Structured propensity for social change, as basis for type of goal-directed social action, by mode of resolving disparities to achieve, maintain or restore social order.

or other-imposed in more "restrictive" societies. The dominant mode is *cooperation or rule by consensus*. Social change in this setting fits an equilibrium model. Midway is the dynamic of *accommodation,* or other, similar forms of stabilizing interaction among and between social elements, including bureaucratization, as the more voluntary dynamic becomes formalized, with tendencies toward oligarchy at the more restrictive end of the social order continuum. The dominant mode is *coordination of diverse elements*. Social evolution is the model of social change in this setting, gradual rather than abrupt. At the other extreme is the mode of *competition or conflict*, with a dynamic of lawlessness, revolution, war and other *violent solutions* within or between societies as competition moves toward conflict. Social change occurs abruptly and disruptively.

Aspects of these three modes are seen in the writings of Parsons, Weber, and Marx, respectively. (*Competition* is more recently addressed in exchange theory, and is basically unstable, tending toward either negotiation or conflict.) Each of these modes varies from self-initiated, goal-directed action in liberating societies, to normatively-guided or coerced, goal-directed action in more restrictive societies. *Individualistic* aspects of this continuum are addressed by Simmel, *normatively-guided* by Mead, and *coerced* by Durkheim.

Members of any society, consisting of individuals, groups, organizations and associations, might be located throughout the grid, whereas representatives of the society as a whole tend to fall within a more limited range. Seeming contradictions in resolving disparities among and between groups can be understood by locating social actors on this grid. Resolving disparities usually requires more than reframing goals and goal priorities, unless the actors are in compatible locations on the grid. Understanding structural differences in propensity for change, and altering the mode of restoring order, may allow participants to negotiate the setting to satisfy essentially compatible goals.

Relevance for U.S. Farm Families:

In mid-20th century, middle America, traditional farm communities would tend to be centrally located on the grid in Fig. G, as follows: *structured propensity for* (agricultural) *change* guided by technology, introduced by government programs and land grant colleges and universities following World War II; *mode of resolving disparities to achieve, maintain or restore social order* cooperative, or coordinated by a smoothly functioning, locally controlled legal system.

For several decades, farm families enjoyed an economic expansion that allowed relative ease in obtaining credit to enlarge their farms, to take advantage of technological innovations that improved the soil and increased productive efficiency while conserving the land. The *structured propensity for change* became liberating, for the business community in general, to meet increasing consumer needs and demands. Agricultural entrepreneurs received land-grant-college information about new technology, government support in subsidies and low interest loans, and agricultural extension help to adopt new farming practices.

The cooperative movement in agriculture at first helped even the small, independent farmer benefit from these developments. But corporate farms eventually gained the greater advantage, in the highly competitive markets of the nation as a whole. Large-scale food transport and processing companies made demands for highly coordinated production efforts that the larger producers could more easily meet. As farm size increased, the number of farms dwindled, with an ever smaller percentage of these producing an ever larger percentage of total farm produce.

In this rapidly changing setting, consider the consequences for farms and farm families in a midwest dairy state, evolving in family structure as economic opportunities both expand and contract. Self-initiated, goal directed action is encouraged for business enterprises in this setting, but within a *mode of resolving disparities* that has moved from cooperative to coordinated to highly competitive. Within the family, a compensating trend occurs in family structure, from a coordinated division of labor with separate, well defined gender roles, to cooperative role sharing in which many farm wives are increasingly involved in most aspects of farming. This trend mirrors changes in the wife's role across America, and the role of women in general, as occupational opportunities have expanded for women and contracted for men, in an increasingly service-oriented, postindustrial society.

Commensurate with these changes, women have experienced new dimensions in their ability to influence the exercise of power, including the contribution of new ideas as well as direct involvement in the decision-making process. Based on earlier research and theory construction, a theory of power sharing is used to differentiate the positive effects of wife influence on creative problem solving as (traditionally) separate, coordinated gender roles change, through phases of transition, to (nontraditional) cooperative role sharing.

The Wife's Farm-Decision Role as an Indicator of Family Type.
Characterization of farm families as traditional if farm decision-making is husband-dominated has been an "ideal typical" portrayal, for discussion purposes, in many references in the literature. However, Beers (1935), Wilkening (1958a, Blood & Wolfe (1960) and Hill (1965) failed to find differences in rural or urban family structure based on culturally-determined patterns of interaction. Wilkening suggested, rather, that husband and wife decision-sharing in farm families is more likely to be determined by their perceptions of joint consequences of decisions for farm and household (1958a). Rural and family sociologists and social historians continue, nevertheless, to make gender-role distinctions when discussing power relations in the home and on the farm (Ferber, 1973; Hannan & Katsiaouni, 1977; Scanzoni & Szinovacz, 1980; Scanzoni, 1982; Bennett, 1982; Gatlin, 1987; Haney & Knowles, 1988; R. Collins in Huber, 1991; Whatmore, 1991; Rickson, 1997).

In a social history of American women since 1945, Gatlin (1987: 6) asserts that a sex-role dichotomy was created in the nineteenth century that gave women a distinctively female 'sphere,' and that the 'functionalist' school, under the leadership of Parsons, upheld this sexual differentiation as 'functional' in maintaining the family and the social order. Moreover, since sexual inequality is reflected in the legal structure, and in many occupational hierarchies, it is relevant to speak of a tradition of male dominance in social relations, and to assume, further, that a degree of female dependence on male authority has affected gender relations in the personal sphere of family life. The research finding of no culturally-produced gender-bias in marital power relations may, itself, be gender-biased (cf. Harding's discussion of erroneous conclusions that have resulted from gender-bias in techniques of scientific investigation, 1986).

In applying the logic of a dual theoretical framework of social action formation and social change to a study of farm families in transition, it will be assumed that the *traditional/nontraditional* dichotomy does differentiate two types of farm-family interdependence, and that high and low levels of husband-wife decision-sharing on farm matters are accurate indicators of this structural difference.

Family Type by Wife's Work Increase, as an Indicator of Phase of Family Transition:

To fully apply the logic of this dual theoretical approach, it is necessary to have evidence of *changes* in farm-family structure through *phases of transition*. Increases in the wife's farm-work and farm-decision roles are selected, in the research application, as evidence of structural change. Due to sample size limitations, only an increase in the wife's farm-work role is used to define phase of transition, as follows, (for a sample of 176 farm families):

Phase of family transition	Low level of H-W farm dec.-sharing	High level of H-W farm dec.-sharing	No increase in Wife's farm work	Increase in Wife's farm work	n
I. Established Traditional	X		X		55
II. Disrupted Traditional	X			X	36
III. Emerging Nontraditional		X		X	40
IV. Stabilized Nontradiitonal		X	X		45

As shown in the chart, changes in farm-family structure begin to occur in phase II, *disrupted traditional,* as the wife's (instrumental) work role increases, and continues to change in phase III, *emerging nontraditional,* with a decision (leadership) role shift: from low to high decision-sharing, but stabilizes in phase IV, with no further increase in the wife's work role. Hypotheses are formulated to predict qualitatively different patterns of wife influence on recent adoption during *disrupted traditional* and *emerging nontraditional* phases of family transition. As noted above, the results may be more indicative of what happens on dairy farms and/or during middle stages of the family cycle, than on nondairy farms and/or during early and late stages of the family cycle. Phases will be discussed further in Chapter 9, Method of Analysis. Hypotheses are presented in Chapter 10, Design of the Analysis.

Background for the Analysis:
The central thesis is that the farm wife's influence on recent adoption of improved farm technology occurs within two very different structures of family organization. One is a *shared-obligations* partnership in which the wife participates fully in financial and management decisions affecting the farm. The other is a *separate-spheres* partnership in which the husband and wife have separate but compatible obligations: his for the overall farm enterprise and hers for specific chores and tasks. The latter is the more typical structure of family organization in rural America prior to World War II.

During World War II (1941-1945), great emphasis was placed on improving farm efficiency and increasing production yields for the war effort. At the same time, there was a manpower shortage due to induction of sons and young husbands into the armed services. As in Pioneer Days, rural women took to the plow, as they often have in times of need. And for many this expanded involvement continued to be a significant part of their farm role after the war ended, as a booming economy provided more off-farm jobs for their men, and the capitalization costs of farming soared.

New technologies were invented, during and after the war, that resulted in rapid mechanization of labor-intensive industries, including not only farming but also agricultural-related food-processing and packaging industries in or near rural areas. Labor-saving devices were also designed for the home, freeing women for greater involvement in the paid work force. So the wife's role in providing capitalization for the farm also expanded, as opportunities for paid employment increased for her as well as for her husband.

Meanwhile, agricultural extension services and university short courses were teaching the new technologies to farmers and farm youth, emphasizing the importance of keeping good records to assess the impact of new practices on yields. Wives and mothers often became the keepers of these records, as well as the managers of cash flow, as farm accounts became increasingly complex.

In twenty years time (1945-1965), as overproduction squeezed the profit margin for small farmers, the number of farm families dwindled as the average farm size doubled, tripled and quadrupled. An 80 to 160 acre farm could no longer support the average farm family, and commercial farms were typically 360 to 480 acres. "Survival" demanded the combined efforts of all family members in whatever capacities they could best serve. The farm wife became flexible and many-talented, and her influence increased. As the second movement of the 20th century for women's equality began in 1966, the American farm wife had earned the right to say that she, too, was a farmer.

But this was a time of transition. Commercial farms continued to grow in size, and newer technologies made it increasingly difficult for the smaller farms to be profitable. Many became "marginal" as younger family members found other occupations and the "old folks" retired. A typical farm couple on these smaller farms was now late middle-aged, with most of their children grown and living elsewhere.

Within this historical-cultural context, then, we will look more closely at farm couples who were farming two decades ago, when large-scale farming was crowding out the small operator, when farming was no longer the most viable occupation for most farm youth, and when success demanded a large capital investment just to "break even." The wife's role in farming, at such a time, might well be considered critical to the success of the operation.

Key Concepts:

The post-World War II economic boom eventually resulted, nationwide, in an expectation of greater equality for women, as economic opportunities for employment of women led to their greater participation in the breadwinner role. In many farm families, too, the wife's involvement in the work of farming had significantly changed her view of the importance of her role. She had become involved to a greater degree in farm management through responsibility for increasingly complex record-keeping. She was able to handle the more mechanized chores, such as operating the milking machines and other livestock equipment. She could do the less physically demanding fieldwork, such as driving the tractor and other specialized farm vehicles. And she, too, became interested in agricultural extension and farm short courses.

Within this context of *shared-obligation* for success of the operation, many husbands and wives began to expect that they should be mutually and reciprocally involved in making important farm decisions. And this became a structural characteristic of their family organization, with the authority structure of the family characterized by an *egalitarian* approach to decision-making. In pretest interviews for the present study, when asked how farm decisions were made, one or the other would say that they were made together, rather than by the husband alone. (This trend was observed in a study of young farm families in Wisconsin as early as the 1950's.)

Within the context of a more *traditional* family organization, where both consider the husband, alone, as the farm operator and family provider, the wife's influence is often exercised indirectly, through helpful hints, suggestions and moral support, whether or not it is recognized as influence by either spouse. But this influence tends to be unstructured rather than structured, and may reflect either their shared interest in the farm or her competing, yet compatible, interests in the home and family. Nevertheless, the structure of family decision-making on farm matters would be regarded by an observer as male-dominated and *authoritarian*.

Conforming this dichotomy of family types to the precepts of exchange theory as expanded to include "conferred exchange" (DeWitt, 1981), the more *authoritarian* couples have accepted a distribution of obligations "*pre*"-*negotiated by cultural traditions,* based on an economy of choices that recognizes the efficiency of a *division of authority into separate spheres of influence.* But the more *egalitarian* couples, responding to greater opportunities for *role sharing* made possible by labor saving technologies, have *coordinated their skills and expertise,* allowing a freer, more reciprocal *negotiation of power relationships* to occur.

Such power relationships, whether entered into interpersonally or culturally, might be defined as voluntary or involuntary *exchanges of obligations,* negotiated contractually or implied in agreements that are entered into informally, consciously adopted or accepted according to cultural conditioning and family tradition. For the purposes of this analysis, it will be sufficient to differentiate the nature of influence in power relationships as either *structurally-based* or *process-oriented.* To the extent *structurally-based,* the wife's influence in farm matters will be seen as culturally determined and secondary to the husband's. To the extent that the wife's power relations are *process-oriented,* her influence will be observed as interpersonally determined, and a function of role sharing.

French and Raven (1959) have identified six dimensions of power and influence. Three of these might be defined as structurally based to the extent that they are ascribed rather than achieved. They are: *coercion, reward power, and legitimacy.* The husband in an authoritarian family has power based on an ascribed (structurally based) *legitimacy*, which gives him an obligation to *reward* family members, and a legally mandated right to *coerce* family members.

The other three bases of power and influence might be defined as *process-oriented* to the extent that they are achieved rather than ascribed. They are *expertise, informational power,* and *referent power*. The husband and wife in an egalitarian family share power based on their achieved (process-oriented) *expertise,* reinforced by their acquired *informational power* (concerning their shared occupation) and strength of *referent power* attained in their relationship.

The nature of the wife's influence, however, depends on the extent of the husband's recognition (legitimization) of her achieved power base and willingness, thereby, to relinquish his structurally determined advantage. For in the more authoritarian family, the wife also has *referent power,* and may indirectly influence farm decisions by providing or withholding emotional support. She might also informally provide *information* and *expertise* while involved in farm tasks. By these means she can affect the outcome of decisions indirectly, even though not formally involved in the decision-making process.

In the more egalitarian family, where decisions as well as farm tasks are shared, the wife has the same recognized power base as the husband, but usually to a lesser degree. (Exceptions might include where she has inherited the farm or provided the capitalization by another means, where she has achieved the skill and training to manage the farm operation on her own, or where she has a specialized skill that is essential to the operation). Thus, the nature of the wife's influence varies along a structure-process continuum differentiated by family type.

Whether structurally-based or process-oriented, decision-making occurs within a family context of interpersonal accommodation that is adapting and evolving over time. In early stages of the family life cycle, *referent power* may be the strongest source of wife influence, regardless of family type, as each tries to please the other. As major changes in the farm operation are considered, sources of *information* and *expertise* may outweigh other considerations. If a wife is disposed to provide these, she may influence the outcome whether or not she is involved in the formal process of decision-making. It is important, therefore, to look for evidence of indirect as well as direct influence in studying the wife's farm role.

Purpose of the Study:

The present study of wife influence on adoption of technological changes in farming was designed to test a *Theory of Power Sharing in Transition*, using a framework of interrelated general theories that describe developmental stages in the formation of social action, and transitional phases of action transformation during periods of rapid social change. These theories were formulated with the help of insights obtained from earlier farm family interviews, and from data analysis that appeared to show both positive and negative effects on overall level of adoption of technological innovations when husband and wife share farm decisions.

The earlier data analysis attempted to approximate the effects of changes in key variables over time. A subsequent analysis of agricultural census data demonstrated that analysis of measures of statistical association of changing behavioral trends (movement out of farming) without such considerations may be misleading (DeWitt, 1967). To assess effects of the time factor more adequately, the present research utilizes respondent recall to approximate recent changes in key variables. Although this technique relies on data that are subject to error, in the absence of longitudinal measures it was deemed necessary to obtain such data to test theories about a process of adaptation to technological change.

Theory of Power Sharing:

Rationale for a Theory of Power Sharing:
In celebrating individualism, independence, and freedom of choice, it is easy to forget that progress is usually a cooperative venture, relying on agreements and consensus, rather than the product of a competitive, "winner-take-all" strategy. Similarly, creativity is often portrayed as a lonely pursuit of isolated artists and geniuses, rather than a team effort by highly motivated partners and coworkers. Only in crisis is there likely to be an urgent realization that problem solving must draw on the resources of everyone present or reachable. The luxuries of individualism, independence, and freedom of choice are sidelined in the interest of a common cause.

Power sharing and collective action are often born of necessity, and thrive on the benefits experienced by those who participate. Whatever the nature of the goal, options for ways to solve difficulties and surmount obstacles increase as power is shared with those who strive for the same goal while committed to a common destiny. The *Theory of Power Sharing* applied in this work is predicated on an assumption that power sharing is entered into voluntarily by participants, in expectation of mutual gain but also in dedication to a shared purpose.

Historically, territorial separation may have impeded recognition of shared purpose, not only geographically but also in gender relations. Segregation during socialization, and adult role differentiation along gender lines in marriage as well as in the work place, may have limited the free exchange of ideas, suggestions and informal expertise that same-sex friends, partners and coworkers have often relied on to respond to daily perplexities, in life as well as in the workplace. In recent years, opposite-sex partnerships, friendships, and colleague relations appear to be receiving serious appraisal as resources for creative problem solving. As such, these associations would seem to be preparing the way for gender power sharing.

Theory of Gender Power Sharing in Transition:
The Theory of Power Sharing applied to gender relations states that, as segregation in socialization breaks down or becomes diffused, expectations for achievement begin to converge. Adult role differentiation is eventually challenged, and instrumental role sharing initiated, setting the stage for disruption of traditional organizational and family structures. This opens up the possibility for opposite-sex contributions in occupational and domestic spheres once labeled gender specific.

The theory does not imply that instrumental role sharing, disruption of traditional structures, and contributions across gender lines will necessarily result in creative problem solving, or ultimately lead to full-scale power sharing. These outcomes depend on perceptions, abilities, dispositions, and other characteristics of the participants, within contextual requirements and constraints of the setting, and eventually on whether new organizational structures emerge that disregard power disparities that have existed.

Initially, contributions across gender lines are assessed as expertise, and accepted or disregarded depending on relative merit and other considerations, including applicability to current concerns, as well as effect on organizational structure. Direct influence by new contributors occurs only after leadership status is obtained or conferred, an indication that a new organizational structure is in the process of emerging. Even then, creative problem solving is problematic, as above.

To apply this theory to farm couples adapting to a changing farm setting requires specifying and measuring the wife's farm roles and role changes, role sharing between husband and wife, the husband's perceptions of the wife's farm-role contributions, and the context of the farm setting in which these role structures and structural changes occur. To test the *Theory of Power Sharing in Transition*, two patterns of wife influence are predicted for farm families in transition, in a midwestern U. S. dairy state, during the mid to late 1970s when expectations for increased farm profits were high. Recent adoption of innovative farm practices is used as an indicator of creative problem solving. Having selected recent adoption as an indicator, the goal is to build models that can predict those combinations of circumstances for which the number of innovative farm practices recently adopted will be highest.

Theories of Social Action and Social Change:

Two general theories have been formulated to provide a theoretical framework for these models (cf. Chapter 2). The first, A Cognitive Contingency Theory of Social Action, describes cognitive response sequences (ordered sets of cognitions of cultural, social, economic and political circumstances) that are necessary for individual, group and collective adaptation to social settings. The second, A Cognitive Inconsistency Theory of Social Change, describes processes of sequence disintegration/ transformation/ reintegration that occur as social settings change.

These general theories help to anticipate and explain human, social evolution at all levels of social organization. For farm families in transition, they help to explain not only the observed changes in farm roles of husbands and wives, but also the significance of these changes for adaptation to a new farming environment.

The first theory, a theory of social action, states that action is part of, and follows from, an ordered sequence of cognitive responses. Social action results when the sequence is completed, contingent on the valence (plus/minus) of some cognitions, the degree (intensity) of others, and the priority of completion relative to other sequences. (In an analogy to neuro-physiology, one may think of a series of *synapses,* each of which must occur, and in sufficient strength, for the series to go to completion.) Consequently, when an action occurs, there may have been a long preparation for what might seem to be triggered in an instant. And that trigger can occur at any place in the series of necessary cognitions. So it is essential, in causal analysis, to examine a full range of controls and conditions that can affect a given series, and to be aware that a change in valence of a single cognition, anywhere in the series, may change the direction of the outcome.

In applying this theory to farm families, therefore, aspects of the wife's farming role will be examined that might affect the direction of her influence when involved in farm decisions. These include: her involvement in farm work, her perception of herself as a partner in farming, her motivation to spend "extra" money for the farm, how she and her husband resolve differences of opinion on farm matters, and even whether they recently spent an evening "just chatting."

The second theory, a theory of social change, recognizes that the *interactive patterns* of the response unit (e.g. the farm family) *are reorganized* as changes in the social setting are perceived to impact the success/failure of action outcomes, and that this reorganization tends to either incorporate or divest unit members *as actors*. The theory describes six transitions that may occur in structural transformation: three of incorporation and three of divestment. Two are especially relevant to this study: incorporation of the wife (more fully) in farm work and incorporation of the wife (more fully) in farm decisions. Included in this research, therefore, are measures of increase in these two variables. These changes may be interpreted as *structural adaptations* of the farm family *to changes in the farm setting.*

The setting, in *the cognitive theory of social action*, consists of four levels of causal factors which consecutively impact on social action: the first level is *cultural,* the second is *social,* the third is *economic,* and the fourth is *political.* Each level consists of an interaction of directives that control and resources that condition the cognitive sequence at that level, eventually to determine a given social act.

According to this theory: The cultural level defines *certainty and uncertainty* (and provides secondary means to assure certainty or alleviate uncertainty). The social level defines *comfort and discomfort* (and provides secondary means to assure comfort or alleviate discomfort). The economic level provides primary means to assure comfort or alleviate discomfort. The political level provides primary means to assure certainty or alleviate uncertainty.

Each response unit (individual, group, or collectivity) has cognitive elements that sense the relevance of directives and availability of resources associated at each level. These sensors (organizational or constitutional) assess *whether* a given directive, and *how much* of a given resource, affect an experienced state of comfort-discomfort or certainty-uncertainty. (Sensors are activated within limits of tolerance, which vary over time, by unit, by setting.)

Action outcomes also impact the setting, altering it in predictable ways by extending or limiting further options. So the theories of social action and social change provide a complex analytical model and predictive framework.

In applying this set of theories to research on farm families, it is expected that *early stage in the family life cycle* (a social variable) and *financial indebtedness* (an economic variable) will determine, respectively, how interested and motivated families are to increase their farm income (to alleviate discomfort). And it is expected that *agricultural education* (a cultural variable) will indicate how knowledgeable they are of ways to do this (to alleviate uncertainty). It is therefore expected that young farm families, those with high farm debt, and those with agricultural education will be more alert to requirements of the setting, and therefore more receptive to innovative ideas that improve their crop yields and increase their farm income.

If the setting, itself, is changing as these adaptations are taking place, the structural organization of the farm family may adapt, as well, to reflect the nature of perceived changes in the setting. As competition and scarcity limit access to essential economic resources, the wife and other family members may increasingly be incorporated into key work roles, including record-keeping and work off the farm, to provide essential services and to broaden the socioeconomic base. As technological advances and government policies create uncertainty in the market, the wife and others may increasingly be incorporated into the managerial, decision-making role, to provide information and expertise and to broaden the politico-cultural base.

These two structural adaptations are more likely to occur as changing circumstances are perceived to limit access to resources and/or create uncertainty in the market. Further, such action-oriented adaptations are more likely to occur during initial orientation to the setting than later, because it is difficult to change, structurally, after initial orientations have been completed, interpreted (culturally) as correct, validated (socially) as acceptable, and reinforced by satisfaction with the outcome.

Are these two adaptations (in role sharing) more likely to occur sequentially or simultaneously? If sequential, in what order? What might the consequences be if the order is reversed? If simultaneous, what is the nature of the combined effect? These are questions of theoretical importance as well as practical significance.

In *primitive social action,* economic access to resources *precedes* political influence over access, which is organized after the fact, *then* culturally rationalized and societally legitimated. But in most response sequences, each cognitive response develops incrementally and affects the incremental development of the others (a *calculus* of social development). So it is possible for two adaptations of farm family structural organization to occur together. And it is also possible for *either* adaptation to move ahead faster than the other, although economic inclusion of family members in farm work will theoretically *precede* political inclusion in farm decisions. But what is the practical significance of this order of development for acceptance of technological innovation?

If the wife becomes more involved in farm decisions without becoming more involved in farm tasks, is her influence on decisions less likely to favor adopting innovative farm technology? In zero-order correlation, the data have shown positive effects of *both* processes of adaptation (decision increase and work increase) on recent adoption (see Table 3a). But in controlled analysis, for that half of the sample in which the husband and wife share most farm decisions, increased decision involvement occurs *only* in combination with increased work involvement, consistent with the *primitive model of social action.* So a deviation from the primitive model does not occur, and the question will therefore not be addressed in this study.

Goal of the Study:

Using theories of social action formation and social change to build predictive models, the goal of the study is to test a *theory of gender power sharing in transition.*

The theory of social action is used to differentiate, within a general framework of social action formation, four dimensions of wife influence on farm outcomes. Also relevant are four contextual dimensions (identified as controls) represented by the husband's age and agricultural education, farm debt relative to farm income, and occupational commitment measured, in part, by plan to continue farming to retirement and, in part, by full-time work off the farm.

The theory of social change is used to identify four phases of family transformation, from separately coordinated, traditional farm roles to nontraditional, cooperative role sharing. In the intermediate, transitional phases of shifting role obligations, the wife increasingly shares responsibilities, first, for farm tasks (an *instrumental* role), and then for farm management (a *leadership* role). During the sharing or transfer of responsibilities, habitual ways of doing things are reviewed, questions asked, insights shared, time and labor-saving helps considered, and flexibility introduced. Creative problem solving is expected to be enhanced as wives become more involved, first in farm tasks and then in farm decisions.

In a multifactor analysis of covariance, a combined, predictive model is tested for unduplicated, interactive effects. The goal is to be able to identify two distinct patterns of family functioning in association with recent adoption of progressive farm technology, both of which are characterized by some measure of increase in husband-wife role sharing.

These two different patterns are expected to include changes in dimensions of the wife's farm role that appear to be structural adaptations to changes in the farm setting. Self-reported assessments of couple interaction are expected to differentiate further the effects of these variations in structural adaptation. If found in the analysis, such adaptations will be interpreted as evidence of gender power sharing in transition.

Focus of the Study:

The focus of the study is on determining the nature of the wife's influence in bringing about technological changes in farming. In earlier assessments of the wife's farm role, adaptation of the farm enterprise to technological change was measured as the overall level of adoption of improved farm practices (Wilkening, 1949, 1953, 1954, 1958b). In the present study, adaptation is viewed as a process that occurs incrementally, over time, and the wife's influence on the number of farm practices adopted is assessed during a specific time period, designated in the study as the five years just prior to the interviews. In addition, the wife is asked to report on ten-year increases in her farm task and farm decision roles, to lend support to predictions that the wife's farm roles affect the rate of adoption of farm practices, rather than the reverse causal sequence.

Initial predictions are that the wife influences progressive farming while involved in essential farm tasks and while involved in farm management decisions, and that these influences take multiple forms, depending on the organization and distribution of major farm responsibilities, i.e., the role structure of the farm enterprise. More specifically, it is predicted that the wife influences recent farm progress favorably when she has primary responsibility for one or more essential farm tasks, and when she is highly involved in making farm decisions.

It is predicted, further, that as the wife's responsibilities for farm tasks increase, and as her participation in farm decisions increase, these role changes also tend to favor farm progress, as the family role structure with regard to the farm enterprise goes through phases of transition. Accordingly, phases of transition are identified as a shift from traditional to nontraditional role structure, differentiated by level of husband/wife decision-sharing on farm matters. Intermediate phases of transition are indicated in the study by a ten-year increase in the wife's farm tasks, first in combination with low decision-sharing ('disrupted traditional' phase II), and then in combination with high decision- sharing ('emerging nontraditional' phase III).

The goal is to demonstrate *two patterns of wife influence on farm innovation* specific to these two phases of transition. Definitions of phases II and III suggest, in the wife's changing farm work role, increased incorporation of the wife into the *instrumental* role of farming. The definition of phase III (the 'emerging nontraditional' phase) suggests, in addition to increased work, inclusion of the wife in a *leadership* role. It is within these two phases that we might expect to find qualitatively different patterns of favorable wife influence on recent farm practice adoption.

First, aspects of the farm setting are expected to interact with wife influence, in phases II and III, to affect the extent of wife influence on recent adoption. Aspects of the farm setting provide a context for husband and wife farm roles and role changes, and may themselves be related to recent adoption of practices. For an analysis of interactive effects, two indicators of farm context are constructed: 'financial risk' (high farm debt relative to low net farm income) and 'commitment to farming as an occupation' (husband plans to continue farming to retirement, and does not work full-time off the farm). Each indicator is expected to qualify, and strengthen, evidence of favorable wife influence on recent adoption in phases II and III.

Next, patterns of wife influence in phases II and III are expected to be differentiated by interactions with additional dimensions of the wife's farm role. Measures of the wife's farm role include: wife and husband perceptions of her farm roles and role changes, and husband and wife assessments of their farm role interactions. From these measures, four indicators are constructed to represent 'collaborative,' 'assertive,' 'consultative,' and 'supportive' dimensions of the wife's farm role.

'Collaborative' wife role is measured by level of wife responsibility for keeping farm records. 'Assertive' wife role is measured by increased wife involvement in farm decisions in the ten years prior to the interviews. 'Consultative' wife role is measured by the husband's assessment of the wife as a source of new ideas in farming. 'Supportive' wife role is measured by reports, of either spouse, that they spent a recent evening "just chatting," and the husband's rating of "completely satisfied" with the way they make farm decisions and settle differences.

Adding these four role dimensions to the analysis of interactive effects, it is predicted that, except for collaborative wife role (high level of wife responsibility for keeping the farm records and/or paying the taxes), wife role dimensions associated favorably with recent adoption are likely to be opposite in phases II and III. Although wives in phase II are increasingly involved in the instrumental role of farming, they are essentially subordinate in decision-making. The pattern of favorable wife influence in phase II, the disrupted traditional phase of family transition, is therefore predicted to be supportive and collaborative, but nonassertive and nonconsultative. In phase III, however, wives are included as essentially equal partners in farm decision-making. The pattern of favorable wife influence on recent adoption is therefore predicted to be assertive and consultative, as well as collaborative, but nonsupportive in that differences of opinion on farm matters are more likely to be expressed openly by wives in an emerging nontraditional phase of family transition.

A final expectation, in the analysis, is that these interactive effects occur relative to preexisting levels of adoption, structural limitations, and resource potentials of the farm enterprise. Measures of these variables are obtained by subtracting estimates of five year changes in adoption, net farm income, and mechanization from current measures, and are therefore subject to two sources of measurement error, (Cohen,

(1988: 537ff), so they are used for the background analysis of predictor intercorrelations only (see Chapter 8). For the analysis of interactive effects on recent adoption, current level of adoption is a more reliable indicator of cumulative, preexisting effects. Entering it into the analysis as a covariate helps to remove the effects of husband characteristics, community contacts, and other external factors found in diffusion studies to be associated with overall level of adoption (Rogers, 1983: 260-261).

This chapter has made reference to the theories of social action and social change presented in Chapter 2. It is hoped that, together, these theories will provide a research method to analyze the complexities of power sharing, and to assess the consequences of power sharing for creative problem solving in farm families in a midwest dairy state in the mid-20th century. In the farm crisis decade that followed the 1970s, many families lost their farms due to overextended farm debt at a time of decreasing land values and an unusually prolonged cost-price squeeze in agriculture. As a survival strategy, power sharing may have helped these families stay in farming. Further research is needed to investigate this possibility.

Statement of the problem:

To achieve the goal of the study, it is necessary to demonstrate, with the data analysis, that *developmental* processes of social action and *transformational* processes of social change are complementary, and that *multidimensional* aspects of social influence evolve as processes of social action and social change evolve. Ideas of *role differentiation* and *spheres of influence*, central to the work of Parsons and other functionalist theorists at mid-century, are set aside in favor of ideas of *goal sharing, role sharing* and *power sharing* in the rational pursuit of shared concerns. Further, in analyzing the data, statistical interactions of predictors rather than techniques of path analysis are employed to test the overall prediction of *two patterns of wife influence on farm innovation*.

In summary, a rationale has been given for an interactive approach to the study of social action and social change, a theory of gender power sharing in transition has been introduced, and key assumptions have been presented for the research that follows, on farm couples adjusting to a climate of economic and technological changes that affected agriculture duning the mid-to-late 1970s.

In Chapter 6, research and theories are reviewed that address the central topics. In Chapter 7 the sample selection is described, a predictive model is presented, and variables are selected to fit the requirements of the model. In Chapter 8, a descriptive analysis intercorrelates thirteen objective predictors and three estimates of pre-study variables, and reports their zero-order associations with recent adoption. Chapter 9 provides the methodological rationale for analyses of interactive and multiple effects. Specifics of the design of analysis are then presented, and hypotheses of multiple patterns of interactive effect are formalized, in Chapter 10. Findings are presented in Chapter 11, and are summarized, with conclusions and suggestions for future research, in Chapter 12.

Chapter 6

Review of the Literature

Innovation and Agriculture:

Adoption of Improved Farm Technology:
Prior to World War II, hybrid corn studies in Iowa were a major source of new ideas and research on the adoption of innovative farm practices (Ryan & Gross, 1943). During and after the war, rural sociologists in Iowa, Wisconsin, North Carolina, New York, Washington, and other farm states studied the diffusion of improved farm practices throughout vast farming areas. As a result of Dust Bowl problems in the 1930's, techniques of soil conservation, pest control, and hybridization of resilient crop varieties were being researched by state-sponsored agricultural experiment stations, and recommended to farmers by university short courses and agricultural extension agents (Fliegel, 1956; Copp, Sill, & Brown, 1958; Rogers, 1962; Wilkening & Guerero, 1969; Katz, Levin, & Hamilton, 1972).

In an attempt to understand the acceptance and diffusion processes better, large-scale surveys were undertaken, and farmers were asked not only about themselves and their farms but also about their families and social networks (Wilkening, 1954; Wilkening & Bharadwaj, 1968;

Abd-Ella, Hoiberg, & Warren, 1981; Carlson & Dillman, 1983). Indices of adoption were constructed and related to various characteristics of farms and farmers. It was determined that some high adopters were opinion leaders in their communities, and influenced other farmers to try new practices, aiding the diffusion process. Early adopters were identified as innovators, and stages in their trial and acceptance of new practices were studied in detail (Beal & Bohlen, 1957). Although most who achieved high levels of adoption were older, with some agricultural education and adequate resources to experiment with new ideas, innovators (early adopters) tended to be young as well as better educated (Rogers, 1962).

In an attempt to reach more of these young farmers with an interest and flexibility to try new ideas, agricultural extension agents launched an ambitious, federally-funded program in the early 1950s to reach not only young farmers but also their wives (Dorner, 1955; Slocum, 1962). In Wisconsin it was called Farm and Home Development, and included a five year, follow-up survey of farmers under age forty-five. From these families we learned that many young wives were highly involved in farm decisions (Wilkening, 1958a); however, wife involvement in farm decisions was not found to be directly associated with overall level of adoption. Further analysis found inconsistent and therefore inconclusive evidence, which helped to inspire the formulation of new, interactive theories of social action and social change. When an opportunity arose, in 1979, to research these theories with responses from farm couples of all ages, variables were included to test earlier impressions of 'two patterns of wife influence,' a theory of gender power sharing in transition, and assumptions (above) of interactive effects.

The dependent variable, recent adoption, was designed to meet the requirements of a limited research objective: to identify family processes associated with the adoption of farm practices during a specified time period, the five years prior to interview. Overall level of adoption is used as a covariate (control variable) to remove the cumulative effects on adoption of factors such as the husband's education, social networks, contacts with agricultural extension services and other community contacts, socioeconomic status, size of farm, level of farm mechanization, and various other characteristics of farm and farmer shown in earlier studies to be directly associated with "innovativeness" (Rogers, 1983: 260-261)

The Concept of Innovativeness in Farming:
Rogers & Rogers (1961) list 28 field studies by rural sociologist that measure what they define as innovativeness with an adoption-of-farm-practices scale. Using data from six of the field studies, supplemented by other published work, they assess the validity, reliability, internal consistency, and unidimensionality of such scales. On the basis of three measures of validity: construct validity (successful prediction), judging by county agents, and self-images of adopters, they conclude that adoption scales "have in some reasonable degree measured the construct of innovativeness" (1961: 329).

Checking reliability with split-half reliability coefficients and test-retest methods they conclude "a fair degree of scale reliability" from coefficients, and a "generally high test-retest reliability" but with an *adoption recall error* of 20% or more for one-third of the test items. As they point out, this may be attributed in part to discontinuance of farm practices during the period between the two interviews (1961: 331).

Internal consistency is checked by intercorrelations of items with one another and with the overall index of adoption score (item analysis). Item-to-total-score correlations vary widely, but are found to be mostly significant. Intercorrelations of single items, however, include 7% to 12% of items in a negative direction. The authors caution that negative correlations suggest that items measure different dimensions, and advise researchers to exclude them from the index (1961: 334).

Unidimensionality is tested with Guttman scaling analysis, factor analysis, and cluster analysis. No clear-cut evidence of a single, general dimension of innovativeness is found, although some of the results are supportive. Since 1961, rural sociologists have differentiated types of farm innovations: environmental vs. commercial and/or profitable vs. unprofitable (Cancian, 1967; Pampel & van Es, 1977; Fliegel & van Es, 1983) and have focused, more recently, on subsets of innovations, such as soil and water conservation practices (Nowak, 1984, 1987). In doing so, Nowak advises that:

> research techniques must be sophisticated enough to distinguish critical differences in the nature of the technology, as well as the institutional context, physical setting, and farm-firm features. (Nowak, 1987: 218).

Innovativeness is accepted as a valid construct for the purposes of this study, based on the conclusions of Rogers & Rogers (1961) that innovativeness can be reliably measured, with adequate internal consistency if reasonable precautions are taken, such as rejecting items that are negatively intercorrelated or negatively associated with the overall index. Unidimensionality is not a concern given construct validity (ability to predict results), as long as the multiple dimensions of the construct are reasonably identified. This is accomplished by factoring the thirteen positively intercorrelated innovative practices in use by the respondents at the time of interview. Factor analysis gives the following loadings on four factors:

	Soil	Crops	Land	Facilities
Soil test, past 3 years	.73			
High nitro side dress	.21		.15	.21
Farm conservation	.46	.16	.30	
Minimum tillage	.43			
Top dress alfalfa	.52	.51	.15	.18
Crop rotation	.29	.35	.13	
Grassed waterways	.29		.41	
Contour farming		.19	.83	
Manure storage			.21	.56
Green-chop feed		.53		
Hay, corn storage	.12	.43	.25	.24
Extra protein		.67	.16	.14
Barn insulation		.13		.62

Rogers & Rogers (1961:335) recommend that weighting adoption scale items is not justified, based on separate studies that found that utilizing judges or factor loadings resulted in correlations of 0.98 and 0.96, respectively, with the unweighted index. They do, however, recommend correcting adoption scores for "don't apply" responses, on the basis of a 0.89 correlation of corrected scores (for dairy practices that do not apply to nondairy farmers) with uncorrected scores (1961:

335). Unfortunately, it was not possible to make this correction. With the second and fourth factors (crops and facilities) heavily weighted by items that are more applicable to dairy farms than to beef and grain farms, their inclusion represents a possible bias in favor of dairy farmers. However, since current level of adoption is a covariate in the analysis rather than the dependent variable, this bias is corrected for in part.

Recent Farm Innovation:
Few indices of farm practice adoption have taken into account the length of time that each innovative practice has been in use (for exceptions see references to Lionberger, 1955, and Rogers, 1961, in Rogers & Rogers, 1961; and Pampel & van Es, 1977). Rogers & Rogers computed adoption scales both ways, using 1955 and 1957 data, and tentatively concluded that adding a measure of the *time of adoption* for each practice adds greater sensitivity to the scale (1961: 336). It is not evident from the literature that any researcher has focused on *recent adoption,* that is, on the number of innovative practices adopted within a recent, set time-frame, as a dependent variable.

Due to the nature of the theory of power sharing in transition, the framework developed to research this theory, and the assumptions that are being made about the requirements of causal analysis, it would seem to follow that hypotheses generated from these theories should be tested only with information about decisions made relatively recently about the farm operation. By asking the farm operator, first, which practices are currently in use, it is relatively easy to ask which of these practices the operator began using "within the past five years" without introducing the bias of an implied value judgment. It is not unreasonable to assume, however, that some decisions have had less salience for the individual operator than others, and are remembered, therefore, within a less accurate time frame. The hope is that such off-estimates balance out, occurring more or less randomly in each direction.

Power Sharing in Farm Families:

Power Sharing in Gender Relations:
Power sharing is a relatively new concept as applied to gender relations (Blood & Wolfe, 1960; Rodrigues, Centers & Raven, 1971; Scanzoni, 1978, 1982; Burr, Hill, Nye & Reise, 1979; Nye & Berardo,

1981; Gillespie, 1984; Hartsock, 1990; Iannello, 1992). Prior to the 20th century, one might say that power sharing connoted some aspect of relations among propertied males, or among collections of male citizens whose territories were defined by legal boundaries (Wollstonecraft, 1792; Goldman, 1885; Donovan, 1986, Tong, 1989). Democracy, representative government, alliances, balance of power, spheres of influence are all political terms that describe some aspect of male power sharing outside the domestic sphere. Within the home, cultural variations might give the woman varying degrees of power over other family members, and this power might be shared with sisters, sisters-in-law or other wives; but this power was usually over children, children-in-law and servants, and subordinate to male authority if there was a male head.

Power sharing between men and women is so new a concept that there is no universally accepted definition, much less an explanation. Terms like suffrage, comparable pay, equal opportunity, and quotas in the workplace address deficits in gender relations outside the home caused by unequal resources for men and women in the larger society. So how do we explain the modern phenomenon, or at least the modern goal, of husband-wife power sharing within the family?

Husband-Wife Power Sharing:

Power sharing within the family has at least three expressions: separate decision-making in separate spheres (e.g., he makes decisions about the farm; she makes decisions about the home), *shared* decision-making in separate spheres (e.g., they make decisions together about the farm, his responsibility, and the home, her responsibility), and *shared* decision-making in *shared* spheres (e.g., they share decisions about their shared responsibilities, whether farm, home, or family). The last includes role sharing within spheres once designated as gender specific (Komarovsky, 1962; Rainwater, 1965; Scanzoni, 1975, 1979; Scanzoni & Szinovacz, 1980; McDonald, 1980; Bianchi & Spain, 1983; Hiller & Philliber, 1986; Hochschild, 1989; Carlson, 1990; Johnston, 1992). Each of these expressions of power sharing is, to some degree, an adaptation to 19th century industrialization and a technological explosion in the 20th century. Expressions of power sharing in the family may reflect, however slowly, new career opportunities for both men and women outside the home, and even outside the immediate community.

Power Sharing in Farm Families:
Power sharing might also be viewed as a survival strategy, as a way to cope with overwhelming odds against survival of the farm enterprise as a family-controlled economic unit (Vogeler, 1981; Bennett, 1982; Brewster, 1983; Rosenfeld, 1985; Barlett, 1987; Haney, 1988; Whatmore, 1988, 1994; Rickson, 1997).

This view of power sharing in farm families does not see the wife as competing in a struggle for equality or dominance. It sees the wife, less burdened by the tasks of child-rearing and food preparation than in past centuries, willing and able to shoulder more of the economic burden, and, with it, more of the mushrooming decisions that accompany a rapid transition to a vastly more complex farming technology (Wilkening, 1958a, 1981; Sawer, 1973; Bokemeier & Coughenour, 1980; Jensen, 1981; Bergson-Larsson, 1982; Bush, 1982; Sachs, 1983; Haney, 1983, 1988; Rosenfeld, 1986; James, 1990; Whatmore, 1991; Barlett, 1993; O'Hara, 1994; Rickson, 1995). Whether the wife works on the farm or off, her contribution is often necessary to the success of the operation (Gasson, 1988, 1992); so it follows that her cooperation is valued as an essential farm resource, within the capabilities of the husband to seek and utilize her help. It is an interactive, integrative, evolutionary process (Boulding, 1978), in which each must be willing to participate for power sharing to work.

Theoretical Support for an Interactive Analysis of Social Structure and Social Process:

A central focus of this work is on the dynamics of social change. The overall conceptual scheme is somewhat compatible with Parsons' AGIL formulation of adaptation and integration (1949), and his structural-functional theory of social systems (1951), but omits the normative assumption that limits functionalism to equilibrium theory, and moves away from his emphasis on role differentiation, to focus on role sharing as a predictor of progressive changes in family farming in the late 1970s. This approach is also somewhat compatible with symbolic interactionist theory (Mead, 1934; Blumer, 1969), in that it identifies cognitions of the actor as central determinants of social action, but expands this approach to include the interactive effects of cognitions with structural and resource determinants of action. This approach is also compatible with social exchange theory (Homans, 1958, 1961; Blau, 1964) by using 'conferred exchange' as a bridging concept to include cultural determinants of negotiated exchange (DeWitt, 1981). This combination of diverse approaches gives the flexibility needed for a multidimensional, process analysis of stages and phases of social change.

Systems theory (Buckley, 1967) provides a general framework for identifying some of the process elements of family adaptation to a changing environment. Propositions presented by Wilkinson, and condensed by Broderick & Smith (1979), include the following:

> The adaptability and hence viability of a (family) system is related:
> 1. positively to the amount of variety in the system, which is related directly to openness to outside input.
> 2. negatively to conflict and tension in the system which is positively related to differentiation and segregation of subsystems and to alienation of units from the decision-making function.
> 3. positively to stability of membership over time.
> 4. positively to number of multiple alternate channels of communication among units, which will most likely be developed with respect to matters most central to their goals and values.
> 5. positively to the efficiency of the subsystem responsible for memory (records, etc.), which unit will have greater access than other units to influence/power in the system. (Wilkinson, 1977)

Looking at the farm wife's involvement in farm work and farm decisions from a systems perspective, one might conclude that: the more involved the farm wife is in farm tasks and decisions, the greater the adaptability of the farm operation to a changing environment. But conflict and tension, in proposition #2 above, is seen as negatively related to adaptability, and positively related to role differentiation. This last proposition has a counter-argument in conflict theory:

From a conflict theory perspective, Farrington and Foss (1977) suggest a set of propositions in which family structure is rigidly determined by "differential access to resources and power," "structural inequality," "age and sex stratification," and "like any other social system... largely integrated through coercion." They view conflict as endemic to social structure, but see positive as well as negative consequences "of each aspect of conflict" for the individual and for the family. If their assumption of rigidly-defined family structure is challenged, using the variability assumption of systems theory, it is

Beyond Equilibrium Theory

possible to modify conflict theory to suggest structural change as a consequence of conflict. The key proposition to be modified is:

#3. Certain structural characteristics of families affect (a) the number of underlying conflicts-of-interest, (b) the degree of underlying hostility, and (c) the nature and extent of social conflict.
(Nye & Berardo, 1981, p.xxi)

Recognizing that structure is variable (systems theory) and therefore subject to change, it is possible that the nature and extent of conflicts-of-interest, and their expression, may conversely affect (bring about changes in) the structural characteristics of families.

Although this proposition is not tested in the research reported here, conflict is recognized as one of the causal factors that may account for increased involvement of the wife in farm decisions, which has the potential of modifying the family's role structure.

Social exchange theory offers an additional perspective on changes in family role structure. Role-taking implies an exchange relation, in which rewards are anticipated as a result of meeting role expectations. In a family social system, role expectations are relatively well-defined and stable, but rewards may not be as great as anticipated.

To the extent that family roles are ascribed to a status position, such as 'husband,' 'wife,' or 'elder son,' *reward disappointment* (failure of rewards to meet expectations) may be rationalized in a way that is not tension producing. This is described by DeWitt (1981) as a 'conferred exchange' relation, in which rewards may be delayed or deferred, for a time, with an expectation of future benefit to self or (significant) others. But, to the extent that these family roles are voluntary and/or shared, it might be anticipated that reward disappointment will result in efforts to affect either the production and/or the (re)distribution of rewards.

In the present study, the initial focus is on an ascribed form of role sharing in farm families, where risk factors and a changing technological environment have combined to create reward disappointment for *all* family members, increasing the demand for greater productivity rather than reward redistribution among family members. The expectation, therefore, is that the structure of family influence will change in the direction of greater participation in decisions for those family members who are increasingly involved in farm production.

Although reward disappointment of family members is assumed to be the motivation for these structural adaptations within the context of exchange relations, other changes might also occur. These could include alternative exchange relations, such as work off the farm, retirement from farming, or sale of the farm to engage in another occupation.

Because of long-held traditions of family member involvement in farming in Wisconsin (Wilkening, 1981a), changes in the structure of influence are expected to be primarily a matter of degree, reflecting compatible rather than conflicting interests.

In contrast to this modified 'exchange relations' perspective of structural change, a less traditional approach would place greater emphasis on equity theory considerations in the sharing of influence and distribution of rewards. This approach relies on resource theory to explain how social roles are negotiated and achieved within a framework of competing interests by whoever has the most power, based on access to superior resources (Blood & Wolfe, 1960). But resource theory can only explain the distribution of power, not its exercise. And neither resource theory nor exchange theory can define those processes whereby structural integration, based on compatible or mutual interests, might occur to obtain common goals.

A more comprehensive theoretical framework is needed to combine these insights with the insights of 'field theory' regarding the importance of the social setting (Lewin, 1951), from which contingency theory evolved (Lawrence & Lorsch, 1967; Duncan, 1972; cf. Hage & Meeker, 1988), and also with developmental (life cycle) theory, with its emphasis on changing family needs (Kirkpatrick, Tough, & Cowles, 1934; Hill, 1965, 1970; DuVall, 1971, 1977). G. Elder and others have begun this work in studies of family transitions (Hareven, 1978; Elder, 1978, 1981, 1987, 1991; Cowan & Hetherington, 1991), with a growing appreciation for the interconnectedness of time, process, and context (Elder, 1991:31). Together, these perspectives require that we take into account, over time, ways in which the family and its members both affect and are affected by the context within which they function.

The next chapter begins to build such a framework, selecting familiar variables to represent not only structural and resource aspects of the setting, but also actor perceived roles, changing roles, and other orientation processes within the setting.

Chapter 7

Research Design

Preview of the Study:

The focus of the study is on the wife's influence in bringing about technological changes in farming. Theories, concepts, and research that bear on the topic have been reviewed. In this chapter a predictive model is presented that defines, consistent with the theory of social action, a causal sequence of social action formation to account for the dependent variable.

Twenty one variables are selected from a survey of 176 Wisconsin farm couples to represent these latent variables (cf. Appendix A, Survey of Wisconsin Farm Families). Intercorrelations of 16 of the more objective of these predictors, and their associations with the dependent variable, are examined in Chapter 8.

The dependent variable, throughout the analysis, is the number of innovative farm practices adopted during the five years immediately prior to the interviews. These practices were selected from a list of fourteen technological improvements recommended, statewide, by Wisconsin agricultural extension agents.

Selection of the Sample:

In the spring of 1978, a mail survey of Wisconsin farm families was conducted to obtain information on how farm families were adjusting to changes in farming (Cell & Johnson, 1979). Interviewees were selected from current lists of farmers reported by township tax assessors to the Wisconsin Department of Agriculture. (A farmer, in this survey, was defined as a person engaged in farming for commercial purposes who makes the management decisions about the agricultural unit that they operate.) Questionnaires were mailed to 1005 farm operators whose names were randomly selected in proportion to the population of each Wisconsin county (Linn, 1983). Of those contacted, 616 or 62% mailed back usable questionnaires. A comparison with the 1974 U.S. Census of Agriculture indicated that this group of farmers was representative of Wisconsin farmers (Cell & Johnson, 1979). In the winter of 1979, a sub-sample of 279 was drawn from the 616 participants in the mail survey. This sub-sample was also randomly selected in proportion to the population of each of the 72 Wisconsin counties. From this group, completed personal interviews were conducted in the spring of 1979 with 181 husband-wife pairs and with 28 additional farm operators living alone or with another family member (Linn, 1983). For the purposes of this investigation, five couples who did not provide reliable information on key variables were dropped from the study (two from the data set prior to access) leaving a total of 176 farm couples in the present study.

Interviews with husband-wife pairs were typically conducted as follows: while the husband was interviewed about the farm operation and his involvement in farm organizations and off-farm work, the wife filled out a questionnaire that included check lists of attitudes and satisfactions; then the wife was interviewed about her farm, home, and off-farm activities while the husband filled out a questionnaire that included check lists similar to hers. Interviews lasted approximately 75 minutes (Linn, 1983). The study was conducted by Professors Charles Cell, Donald Johnson, A. Eugene Havens and Eugene A. Wilkening of the Department of Rural Sociology, with the support of the Research Division of the College of Agricultural and Life Sciences and the Research Committee of the Graduate School of the University of Wisconsin (Wilkening, 1981a).

The 1978 mail survey and the 1979 interviews obtained information on topics included in earlier surveys of Wisconsin farm families, dating back to a 1954 survey of young farm families where the farm operator was age 45 or younger (Wilkening, 1958a), and a 1962 survey of farm families where the male operator was age 65 or younger and had an annual gross farm income of $2,500 or more (Wilkening & Bharadwaj, 1966). Information on farm work roles, husband-wife farm decision-sharing, and adoption of innovative farm practices were obtained in each survey. The largest increase in the wife's farm role was reported to be in farm record-keeping, with 44% of the wives assuming major responsibility for this task in 1979 compared to 32% in 1962. An increase in the wife's involvement in farm decisions was reported for some farm purchases, but a decrease was reported for deciding whether to borrow money for the farm, although the data are not entirely comparable since the 1962 data were reported by wives, whereas the 1979 data were reported by husbands. The 1978-1979 surveys had no limits on age of operator or gross farm income, so the data on work and decision roles were made more comparable to data collected in 1962 by using a reduced sample equivalent. (Wilkening, 1981a). Results of the 1978-1979 surveys, and of a 1950-1975 panel study of Wisconsin dairy farmers (Dorner & Marquardt 1977, 1978, 1979, 1981) were summarized by Wilkening, who concluded that:

> Both the family farm and farm family have changed considerably in the past two decades. The same economic and social forces affecting the larger society have affected the farm family. Although there is value placed upon the family farm and upon traditional family patterns, both have been affected by processes in the larger society. (Wilkening, 1981b: 35)

Dorner & Marquardt (1977, 1981) reported that, while the labor input on the farms studied changed little during the period, the share of the wife's labor increased from 9.3% of the total farm work load in 1950 to 16.4% in 1975.

Questions were added to the 1979 survey to specifically test the "two patterns of wife influence" thesis. These included an expansion of the list of farm decisions, and new questions about ten-year increases in the wife's farm and decision roles, how the wife sees her role in farming (as a farm helper or as a farm partner), whether or not the husband sees his wife as a source of new ideas in farming, how satisfied the husband is with the way he and his wife make farm decisions and settle differences, how often they disagree on farm matters, who wins when they disagree, and which of a list of thirteen innovative farm practices they began using in the five years just prior to the interview.

All questions were pre-tested in interviews with farm families in Dane County who were not part of the sample, using two-person teams with at least one experienced interviewer, as part of the interviewer training process.

Profile of Wisconsin Farms:

Three fourths of the 616 farm units surveyed by mail questionnaire in 1978, from which a sample was drawn for intensive interviews in 1979, were owned rather than rented, and almost all (95%) were owned at least in part. Two thirds included dairying as a major enterprise, and half supplied all of household income (see Table 1). Typical farms in the 1979 survey varied in size from 80 acres to 400 acres, farmed with two to five tractors, of 100 to 300 horsepower. They were improved by three to nine soil-conservation or other recommended farm practices, of 14 inquired about in the survey. One third of these practices, two on average, were adopted within five years prior to the 1979 interview (see Table 2).

Profile of Wisconsin Farm Couples:

Most of the 176 farm couples interviewed in 1979 were raised on a farm (87% and 71%, respectively), and two thirds of the husbands reported their first full-time occupation as farming. Most husbands farmed full-time at the time of interview (70%); however, more than half (55%) saw farming as a way of life rather than as primarily a profit-making business (not shown), and less than half (48%) planned to farm full-time to retirement. Only one third of farm husbands had some college or vocational agricultural training beyond high school (see Table 2).

Most of the couples interviewed had children living at home (89%), but less than half (38%) were in early stages of the family cycle, with oldest child (at home) younger than eighteen. Still, a continuing need for farm investment is reflected in the choice of farm rather than home or family for use of extra funds by 47% of husbands and/or wives (not shown).

TABLE 1. Characteristics of 616 Wisconsin farm families, 1977.

	Central Tendency	Percentage
Average number of acres operated	256 acres	
Main enterprise (more than 50% of farm income):		
Dairy		66%
Beef cattle		11
Cash grain		12
Average number of years in farming (farm husband)	22.8 years	
Farm tenure:		
Own all of land farmed		76%
Own part of land farmed		19
Rent all of land farmed		5
Income characteristics:		
Median net farm income (1977)	$2,725	
Median family income (1977)	$9,600	
Households with only farm income		50%
Family life cycle:		
Mean age of farm husband or male head	49.1 years	
Mean age of farm wife or female head	46.2 years	
Married household heads		87%
Households with children at home (includes adult children)		57

SOURCE: Cell, C. P. & Johnson, D. E. (1979). Wisconsin farmers in 1977: A regional profile. *Population Notes, #9*. Madison, WI: University of Wisconsin Agricultural Extension.

TABLE 2. Characteristics of 176 Wisconsin farm couples, 1979.

	Central Tendency (arithmetic mean)	Dispersion (one S. D.)	Percentage
Size of farm operated:			
Mean number of acres	250 acres	+/- 186 acres	
Mean number of tractors	3.4 tractors	+/- 1.3 tractors	
Mean tractor horsepower	200 HP	+/- 112 HP	
Farm background:			
Husband was raised on a farm			87%
Wife was raised on a farm			71
Husband's first occupation was farming			66%
Husband has some college or vocational ag training			33
Occupational commitment to farming:			
Husband farms full-time			70%
Husband plans to farm full-time to retirement			48
Adoption of innovative farm technology:			
Number of 14 recommended farm practices adopted	6.2 practices	+/- 2.9 practices	
Number of practices adopted within the past 5 years	2.1 practices	+/- 2.4 practices	
Husband's perception of wife's farm role:			
Wife is equally involved (with husband) in farm decisions:			
Resource allocation decisions			49%
Operation change decisions			46
Operation management decisions (65% discuss farm management decisions with wives)			9
Wife is equally or mostly responsible for farm records and/or tax forms			53%
Wife's perception of her farm role:			
Wife's farm-work role has increased in past ten years			43%
Wife's farm-decision role has increased in past ten years			23
Wife sees herself as a partner in farming			58
Wife sees herself as a farm helper			18

Nearly three of five farm wives saw themselves as partners in farming (58%), and over half of the husbands reported that their wives equally or mostly keep the farm records and/or make out the tax forms (53%). Almost half of the wives were seen by their husbands as equally involved in farm decisions on resource allocation and operation changes (49% and 46%, respectively); and, although only 9% of wives were seen as equally involved in decisions on operation management, two-thirds of the husbands (65%) reported discussing these daily operations with their wives. In addition, almost one in four farm wives (23%) reported a ten-year increase in their involvement in major or daily farm decisions, while more than two in five (43%) reported a ten-year increase in their involvement in some aspect of farm work, which may have included chores, field work, or record-keeping (see Table 2).

Latent Causal Chain and Selection of Variables:

A latent path model (cf. Path Diagram 1, Appendix B) is derived from the theory of social action. It consists of an ordered sequence of object and action orientations, formed within a contextual setting of directives and resources, to account for the qualitative and quantitative performance of any given social act (cf. Model of Interactive Effects, Chapter 9). This causal chain will be separated into two, essentially different patterns of predicted interactive effect on the dependent variable: recent adoption of innovative farm practices.

First, operationalizing the latent variables requires an examination of distributions and intercorrelations of variables that match the theoretical constructs, using data obtained from the questionnaires and interviews of the 176 farm couples. (Three of these couples are omitted from the background analysis due to decision-sharing response item inconsistencies, but included in the combined analysis since the two-level decision-sharing indicator of family type was not affected by inclusion or exclusion of the seemingly discrepant responses.)

Measures are selected for further study based on suitable distributions and acceptable correlations with related measures. Thirty of these are used to construct indices to measure four key variables: current level of farm practice adoption, current level of husband and wife farm decision-sharing, the wife's changing farm-work role, and the wife's changing farm-decision role. Additional variables are selected from single-item measures. Pre-study variables are constructed from current-level and recent-change data. Sixteen predictors, in all, are selected for the background analysis reported in Chapter 8 (cf. Tables 3a and 3b). Number of farm practices recently adopted, the dependent variable, is obtained from the number of double-checked items in a list of practices reported as currently in use (cf. v0, following v1, Appendix A). Double-checks are in response to the Q. "Which of these practices have you started using within the past five years?"

From these, and three self-reported role-interaction-assessment measures, seven key predictors are selected or constructed for tests of hypotheses of interactive effects (cf. Chapter 10, Design of the Analysis). Measures omitted from the study include: subjective measures of values, attitudes and satisfactions, the wife's involvement in doing chores and field work, her farm background, her work off the farm, the husband's first occupation, the children's involvement in farm work, and the family's level of living.

Measurement of the Study Variables:

Study variables are identified by variable number (v#) in the Survey of Wisconsin Farm Families (Appendix A), in Path Diagrams (Appendix B), and in the background analysis reported in Chapter 8 (cf. Tables 3a and 3b).

Current Adoption, Recent Adoption, and Pre-study Level of Adoption:
In 1979 the farm husband was asked which of thirteen recommended practices he was currently using on his farm. He was then asked which of these practices he had started using within the past five years. To complete this question he was asked if he had started using any other new farming techniques within the past five years. All answers were recorded and later evaluated. Forty five farmers described a new practice that qualified as an improved farm practice. This practice was added to their total number and to the number of practices recently adopted.

On average, six improved practices were checked, two of which were checked twice, to indicate that they were adopted during the five years just prior to the study. From these responses an overall level of adoption index was constructed with equal weighting, for a maximum score of fourteen. This index was separated into two parts to obtain the dependent variable (v0): number of practices adopted within five years of the interview and (v1): pre-study level of adoption of practices currently in use (cf. Appendix A, Survey of Wisconsin Farm Families). These measures are considered to be reasonably objective, within acceptable limits of recall, with an error term increase for the pre-study measure (cf. discussion of implications for reliability coefficients in Cohen & Cohen, 1983). To minimize measurement error, overall level of adoption is used as the covariate in the analysis of interactive effects (cf. Cohen, 1988: 537-542 for an example of the inadvisability of using the difference between two measures to qualify one of the measures).

Problems Associated with Use of Respondent Recall:
Concern about problems in obtaining reliable data on the time of adoption in diffusion studies has been expressed by researchers in several fields (Gray, 1955; Menzel, 1957; Jaeger & Pennock, 1961; Coughenour, 1965; Rogers, 1971, 1983). When asked to recall the year of first use of a new farm practice, for example, in three successive surveys (1957 to 1962), the respondents varied from the estimated true dates by, on an average, one to one-and-one-half years in either direction (Coughenour, 1965: 188). For soil tests and a type of seed oats, disproportionate numbers of farmers reported progressively later adoption dates with each survey. The author concludes, after assessing means and standard deviations of dates of adoption for four farm practices, that errors in reporting dates of adoption increase as the time between the survey and the dates of adoption increase. Average dates of adoption for all but the type of seed oats, however, were *five years or more prior to the year of first interview*; whereas average date of adoption of the type of seed oats was always *within* five years of the date of *(each successive)* interview (Coughenour, 1965: 192). Systematic errors of this nature would not seem to affect the dependent variable, number of practices adopted within five years of the interview.

Jaeger & Pennock (1961), in a study of response consistency of nearly 3,000 households interviewed twice, 11 months apart, found that, for about two-thirds of their sample, washing machines that were reported as *five years old or less* in the first survey tended to be reported with an earlier date of purchase during the re-interview, whereas *older* machines tended to be reported as newer than previously reported. In each case, the discrepancy occurred in the direction of the overall sample mean. The net effect of the second interview was to make the average date of purchase somewhat earlier. Assuming less error in the first date of reported purchase than in the second date, it might be concluded that five years is a relatively good cutting point for accuracy of recall.

There are two types of error in recall data: random error and systematic error. Random error has the effect of reducing the strength of an observed statistical association, whereas systematic error can lead to a false conclusion about the relative strengths of two or more associations. Concerned primarily with the latter, the precaution is taken of introducing overall level of adoption as a covariate. This not only has the effect of reducing variation within and between groups due to errors of recall, but removes variation in the dependent variable that is due to factors associated with the covariate (Hays, 1988: 138).

Pre-Study Levels of Net Farm Income and Tractor Horsepower:
Pre-study levels of income and tractor horsepower are calculated by subtracting reported five year changes from reported 1979 levels. With categorical data reported for net farm income in the 1979 study, this measure is admittedly imprecise (cf. v2 & v3, Appendix A).

Pre-study level of net farm income, as an indicator of need, is expected to be negatively associated with recent adoption. Tractor horsepower, as a resource, is expected to be positively associated with recent adoption.

Measures of the Wife's Farm Role and Farm Role Context:
These measures fall into several categories: a measure of husband and wife decision-sharing; two measures of the wife's farm role; two measures of role increases; and two measures of role context. Decision-sharing is measured by level of farm decision-sharing reported by the husband. He was asked whether the couple discuss and who decides each of ten matters in three areas of farm management. These three areas, weighted equally in the index, are: daily farm operations, resource allocation, and major operation changes (v4, Appendix A). For the analysis of interactive effects, level of decision-sharing is dichotomized as high and low, *as an indicator of nontraditional and traditional family type*, to test the theory of creative effects of gender power sharing in transition.

Measures of wife farm role changes expected to favor recent adoption are: the wife's report of ten-year increases in her work and decision roles (v5 & v6, Appendix A). Almost half (43%) report increased involvement in farm work; about one fourth (23%) report increased involvement in farm decisions. Role context variables expected to favor recent adoption are: early stage in the family life cycle, indicated by oldest child under age eighteen, and motivation to spend extra money for the farm (v7 & v8, Appendix A). Farm roles expected to favor recent adoption are: the wife's responsibility for keeping farm records and/or doing the taxes, and her perception of herself as a partner in farming (v9 & v10, Appendix A).

Implications of Dairy vs. Other Farms, and Stage in the Family Cycle, for the Wife's Farm-Work Role:

Although most of Wisconsin's farms are dairy farms, with two-thirds receiving more than half of their farm income from dairy, nearly one in four receive more than half of their farm income from beef cattle or cash grain (cf. Table 1). Since these operations are not as labor-intensive as dairy operations, the farm wife may be less involved in daily farm chores. Involvement of the wife in chores and fieldwork may also vary with stage in the family cycle, decreasing when there are children under age six or over age twelve (Wilkening & Ahrens, 1979). For these reasons, level of the wife's responsibility for record-keeping is chosen, rather than her level of involvement in chores and/or field work, to achieve comparability in the measure of what is regarded, here, as an economic dimension of the wife's contribution to the farm operation. Not only is record-keeping an essential farm task, regardless of farm type, but the ages of children would presumably not affect the extent of the wife's involvement.

However, the measure of *increase* in the wife's farm-work role includes her reported ten-year increase in any or all of the three areas: farm chores, field work, and record-keeping. An advantage, for balancing categories in the analysis of categorical data, is that this measure represents 43% of the families (cf. Table 2). A possible disadvantage is over representation of families in middle stages of the family cycle and on dairy farms. Since this measure is used in combination with family type as an indicator of phase of family transition (see definitions in Chapter 5, Focus of the Study), there are implications for the generalization of results.

The Husband's Farm Role Context:

The husband's role context variables consist of characteristics of himself and the farm, his long-term plan for the farm, and his reason for farming (v11 to v16, Appendix A). The husband's reported long-term plan for the farm is to continue full-time, continue part-time, or quit farming before retirement. He reportedly sees farming as either a way-of-life or as primarily a profit-making business. It is expected that 'plan to continue farming' and 'profit orientation' will favor recent adoption. Husband characteristics expected to favor recent adoption are: age under 50, and 'agricultural training beyond high school or some college,' characteristics that are known to be associated with either new adoption or high level of adoption (Rogers, 1972). Farm characteristics that indicate a resource and/or need to improve farm income are: farm debt over $40,000, and recent net farm income of less than $10,000. These indicators, in combination, are expected to favor recent adoption.

Subjective Assessments of Husband and Wife Role Interaction:
In addition to the more objective measures of roles, role changes, and role contexts, there are five self-reported assessments of husband-wife role interaction. These include the wife's report of how often they disagree on farm matters, who wins out when they disagree, and whether they recently spent an evening just chatting. In addition, the husband reported on how satisfied he is with the way they make farm decisions and settle differences, and whether the wife is a source of new ideas about farming (v17 to v21, Appendix A).

Deriving Hypotheses of Higher-Order Interactive Effects:

From predictions of interactive effects (pp. 114-116, in Focus of the Study, Chapter 5), and selection of variables (above), a formula is constructed from which to derive a series of hypotheses of three-way and higher-order interactive effects. This represents an alternative approach to path analysis as conceived by Duncan (1966) and Blalock (1971). It focuses on interactive effects rather than on direct and indirect effects. Unlike LISREL models, the goal is to demonstrate that direct effects are qualified by interactions of role variables with actor orientations and contextual variables that either moderate (significantly enhance or diminish) or mediate (explain) observed, direct effects.

A *general formula*, incorporating all of the relevant statistical interactions of predictor variables, takes the form: extent of recent adoption is a function of phase of family transition (x) contextual variable (x) dimension of the wife's farm role (in each of the four domains of social action formation). Specific hypotheses of higher-order interactive effects on the dependent variable are derived from assumptions about the interconnections of latent variables, shown in Path Diagram 1 (Appendix B), modified to include multiple paths of positive effect. Multiple paths are differentiated by level of decision-sharing, as an indicator of family type. (This approach is consistent with the contingency model of leadership effectiveness, Fiedler, 1966, 1967, 1978, 1981).

The logic and theoretical rationales for more complex hypotheses are presented in Chapter 9, Method of Analysis. Sixteen hypotheses are derived from the general formula of interactive effects, using the models and theoretical framework provided in Chapter 9. Formulas for generating these more specific hypotheses are presented in Chapter 10, Design of the Analysis.

Chapter 8

Background Analysis

Introduction:

The focus of the study is on the wife's influence in bringing about technological changes in farming as reflected in recent adoption of farm practices. As co-determinants of recent adoption, farm roles and role contexts are taken into account, as these change through time and over the family life cycle. Role variables and contextual variables are examined for combined effects that are interactive rather than additive in their effects on recent adoption.

The theoretical framework for the analysis predicts that wives influence recent adoption of farm practices not only through involvement in farm decisions but also through involvement in farm work. In addition, husband and wife perceptions and assessments of the wife's participation further specify the effects on adoption of each of these sources of wife influence. As background to this analysis, it is interesting and informative to first look at the intercorrelations of objective predictor variables, and their direct (zero-order) associations with recent adoption.

144 Beyond Equilibrium Theory

Farm Development and the Family Life Cycle *(see Table 3a):*

Farms and farm families tend to go through parallel stages of expansion and contraction, as the requirements of both the enterprise and the family change with cycles of growth and decline. In recent decades, scientific and technological innovations in agriculture have added a spiraling nature to these cyclical effects, further impacting on the organization of both farm and family.

Understanding the farm and the family as closely interconnected, evolving systems, it is not surprising to find farm indebtedness of over $40,000 positively associated with the farm husband's age under fifty (.38) and with early stages in the family life cycle (.30). High farm indebtedness is also associated with agricultural education beyond high school (.34), which in turn appears to be associated with the husband's age under fifty (.21), supporting a view that borrowing is an accepted means of obtaining capital for early farm development.

Corresponding to early stages of farm development, the wife's increased involvement in farm work appears to be associated with high farm debt (.29), the husband's age under fifty (.27), and early stages of the family cycle (.25). Similarly, the wife's increased involvement in farm decisions may be somewhat positively associated with farm debt (.19) as well as the husband's age under fifty (.34) and early family cycle (.26). Functionally, her increased role involvements in both farm work and farm decisions appear, along with high indebtedness, to be part of the resource structure of early farm development.

Given this set of relationships, it is interesting to note that the wife's choice of farm over home or family for use of extra funds appears to be associated with the agricultural training and education of her husband (.23), their farm indebtedness (.23), and her perception of herself as a partner in farming (.21). Further, her increased farm work involvement may be also associated with the husband's agricultural education (.23) and with her perception of herself as a partner in farming (.19). These relationships support the premise that farm and family evolve together, in a functional way, through periods of technological progress as well as through cycles of family change. And they suggest that the wife is an active and intentional participant in this evolution.

On the other hand, the wife's farm roles *at the time of interview* are not as highly or as uniformly associated with the husband's age and education, farm debt, and family life cycle as are *changes* in her farm

TABLE 3a Family context for new adoption: I. The wife's farm role, role changes and role context, and the husband's farm role context (correlation matrix).

Predictors	New Adopt v0	H/W Incr. D-Sh v4	Incr. Dec.Work v5	E.Fm. Cycle v6	Farm Goal v7	Farm Rcds. v8	Farm Part. v9	H's Ed. v10	High Debt v13 v14

1979 INTERVIEW:

Wife's farm role and role context

v4 H/W share most
farm decisions   -.02   --

v5 10-year increase
dec. inv'ment   .16* -.04   --

v6 10-year increase
in farm work   .20*   .09   .42*   --

v7 Early family
life cycle   .22*   .05   .26* .25*   --

v8 Use extra $
for farm   .12   .18*   .10   .14+ -.01   --

v9 Wife keeps the
farm records   .08   .16*   .10   .22*   .12   .12   --

v10 Wife sees self
as farm partner .05   .18*   .12   .19* -.03   .21* .16*   --

Husband's role context

v13 Education
past H. S.   .32*   .12   .09   .23* .15+   .23*   .00   .13   --

v14 Farm debt
> $40,000   .25* -.02   .19* .29*   .30*   .23*   .05 -.02   .34*   --

v16 Less than
age fifty   .21*   .11   .34* .27*   .47*   .14+   .20*   .05   .21*   .38*

*P < .05   +P < .10

roles. Only the wife's level of responsibility for chores and fieldwork (not shown), and the extent to which she shares decisions about major changes in the farm operation (not shown), suggest positive association with early stages of the family cycle (.19 & .19). Responsibility for record-keeping, and for sharing operation management decisions (not shown), seem not to be significantly higher in early stages of the family cycle (.12 & .13), while responsibility for obtaining information on farm matters and sharing resource allocation decisions (not shown) appear not to vary with the family cycle (-.01, .03). Viewed from a functionalist perspective, it seems reasonable to assume that not all of the wife's farm work and farm decision roles change over the family life cycle.

Similarly, farm indebtedness and the husband's agricultural education seem to be not associated with level of wife responsibility for farm records or level of husband-wife decision-sharing. Although wives of husbands under age fifty do tend to share in keeping the farm records (.20), they appear to not significantly share in most farm decisions (.11); and wives of husbands with some college or agricultural training, also, seen to not significantly share in most farm decisions (.12).

To some extent, level of decision-sharing appears to differentiate traditional from nontraditional life style, rather than the changing requirements of the family cycle, a possibility that will be examined further. But it should also be noted that for the two thirds of the sample in which husbands have not had training or education beyond high school, high decision-sharing may be associated with the middle stages of the family cycle; whereas, for the more educated third the association seems to be positive with husband's age under fifty (from a preliminary analysis not shown).

The Wife's Farm Roles *(see Table 3a):*

As suggested above, farm decision-sharing is a multidimensional variable, part of the resource structure of the family, but also a reflection of family lifestyle. Theoretically, decision-sharing would seem to indicate a *mutual* willingness to share influence over matters affecting the farm operation. In this study, however, the major correlates of husband-wife decision-sharing (as reported by the husband) appear to be characteristics of the wife: her choice of the farm for use of extra funds (.18), her perception of herself as a partner in farming (.18), and her level of responsibility for keeping farm records and/or filling out tax forms (.16).

Since the husband's characteristics are not significantly associated with level of husband-wife decision-sharing, it may be that the wife's role in decision-making reflects an active rather than a passive involvement. In families where the husband is younger and also better educated, it may also reflect a historical development, a cultural shift in emphasis from one-person head of household to two-person head.

Another relevant historical development is that record-keeping and tax filing have increased in complexity in recent years, requiring greater knowledge of the details of the farm operation, and a greater investment of time and effort. Responsibility for this role also places the wife in a position to supply essential information for key decisions. It is reasonable to assume, therefore, that the wife will see this role as important. In addition to being related to decision-sharing (.16), the wife's responsibility for farm record-keeping appears to be positively associated with her increased involvement in farm work (.22) and with her perception of herself as a partner in farming (.16).

Progress, Productivity, and Farm Continuity (see Table 3b):

The second theme of farm development, its association with a historical period of technological progress, is further illustrated in the intercorrelations of (estimated) pre-study levels of net farm income, tractor horsepower, and adoption of improved farm practices with 1977 net farm income and 1979 plan to continue full-time to retirement. Viewed as a causal sequence, tractor horsepower and level of farm practice adoption in 1974 seem to be positive predictors of net farm income in 1977 (.24 & .23); and 1974 tractor horsepower and 1977 net farm income may, in turn, be positive predictors of the husband's 1979 future plan (.20 & .27). But pre-study level of adoption does not significantly predict the husband's future plan (.15).

Not unexpectedly, 1974 tractor horsepower appears to be related to high 1977 farm debt (.21), as well as to 1974 level of adoption and 1973 net farm income (.28 & .22), but not to early family cycle (-.07), which, as we have seen, appears to be related to high farm debt (.30).

Pre-study levels of farm practice adoption and net farm income are not associated with either early family cycle (-.13 & -.11) or high farm debt (.10 & .06). Negative associations of pre-study variables with the husband's age under fifty are also not significant (-.10, -.08, & -.11, not

TABLE 3b. Family context for new adoption: II. Past farm progress, present roles and role contexts of husband and wife, and future farm plan (correlation matrix).

Predictors	New Adopt v0	Pre-study Adopt v1	H/W NFIMech. v2	E.Fm. D-sh. v3	Wife Cyc. v4	Farm Recd. v7	Farm Bus. v9	High Plan v11	Debt v12	v14

PRE-STUDY (1974):

v1 Prior level of farm
practice adoption   -.40* - -

v2 Net Farm Inc.'73   -.17* .00   - -

v3 Prior mechaniz'n.   .05   .28*   .22* - -

1979 INTERVIEW:

Wife's farm role and role context

v4 H/W share most
farm decisions   -.02   -.07   -.09   -.18*   - -
v7 Early family life
cycle   .22* -.13⁺ -.11   -.07   .05   - -
v9 Wife keeps the
farm records   .08   -.08   -.11   -.04   .16*   .12   - -

Husband's farm role and role context

v11 Farming: a profit
making business   .06   -.01   -.11   -.04   -.02   .15*   .12   - -
v12 Farm full-time
to retirement   .04   .15⁺   .03   .20*   .08   .00   .00   .05   - -

v14 Farm debt
> $40,000   .25*   .10   .06   .21*   -.02   .30*   .05   .16*   .05   - -
v15 Net Farm
Income'77   -.12   .24*   .08   .23*   -.11   -.14⁺   -.07   .08   .27*   -.09

*P < .05   +P < .10

shown). These correlations help to define the scope conditions of the study (cf. Walker & Cohen, 1985). Each of the pre-study levels reflects cumulative changes during stages of farm development prior to 1974. With more accurate measures, they could be entered as covariates in the analysis of interactive effects, to remove their combined effects on recent adoption.

Progress, Productivity and Husband-Wife Decision-Sharing
(see Table 3b):

It should be noted that tractor horsepower in 1974, while it may be a positive predictor of the husband's plan to continue farming full-time to retirement, it appears to be a negative predictor of level of husband-wife decision-sharing in 1979 (-.18). The type of decision-sharing most affected may be the sharing of operation management decisions: when to sell crops or livestock, how much fertilizer to use, what make of equipment to purchase, whether to rotate crops, and whether to try a new farm practice (-.16, not shown). Type of enterprise, size and/or mechanization of operation, and whether the operation is a partnership with a separate family unit might help to explain this relationship. To the extent that decision-sharing has been a relatively stable characteristic over the family cycle, however, it may mean that a high level of husband-wife decision-sharing has inhibited the purchase of tractors.

Other measures of farm progress and productivity: pre-study level of farm practice adoption, and net farm income in 1973 and 1977, seem to be not significantly related to husband-wife decision-sharing (-.07; -.09 & -.11). In further analysis, however, variations in this important aspect of husband-wife cooperation will appear to "set the stage" for two distinctly different types of positive wife influence on recent adoption of improved farm technology, and these will appear to vary within changing developmental and cultural-historical contexts.

Direct Effects of Contextual Variables on Recent Adoption
(see Tables 3a & 3b):

The background analysis also includes observed direct effects of contextual variables on the dependent variable: recent adoption of improved farm practices.

In reviewing the resource structure of early farm development, we see significant intercorrelations of early family life cycle, the husband's age under fifty, his agricultural training and education beyond high school, high farm debt, and ten-year increases in the wife's involvement in farm work and farm decisions. It is not surprising, then, that each of these variables is significantly associated with recent adoption (see Table 3a).

In reviewing past progress and productivity, reflecting cumulative changes during stages of farm development prior to 1974, we see what appears to be a causal sequence, predictive of 1977 net farm income and the husband's 1979 plan to continue farming full-time to retirement. However, early progress and productivity, as indicated by pre-study levels of farm practice adoption and net farm income, are negative predictors of recent adoption (see Table 3b). These findings underscore the cyclical nature of farm development, in that, after a series of improvements have been made to the farm, during early stages of farm development, additional improvements may be less likely (although, since the pre-study measures are only estimates, caution is suggested in accepting this conclusion).

Observed direct effects on recent adoption help to further define the scope conditions for an analysis of interactive and multiple effects of contextual variables on recent adoption (cf. Walker & Cohen, 1985, on the importance of identifying scope conditions; Hage, 1988: 71, on the need to consider scope conditions and multiple paths; Cohen, 1989, on developing sociological theories and methods).

In the next chapter, models of interactive and multiple effects are derived from the theories of social action and social change presented in Part One (cf. Chapter 2), to test the theory of power sharing in transition (cf. Chapter 5).

Chapter 9

Method of Analysis

Introduction to the Method:

The research is guided by a *model of interactive effects*, derived from a 'contingency' theory of social action, and by a *model of multiple effects,* derived from an 'inconsistency' theory of social change. To trace a pattern of influence, it is necessary to study the interactive effects that determine the outcome of that pattern. At the same time, one must be aware of alternative patterns of influence, each uniquely combining sometimes opposite interactive effects.

This approach, which is appealing from both a practical and a theoretical standpoint, is not possible if the research is limited to linear path models. However, multiple paths have proven to be difficult to conceptualize and operationalize (e.g., Parsons' pattern variables). Organizational theorists have discovered the usefulness of dual approaches in research on open and closed systems (Woodward, 1958, 1965) but have rejected contingency theory (cf. Hage & Meeker, 1988). Methodologists have relied on intervening variables and data transformations to adapt their models to their data, and systems theorists have tended to rely on feedback effects. For the most part, these adjustments do not fully anticipate or adequately account for multiple paths or multiple effects.

Early functionalists were too restricted by the normative, equilibrium-model determinism of their day to realize the flexibility encompassed in Toënnies gemeinschaft/geselschaft or Parson's pattern variables. But even conflict theorists and class-struggle theorists have seemed hesitant to apply value-free dualisms to resolve the contradictions found in their phenomena of interest. Lacking a methodology that examines interactive effects, 'grand theory' bowed to 'social facts' as the basis for collecting and interpreting social data. It was intended that from this research 'theories of the middle-range' would be developed from which to formulate more workable theories on a grander scale (Merton, 1957). But that has not happened. Instead, researchers have relied increasingly on multiple regression analysis (in which it is easy to ignore the complexity of interactive effects) and have been satisfied with one path models: equilibrium, moving-equilibrium, and semi-equilibrium models that failed to predict the many cultural, social, economic, and political upheavals of recent decades.

As a remedy, theory-based models of interactive and multiple effects are proposed, to identify 'patterns' of response that predict and explain personal and societal transformations, including radical social change. (Others who have addressed the need for greater complexity of analysis include Hage, 1988; Coleman, 1991; Skvoretz & Fararo, 1991; and Young, 1991).

The Model of Interactive Effects:

The conceptual scheme for the theory of social action is based on an ordered sequence of twelve necessary but not sufficient causes of any given social act. At each of four levels (cultural, social, economic, and political) a set of three cognitive responses necessary to a given act develops as a growing perception of available resources, within an optimum threshold of awareness, subject to the recognition of a directive (i.e., to obtain and use available resources).

It might be helpful to think of a set of descending stairs, with each step representing one of the four levels: cultural, social, economic and political. Each step is comprised of a set of recognized controls *(directives)* and perceived conditions *(resources)* connected by a (sensitivity) threshold of awareness. The actor responds cognitively at each step with 1) recognition of a directive that utilizes resources from the previous step, 2) awareness of a degree of sensation (not too great or too small), and 3) perception of the amount of resources available to

Beyond Equilibrium Theory 153

carry the directive to the next level. (Our focus is only on directives and resources.)

As each step is completed, the initial directive is qualified at the next level, and additional resources are assessed, until it is possible to carry out a social act that satisfies all four directives. Social action occurs when the fourth step, at the personal/political level, is completed. It is interpreted *in the next first step, the cultural level*, and is validated or invalidated *in the next second step, the social level*. From this process it eventually becomes, with repetition, a predictable causal sequence for a given social action.

Each cognitive response is *contingent* on a progression of preceding cognitive responses, each with a set of three immediate causes: a directive, a sensitivity, and one or more resources, as explained above. Each cognitive response therefore represents a series of interactive effects, as part of a logical "pattern" (developmental sequence) of responses, as follows:

Developmental Sequence of Cognitive Responses, within a Social Context (Environment) of Directives (Controls): >

```
                  CULTURAL    SOCIAL      ECONOMIC    PERS./POLIT.
                  TRADI-      EXPECTA-    NEED        COMMIT-
                  TIONS       TIONS       PRIORITIES  MENTS
and Resources       .           .           .           .
(Conditions):       v           .           .           .
       v          Concepts      .           .           .
                  Values        .           .           .
INFOR -             v           v           .           .
MATION . . . . . .> Ideas......> Beliefs    .           .
                              Attitudes     .           .
SOCIAL                          v           v           .
ACCESS . . . . . . . . . .> Interests......>Goals       .
                                          Motivations   .
ECONOMIC                                  Responsi-     v
MEANS . . . . . . . . . . . . . . .> bilities......> Obligations
                                                     Intentions
PERSONAL/ POLITICAL                                    v
INFLUENCE . . . . . . . . . . . . . . . . . . ..>ACTIONS..>
```

....> (Sequence continues as actions are culturally interpreted as to meaning, socially assessed as to acceptability, etc.)

Pattern connotes reproducibility, not only of a response sequence but also of the social context that produced it. To fully represent the model, social context is included as well as the response sequence (see previous page).

Interactive effects imply that single factors do not, alone, produce effects. It is assumed, in this approach, that social context (controls and resources) as well as cognitive responses are interactive. Both types of interactions are included in the study.

Application of the Model of Interactive Effects:

In the following presentation a letter and number are enclosed in parentheses next to each of the study variables to indicate its location in the model. The number indicates the step-level or domain: (**1**) = the cultural domain, (**2**) = the social or societal domain, (**3**) = the economic domain, and (**4**) = the personal/political domain.

The letters in parens with the numbers distinguish between *resources* (**R**) and *directives* (**D**). The letter (**C**) for *cognition* is added to indicate perception or assessment of a resource (**RC**), or acknowledgment of a directive (**DC**). [Stable boundaries (**B**) of sensitivity thresholds are assumed in the study.]

Resources in the cultural domain are categorized as *information* and designated (**R1**). Those in the social domain are categorized as *social access* and designated (**R2**). Economic resources are referred to as *means* and designated (**R3**). Political resources are referred to as *influence* and designated (**R4**).

In the social action schema, influence is the resource immediately preceding the social act, and therefore of major interest as an independent variable. However, the direction of influence is determined by a (**D4**) directive, i.e., by a *personal commitment*, contingent on actor assessment of a (**D3**) *need priority*, within the limits of (**D2**) *social expectations* and (**D1**) *cultural traditions*.

This schema describes a causal context in which patterns of response are formed that result in social acts. It is self-deterministic, in that sensitivities of the social entity determine whether a response sequence will proceed. It is a reflexive context, in that resources and directives may be altered as a consequence of the social acts that they help to cause. It is likewise a personalized context, in that past responses to situational controls and conditions (directives and resources) have individualized the context, accommodating it to the uniqueness of that social entity. Each social act is therefore a creation of that entity, affected by current setting as well as by past responses of that entity.

So the word *pattern* also connotes an approximation, reproducible within a range of variation that might be expected for a given population or subpopulation knowing their common experiences and setting. *A pattern consists of a set of (sequentially interrelated) object and action orientations that precede any given social act.* Each orientation is formed by a directive, a sensitivity, and a resource, in stair-step fashion, as mentioned above.

For simplicity, each cognition is identified with its cultural, social, economic, or personal/political domain, rather than with the most immediate of its three causal elements. For example: "Farms primarily as a way of life rather than as a way to make a living" is designated (**DC1**), to indicate a *concept* or *value* from the cultural domain. [NOTE: *value* is here defined without valence, since valence is assigned to *value* in the social domain.] *Concept* is a tradition-structured interpretation of past action, and signifies acknowledgment of that action. *Value* signifies awareness that the interpretation has either reduced uncertainty or has increased the entity's tolerance for uncertainty.

Since a cognition implies a prior directive or resource, such references are given. For example: Husband's plan to continue farming is designated (**DC4**) to show the (**D4**, political domain) personal commitment relevant to this awareness of an *intention* (**C4**). [NOTE: Other multiple references are used to show multiple contextual inference. For example: "husband's age under fifty" is designated (**D2/3**) to show that not only social expectations but also economic need priorities are represented by this measure.]

Reported change in a resource variable is shown with the notation " ' " after the letter R, shown as (**R'C3**) and (**R'C4**) below. The importance of this notation is explained when the model is expanded to include multiple paths. To simplify the model, *context variables are placed within each step rather than outside.* One might visualize a three dimensional helical structure of (process-necessary) resources and (structurally-determined) directives on the outside, actor cognitions within.

Study variables are now inserted into the combined, generalized model of interactive effects on recent farm practice adoption, which does not yet differentiate between two patterns of wife influence, the primary focus for further study. Due to sample size, not all study variables will be included in the analysis of interactive effects.

Study Variables placed within the Model of Interactive Effects:
CULTURAL DOMAIN (concepts, reinforced or modified by information, ideas)
Concept of farming. Husband: 'farming is primarily a profit-making business,' or 'farming is a way of life' (**DC1**)
Information. Husband has agricultural training or some college (**R1**)
Ideas. Husband's assessment of wife as a source of new ideas in farming (**RC1**)

SOCIAL DOMAIN (expectations reinforced or modified by attitudes, social access)
Expectations/Priorities. Husband is younger than age 50 (**D2/3**)
Attitude. Husband's level of satisfaction with the way he and his wife make farm decisions and settle differences (**DC2**)
Social access. H/W did or did not spend a recent evening 'just chatting' (**RC2**)

ECONOMIC DOMAIN (need reinforced or modified by means, responsibility, responsibility change)
Need. Net farm income is less than $10,000 or negative (**D3**)
Means (through borrowing). Farm debt is greater than $40,000 (**R3**)
Responsibility. Wife mostly keeps the farm records (**RC3**)
Responsibility change. Ten year increase in wife's involvement in farm chores, field work, &/or record-keeping (**R'C3**)

PERSONAL/POLITICAL DOMAIN (commitment reinforced or modified by intention, influence, influence change, action, action change)
Commitment (to farming as an occupation). No full-time work off the farm, farm husband (**D4**)
Intention. Husband plans to continue farming full-time or part-time to retirement (**DC4**)
Influence. Level of H/W decision-sharing on farm matters(**RC4**)
Influence change. Ten year increase in wife's involvement in farm decisions (**R'C4**)
Action. Overall adoption of farm practices (**R4**)
Action change. 5 year increase in adoption (**R'4**)

Procedures for Application of the Model:

1) The social setting is differentiated by structural requirements manifested as directives, and by resources manifested as processes and roles.

2) Directives are recognized, resources perceived, and roles acknowledged by some component or combination of components of the acting unit.

3) Such cognitions occur at each of four levels: at the level of reason (cultural domain), at the level of feeling (social domain), at the level of movement toward goals (economic domain), and at the level of planned effort to attain goals (personal/political domain).

4) Cognitions occur at three progressive states of awareness at each response level: awareness of a sensation (e.g., hunger), perception of a resource to increase or decrease the sensation (e.g., food), and recognition of a directive regarding use of the resource (e.g., ingest).

5) Measurement criteria for the study variables include, whenever possible, validity checks of cognitive definition of the setting by the actor(s).

Before using this model to develop a predictive model that includes multiple paths, it is necessary to consider a *Model of Multiple Effects.* Where a social environment is changing, and the population is not entirely homogeneous and immobile, there may be multiple strategies for either adapting to or attempting to change the new environment. Further, given a specific strategy, there may be multiple ways of arriving at that strategy.

Introduction to the Model of Multiple Effects:

This model is visually more complex. Building on the previous model, this model requires visualization of select combinations of response categories, of a manageable subset of the study variables hypothesized to result in greatest incidence of a given social act. The social act of interest is recent adoption of innovative farm practices. Tests include a multifactor analysis of covariance and sixteen planned means comparisons, adjusted for the covariate, selected from higher-order interactive effects.

Alternatively, the model can be used to test patterns of effect associated with more than one outcome, including effects not categorized as acts. (The initial study design included, as farm outcomes, changes in net farm income, number of crop acres, and tractor horsepower. However, these changes require minimal or no integration of new cultural concepts so were eliminated for the sake of simplifying the study design.)

The model can also be used to study 'negative' effects, that is, low quantitative change in the outcome variable; and it can be used to study decreases as well as increases in social acts or other outcomes. Any change can be studied using this model, whether adaptive, integrative, disintegrative or reintegrative. This is where discussion of the theory of social change becomes relevant.

The theory of social change is a stage and phase theory. It looks at the social actor as going through highly predictable *developmental stages of actor formation*, and also less predictable *transitional phases of actor disintegration, transformation, and reintegration*. And, whereas social action is seen to result from attempts to reduce *discomfort* and/or *uncertainty*, social change results from attempts to reduce *inconsistency*, which may require structural adaptation or radical structural change.

These separate insights impact the study in two very different ways. *Developmental stage* is initiated by social and economic directives, represented by 'socioeconomic status' indicators in the social and economic domains of the model of interactive effects. *Transitional phases* are more likely to be initiated in the cultural and political domains, and to affect the distribution of influence within (and between) social entities, the essential resource of the political domain.

For purposes of prediction, it is assume that younger farm husbands, and farm families in the early stages of the family cycle, are developmentally more flexible (social domain) as well as more motivated (economic domain) to adopt innovative farm practices, an indicator of acceptance of technological change. In similar economic circumstances, older farm husbands, and couples in later stages of the family cycle, may be less sensitive to economic hardship or may tend to adapt in less financially risky ways, such as renting more acreage to increase yields.

Using *developmental stage* theory helps to differentiate the population of interest within domains most familiar to sociologists, the social and the economic. But these domains are not the ones that help to explain rapid technological change. For this focus one must look to the cultural and political domains. Assuming that there is equally available knowledge of and information about innovative farm practices, the primary focus will be on the political domain, including evidence that the farmer has a plan to continue farming as an occupation as well as the ability to mobilize family resources to make this possible.

At this point, one should differentiate between two kinds of influence referred to above. Influence within the social entity implies that the social actor *has the use of* resources available to the social entity to achieve the ends toward which he (they) are committed. Influences beyond this boundary may be relevant but are not included in this study. (These include the dynamics of farm co-ops, extended family partnerships, family-owned corporations, and other cooperative arrangements.)

Next, one should define the social entity and the social actor. The entity is the farm family, specifically the husband and wife. But the actor may be either the husband or the husband/wife acting as one. It is important to know which, but it is also important to know *whether the structure of influence is changing,* for this has implications for identifying transitional phases of 'actor' disintegration and transformation that may affect the acceptance of technological change.

To identify 'two patterns of wife influence,' it is necessary to examine the structure of family influence associated with each of two phases of family transition. The first phase is characterized by increased participation of the wife in the work of farming, an instrumental role. Although work is associated with the economic domain, such incorporation into the role of 'actor' represents not only a change in the role structure of the acting unit, but also a secondary change in the structure of influence, since it increases the wife's indirect influence while at the same time enhancing the husband's ability to carry out, in the political domain, his commitment to farming as an occupation.

The second transitional phase of interest, in studying the wife's influence on farming, is characterized by an increased incorporation of the wife into the role of deciding farm matters, a leadership role. This, too, represents not only a change in the role structure of the acting unit, but also a primary, process-oriented (achieved rather than ascribed) change in the structure of influence that potentially *redefines the 'actor.'*

Changes in the wife's involvement in these instrumental and leadership roles, combined with a consideration of levels of husband-wife role-sharing, help to indicate whether the social actor is entering a final phase of disintegration (of traditional gender roles) or an emerging phase of new integration, phases of system change most likely to be reflected in innovative acts.

Phases of social structural change have earlier been identified as *Vacillating, Disrupted, Emerging, Fluctuating,* and *Stabilized;* with a sixth, *Established,* being an 'equilibrium' phase where stabilized structural changes become socially reinforced (cf Chapter 2). Of course, one should distinguish between major social disruptions and minor adjustments. In the present study the concern is with increased innovative behavior in only one sphere of farm family activity, related to operation of the farm enterprise. The focus is on increased incorporation of the wife in farm roles, which may be either disintegrative or transformative within the sphere of family income-generating activity. The summary analysis will distinguish between disintegrative (instrumental role reorganization in the *Disrupted* phase), and transformative (leadership role redefinition in the *Emerging* phase), with positive implications of both adjustments for acceptance of technological change.

Although multiple and even opposite social actions can occur in similar social settings as a result of altering only one or two actor responses, there can be identical actions resulting from what appear to be different settings and different responses. The goal of this study is to demonstrate the latter with reference to the adoption of new farm practices, and to interpret the results according to stated theories.

A Logic of Causal Analysis of Social Change:

For the purpose of discussion it can be said that social change is produced in basically two ways: qualitatively and quantitatively. **Qualitative** change indicates a change in the *direction* of an effect, and represents an *alternative option,* even if it is only a variation of what was, such as a move to a different house in the same village. **Quantitative** change indicates a change in the *resource base required* for an effect, and represents a *greater or lesser opportunity,* for example, more or less time or money to pursue a pet project.

Accordingly, the causal analysis for each type of social change will vary. Using the theoretical framework presented, the emphasis in an analysis of **qualitative** change is on change in the requirements of a structural directive, e.g., of a cultural tradition, a societal expectation, a need priority, or a personal commitment. The pattern of change is characterized by ways in which information, social access, economic means and personal/political influence enhance or obstruct the change. So the focus of the analysis is on these interactive effects.

In contrast, the emphasis in an analysis of **quantitative** change is on change in the availability of a resource: e.g., of an information source, a social position, a material asset or a source of personal influence. The pattern of change is characterized by the way in which cultural traditions, societal expectations, need priorities and personal commitments direct the use of the additional or diminished resource. The focus of the present analysis is on these interactive effects, which are quite different from those mentioned above, in that the key variable or variables that trigger the social change are changing resources rather than changing directives.

A third possibility is one in which change is both quantitative and qualitative, requiring a simultaneous analysis of changes in both the structure of directives and the availability of resources. It is helpful to know if one change preceded the other, if either was necessary for the other, and if one or both is a recurring change (e.g., cyclical and anticipated) or essentially new.

The research problem is focused on quantitative acceptance of a resource that is essentially new: innovative farm technology. For the purpose of the analysis, it is assumed that qualitative change is a precondition rather than a simultaneously occurring change, and that it has already occurred, to varying degrees, for most of the population of farm families under study. This involves two assumptions: 1) some degree of recognition, by all families, that innovative farm technology exists, and 2) some degree of perception, by all families, that information is available regarding its applicability and use.

For the analysis of quantitative change, a logic formula is presented for only this possibility. Briefly, given an effect (E) that is a quantifiable level of performance of some social act, such as adoption of innovative farm practices, then (E) is a summation of all incremental increases and decreases in the attainment of that level of performance. Showing the net change in level for each given time period as E prime (E'), the formula: $E = \Sigma E'$ is used to represent the relationship of E to E'.

With E' as the dependent variable, the interactive effects on E' of resources (R), directives (D), and cognitive responses (RC and DC) can be shown in notation form, noting a balance (B) in the sensitivity thresholds required for cognitive response to the setting. Also noted are the interactive effects of quantitative *changes* in resources (R'). Current or preexisting E level is entered into the equation as a covariate (depending on reliability of measurement) along with (optional) preexisting R levels and D values whose effects on E are known, and whose effects on E' do not interact significantly with the effects on E' of key predictors. A general formula for quantitative E' is as follows:

Given B, balanced sensitivity thresholds,
$$E' = f \text{ Cov: } (E+R+D) + \text{Direct effects: } (R+R'+D+RC) +$$
Higher-order interaction combinations: **(R x R') x (D x RC)** + e

Covariates and direct effects "set the stage" for the analysis of interactive effects. The first interaction term, R x R', identifies primary and secondary pattern variables, and is used to define phase of family transition in the analysis. The second interaction term, D x RC, may be expanded to include a set of structural variables, as directives for continuity or change, and a set of process variables, as resources for change. Both are included in the study design, with farm context variables defined as directives for change, and wife role dimensions (shown as cognitive variables, RC) defined as resources for change.

Cognitive measures are interchangeable with R and D study variables (as distinguished from covariates). Other variations include RD combination variables as either R or D, depending on how that variable (which implies both a resource and a directive) is to be interpreted in the discussion.

In Design of the Analysis (Chapter 10) it is shown how measures in all four domains of the interactive model: cultural, social, economic and personal/political are used to refine this formula, to generate specific hypotheses of interactive effect that predict higher (as indicated by group means) attainment of E', a quantitatively measured, time specific increase in the adoption of innovative farm practices.

NOTE: D' is not included in the general formula for **quantitative** change. Reversing Rs and Ds gives the general formula for **qualitative** change, to show the effects of changes in directives, predicted to affect the structure of *alternatives* for E'.

Summary of the Logic of Causal Analysis of Social Change:

The Logic of Causal Analysis of Social Change identifies changes that are qualitative, quantitative, or both. Qualitative change results from a *structural* change that changes a *directive* that changes a *role selection*. Quantitative change results from a *resource* change that changes a *process* that changes a *role performance.*

Structure and process tend to be abstract concepts that are hard to operationalize. Directives and resources tend to be concrete and measurable, and therefore are used to define social context in the formulas and models developed for the analysis.

Frameworks for the two types of change are differentiated as follows:

	Structural Change:	*Process Change:*
	STRUCTURES	**Resources**
	are manifested as	
	Directives	**PROCESS**
	cognated as	
Cultural:	Concepts...	Ideas...
Social:	Beliefs...	Interests...
Economic:	Goals...	Responsibilities...
Political:	Obligations...	Actions...
	and expressed as	
	Role Selections	**Role Performances**

Qualitative change is a function of a *structural change* interacting with 1) recognition of the *current directive,* 2) perception of *current resources,* and 3) subjectively assessed social interactions, all relative to the preexisting social setting and *prior role selection.* Qualitative change, however, is not the focus of the present study.

Quantitative change is a function of a *changing resource* interacting with 1) perception of the *current resource,* 2) recognition of *current directives,* and 3) subjectively assessed social interactions, all relative to the preexisting social setting and *past role performance.* Quantitative change is the only focus of the present study.

Rationale for a Logic of Multiple Causal Analysis of Social Change:

The logic of causal analysis of social change, just summarized, is a model of zero-order (main) effects and higher-order (interactive) effects. The present analysis begins with level four, the personal/ political domain, in which the resource *influence* and the structure of *role commitments* interact with role changes to affect size and direction of behavioral change. The model of interactive effects then extends to include the economic, social and cultural domains, each domain mediated by measures of cognitively assessed relevance (of resources) and salience (of directives).

For change that is quantitative, such as increased adoption of innovative farm practices, the first concern is with the exercise and increased exercise of influence in the personal/political domain. Since the research focus is on the secondary actor within the acting unit: the wife, this requires looking at her level of involvement and increased involvement in farm decisions. Moving to the economic domain, it includes looking at her farm-work role and role increase. In the social domain, it includes assessing her as a source of social-emotional support for the primary actor. And finally, in the cultural domain it includes assessing her as a source of new ideas. Indication of the wife as a resource in any of these domains provides the basis for predicting an effect on quantitative change in the model of interactive effects. (See Appendix B, Path Diagram 2, for an undifferentiated general model.)

The first concern, then, in analyzing quantitative change, is with the resource *influence*. And since the focus is on the wife as secondary actor, it is the nature of her influence that is examined.

As indicated above, power is a multi-dimensional resource (French & Raven, 1959), with some aspects primarily *ascribed,* that is, assigned to position, and other aspects primarily *achieved,* that is earned by the individual. In the study, it is assumed that the farm husband's power in deciding farm matters is primarily ascribed, as part of his role as farmer and traditional household head. As such, his power is *legitimated*, giving him power to *reward* family members for playing helpful although subservient roles, and to even *coerce* them when necessary. On the other hand, it is assumed that the wife's power in deciding farm matters is primarily achieved, by virtue of her practical know-how and experiences in farming *(expertise),* her access to media and farm extension reports *(information),* and her importance to her husband as a helpmate or life-partner *(referent* power).

Influence is manifested from each of these six power bases, while differentiated as to its direct or indirect expression. By wife's influence is meant the exercise of her ability to affect farm outcomes, and this includes indirect influence as well as direct influence. The wife's source of direct influence on farm matters is indicated by the level of husband-wife decision-sharing on farm matters, which is also a measure of her level of decision involvement, since the husband is essentially the 'task leader'.

One source of indirect wife influence is through involvement in carrying out farm tasks. One task that is critically important to the success of farming, and applicable for all types of farms, is the keeping of accurate and up-to-date farm records. This role can affect economic decisions and their outcomes.

Another source of indirect influence is the wife's prescribed role as a source of social-emotional support for her husband. And a third is her role as a supplier of business-relevant information, including information from informal sources in the community.

These three indirect sources of wife influence: task, social-emotional, and informational, have direct power implications as expressions of influence to the extent that the wife is involved in farm decisions, i.e. has power to persuade. To the extent that she is not, they are still sources of influence. They may or may not be exercised consciously and deliberately by the wife, and may or may not be recognized as influence by the husband. But regardless of their intended or perceived use, they have a potential to affect farm outcomes, even though this influence is indirect.

Accordingly, the model of interactive effects will be tested for *multiple paths to the same outcome*. (This is a variation of the model of multiple effects, which can be used to predict negative outcomes, as well. But for the purposes of this study, predictions will be limited to positive outcomes.)

In contrast to the Logic of Causal Analysis of Social Change, the Logic of Multiple Causal Analysis of Social Change combines two or more models of main and interactive effects. Interactive effects in combined, multiple models include the possibility of disordinal (opposite) effects.

For the analysis of quantitative change, depending on the nature of the wife's influence, whether direct or indirect, not only should we expect to find different farm settings and different patterns of husband-wife response to those settings that explain positive effects of the wife's influence on farm outcomes, but also we should anticipate that, in some respects, these patterns of effect will be exactly opposite. For example, a husband who enjoys farming but is not counting on farm income to support his family may be more receptive to new farming ideas if his wife does not help make farm decisions. But one who makes his living from farming and expects to stay in farming may be more receptive to new ideas if he and his wife are farming as a team.

Before explaining how multiple paths, or patterns, of interactive effect are used to interpret the meaning of disordinal effects, it is essential to describe the *model of multiple effects* in more detail.

The Model of Multiple Effects:

In this section quantitative change is analyzed first, then qualitative change is reviewed briefly. The *model of multiple effects*, derived from the theory of social change, requires a closer look at phases of structural reorganization and transformation. Elements of social action formation and the *model of interactive effects* are referred to throughout.

Quantitative effects on behavioral change often come into the system at the level of *information,* and are interpreted within the limits of conceptualized experience. If new information does not fit within the existing mind set, it might be interpreted as meaningless and forgotten. Or it might be interpreted as meaning something quite different than - and even opposite to - its intended meaning.

An example is information about birth control. Such information might be interpreted as a threat to her position, by a woman whose status in the village increases with each child she bears. She will not only reject the information, but may seek social support to resist it. If she mobilizes economic resources and political influence, as well, the source of the information may be attacked, and a confrontation ensue.

The potential for resistant social action as a result of new information should not be underestimated. Resistance can have major consequences for social change. The religious wars of medieval Europe are one example. The ideological wars of the 20th century are another.

Even new information that is interpreted as useful and helpful has the potential of destabilizing the individual, group, or collectivity that incorporates it into its mind set. An example is Austrian physicist Lise Meitner's insights, from laboratory experiments, into the potential of splitting the atom. Shared eventually with Albert Einstein during World War II, who then shared it with U. S. President Franklin Roosevelt, this information culminated in successful U. S. efforts to produce nuclear fission. This success heralded a Nuclear Age of intense international competition to produce weapons of mass destruction, and the risk of nuclear holocaust.

From these examples it is evident that when new information is shared, and its interpretation (favorable or unfavorable) validated by others, it may eventually have an effect on social action. The simple act of sharing information can begin to move an entity from a traditionally determined, socially reinforced *Established* phase of social action formation to a *Vacillating* phase, if, *in the economic domain*, there is a compelling need, and means are available to satisfy the need.

This has occurred in farm communities with 30 to 40 years of experience with 'new' farm technology, with no evidence of organized resistance during the *Vacillating* phase, as farmers recognized a need to increase income from farming, and gradually accepted new technology as a way to do this. (An exception is resistance of some dairy farmers in Wisconsin to genetically engineered growth hormones, rBST and rBGH, to increase dairy herd production.)

In the cultural domain, in contrast, a *Fluctuating* phase manifests, initially, as conflict between new ideas and old beliefs, with confusion eliminated by sharing views with significant others until contradictions are resolved. A *Fluctuating* phase may culminate in attitudes that accept new ways of doing things, with discontinued interest in the old ways. For example, by 1957 less than 1% of Wisconsin farms relied on horses for plowing, so resistance to mechanization was almost nonexistent. Only in culturally isolated ethnic groups farther east, in Indiana and Pennsylvania, are tractors regarded as objectionable, e.g., members of Amish communities continue to travel and farm with horse-drawn vehicles, rejecting the convenience and efficiencies of mechanization.

This does not mean that social disintegration does not occur in farm communities, only that it is not initiated by new information about improved farming methods. Structural changes account for the qualitative decisions that farm families make, not always voluntarily, to leave farming. But the focus of this study is not on these qualitative changes. The transformational phases of primary interest, in the present study, are the *Disrupted* and *Emerging* phases, in which social change is initiated as action orientations. These orientations are expressed through instrumental roles in the economic domain and through leadership roles in the personal/political domain.

Quantitative change affects the performance, rather than the distribution, of these roles within the acting unit, so the primary predictors of social change are indicators of role intensification, within the economic and political domains. Since the focus of interest is on the effects of the wife's roles, as secondary actor, it is the intensification of her instrumental and leadership roles that are measured in the study.

But how are the *cultural and social domain* object-orientations differentiated for these action-oriented aspects of phases of change? So far, the potentially disintegrative effects of new information on the beliefs, attitudes, and interests of this farm population have been discounted. It is assumed that farm values, although changing to emphasize a more modern, business-efficient orientation, are still compatible with the older, more established farm traditions. New ideas of soil conservation, crop improvement, optimum use of land, and improvement of facilities are assumed to be compatible with traditional rural values and socially accepted beliefs about farming. And it is assumed that there is still a love for the land, and an interest in preserving it, as well as an interest in making it more productive.

Patterns of change of interest in the study begin, therefore, with evidence, in the economic domain, of a *need to increase farm income* (low net farm income) combined with *willingness to risk financial indebtedness* (high farm debt). Crisis in goal selection and risk in goal pursuit are initial expressions of a **Vacillating** phase of system change. While there is no separate indicator for families in this phase, it would be predicted that husbands whose wives are minimally involved in farm work and decisions, with no increase in work or decisions, will be higher recent adopters if income from farming is not their primary source of family income, that is, if the financial risk of adopting new practices does not have consequences for the family.

It is primarily in the later, action-oriented aspects of phases of system change that the wife is predicted to make a difference. First, there is the **Disrupted** phase, in which the wife becomes fully involved as instrumental actor, expressed initially as a shift from sharing responsibilities for tasks to taking on task obligations. The latter indicates a role commitment, with an investment in the quality of outcomes.

An example of a shift from shared responsibility to full commitment might be a father who occasionally 'babysits' his child in the absence of the mother, but who gradually assumes a role as fully involved, dedicated parent. If this degree of involvement was not part of his family tradition, it may take time to make the shift.

When the wife's changing instrumental role in farming is assessed, therefore, current role commitments as well as increased involvement are examined, to determine how far the wife has recently progressed in assuming this role. To the extent that the wife is being incorporated as instrumental actor, it is anticipated that her *increased investment in farm outcomes* will favor the use of new technology to improve farming. But, logically, there is no necessary relationship between incorporating the wife as instrumental actor and adopting new farm technology. The husband's role context, including his plan to continue farming as an occupation, is expected to be a factor in explaining such an effect.

Next, there is an ***Emerging*** phase of system change expressed, initially, as the *empowerment* of wives who have assumed obligations for farm outcomes. In this study, the level of empowerment of the farm wife in a shared leadership role with the farm husband is indicated by level of decision-sharing on farm matters. And increased farm decision involvement of the wife, in relation to current decision-sharing, is viewed as evidence that this process of incorporation is ongoing.

As the process of role inclusion evolves through these two phases, and given a favorable role context such as the husband's plan to continue farming, it is expected that the wife's *increased empowerment* will additionally favor the use of new farm technology.

Points of entry of the six phases of structural transformation into response sequences are shown in Figure H, starting in the economic domain. Each initiation of a transitional phase of system transformation has different implications for the acceptance of new technology. During each phase entry, there is an opportunity for the wife to influence the results. In early phases of system change she might suggest new goals, provide technical skills, or directly participate in a decision to try out something new. In later phases she might be a source of helpful information and ideas, social validation, or emotional support, dimensions of the wife's role in the cultural and social domains. At the pivotal point of family *need* redefinition, where farm priorities are reviewed and revised, her influence may be felt rather than expressed, depending on the nature of family communication. But in immediately subsequent phases her input becomes increasingly role-structured and action-oriented.

Throughout the study, the focus is on evidence of the wife's influence on recent adoption, but the emphasis is on action-oriented influence, in the economic and personal/political domains, and the analysis begins by focusing on direct influence in the political domain. Accordingly, the Logic of Multiple Causal Analysis of Social Change is used to separate the analysis in this domain.

PHASE::	(DOMAIN:)	COGNITIVE RESPONSE SEQUENCE:
	(Social)	*beliefs* validated by social consensus
(Old)ESTABLISHED		*attitudes/feelings* reinforce beliefs
		interests supported in social settings

Disintegrative Phases are initiated in response to recognition of a compelling need: (Economic)   *new goals* conditionally selected

VACILLATING .... *motivations* conditionally redirected

responsibilities increase>

DISRUPTED........(Political)...........................>*obligations* are redefined

Transformational Phases are initiated in response to redefinition of leadership roles: *intentions* are reconsidered

EMERGING...*actions* are redirected >

(Cultural)   >*new concepts* are formulated to interpret actions

FLUCTUATING...................... *new concepts* are challenged by old traditions

old values extend to accommodate new concepts

Reintegrative Phases are initiated as a result of value resolution:

STABILIZED...........................*new ideas* are supported by new information>

(Social)   >*beliefs* are validated by social consensus

(New)ESTABLISHED........................*attitudes/feelings* reinforce beliefs

interests are supported in social settings

Figure H. Points of Entry into Response Sequences of Six Phases of Structural Disintegration, Transformation, and Reintegration

Beyond Equilibrium Theory 171

In the next section the formula for a *Logic of Causal Analysis of Social Change* is expanded to include multiple paths.

A Logic of Multiple Causal Analysis of Social Change:

This logic is derived from both the *model of multiple effects* (just presented) and the Logic of Causal Analysis of Social Change. It provides for an expansion of the basic formula to include multiple patterns of effect. The goal is to differentiate between the wife's indirect influence, associated with sharing an instrumental role in the economic domain, and direct influence, associated with sharing a leadership role in the political domain.

For an analysis of quantitative change, the most immediate as well as the most pervasive determinant of social change is the resource *influence*. Although it is shown as a single element in the political domain of the Model of Interactive Effects, it is described as a multidimensional resource, contained in other elements of the model, as well. P*attern of influence* is used to refer to elements that have a shared explanation for their impact on action outcomes, such as the 'wife's supportive role.' But for purposes of presenting the logic of the analysis, the definition of influence is limited to direct influence.

A measure of the wife's source of direct influence is level of husband-wife decision-sharing on farm matters. To the extent that the wife shares in making farm decisions, she is empowered to influence farm outcomes directly. All other influences are indirect.

Multiple patterns of effect are differentiated, in the analysis, by controlling level of farm decision-sharing, selected as the indicator of traditional and nontraditional family type (RC4). As before, operational thresholds of sensitivity (B) are assumed, so the basic formula for *differentiated* quantitative change, is as follows:

Given B, and a specified value range for level of Husband/Wife decision-sharing, **RC4,**

$\mathbf{E'} = f$ Covariate (**E**) + (Simple Main Effects) + 2-way and
3-way interaction combinations:
(**R'**) x (Farm Context) x (Wife Role Dimension) + **e**

which is similar to the general formula for quantitative change, except that we now have 'simple main effects' of interactions of other predictors with RC4, and as many formulas as there are value ranges of RC4. This control of RC4, as the pattern variable, differentiates between direct wife influence (in domain four) and indirect wife influences (in domains one, two and three: the cultural, social, and economic domains).

With a large enough sample we might control (as a blocking factor) the interactions of RC4 and RC3, to differentiate action-oriented effects (in domains three and four) from resistance effects (in domains one and two, the object-oriented domains). But the study design does not require this degree of complexity.

The focus is on the effects of structural changes in the wife's farm role during the *Disrupted* and *Emerging* phases of farm family transformation. To maintain this focus, the analysis is limited to two patterns of effect, controlling level of husband-wife decision-sharing (RC4) as the indicator of direct wife influence, and increased wife work role (RC3) as the indicator of phase change within each level.

The immediate *context* in which effects of phase changes occur is measured by farm debt relative to net farm income (R3 x RD3) in the economic domain, and the husband's commitment to farming as an occupation (DC4 x D4) in the personal/political domain. [Context variables omitted from the study due to limitations of sample size include: the husband's agricultural education (R1) in the cultural domain, and his age under fifty (D2/3) in the social and economic domains.] Further differentiation, of patterns of interactive effect, includes measures of the wife as a farm resource (dimensions of the wife's farm role) in all four domains.

For Traditional Farm Couples (low level of husband-wife decision-sharing on farm matters), the predicted pattern of wife influence on recent adoption of farm practices is based on an assumption that the wife's influence is indirect, expressed most effectively as a *subordinate*, in that recent adoption is greatest when she is supportive in the social domain and helpful in the economic domain but refrains from suggesting ideas in the cultural domain or asserting herself in the personal/political domain (see Figure I-1, for a profile of expected high recent adopters among traditional farm couples.)

For Nontraditional Farm Couples (high husband-wife decision-sharing), the predicted pattern of wife influence on recent adoption is based on an assumption that the wife's influence is direct, as well as indirect, and is expressed in all domains as an *equal partner* in farming (see Figure I-2, for a profile of expected high recent adopters among nontraditional farm couples.) Again, the predicted profile of high recent adopters includes variables omitted from the analysis due to limitations of sample size.

For the statistical analysis, uniform measures of contextual variables are constructed to reduce the number of categories in the model of higher-order interaction effects. Wife role variables are selected from each of the four domains, in the following profiles, to test the thesis of 'two patterns of wife influence on recent adoption.' Hypotheses include predictions of *disordinal* effects of wife roles in the cultural, social, and personal/political domains, as well as *ordinal* effects (effects in the same direction) in the economic domain, where farm wives in the geographic area of study have traditionally played an important farming role (cf. Chapter 10, Design of the Analysis). Group means, of the number of farm practices recently adopted, are compared within high and low levels of husband-wife decision-sharing, as the indicator of family type, to assess each *pattern of wife influence* separately, after first qualifying the analysis with significant evidence of higher-order interaction effects. For the qualifying analysis a standard, analytical computer program is used: ANOVA (actually MANOVA, to include overall level of farm practice adoption as a covariate, see Chapter 11, Tests of Hypotheses).

Before building a predictive model, using the concepts and variables already presented, it is necessary to develop the concept of *pattern variables* further, to explain their nature, how to identify them, how they impact response sequences, and how to incorporate them into models that predict social change. This will provide the *theoretical* rationale for using multiple models of interactive effect in the present study. Pattern variables are associated, for this purpose, with six bases (dimensions) of power identified by French and Raven (1959), rather than with the descriptive dichotomies identified as pattern variables in the work of Parsons (1948). Further, a *shift* in each of these six power bases is associated, respectively, with the start of each of six *phases of structural change* (see next section and Figure J).

Resources/Process   *Directives/Structural*
variables :   *variables:*

CULTURAL DOMAIN

Husband has agricultural training past H. S.   Husband: farming is a way of life

*Wife is not seen as a source of
new ideas in farming*

SOCIAL DOMAIN

Husband is younger than age 50

*H is completely satisfied with how
H/W make farm decisions*

H/W spent recent evening 'just chatting'

ECONOMIC DOMAIN

Negative net farm income

Farm debt over $40,000

Wife mostly keeps the farm records

Wife's farm-work role has increased

PERSONAL / POLITICAL DOMAIN

Husband does not plan to farm
full-time to retirement

Low H/W farm decision-sharing

No increase in wife's farm-decision role

High recent adoption of innovative farm practices

Figure I-1. Profile of Expected High Recent Adopters Among
        Traditional *Farm Couples*

Resources/Process   *Directives/Structural*
variables: *variables:*

CULTURAL DOMAIN

                                       Husband: farming is primarily a
                                               profit-making business
Husband has some college education

Wife is seen by husband as a source of new
ideas in farming

SOCIAL DOMAIN

                                                Husband is younger than age 50

                                          H is not completely satisfied with how
                                                H/W make farm decisions
H/W did not spend a recent evening
'just chatting'

ECONOMIC DOMAIN

                                                 Low net farm income (< $10,000)
Farm debt over $40,000

Wife mostly keeps the farm records

Wife's farm-work role has increased

PERSONAL / POLITICAL DOMAIN

                                       Husband plans to farm full-time to retirement
High H/W farm decision-sharing

Wife's farm-decision role has increased

         High recent adoption of innovative farm practices

Figure I-2. Profile of Expected High Recent Adopters Among
           NONTRADITIONAL *Farm Couples*

Dimensions of Power as Initiators of Social Change; Implications of 'Power-Shift' for Social Transformation:

We are looking at changes in social action as the dependent variable, the E' effect. But we can look at changes in any of the twelve response categories in the cognitive response sequence, and use the logic of causal analysis or logic of multiple causal analysis to construct predictive models. This not only extends the usefulness of the models of interactive and multiple effects, it helps to explain the nature of pattern variables, how to identify them, and how to incorporate them into models that predict social change. It also provides a *theoretical* rationale for using multiple models of interactive effect in the present study.

First, consider that each changing response has a unique set of immediately prior conditions, controls and contingent responses. Next, consider that one of six phases of system transformation (newly **Established** being the last) is initiated at or near each of the twelve response categories. Finally, consider that a specific *power-shift* is associated with each phase of transformation (as shown in Figure J).

An adjustment is made to the six power bases identified by French and Raven (1959) to include *persuasion* with coercion, to show a power-shift in *volitional* power. Volitional power implies the ability to exercise one's will, and is therefore a *resource in the political domain*. It is the only indicator of direct influence over the actions of others, in the cognitive contingency theory of social action.

Legitimate power, a *structural variable in the cultural domain*, directly affects how actions are interpreted, and indirectly affects value formation. *Informational* power, a *resource in the cultural domain*, directly affects the formation of ideas, and indirectly affects their acceptance as beliefs.

Referent power (identifying with and wanting to be like another), an *internalized social structural component*, directly affects the formation of attitudes (the valence component of like or dislike concerning beliefs), and indirectly affects the formation of interests.

Reward power, an *internalized economic structural component* (in the broadest sense of economic), directly affects motivation to achieve goals, in accordance with need priorities, and indirectly affects willingness to work toward goal achievement.

STRUCTURAL CHANGE PHASE:	Power Base:	Power-Shift:	Responses Affected:
	(ECONOMIC DOMAIN) (new opportunities for satisfying need priorities interrupt previous orientations, and introduce variations in action-oriented responses)		
VACILLATING	Rewards.........	from **Predetermined to Earned**	Goals Motivations Responsibilities
	(PERSONAL/POLITICAL DOMAIN)		
DISRUPTED	Expertise.........	from **Old methods to New methods**	Obligations Intentions
EMERGING	Volition.............	from **Coercion to Persuasion**	[ACTIONS]
	(CULTURAL DOMAIN)		
FLUCTUATING	Legitimacy.........	from **Ascribed to Achieved**	Concepts Values
STABILIZED	Information.......	from **Old sources to New Sources**	Ideas
	(SOCIAL DOMAIN)		
(newly) ESTABLISHED	Referents.........	from **Pre-chosen to Selected**	Beliefs Attitudes Interests

Figure J. Power-Shifts associated with each Structural Change Phase

Expert power, a *structural variable in the political domain* (associated with individual role commitments), directly affects ability to fulfill role obligations, and indirectly affects intentions to do so.

At this point, it is those actors with *volitional* power who move actions toward completion, using *coercion or persuasion* to mobilize other power sources. Subsequently, they may try, by indirect means, to affect how those actions are interpreted by those with *legitimacy,* or they may strive to obtain legitimacy, to have influence in both domains.

It might be argued that legitimacy provides for direct employment of volitional and other sources of power, but it has been shown that endorsement of legitimacy is mediated by perceptions of *fairness in distributing rewards* and *competence in performing tasks* (Michener & Burt, 1975), which are two of the three action-oriented power bases: reward and expert, volitional being the third. So the direction of causal linkage is not as clear-cut as might appear, is probably interactive, and may be mutually reinforcing.

As discussed, two of the six power bases are structural and two are resource based. All four of these are located within the political and cultural domains, and therefore concerned primarily with the uniquely human endeavor of managing *uncertainty.* The linkage combinations are important to consider, especially when studying power-shifts and patterns of change, where management of ambiguity (cognitive *inconsistency)* also comes into play.

But the focal point of system change is not within either of these domains. It occurs in the *socioeconomic sphere* where attitudes and motivations are directly affected by power bases that reflect social and need structures. Thresholds of tolerance for *discomfort* are increased or decreased by the strengths or weaknesses of referent and reward power, based on hopes and fears (anticipations) regarding social approval and need fulfillment. These are internalized, usually together during periods of personal, social and societal formation. If referent power is weakened or disrupted, for example, as when all members of one's reference group are lost by tragedy or relocation, reward power may destabilize and re-form, based on a redefinition of needs, or a redetermination of need priorities.

Referent and reward power may be exercised (by self and others) by manipulating symbolic reminders of the accepted requirements for receiving approval and satisfying needs, as happens, for example, in religious worship. These requirements might be reinforced by some system resources and offset by others. Access to social approval that does not conform to internalized requirements for approval may weaken the structure of referent power. Similarly, means to satisfy needs that do not conform to those requirements may weaken the structure of reward power. System tolerance of discomfort may be reduced as a consequence of these non-system-conforming temptations. Being structurally determined, however, both referent power and reward power are relatively resistant to change. This provides stability during times of changing resources, whether expanding, diminishing, or changing in nature. The potential for change increases as other domains are affected.

The consequences of system change are played out in the *politico-cultural sphere*, where actions occur, and are either accepted or challenged. Here, there are no direct effects of *power-shifts* on the formation of values and intentions, which occur in relation to thresholds of tolerance of uncertainty. But values are structured by cultural traditions, and intentions are structured by role commitments. Whatever changes the limits of tolerance of uncertainty strengthens or weakens these effects. Informational and volitional power-shifts do this directly, and shifts in legitimacy and expert power directly affect the structures of traditions and commitments.

Therefore, changes in the politico-cultural sphere can begin with power-shifts in any or all of these four power bases. The combinations are more complex than the single linkage of power-shifts in the socioeconomic sphere, but only two linkages are of primary interest in the study. One is the linkage between a *shift in informational power,* that provides new information about farming, and a *shift in expert power,* that changes the structure of role commitments, incorporating the wife more fully in farm work. The other is the linkage between a *shift in informational power,* as above, and *a shift in volitional power,* that changes the nature of influence, incorporating the wife more fully in making farm decisions.

It is assumed, here, that pattern variables are identified as *variations in any of the six power bases,* and that these interact with one another and with their respective power-shifts, in either direction. These assumptions have guided the formulations of the theories, the design of the study, and the analysis of the data. They account for an expectation of disordinal effects, and provide the theoretical rationale for a multiple causal analysis design. Accordingly, these assumptions are included in the criteria for using multiple models of interactive effect.

Criteria for Using Multiple Models of Interactive Effect:

How is it determined that multiple patterns exist in the data? How are pattern variables recognized? When is an analysis separated to examine multiple effects? How are the results interpreted?

It might seem evident, from the discussion of multiple effects, that multiple models are needed. But when, precisely, do we make this decision, and how do we proceed?

This decision is made whenever there is evidence of power-shifts in the political and cultural domains. [In the next section, power-shifts in the social and economic domains are discussed.] In quantitative analysis, R variables are tested for disordinal interactions with other predictors, to confirm them as primary pattern variables; R' changes are tested for higher-order disordinal interactions with primary (R) pattern variables and other predictors, to confirm R' changes as secondary pattern variables. (In qualitative analysis, D variables are potential primary patterns variables, and D' changes are potential secondary pattern variables.)

A basic assumption of the logic of multiple causal analysis of social change, with regard to the six power bases, is that power-shift variables are associated with social change in multiple ways, sometimes in opposite directions. Unless concomitant changes and contextual variables are taken into account, research findings may evidence little or no effect.

Consequently, if a power-shift variable shows no observed direct effect on the dependent variable, it should be tested for a disordinal interaction effect. Even if it does have a direct effect, it should be tested for an interaction. Pattern variables always interact with other variables to produce effects. Whether the effect is disordinal will depend on the range of variability of the power-shift variable.

It might be asked: are structural variables and resource variables pattern variables only to the extent that they imply a power dimension? Logically, yes, but this question can only be answered by research.

A Logic of Causal Analysis of Social and Personal Change:

In addition to qualitative and quantitative changes, initiated in response to contextual variables and to power-shifts in the political and cultural domains, there may be changes to the internalized structures of referent and reward power that are deeply embedded during system formation.

These are not easily changed, but are relevant to predictive models. Experiments with operant conditioning, behavior modification, mind control, and the various psychotherapies *basically* attempt to re-program physiological reactions to life situations by changing the internalized *referent and reward structures* that 'trigger' problem feelings and problem motivations, i.e., impulses over which the person, group or collectivity appears to have no control. Mental dysfunction is restructured by providing a new structure of social-emotional support. Aberrant behavior is restructured by providing a new structure of rewards.

The success of these strategies and their techniques requires coordination of three objectives: 1) remove old referent and reward structures, 2) provide new referent and reward structures, and 3) change the upper and/or lower boundaries of sensitivity thresholds to allow or require system integrative responses.

This represents a transformation in the developmental processes of the social entity at a deeper (natural) level of existence than at the (rational) levels of thought and action. The success or failure of these transformations spreads to the rational levels, but does not begin there. Any changes that occur at the rational levels, alone, are superficial and transitory, a product of thought and design.

The *Logic of Multiple Causal Analysis of Social and Personal Change* incorporates (adds) terms for B (sensitivity thresholds and limits of tolerance) and B' (changes in these levels) as follows:

$$E' = f \text{ Covariate } \mathbf{B} + \text{Direct Effects } (\mathbf{B+B'}) + \text{Interactions } (\mathbf{BxB'}) \times (\mathbf{BxD}) \times (\mathbf{BxR}) + e$$

This completes the full range of possibilities for the combined theory of social action and social change. The final sections build a predictive model, apply the predictive model to the analysis, and provide criteria that may be used to falsify this approach.

Building a Predictive Model:

Reconciling data to complex theory without a predictive model would be a difficult task. Model building is a way to look at the whole before and after, to be clear about what researchers are striving to achieve, and to see how far they have come. Chapter 5 included a summary of expected interactive effects of key predictors on the dependent variable, after stating a set of general assumptions about such effects. Chapters 7 and 8 included a look at characteristics of the sample, and intercorrelations of all but the subjective study variables. A theoretical rationale for the analysis of interactive effects is given in the present chapter, from which hypotheses are derived in Chapter 10.

First, to reconcile the data with the theories, a multiple-pattern predictive model of interactive effects must be provided. When the study variables were listed, to illustrate the *model of interactive effects*, it was not specified which variables, or which values of the same variable, belonged to any given pattern of effect. This was begun with a description of two paths to higher increase in the adoption of new technology during a five-year period, each involving the wife. One is an indirectly-shared path, in which the wife's influence may be felt but not formally acknowledged. Another is a directly-shared path, in which the husband is fully aware of the wife's participation in the decision-making process. This does not preclude paths in which the outcome is achieved in other ways, but those are not the focus of this study. Rather, it is to show under what circumstances each of two paths that involve husband and wife, together, resulted in higher adoption of new practices during a specified five-year period.

In the cognitive inconsistency theory of social change, two phases of system transformation were differentiated, **Disrupted** and **Emerging**, with implications for changes in the structural organization of work and decision roles. In the *model of multiple effects*, the **Disrupted** phase was identified as one in which the farm wife increasingly takes on an instrumental farm role, and the **Emerging** phase was identified as one in which the wife increasingly shares a leadership role. Two patterns of interactive effect, associated with these two phases, are expected to be predictive of high recent adoption.

One pattern might be described, in popular terms, as a "pioneer spirit," in which husband and wife work together to farm the land. There are traditional ties to farming, and a commitment to farming as a way of life. In this pattern, the level of wife responsibility for an essential farm task, such as record-keeping, is expected to interact with the wife's increased farm-work role to favor acceptance of technological change. The other pattern might be described, in popular terms, as a "modern-day partnership," in which the husband and wife are more equal in their contributions to farming. Commitment is primarily to farming as a way to make a living, rather than as a way of life, and level of wife participation in farm decisions is expected to interact with an increase in her decision role, to favor acceptance of technological change.

The implications of the cognitive inconsistency theory of social change, for these two patterns of effect, are that the process of acceptance of change is affected by the changing roles of those who participate in the process. In the *Disrupted* phase, work obligations coincident with family ties provide instrumental means toward shared ends. As learned obligations are instituted in a new marriage relationship, new expectations arise. As they are reconciled with traditional values there are opportunities for new thinking, new ways of doing things, new methods to achieve traditional goals. As work is shared, thoughts are shared, and accommodations are made.

In the *Emerging* phase, pragmatic solutions outweigh traditional considerations, and the process of acceptance of change becomes more conscious and more intentional. The husband becomes more aware of his wife as a source of ideas, as someone with expertise, as a business partner in every sense. As this occurs, she exerts a direct influence on the decision process. This may result in more options considered, with a greater likelihood that rational choices will be made.

One objective of this research is to show under what circumstances the wife's direct participation in farm decisions results in greater increase in the adoption of innovative farm technology. This pattern is designated: "Wife as Equal Partner," in which the wife plays a direct role in the process of accepting change.

Another research objective is to show under what circumstances the wife influences recent adoption favorably with only minimal involvement in farm decisions. This pattern of wife influence is designated: "Wife as Subordinate," in which the wife plays an indirect but nevertheless effective role in the process of accepting change.

From the combined rationales of theories, models, and logics presented thus far, eight predictive formulas and sixteen hypotheses are constructed in Chapter 10, Design of the Analysis.

Applying the Predictive Model to the Analysis:

1) Deductions from the above theories of social action, social change, and power sharing in transition, with reference to Wisconsin farm families, are as follows:

a) there are at least *two processes of social action formation in farm family systems in which wives are influential in affecting recent adoption of farm practices*, and

b) *these processes are distinctly separate, representing different phases of family transition*, in both of which the wife's involvement in farm work is increasing.

In the theory of social change, high decision-sharing within a social unit is characteristic of an **Emerging Nontraditional** phase of social change, in which a new system is evolving. For these social units, sharing information and building consensus is an adaptive strategy. In contrast, low decision-sharing is more characteristic of a **Disrupted Traditional** phase, where old ways of doing things are still competing with the new, making 'separate spheres' and 'chain of command' more efficient and possibly more effective. An interactive analysis will seek to differentiate these adaptive strategies by using multiple models of interactive effect.

2) Accordingly, *two patterns are predicted, of favorable wife influence on recent adoption of innovative farm practices* by Wisconsin farm families, during a five-year period in American agriculture: 1974 to 1979.

a) One pattern, in which farm decision-sharing between husband and wife is high, in an **Emerging Nontraditional** phase of family transition, predicts greater increase in farm practice adoption when decision-sharing is increasing, suggesting an *assertive* wife role in the personal/political domain of social action formation, where responses to need recognition are translated into courses of action through a decision-making process in which the wife increasingly takes part.

In this pattern, greater increase in farm practice adoption is predicted, also, when husbands regard their wives as sources of new ideas in farming, suggesting a *consultative* wife role in the cultural domain, where past social actions are interpreted and new ideas considered, according to the theory of social action.

In this pattern, some husband dissatisfaction with the way they make farm decisions and settle differences may be functional, and indicate a free exchange of ideas in the decision processes required for adaptation to a changing agricultural environment. The wife's role, in this pattern, might therefore be described as *nonsupportive*, insofar as she may be willing and able to present and defend divergent points of view, allowing consideration of more options for solutions to farm problems than might occur if she was less involved.

b) Another pattern of wife influence, in which farm decision-sharing between husband and wife is low, in a **Disrupted Traditional** phase of family transition, predicts greater increase in farm practice adoption when there is no increase in the wife's involvement in farm decisions, and when the husband does not regard his wife as a source of new ideas in farming, suggesting *nonassertive* and *nonconsultative* wife roles.

The wife, in this pattern, is likely to be involved in farm decisions only to the extent that her husband wishes, and is unlikely to offer ideas that might challenge his own. As a result, he is able to exercise his independent judgment, free of competing interests that might inhibit his decisions or restrict his expenditures, particularly where a risk is involved, as may occur in trying a new farm practice.

In this pattern, any dissatisfaction of the husband with the way he and his wife make farm decisions might be dysfunctional, detracting from the climate of acceptance that a husband making most of the farm decisions might want from those involved in the work of farming, and possibly in the work of carrying out the decisions. It is predicted for this pattern, therefore, that high recent adopters have wives who, while being accessible, are non-confrontative and *supportive* when involved in farm decisions, as reflected in their husbands' being completely satisfied with the way they make decisions and settle differences.

c) Essential to both patterns is the wife's responsibility for keeping farm records, a resource dimension of the wife's farm role in the economic domain, suggesting a *collaborative* wife role. The rationale to include this measure as a resource indicator is that roles in farming that include critical skills (means of getting things done) and discretionary power (expertise: a power-shift variable in qualitative analysis) are expected to enhance the effects of wife influence in either tradition, old or new, regardless of any formal, acknowledged role in decision-making.

3) Further, it is anticipated that *the interface of the farm family system with external systems will mediate effects of the wife's farm*

roles on recent adoption, within disrupted traditional and emerging nontraditional phases of family transition.

System resources and rewards in the cultural and economic domains are relevant. These include access to information and education, in the cultural domain, and access to farm income and farm loans, in the economic domain:

a) *In the cultural domain*, the husband's agricultural training and education beyond high school are indicators of his access to information about changes in agriculture and new farm technology.

For low-decision-sharing (traditional) couples, agricultural training beyond high school, interacting with a favorable pattern of wife roles in the disrupted phase of family transition, is expected to be associated with high recent adoption.

For high-decision-sharing (nontraditional) couples, some college education, interacting with a favorable pattern of wife roles in the emerging phase of family transition, is expected to be associated with high recent adoption.

Due to limitations of sample size these expectations are not tested.

b) *In the economic domain*, net farm income and farm indebtedness are used as indicators of rewards and resources in the market and financial systems of the larger economy.

For low-decision-sharing (traditional) couples, high financial risk-taking, as indicated by high debt with negative net farm income, interacting with a favorable pattern of wife roles in the disrupted phase of family transition, is expected to be associated with high recent adoption.

For high-decision-sharing (nontraditional) couples, more conservative risk-taking is observed for high adopters, such that high farm debt with low but positive net farm income is expected to interact with a favorable pattern of wife roles in the emerging phase of family transition, to predict high recent adoption.

In the analysis, the degree-of-risk-taking distinction is omitted, due to sample size limitations, and the measure *financial risk* is a combination of high farm debt with either low or negative net farm income.

4) *Finally*, it is anticipated that within the farm family system, the husband's *structurally determined orientations toward farming will mediate effects of the wife's farm roles on recent adoption*, within disrupted and emerging phases of family transition.

The husband's farm orientations in all domains are relevant. These include his reason for farming, in the cultural domain, farm expectations and priorities associated with his age level, in the social and economic domains, and his occupational commitment to farming, in the personal/political domain.

a) *In the cultural domain,* the husband's reason for farming was included in preliminary analysis to explain the more conservative risk-taking behavior of innovative, high-decision-sharing (nontraditional) couples, in that these couples seem to be farming primarily as a way to make a living, whereas innovative, low-decision-sharing (traditional) couples seem to be farming as a way of life, with income from farming more likely to be supplemented, perhaps, by other income (see Tables C-2 & C-3, Appendix C). This seeming difference in value orientation of recent adopters by family type may reflect a somewhat marginal status of family farms on which the wife plays a more traditional, supportive role. Further analysis was not attempted due to limitations of sample size.

b) *In the social and economic domains,* the husband's age under fifty, reflecting expectations and priorities for insuring some degree of socioeconomic success and stability from farming, is expected to interact with favorable patterns of wife roles in both the disrupted and emerging phases of family transition, in association with high recent adoption. The husband's age is omitted from the analysis, however, due to limitations of sample size.

c) *In the personal/political domain,* the husband's commitment to farming as an occupation represents a strong directive to mobilize whatever resources are available to make or keep the farm operation viable.

For low-decision-sharing (traditional) couples, the husband's plan to continue farming *at least part-time* to retirement, interacting with a favorable pattern of wife roles in the disrupted phase of family transition, is expected to be associated with high recent adoption.

For high-decision-sharing (nontraditional) couples, the husband's plan to continue farming *full-time* to retirement, interacting with a favorable pattern of wife roles in the emerging phase of family transition, is expected to be associated with high recent adoption.

Assessment of the husband's commitment to farming as an occupation is, also, more complex than the study design allows. In the analysis, the distinction between part-time and full-time is therefore omitted, and the husband's *occupational commitment to farming* is a combination of plan to continue farming either part-time or full-time to retirement, with, at the time of the study, no full-time work off the farm.

In a more comprehensive analysis, one might expect the husband's plan to farm *full-time* to retirement to interact with assertive wife influence, his plan to farm *part-time* to retirement to interact with supportive wife influence, and his plan to *quit* farming before retirement to interact with no wife influence, to predict high recent adoption. This *third pattern* might represent "investment" farming, in which the property is being developed primarily to enhance its profitability at the time of sale. In the theoretical scheme, this third pattern would represent a VACILLATING phase of family transition, in which income needs and farming goals are being reassessed and occupational plans redirected.

5) *In summary*, the meaning of level of farm decision-sharing for recent farm practice adoption is qualified, in the study design, not only by interactive effects with dimensions of the wife's farm role, but also by interactive effects with the husband's role context. In combination, these interactive effects are expected to show that a low-decision-sharing (traditional) wife whose farm work role has increased (in phase II) affects change in a subtle way, by being supportive in what is probably a more 'life style' oriented farm setting; whereas a high-decision-sharing (nontraditional) wife whose farm work role has increased (in phase III) affects change directly, by being assertive in what is probably a more 'profit' oriented farm setting.

Since two contrasting combinations of wife roles and role changes are expected to be associated with high recent adoption, at least two patterns of positive wife influence are anticipated. (Negative effects are observed in the data, but are beyond the scope of this study.) By nesting the data on level of decision-sharing to explore each of these patterns separately, it is possible to assess individually two patterns of alternative processes of social adaptation to a changing technological environment.

Multiple patterns are summarized in Path Diagrams 3a & 3b (Appendix B). These models include all of the study variables, extending the 'two patterns of wife influence' thesis beyond the scope of the present analysis, to suggest hypotheses for further study.

Falsifying the Models of Interactive and Multiple Effects:

The *model of interactive effects* is called into question if main effects explain more of the variance, in the combined regression analysis, than interactive effects, i.e., if they enter the regression equation over interactive effects at the chosen confidence level (as determined by level of significance of the F test).

The *model of multiple patterns of effect* is called into question if no variable qualifies as a pattern variable, to differentiate multiple patterns, even though sufficient variation exists in the proposed pattern variable or variables.

Discussion: For relatively homogeneous populations, there may be data for which the model of multiple effects does not apply. If we could be certain that there is only one way to achieve a given outcome, then we would not expect to find multiple patterns of effect that lead to that outcome.

Where anticipated change is developmental, first we would look for one (interactive) growth pattern, with minor variations. But if the anticipated growth pattern is blocked to a portion of the population, such as skill-enhancing education for a racial group, or role-enhancing employment for a gender group, then we would look for evidence of qualitatively different growth patterns for the less-advantaged groups, and anticipate that power-shift variables (pattern variables) will differentiate these multiple patterns at each developmental stage.

In looking at transformational change, multiple patterns might originate at any developmental stage, and lead to multiple outcomes. For example, acceptance of technological change might be expressed as a decision to leave farming before retirement as well as adopt improved farming practices, with both outcomes seen as a way to maximize benefits. The role commitment assumption, in the model of interactive effects, is thereby negated for the pattern of change in which farming is seen primarily as a way of life with some other occupation seen as a more viable source of income.

So falsification is viewed in pragmatic terms. It is essential that reason as well as logic guide the interpretation of results. If the models do not apply, it is unreasonable to expect the data to fit. But if the models do apply, it is still necessary that interpretations of results be reasonable. If interpretations are not consistent with the logic of the theoretical framework for the models, from which predictive formulas have been derived and hypotheses generated, one should not then use circular reasoning to conclude that the models are false.

It is therefore necessary to determine if the models apply before looking for patterns of interactive effect. Once variables are selected to represent the latent variables, a variable might be disqualified during the analysis, but the models themselves should be considered applicable and therefore falsifiable using the above criteria.

Chapter 10

Design of the Analysis

Preview of the Analysis:

Variables for hypothesis testing have been selected and defined for a tripartite unit of analysis, the wife, the husband, and both as a farm couple. As background for the analysis, objective predictor variables have been intercorrelated, and their zero-order association reported with the outcome variable: number of innovative farm practices adopted within a five-year time period (cf. Chapter 8, Background Analysis).

A theory of gender power sharing in transition has guided the study, intending to show that the wife's role in farming is not only multi-dimensional but also changing over time, as farming as a business enterprise is itself undergoing change (cf. Chapter 5). The challenge is to study the interconnection. The theory suggests that power sharing is a survival strategy that incorporates the problem-solving skills of all who are engaged in a common purpose, when achieving that purpose has become problematic. To complicate an understanding of this complex phenomenon, the theory assumes that *ways* of sharing power change as various system elements, such as role obligations, are restructured. To complicate the matter further, it is assumed that the *contexts* in which these changes occur help to determine if power sharing will, in fact, have a positive effect on creative problem solving, represented in the study by recent adoption of innovative farm practices.

A method developed to study the interactive and multiple effects of diverse elements has guided the approach. A *model of interactive effects* specifies a four-level progression of social act formation (cf. Chapter 9). Each level is defined as an exact configuration of controls, sensitivities, and conditions resulting in cognitions, upon which the next level is contingent. At each level the unit of analysis may grow in complexity, from cognitions of individuals at level one (the cultural domain) to a potential for multiple-actor responses at level four (the political domain). Upon identifying primary and secondary power-shift variables associated with levels three and four, this four-level progression is used to differentiate *multiple patterns* of adaptive response to technological changes in farming, given specified characteristics (contexts) of the farm setting. This is accomplished using a *model of multiple effects* (cf. Chapter 9).

For the analysis of interactive effects, predictors are the wife's farm roles and role changes, level of farm decision-sharing, husband and wife assessments of their role interactions, the husband's plan to continue farming, and an indicator of the financial risk involved: a measure of farm debt relative to net farm income. Two patterns are differentiated by high and low levels of husband-wife decision-sharing on farm matters, selected to represent nontraditional and traditional family types. Disordinal effects of level of decision-sharing, interacting with three of four dimensions of the wife's farm role, qualify level of decision- sharing as a power-shift variable.

Unduplicated, higher-order interactive effects on recent adoption are tested in a multifactor analysis of covariance. Disordinal interactive effects are examined by level of farm decision-sharing, to differentiate by family type and phase of family transition the interpersonal dynamics of the wife's influence on recent adoption, within a context of high financial risk and high occupational commitment.

In future analysis, additional variables may be substituted or added to the model to test their efficiency as predictors. A larger sample is advised, to increase the number of planned comparisons from the analysis of higher-order effects.

Throughout the analysis the data are discussed at more than one level of abstraction, to interpret the findings and assess the multi-layered theoretical framework more comprehensively.

Criteria for Variable Selection:

Theoretical:
- A balanced selection of farm *resources* and *directives*, in each of the four domains: cultural, social, economic, and personal/political.
- A quantitative measure of change in the outcome variable.
- Quantitative measures of role sharing, role changes, process-oriented variables, and overall (or pre-study) attainment of the outcome variable.
- Qualitative measures of need priorities, role commitments, and other structurally determined (cognitive and contextual) variables.

Methodological:
- Distributions 'normal.' i.e. dichotomies close to 50-50 or trichotomies close to 33-33-33.
- Validity checks (including factor analysis): do the variables measure what the researchers want them to measure?
- Reliability checks (including correlation matrix checks): do the predictors relate to similar measures as expected?

Practical:
- Familiarity to other researchers, building on past research.
- Of interest to extension agents, farm families, and the public at large.
- Responsibility, and other ethical considerations.

Selection and Use of Statistical Tests and Techniques:

Significance:
Two-tailed tests of significance are reported for computer-generated correlations (cf. Tables 3a & 3b) and analysis of covariance (cf. Table 4 & Appendix Table C-l). Means comparison tests are one-directional, and are reported as one-tailed tests (cf. Table 5).

Factor Analysis and Index Construction:
Factor analysis is used to assist in developing indices of 1) level of adoption of improved farm practices, 2) level of decision-sharing on farm matters, 3) increase in wife's decision role, and 4) increase in wife's work role. Factor analysis is used to confirm underlying dimensions, clarify meaning, and exclude variables that do not belong in the index. For example, "irrigation" does not factor load in the adoption index since it does not generally apply to Wisconsin farms.

Factor analysis provides a better understanding of what each index contains. The adoption index includes four factors, as indicated above (cf. p. 122, Innovation and Agriculture, Chapter 6), with six to nine of 13 items loading on each factor. This is useful for interpretation and also for replication since, for example, the index does not include specific practices on disease and pest control, which require more discretion and qualitative assessment in their application than the more generally applicable practices included.

For purposes of the study, the factor loadings are not used for index construction. All items are included in the index of adoption and are weighted equally, since the focus is on quantitative change in this variable. The index of decision-sharing also includes multiple factors, two on major farm matters and one on day-to-day farm management. These are relatively well differentiated in the factor loadings, so each factor has been given equal weight in the index, lessening the weight of daily farm operation decisions (represented by more items) and making the index easier to replicate.

Level of Decision-sharing as a Blocking Factor.
Level of husband-wife farm decision-sharing is used as a blocking factor, after qualifying level of decision-sharing as a pattern variable. This is also defensible from a theoretical standpoint. Building a predictive model of interactive effects requires that blocking factors be discovered early in the analysis. These are key variables that represent or are closely associated with *power-shifts,* according to the theories of social action and social change.

Analysis of Covariance:
A multifactor analysis of covariance is used to test the combined model of interactive effects (MANOVA, since SPSS for ANCOVA does not adequately test for covariate interactions with predictors). The computer program used is SPSS for MS Windows, Release 6.14. All

main effects and interactions of predictor variables are entered simultaneously. Level of adoption at the time of interview is entered as a covariate, to remove the effects of factors associated with overall adoption.

Seven predictors, two constructed from significant predictor interactions, are selected to satisfy or balance theoretical considerations. *Phase of family transition* is constructed from level of decision-sharing x increase in the wife's farm-work role, consistent with the theory of social change and model of multiple effects. *Financial risk* is constructed from high farm debt x low net farm income. Financial risk and the husband's commitment to farming as an occupation represent contextual variables in the economic and political domains, domains that are most immediately relevant to social action formation in the theory of social action. Two additional wife role variables and two assessments of couple role interaction are selected to represent wife role dimensions in all four domains of social action formation, to complete the combined analysis of higher-order interactive effects.

Sample size is increased from 173 (cf. Tables 3a & 3b) to 176, to include three couples for whom an inconsistent response was reported for one or more of the farm decision-sharing questions, after omitting the inconsistent response(s) did not change the binary coding of level of decision-sharing for purposes of the analysis of interactive effects.

Means Comparisons:

Hypotheses of mean differences are derived from the formulas (below) for predicting higher-order, interactive effects. Means adjusted for the covariate are provided by the keyword PMEANS after the PRINT = subcommand in the MANOVA subprogram of SPSS. For all means comparisons a one-tailed t-test is used, adjusted for the covariate (cf. Kennedy & Bush, 1985: p. 408 ; Winer, 1971: p. 786).

Formulas for Predicting Higher-Order Interactive Effects:

Three interaction terms are shown in the following generalized formula for quantitative change (excluding terms for covariates, main effects, and error):

$$E' = f \text{ Phase } (\mathbf{R} \times \mathbf{R'}) \times \text{Farm Context } (\mathbf{D}) \times \text{Wife Farm Role Dimension } (\mathbf{RC})$$

where **E'** is a quantitative change in level of an outcome variable E, and predictors of the change include resources **R**, changes in resources **R'**, directives **D**, and perceptions of resources **RC**.

The central focus of the analysis is on interactive effects of predictors, expected to outweigh main effects (included in the analysis but not in hypotheses), to demonstrate the applicability of models of interactive and multiple effects. All three interaction terms are part of the analysis of higher-order interaction effects reported in Chapter 11.

The first interaction term, (R x R'), may include cognitive indicators **RC** and **R'C** (perceived resources and perceived resource changes) as follows: (R or RC x R' or R'C). The expression represents one or more resources interacting with one or more resource changes. These may be incorporated by the acting unit as *process* interacting with *process changes* or, more specifically, in the economic and political domains, as *perceived roles* interacting with *perceived role changes*. The latter may be used to identify phases of transition in family structural change.

The resource term, R, is represented in the study by two role variables: husband-perceived level of husband-wife farm decision-sharing on farm matters (RC4), in the personal/political domain, and husband-perceived level of wife responsibility for keeping farm records and/or completing tax forms (RC3), in the economic domain. (The latter might also be regarded as a directive, D, representing a wife role commitment (D4), in the personal/political domain, but for purposes of the analysis, an R designation (RC3) is used, and this variable is included in the third interaction term, as a dimension of the wife's farm role in the economic domain.) The changing resource term, R', is represented by two wife-perceived role changes during the ten years prior to the study: increase in her farm-work role (R'C3) and increase in her farm-decision role (R'C4)

In applying the theoretical scheme, level of husband-wife decision-sharing is identified not only as an indicator of the wife's decision role, but also as a power-shift variable and as a pattern variable that differentiates traditional and nontraditional family types. Decision-sharing is then used as a blocking factor, to differentiate multiple patterns of effect by family type. Incremental role changes, interacting with the wife's decision role, can then be used, as secondary pattern variables, to identify phases of change in family type from *established traditional* to *stabilized nontraditional*, including two intermediate phases: *disrupted traditional* and *emerging nontraditional*. Due to uneven distribution of the wife's decision role increase, and sample-size limitations, only the wife's work role increase is used to differentiate phases of family transition, for the combined analysis of higher-order interactive effects. (The wife's decision role increase is included, instead, in the third interaction term, as a dimension of the wife's farm role in the personal/political domain.)

The second interaction term, (D), may include perceived directives **DC** and implied directives **DR** as follows: (D or DC or DR). The terms D and DC represent one or more directives (internalized structure). The term DR represents a structured aspect of the resource base, i.e., implies a directive in the same domain. Examples: education for farming implies an agricultural conceptual framework; low income from farming and farm financial debt imply a need to increase farm income. The term DR is interchangeable with the D and DC terms. Directives help to further specify the context, or scope conditions, for change.

Variables in this interaction term represent choices that have been *structurally determined*, and therefore *control* the 'object' oriented processes and 'action' oriented roles *conditioned by* (manifested from) *resources*. These D variables are primarily qualitative, comprised of discrete categories that are easily determined or easily approximated. The quantitative (resource) aspect of the DR term is reduced to categories according to meaningful structural criteria, e.g., farm debt over $40,000 represents a 'financial risk,' indicating a choice to go beyond the median (1977) debt load to finance farm operations.

According to the conceptual models, this interaction term, in combination with the R x R' (phase of transition) term, defines the context within which social changes are likely to occur, and discloses the more objectively observable characteristics of the acting unit associated with change.

In the study design, the directive term, D, is represented by characteristics of the husband, wife or family that indicate probable (D) or perceived (DC) concepts, values, and beliefs ('object' orientations) and goal priorities, motivations, and plans ('action' orientations). The directive term DR is represented by variables that reflect qualitative choices that one or both (husband and wife) have made regarding development and use of family resources.

Each of these measures is definitive, in that the presence of a given value or value range is expected either to predispose (create favorable 'object' orientations) or to provide an incentive (create favorable 'action' orientations) to farm husbands and wives to adopt improved farm practices. For four of these measures: family life cycle, husband's age, husband's education or agricultural training beyond high school, and farm debt, zero-order correlations confirm this expectation (cf. Chapter 8), but differences by family type and phase of family transition are expected to refine these associations, consistent with the theoretical models. For the remaining six: net farm income, level of wife responsibility for record-keeping, and four cognitive measures (of object and action orientations), differences by family type and phase of transition are expected to uncover higher-order effects on recent adoption that are not evident in zero-order correlations.

Six of these initial predictor variables were selected to represent D, DC and DR variables. The two D variables, level of net farm income (D3) and husband's age (D2/3), suggest *degree of expectation of farm success*, in the social domain (D2), and *level of need to secure an income*, in the economic domain (D3). The two DC (cognitive) variables are: the husband's concept of (and reason for) farming, a value indicator in the cultural domain (DC1), and the husband's plan to continue farming, an intention and indicator of occupational commitment in the political domain (DC4). The two DR variables (resource with implied directive in the same domain) are: husband's education or agricultural training beyond high school, as an information resource with implied conceptual orientation in the cultural domain (DR1), and level of farm debt, as a financial resource and indicator of willingness to borrow to improve farm income, with an implied need to increase income to repay the debt, also in the economic domain (DR3).

Due to sample size limitations, effects of predictors in the social and cultural domains were subsequently omitted, to simplify the analysis. The remaining predictors, in the economic and political domains, were restructured as two *role context* variables: 1) level of *financial risk*, as indicated by high farm debt (D3) with low or negative net farm income (DR3), and 2) *occupational commitment to farming*, as indicated by the husband's plan to continue farming either part-time or full-time to retirement (DC4) with, currently, no full-time work off the farm (D4).

The third interaction term, perceptions of resources **(RC)**, may include perceptions of resource *changes* **(R'C)**, and perceptions of resources qualified by structurally-determined perceptions **(RC x DC)**.

As mentioned in the discussion of the first interaction term, the (husband-perceived) level of wife responsibility for keeping farm records (RC3) is included in the third interaction term, as a dimension of the wife's farm role in the economic domain. Also, the wife's perceived increase in her farm decision role (R'C4) is included as a wife role dimension in the personal/political domain. Her farm record-keeping role is called a *collaborative* role and her increased farm decision role an *assertive* role, for purposes of the discussion.

The third interaction term includes *assessments of role interactions,* as well as role perceptions. Role interaction assessments may have a combination of resource **(RC)** and directive **(DC)** implications, suggesting both a resource aspect and a structural aspect. It is not always easy to distinguish between the two, but the resource component is easier to identify, and perhaps easier to interpret.

In the study, resource assessments of farm role interactions are measured in two ways: the husband's view of the wife as a source of new ideas in farming, in the cultural domain of social action formation (RC1), and a report by either spouse that they spent a recent evening "just chatting," an indication of social access for a supportive spousal relationship, in the social domain (RC2). The wife's role as a source of new ideas in farming is called a *consultative* role. Social access for a supportive relationship is qualified, further, by the husband's attitude regarding their interaction when involved in farm decisions. Structural assessment of their decision-making interaction is measured by his rating of how satisfied he is with the way they make farm decisions and settle differences (DC2), designated in the *predictive model* as an attitude rating. As such, it represents a structurally-determined cognitive response in the social domain of social action formation. Together, social access and the husband's satisfaction with the way they make farm decisions suggests, for the purposes of the discussion, a *supportive* dimension of the wife's farm role.

Role interaction assessments, while subjective in nature and not easily observed or interpreted, are important to the understanding of the dynamics involved in acceptance of technological change. Future studies might attempt to refine measures of role interaction assessment as a means of helping families and groups determine how these factors improve or impede their acceptance of change, their adaptation to specific changes, and their ability to initiate effective strategies to cope with change.

Perceptions of the wife's farm role in the economic and personal/political domains, and role interaction assessments in the cultural and social domains, are expected to interact with phase of family transition, and indicators of farm context, to test the thesis of two patterns of wife influence on recent adoption.

For an analysis of unduplicated effects, the following three-way interactions are predicted (predictor combinations are shown in parens):

Four predictive formulas, by phase of transition, within a context of high financial risk:

(1) $E' = f$ (R4xR'3)x(D3xDR3)x(RC3): Phase of family transition x financial risk x *collaborative wife role*: does the wife keep the farm records &/or pay the taxes?

(2) $E' = f$ (R4xR'3)x(D3xDR3)x (RC'4): Phase of family transition x financial risk x *assertive wife role:* did the wife's farm-decision role increase within the past ten years?

(3) $E' = f$ (R4xR'3)x(D3xDR3)x(RC1): Phase of family transiiton x financial risk x *consultative wife role*: does husband see wife as a source of new ideas in farming?

(4) $E' = f$ (R4xR'3)x(D3xDR3)x(RC2xDC2): Phase of family transition x financial risk x *supportive wife role:* did H/W spend a recent evening just chatting, and is he completely satisfied with how they make farm decisions and settle differences?

Four predictive formulas, by phase of transition, within a context of high commitment to farming:

(5) $E' = f$ (RC4xR'C3)x(DC4)x(RC3): Phase x H's occupational commitment x *collaborative wife role*: does the wife keep the farm records &/or pay the taxes?

(6) E' = ƒ (RC4xR'C3)x(DC4)x(RC'4): Phase x H's occupational commitment x *assertive wife role:* did the wife's farm-decision role increase within the past ten years?

(7) E' = ƒ (RC4xR'C3)x(DC4)x(RC1): Phase x H's occupational commitment x *consultative wife role*: does husband see wife as a source of new ideas in farming?

(8) E' = ƒ (RC4xR'C3)x(DC4)x(RC2xDC2):Phase x H's occupational commitment x *supportive wife role:* did H/W spend a recent evening just chatting and is he completely satisfied with how they make farm decisions and settle differences?

Sixteen hypotheses of predicted highest group means are derived from these eight formulas, using traditional/nontraditional family type as a blocking factor, to test the central thesis of "two patterns of wife influence" and the theory of power sharing in transition (see Figures K-1 and K-2).

The predictive model has been derived from an interactive theoretical framework provided by theories of social action and social change. Interactive effects have been selected that are most relevant to the research problem. An analysis of these effects is expected to show that they combine to reveal two distinctly different patterns of farm couple response to a changing agricultural environment, each associated positively with recent adoption of innovative farm technology.

Fitting the Analysis to the Theories:

According to The Logic of Causal Analysis of Social Change, a change in the quality or quantity of a given social act occurs as the result of change in one or more cognitive responses of the actor to a social setting of structural controls (internalized as directives) and resource conditions (cf. Chapter 9). In testing hypotheses for a given population of social actors, researchers should look for multiple patterns of cognitive response that may result in the given social act (cf. Chapter 9). Ideally, researchers would hold constant pre-study levels of the activity, and pre-study measures of one or more conditions and controls to remove their prior effects. In this analysis, only the overall level of farm practice adoption is held constant, a more reliable measure than pre-study estimates.

In studying Wisconsin farm families, a preliminary assumption might be made of one causal sequence of interactive effects. Comparing latent and operational variables shown in Path Diagrams 1 and 2 (cf. Appendix B), one would then look for evidence of interactive effects of study variables, shown in Path Diagram 2, to provide support for the sequence of latent variables shown in Path Diagram 1. The assessment is complicated, however, by a need for multiple models, to test the theory of power sharing in transition.

To accomplish this, a power-shift variable is selected to distinguish multiple models (cf. Chapter 9). In Path Diagram 1, *influence* is shown as the resource that most immediately affects recent adoption. In Path Diagram 2 there are three indicators of *influence sharing*. Level of husband-wife decision-sharing on farm matters is selected as the one to represent a power-shift, from traditional, husband-dominated decision-making to nontraditional, egalitarian decision-making.

Applying the theory of power sharing in transition, within the theoretical framework provided by the theories of social action and social change, the power-shift indicator, qualified as a pattern variable using required criteria, is used as a blocking factor to test two patterns of interactive effect: of role changes, role context, and dimensions of the wife's farm role on acceptance of technological change.

After confirming disordinal effects on recent adoption, of levels of decision-sharing interacting with combinations of these variables, two models of interactive effect are constructed (cf. Path Diagrams 3a & 3b) from which key variables are selected to test, in a combined analysis of interactive effects, for qualitatively different patterns of association with the dependent variable.

Ten predictor variables are selected for the combined analysis of unduplicated, higher-order interactive effects. These include: two measures of the wife's farm role, two measures of her farm role changes, three assessments of husband-wife farm role interaction, and three indicators of farm role context. These ten predictors are reduced to seven, through conceptually meaningful variable combinations, as follows:

(1) Two role interaction assessments, in the social domain of social action formation, are combined to measure a *supportive* dimension of the wife's farm role. These are: a) husband and/or wife recall spending a recent evening just chatting, as a measure of access, a social domain resource, and b) the husband is completely satisfied with the way they make farm decisions and resolve differences, representing his attitude of complete acceptance regarding their current level of power sharing.

(2) Two role context variables, in the economic domain, are combined to measure level of financial *risk-taking*. These are: high farm debt and low net farm income two years prior to the interview. In addition, the third role context variable, *commitment to farming as an occupation*, is qualified by consistency with earlier questionnaire data and evidence, either year, of full-time work off the farm.

(3) Level of husband-wife decision-sharing, the indicator of family type, is combined with ten year increase in the wife's farm-work role, an indicator of wife incorporation into the instrumental role of farming, to identify four phases of family transition: *established traditional*, *disrupted traditional* (increased wife instrumental role), *emerging nontraditional* (new wife leadership role with increased instrumental role), and *stabilized nontraditional*.

Phase analysis helps to differentiate, further, multiple patterns of effect, to demonstrate the researchability of the theory of social change. *Disrupted traditional* and *emerging nontraditional,* as indicators of structural transformation, help to specify two patterns of wife influence to test the theory of power sharing in transition.

In the next section, sixteen hypotheses of mean difference are generated from the theories, the models, and eight predictive formulas of three-way interactive effects. Eight hypotheses test a pattern of subordinate, traditional wife influence on recent adoption; the other eight test a pattern of equal partner, nontraditional wife influence.

Hypotheses for Predicting Two Patterns of Wife Influence:

Hypotheses for predicting highest recent adoption of new farm practices are derived from theories and general predictions (cf. pp. 107-116, Chapter 5), a general formula (cf. pp. 140-141, Chapter 7), models of interactive and multiple effect (cf. Chapter 9), and eight specific formulas, above. Proposed in this section are predictions, in the form of hypotheses differentiated by family type, of highest group means compared to mean levels of recent adoption for couples in all other groups of that family type. Means, adjusted for the covariate, overall level of adoption, are partitioned (nested) on level of decision-sharing (the pattern variable and indicator of family type), to test the thesis of *two patterns of wife influence on recent adoption of farm innovation*s.

For reference, the formula numbers (1) to (8), above, are used to identify hypotheses. A letter code is added to the formula code to represent the nested variable, family type, as indicated by level of decision-sharing: an "A" for low-decision-sharing (traditional) couples, a "B" for high-decision-sharing (nontraditional) couples. Hypotheses are identified, in all subsequent presentations and discussions, as Hypotheses (1A) to (8A) for traditional couples, and (1B) to (8B) for nontraditional couples.

Three-way interactions, corresponding to the eight formulas, above, are entered along with main effects and relevant two-way interactions in a multifactor analysis of covariance, with overall level of adoption (number of innovative farm practices in use at the time of interview) entered as the covariate (control factor). From this analysis, group means are obtained of numbers of farm practices recently adopted, adjusted for the covariate, to test the hypotheses shown in Figures K-1 and K-2. Each set of eight comparisons tests a predicted pattern of influence on recent adoption, of four dimensions of the wife's farm role by phase of family transition (within family type), first under conditions of high financial risk and then under conditions of high occupational commitment to farming. The first eight comparisons test Hypotheses (1A) to (8A), for traditional couples; the second eight comparisons test Hypotheses (1B) to (8B), for nontraditional couples.

NOTE on construction of interaction terms:

Phase of family transition is constructed as a four-category interaction of level of husband-wife decision-sharing, representing family type, x ten year increase/no increase in the wife's involvement in farm work.

Financial risk is constructed as a two-category interaction of 1978 farm debt more than $40,000 x 1977 net farm income less than $10,000.

Farm commitment (plan to continue farming) is a two-category interaction of husband's plan to continue farming part-time or full-time to retirement with (currently) no full-time work off the farm, (also referred to as the husband's *occupational commitment to farming*).

The first comparison, in each set of four, tests the effect of the wife's record-keeping responsibilities (*collaborative* role) interacting with the wife's work role increase, in the economic domain of social action formation, where most new actions are initiated in response to identification of a need priority, according to the theory of social action. *Financial risk* and *occupational commitment* are tested as role-context variables that mediate the wife's economic role in facilitating change. When the wife's influence is based on expertise associated with task sharing *(instrumental role sharing)*, represented in the study by the wife's greater responsibility for keeping the farm records and/or filling out the tax forms, favorable effects on recent adoption are predicted in both the 'disrupted traditional' and 'emerging nontraditional' phases of family transition (Hypotheses 1A, 5A, 1B, and 5B).

In all other comparisons, disordinal effects are anticipated by family type, as a result of a power-shift in the personal/political domain of social action formation from low to high husband-wife decision-sharing *(leadership role-sharing)*. For low-decision-sharing couples, positive wife influence on recent adoption is predicted in the social domain when the wife plays a *supportive* role, during a 'disrupted traditional' phase defined by increased task-sharing (Hypotheses 4A, & 8A). For high-decision-sharing couples, positive wife influence is predicted in the personal/political domain when the wife plays an *assertive* role (Hypotheses 2B & 6B), and in the cultural domain when she plays a *consultative* role (Hypotheses 3B & 7B), during an 'emerging nontraditional' phase defined by leadership role-sharing as well as increased task-sharing. Further, positive effects are predicted during these transitional phases when *traditional* wives are unassertive or are not perceived as sources of new ideas (Hypotheses 2A, 3A, 6A & 7A), and *nontraditional* wives do more than simply agree with their husbands when giving moral support (Hypotheses 4B & 8B). Again, effects on recent adoption are expected to be mediated by *high financial risk*, as an indicator of need to improve the income-generating capacity of the farm, and by *high occupational commitment*, as an indicator of husband's long-term plan to farm as a primary occupation.

NOTE: Null hypotheses take the form: predicted highest group mean is equal to or less than the mean of all other recently adopted practices for the given family type, i.e., traditional or nontraditional.

For TRADITIONAL farm couples, the largest group means (average #s) of innovative farm practices recently adopted are expected to be in the *disrupted phase* (phase II) with *high financial risk* and...

(1A) ...the wife keeps the farm records and/or fills out the tax forms
 E' =f phase II x hi risk x collaborative wife role

(2A) ...there was *no* ten-year increase in the wife's farm-decision role
 E' =f phase II x hi risk x nonassertive wife role

(3A) ...wife is *not* seen by husband as a source of new ideas in farming
 E' =f phase II x hi risk x nonconsultative wife role

(4A) ...H/W spent a recent evening 'just chatting,' and husband is completely satisfied with the way they make farm decisions and settle differences
 E' =f phase II x hi risk x supportive wife role

...and also for those in the *disrupted phase* (phase II) with *high farm commitment (husband plans to continue farming until retirement, with no full-time work off the farm)* and...

(5A) ...the wife keeps the farm records and/or fills out the tax forms
 E' =f phase II x farm plan x collaborative wife role

(6A) ...there was *no* ten-year increase in the wife's farm-decision role
 E' =f phase II x farm plan x nonassertive wife role

(7A) ...wife is *not* seen by husband as a source of new ideas in farming
 E' =f phase II x farm plan x nonconsultative wife role

(8A) ...H/W spent a recent evening 'just chatting,' and husband is completely satisfied with the way they make farm decisions and settle differences
 E' =f phase II x farm plan x supportive wife role

Figure K-1. Hypotheses for Predicting Pattern of Wife Influence on Recent Adoption for TRADITIONAL *Farm Couples*

For NONTRADITIONAL couples, the largest group means (average #s) of innovative farm practices recently adopted are expected to be in the *emerging phase* (phase III) with *high financial risk* and...

(1B) ...the wife keeps the farm records and/or fills out the tax forms
E' =*f* phase III x hi risk x collaborative wife role

(2B) ...there was a ten-year increase in the wife's farm-decision role
E' =*f* phase III x hi risk x assertive wife role

(3B) ...the wife is seen by husband as a source of new ideas in farming
E' =*f* phase III x hi risk x consultative wife role

(4B) ...*no* recent evening chat, and/or husband is *not* completely satisfied with the way they make farm decisions and settle differences
E' =*f* phase III x hi risk x nonsupportive wife role

...and also for those in the *emerging phase* (phase III) with *high farm commitment (husband plans to continue farming until retirement, with no full-time work off the farm)* and...

(5B) ...the wife keeps the farm records and/or fills out the tax forms
E' =*f* phase III x farm plan x collaborative wife role

(6B) ...there was a ten-year increase in the wife's farm-decision role
E' =*f* phase III x farm plan x assertive wife role

(7B) ...the wife is seen by husband as a source of new ideas in farming
E' =*f* phase III x farm plan x consultative wife role

(8B) ...*no* recent evening chat, and/or husband is *not* completely satisfied with the way they make farm decisions and settle differences
E' =*f* phase III x farm plan x nonsupportive wife role

Figure K-2. Hypotheses for Predicting Pattern of Wife Influence on Recent Adoption for NONTRADITIONAL *Couples*

Effects in the predicted directions will be interpreted as support for the thesis of two patterns of wife influence on farm innovation and for the theory of gender power sharing in transition. Further, such effects will satisfy two, interdependent criteria for applying the theoretical framework to an empirical study. Briefly these are: to have provided not only an overall logic for the interconnectedness of the hypotheses, but also a set of logically consistent rationales for the findings. In simplest terms, these criteria require a combination of correct prediction and cogent explanation, a necessary combination for broad-based, overarching theoretical frameworks to achieve.

The findings are presented in the next chapter, and interpreted as to their practical and theoretical significance.

Chapter 11

Tests of Hypotheses

Introduction:

A primary objective of the study is to find evidence of a predictable evolution of farm family systems in response to a changing economic environment of risks, challenges and opportunities. Another is to show that the task and power structures of the family determine how these challenges are met. And a third is to demonstrate that factors that influence these adaptations are interactive and not simply additive.

A theory of power sharing and two general theories guide the research. The general theory of social action describes how object orientations are created within cultural and social contexts, selected to satisfy need priorities, and developed further as action orientations within contexts of economic opportunities and political requirements. The general theory of social change states that systems move through phases of disintegration, transformation, and reintegration as crises occur. The theory of power sharing in transition, within the framework provided by the two general theories, predicts that, as families move through phases of change, power is shared in direct or subtle ways in one or more domains of social action formation. Further, these ways change dramatically with structural changes in the family that include increased involvement of wives in making farm decisions.

As family systems evolve, by a series of rational choices and/or their approximation in each of four domains, structural variations may either encompass or operate independently of the occupational commitments of family members. Farm families have traditionally relied on family members to help with at least some aspects of the farm operation, so it is not unusual for the farm wife to be a resource in the economic domain of farm system social action formation. If this is the extent of her farm role, family structure is identified as traditional in relation to the farm enterprise. In terms of the theories, the traditional wife is involved primarily in *processes of sensing discomfort and problem solving in the economic domain*, and *reducing discomfort in the social domain*. Correspondingly, the traditional husband is more involved than the wife in *processes of sensing uncertainty and problem solving in the political domain*, and *reducing uncertainty in the cultural domain*.

This division of gender role emphasis by separate domains reflects the culture of the larger society prior to World War II. After the war this division began to break down (cf. Chapter 5). Wives became more active outside the home, and became more involved in the political domain of shared system social action formation. To the extent that the farm wife, as a decision maker, has become a resource in the political domain of farm system formation, the farm family is identified as nontraditional. This role extension often carries into the cultural domain, as well, to include her as an interpreter of new concepts and a source of ideas affecting the farm operation. Involvement in the economic and social domains continues, but as more of an equal partner than as a subordinate.

In the analysis to follow it will be shown how this shift in family structure, as indicated by changes in the wife's farm roles in combination with other wife role variables, together with key characteristics of the farm setting, affected adaptation to a changing farm technology in a Midwest dairy state in the late 1970s.

Findings:

In the overall statistical analysis of direct, two-way, and three-way effects, all significant main effects and two-way interactions are found to be qualified by three-way interactions (see Table 4), as the theory of social action predicts. This means that main effects and two-way interactions must be interpreted with caution.

TABLE 4. Analysis of wife influence on recent farm practice adoption, 1974-1979 (ANOVA)

Source of variation:	SS	DF	MS	F	Sig. of F
Within + Residual	346.17	116	2.98		
Regression: 1979 adoption level	50.93	1	50.93	17.07	.000 *
Phase of family transition	13.11	3	4.37	1.46	.228
Risk: high debt, low farm income	32.96	1	32.96	11.04	.001 *
Plan to continue farming	.33	1	.33	.11	.741
Collaborative wife role	4.67	1	4.67	1.56	.214
Assertive wife role	3.31	1	3.31	1.11	.295
Consultative wife role	7.08	1	7.08	2.37	.126
Supportive wife role	.65	1	.65	.22	.641
Phase x Risk	25.15	3	8.38	2.81	.043 *
Phase x Plan	20.83	3	6.94	2.33	.078 +
Phase x Collaborative	98.45	3	32.82	11.00	.000 *
Phase x Assertive	8.12	3	2.71	.91	.440
Phase x Consultative	4.54	3	1.51	.51	.678
Phase x Supportive	6.06	3	2.02	.68	.568
Risk x Collaborative	14.39	1	14.39	4.82	.030 *
Risk x Assertive	9.27	1	9.27	3.10	.081 +
Risk x Consultative	.41	1	.41	.14	.711
Risk x Supportive	1.06	1	1.06	.35	.553
Plan x Collaborative	.02	1	.02	.01	.937
Plan x Assertive	1.87	1	1.87	.63	.430
Plan x Consultative	.72	1	.72	.24	.624
Plan x Supportive	11.42	1	11.42	3.83	.053 +
Phase x Risk x Collaborative	88.70	3	29.57	9.91	.000 *
Phase x Risk x Assertive	43.68	2	21.84	7.32	.001 *
Phase x Risk x Consultative	28.15	3	9.38	3.14	.028 *
Phase x Risk x Supportive	4.04	3	1.35	.45	.717
Phase x Plan x Collaborative	11.44	3	3.81	1.28	.285
Phase x Plan x Assertive	27.59	3	9.20	3.08	.030 *
Phase x Plan x Consultative	22.71	3	7.57	2.54	.060 +
Phase x Plan x Supportive	31.33	3	10.44	3.50	.018 *
(MODEL)	650.37	59	11.02	3.69	.000 *
(Total)	996.55	175	5.69		

$R^2 = .653*$ Adjusted $R^2 = .476*$

NOTES: *P<.05 +P <.10

Direct effects, two-way interactions, and alternative explanations of findings:

The only direct effect on recent adoption, in the interactive analysis, is *financial risk* as measured by high farm debt with low net farm income (see Table 4). It is assumed that, as a contextual variable, financial risk-taking is concomitant with taking a chance on adopting new farm practices, that is, they occur together. It might also be argued that adopting new practices causes farm debt to increase relative to net farm income, at least in the short-term. To explore this possibility, one would need to measure *change* in the ratio of farm debt to net farm income during the period of adoption (some researchers might prefer a *changing debt-to-assets* ratio). One might argue, too, that financial risk and high recent adoption are both characteristic of early stages of farm development, equated somewhat with phases II and III of farm family transition, in that the wife's farm work role has been increasing. Checking this possibility with an analysis by phase of transition, however, it is found that a two-way interaction of phase and risk, observed in Table 4, is reflected in greater differences in average recent adoption between high and low risk-takers in phases III and IV (nontraditional couples) than between high and low risk-takers in phases I and II (traditional couples):

	Traditional couples		*Nontraditional couples*	
	Phase I	Phase II	Phase III	Phase IV
High financial risk	1.997	2.862	3.352	2.970
Low financial risk	1.777	2.057	1.585	1.612
Mean difference:	0.220	0.805	1.767	1.358

The assumption of concomitant effect is thereby qualified, initially, by family type, rather than by other considerations, but is qualified further when interpreting three-way interaction effects, within family type, by dimensions of the wife's farm role.

A two-way interaction of phase and husband's *occupational commitment/plan to continue farming* (see Table 4) does appear to differentiate recent adoption by couples in phases II and III from those in phases I and IV, suggesting a possible concomitant effect of occupational commitment and early stages of farm development on recent adoption. However, a greater difference in average recent adoption is observed in phase III, between husbands who plan to continue and those who plan to quit (or work full-time off the farm), than are observed in phase II:

	Traditional husbands		Nontraditional husbands	
	Phase I	Phase II	Phase III	Phase IV
Plan to continue	1.669	2.705	2.824	1.930
Plan to quit	2.007	2.153	1.641	2.035
Mean difference:	- 0.338	0.552	1.183	- 0.105

Emerging nontraditional couples where the husband plans to quit farming may be more likely than other couples to plan on selling the farm, rather than live in the farm house and rent out the land as other couples might do to preserve a rural lifestyle, and therefore less likely to improve the farm before completing these plans. It would be helpful to know what options are being considered by those who plan to quit, and whether they have a plan to transfer farm ownership to a family member. For those in phases II and III who plan to continue, the effect on recent adoption is qualified further, within family type, by dimensions of the wife's farm role.

A two-way interaction of phase of family transition and level of wife's responsibility for farm records (*collaborative* wife role) appears also to differentiate recent adoption by couples in phases II and III from those in phases I and IV, showing a combined effect of wife's *collaborative* role and increased involvement in farm tasks on average recent adoption. For nontraditional couples, however, although recent adoption is lower for couples in phase III when the husband keeps the farm records, it is higher in phase IV when he keeps the records:

	Traditional couples		Nontraditional couples	
	Phase I	Phase II	Phase III	Phase IV
Collaborative wife	1.678	2.761	2.654	1.768
Noncollaborative wife	1.945	1.824	1.435	2.431
Mean difference:	- 0.267	0.937	1.219	- 0.663

The higher than expected effect in phase IV is inflated by two very high recent adopters. One possible explanation is that capital being used to improve these farms may be coming, in part, from the wife's off-farm work (an important factor omitted from the analysis). This would account for her relative noninvolvement in record-keeping and non-increase in farm work. Not shown: high *financial risk* is a factor in both of these two cases, with each wife seen by her husband as a source of new ideas in farming (*consultative* role) without having increased her involvement in farm decisions (a *nonassertive* role). Such exceptions sometimes reveal the start of a new trend.

As effects of wife farm role dimensions on recent adoption are discussed, it is important to keep in mind that three of the four measures describe current states: keeping records, being an idea source, being in a supportive relationship as indicated by being socially accessible and not a source of dissatisfaction when farm decisions are being made. To make the case that these are causal factors in recent adoption, and not consequences of the adoption process, requires that constancy is assumed in these activities. And yet, each of these role dimensions may change over time. Some innovations require that careful records be kept and results monitored, a task that may increase the wife's farm work. Being a source of new ideas may result from and/or result in greater contact with media, neighbors and community leaders, agricultural education and extension agents, and other sources of information about new practices. Supportive relationships can be tenuous, strained by hardships and unexpected events, or even by expected events that are stressful. Assertiveness is very loosely defined in the study, as increased involvement in farm decisions. Better measures can be constructed for each of these wife role dimensions.

Interpretations are offered, therefore, as one way to look at the interactive effects of changing family structure, farm context, and wife farm roles on recent adoption of new farm technology in an environment of high risks and limited opportunities for success. The fact that an approach has been used successfully to differentiate two patterns of effect may challenge other researchers to use similar techniques, to uncover multiple patterns of effect associated with other social phenomena. As mentioned above, care must be taken in defining the dependent variable. Multiple factors are knowingly combined in the measure of adoption, in an effort to show that "innovativeness" can be studied as an incremental process without reference to individual practices or limited types of practices. Each farm is unique. By including a variety of practices in the adoption index, an attempt was made to maximize opportunities for respondents to describe their unique experiences. An open-ended index item was included, and carefully checked for content, to further this goal.

Three more two-way interactions (see Table 4) are presented briefly before testing hypotheses of three-way interactive effects. *Financial risk* interacts with *collaborative* and *assertive* wife roles, and *plan to quit* interacts (negatively) with *supportive* wife role. These associations with average recent adoption will be qualified in further analysis by phase of family transition.

	Collaborative wife	Noncollaborative wife
High financial risk	3.046	2.461
Low financial risk	1.747	1.696
Mean difference:	1.299	0.765

	Assertive wife	Nonassertive wife
High financial risk	3.090	2.690
Low financial risk	1.824	1.710
Mean difference:	1.266	0.980

	Supportive wife	Nonsupportive wife
Plan to continue	2.152	2.320
Plan to quit	1.483	2.216
Mean difference:	0.669	0.104

Although not by themselves of theoretical interest, two-way associations of contextual variables with wife role dimension variables prompt the researcher to differentiate these effects further by family type and phase of family transition. (Without such tests of higher-order interactions there is little to interpret.) The novelty of this approach is that a process is *assumed* in which family structure is evolving in response to changes in the setting, rather than one in which families are merely reacting to the setting, and *it is assumed* that as family structure evolves, role changes occur that have predictable consequences for creative problem solving, through one pattern of effect as instrumental roles are shared, and quite another as leadership roles are shared. Flexibility is introduced with each type of structural shift.

This does not imply that structural shifts occur in only one direction. As the setting becomes more predictable (not necessarily more favorable), efficiencies of effort are likely to result in new forms of role specialization, not necessarily gender specific. A wife may become the primary farm operator when her husband take a full-time job off the farm; or a wife may have no time for the farm if she, herself, works full-time away from home. This study does not attempt to identify such structural changes, but their importance for survival of some family farms is recognized.

Three-way Interactions:

The effect of economic need, as indicated by high *financial risk*, on recent adoption appears to be qualified further by three-way interactions with phase and *collaborative, assertive,* and *consultative* dimensions of the wife's farm role (see Table 4). Three-way interactions of phase x risk x wife role dimensions visually support the predicted patterns of ordinal and disordinal effects on recent adoption by family type (see Appendix B, Graphs 1 to 4). An overall nonsignificant interaction with *supportive* wife role (see Table 4) may be due to an unanticipated positive effect of *nonsupportive* wife role in phase IV (Graph 4). One-way tests of Hypotheses 1A to 4A and 1B to 4B, of mean differences within family type, all appear to be significant, however, at the .05 level or better (see Table 5).

The effect on recent adoption of *occupational commitment*, indicated by plan to continue farming to retirement, appears to be qualified further by three-way interactions with phase of transition and *assertive, consultative,* and *supportive* dimensions of the wife's farm role (Table 4). Three-way interactions of phase of transition x plan to continue farming x wife role dimensions support the predicted patterns of ordinal and disordinal effects on recent adoption by family type, as above, (see Appendix B, Graphs 5 to 8). An overall nonsignificant interaction with *collaborative* wife role (see Table 4) may be due to an unanticipated positive effect of *noncollaborative* wife role in phase IV (Graph 5). One-way tests of Hypotheses 5A to 8A and 5B to 8B, of mean differences within family type, all appear to be significant, however, at the .05 level or better (see Table 5).

Discussion of the Findings:

The overall statistical model appears to explain nearly half of the variance (47.6%) in the dependent variable "recent adoption" (see Table 4). Having identified two qualitatively different patterns of effect, one could now separate the data on family type to compare the predictive power of each pattern if the sample was large enough to

TABLE 5. Tests of hypotheses of predicted highest average recent adoption of farm practices, within family type, by phase of family transition, by contextual variables, by dimensions of the wife's farm role.

TRADITIONAL COUPLES (low farm decision-sharing)

Hypo-thesis	Family phase x	Farm context x	Wife farm role dimension	Ave. # new practices	Mean difference /a	t-test
1A	II	High Risk	Collaborative	3.2	+1.4	2.801 **
2A	"	"	Nonassertive	3.9	+2.0	3.332 ***
3A	"	"	Nonconsultative	4.1	+2.3	4.006 ***
4A	"	"	Supportive	3.6	+1.7	2.562 **
5A	"	Farm Plan /b	Collaborative	3.0	+1.1	2.316 *
6A	"	"	Nonassertive	3.0	+1.1	2.077 *
7A	"	"	Nonconsultative	3.4	+1.6	3.110 **
8A	"	"	Supportive	4.4	+2.5	3.823 ***

NONTRADITIONAL COUPLES (high farm decision-sharing)

Hypo-thesis	Family phase x	Farm context x	Wife farm role dimension	Ave. # new practices	Mean difference /c	t-test
1B	III	High Risk	Collaborative	4.1	+2.3	4.230 ***
2B	"	"	Assertive	3.9	+2.0	3.564 ***
3B	"	"	Consultative	3.9	+2.0	3.720 ***
4B	"	"	Nonsupportive	3.8	+1.9	3.825 ***
5B	"	Farm Plan /b	Collaborative	3.2	+1.3	2.975 **
6B	"	"	Assertive	4.0	+2.1	3.844 ***
7B	"	"	Consultative	2.9	+0.9	1.883 *
8B	"	"	Nonsupportive	3.1	+1.1	2.227 *

NOTES: /a Compared to average recent adoption by all other traditional couples
        /b High commitment to farming as an occupation
        /c Compared to ave. recent adoption by all other nontraditional couples
        *   P < .05 (one tail test)
        ** P < .01 (one tail test)
        *** P < .001 (one tail test)

sustain further analysis. With a small sample, family type has been used as a blocking factor to test the predictions of largest group means within family type.

Assessing the relative importance of each predictor, it is found in the overall model that *financial risk* seems to be the best contextual predictor of recent adoption, *collaborative* role in *phases II and III* (wife mostly keeps the farm records, and the wife's farm-work role has increased) the best combination of wife roles as predictors, and *phase* by *risk* by *collaborative* role the best three-way predictor-interaction combination. All three predictors are located within the economic domain of social action formation in the model, and appear to be positively associated with recent adoption regardless of traditional or nontraditional family type, as predicted.

Qualitatively different patterns of wife influence appear to be observed, however, in the personal/political, cultural, and social domains, by family type, supported by comparisons of predicted largest group means (see Graphs 2 through 4 and 6 through 8, Appendix B) tested for mean differences (see Table 5). For traditional couples in phase II, identified as a 'disrupted' phase of family transition, the largest group means are observed for *nonassertive, nonconsultative,* and *supportive* wives, whether the context is high financial risk or high occupational commitment. Similarly, for nontraditional couples in phase III, identified as an 'emerging' phase of family transition, the largest group means are observed for *assertive, consultative,* and *nonsupportive* wives, whether the context is high financial risk or high occupational commitment. All mean differences are significant at the .05 level or better (one-way tests).

These two patterns, disordinal for all but the economic, *collaborative* dimension of the wife's farm role, are observed when the wife's farm-work role is increasing, in phases II and III, in support of the theory of power sharing in transition.

NOTE: two out of four high group means observed in phases I and IV have low group frequencies (Graphs 2 and 5); the other two, in phase IV, are contained in three-way interactions that are not significant in the overall model, and may help to explain the nonsignificance of those three-way interactions.

Statistical tests of predicted highest group means, compared to summary means of remaining scores within family type, lend support for all sixteen of the hypotheses of interactive effects of farm context and wife role dimensions by phase of family transition. For couples in the 'disrupted traditional' phase (phase II), the best predictors of recent adoption when farm debt is high and net farm income is low (high *financial risk)* appear to be *nonassertive* and *nonconsultative* wife roles; and the best predictor when the husband plans to continue farming to retirement (high *occupational commitment*) appears to be a *supportive* wife role. Although keeping the farm records (*collaborative* role) is not as strong a predictor in phase II, the wife's farm-work role has increased in the past ten years, which may include an increase in farm chores and fieldwork as well as record-keeping (see Table 5).

For couples in the 'emerging nontraditional' phase (phase III), a *collaborative* wife role appears to be the best predictor of recent adoption, when farm debt is high and net farm income is low (high *financial risk*), although *assertive, consultative* and *nonsupportive* roles also seem to be strong predictors. When the husband plans to continue farming to retirement, an *assertive* wife role (increased involvement in farm decisions) appears to be the best predictor of recent adoption (see Table 5).

NOTE: These measures are somewhat representative but not all-inclusive. There are important additional ways in which wives contribute to the success of the farm operation, such as providing investment capital from off-farm employment.

Interpretation of the Findings:

In studying farm families in a Midwest dairy state, it is known that farm wives are engaged in many of the essential tasks of farming, including chores, fieldwork, and record-keeping (Wilkening, 1981a). It is not surprising that they are also involved in farm decisions. How does this affect the farm operation? The present study was designed to investigate multiple answers to this question. The focus is on the number of innovative farm practices adopted during a five year period in the mid-to-late 1970s, improvements that were recommended by university agricultural extension services to meet the challenges of technological advances in agriculture, part of what is now described as a post-industrial revolution affecting all segments of society (Hage & Powers, 1992).

Families, too, are changing, including the wife's role in farming. Introducing this research, a framework was provided for identifying a variety of societal traditions, including a tradition of interdependence in 19th century rural America, rooted in pioneer beginnings (cf. Figure G). Relationships between farm husbands and farm wives are part of this tradition, as they work together, face hardships together in years when crops fail, and act as one in this somewhat precarious occupation known as farming. When asked in a pretest interview "Who makes the following farm decisions? You only, you mostly, or you and your wife together?" a farmer replied without hesitation: "I make all of those." And yet, throughout the interview he turned frequently to his wife for concurrence about what they do. It was evident that they work as a team.

Many of the farmers interviewed for this study acknowledged that their wives were involved in most of the farm decisions. For lack of a better term these families are called *nontraditional* (Barlett, 1993, has used the term "symmetrical" to identify this marital model for third generation farm couples with agrarian value orientations.) Sharing decisions is a further expression of their interdependence, but one in which the wife is recognized as a separate entity, more than just an extension of her husband. How does this new tradition evolve? It is assumed, here, that the wife's increased involvement in farm work is a necessary but not sufficient cause. Societal factors are also at work, redefining the person-hood of women in marriage relationships. What effect does this have on the farm operation?

In this analysis, two patterns of wife influence on recent adoption have been tested, one for high-decision-sharing couples, the other for low-decision-sharing couples. These patterns are evidenced by a series of statistically significant effects of wife farm role variables interacting with farm context to explain recent adoption. In the analysis these patterns are differentiated by phase of family transition: 'established traditional,' 'disrupted traditional,' 'emerging nontraditional,' and 'stabilized nontraditional.'

By definition, the wife's farm work has increased in both the 'disrupted' and 'emerging' phases of farm family transition. In the analysis, increased involvement of the wife in farm decisions (viewed as an *assertive* wife role) identifies an intermediate step in the shift from 'disrupted traditional' to 'emerging nontraditional,' suggesting an even greater contrast in patterns of effect on recent adoption *as the shift occurs*. (In a larger study it might be possible to examine such contrasts in greater detail.)

If the wife's decision involvement is a direct result of her work contribution (cf. Resource Theory, Blood & Wolfe, 1960), one might expect a simultaneous increase in both roles to have parallel effects on recent adoption, regardless of phase of family transition. The reasoning might be that any work-related increase in farm-decision role will have functional consequences. Instead, tradition intervenes to mediate the effects of decision role increase on recent adoption. The findings suggest that, for traditional families, role consistency in decision-making is more functional than increased decision role, when no change in family structure has occurred. In future research one might study effects of decision role increases that alter family structure, i.e., that shift families from low decision-sharing to high decision-sharing.

For this analysis, resource dimensions of the wife's farm role have been selected in all four domains of social action formation. Economic means, personal/political influence, cultural information, and social access are each defined as resources, conditions *for* action rather than controls *of* action. Each role variable identifies the farm wife as a direct source of, or as a direct participant in, one of these four types of resources. By phase of family transition, the effects on recent adoption of all four dimensions of the wife's farm role have then been assessed, interacting with the husband's role context in two domains: economic (risk-taking) and political (commitment to farming). The focus is primarily on two phases of family transition: the 'disrupted traditional' and 'emerging nontraditional' phases in which, by definition, the wife's farm-work role has increased.

The results, which locate two qualitatively different patterns of positive wife influence, support hypotheses of wife influence on recent adoption during phases of structural transition. Further, the results suggest that these effects are interactive rather than merely additive. Positive wife influences on recent adoption in phases I and IV (established traditional and stabilized nontraditional) appear minimal. [NOTE: assessing negative effects in these phases is beyond the scope of this work].

The goal has been to simulate a causal analysis of change over time, using point-in-time survey data. Given this limitation, the risks of making erroneous assumptions about cause and effect might seem to outweigh the potential gains. To reduce the risks, a multidimensional theoretical framework was crafted with the research objectives in mind. Questions were asked of farm couples, and composite variables constructed, to put assumptions of causal sequence based on past observations to the test. Rather than weigh the pros and cons of one interpretation as opposed to possible others in each instance, findings are assessed for consistency with the overall logic presented.

A central requirement of the study, as stated in Chapter 5, has been to balance structural factors, as they define context, with process variables, as reflected in the use of resources. Another requirement has been to use evidence of family structural variations to infer a natural progression, through phases of structural change. These three types of variables have been combined in the analysis of higher-order interactive effects, to explain changes in the variable chosen to represent creative problem solving. Rationales for procedures and methods have been provided throughout.

As a further requirement, to test the theory of power sharing in transition, a distinction has been made between sharing an *instrumental* role and sharing a *leadership* role, to differentiate between the exercise of indirect influence and direct influence in power sharing. Finally, subjective assessments of couple role interaction have been added, to help define the process elements of social action formation. As such, they may seem more tenuous than the more objectively measured elements of roles, role changes, and role contexts. Nevertheless, how the husband and wife assess their time together has implications for their working relationship as a farm couple. These measures were included for the insights they offer into the interpersonal dynamics involved in creative problem solving.

Any of the interpretations that have been offered may be challenged. Whether the theories are the best possible theories, or the methods the best possible methods, can only be decided when comparable, broad-based theories and methods have been demonstrated to be not only logically consistent but also applicable to the many kinds of research questions suggested by this approach.

Chapter 12

Summary and Conclusions

Summary:

In the early 1950s, agricultural extension programs sensitive to the potential of family influence on acceptance of new farm technology (Wilkening, 1949, 1950) launched an ambitious, new, federally-funded program of farm and home development that advocated the wife's participation in making farm decisions (Dorner, 1955; Slocum & Brough, 1961, Slocum, 1962). Studies since that time have not demonstrated a clear association between the wife's participation or non-participation in farm decisions and adoption of agricultural innovations (Wilkening, 1953, 1954, 1958b; Sawer, 1973; Lyson, 1985).

As an alternative approach, the present study has examined husband-wife decision-sharing on farm matters in relation to recent adoption, rather than to overall level of adoption, taking into account the changing nature of farm family roles as well as the incremental nature of technological change (Rogers, 1962; Hannan & Katsiaouni, 1977; Summers, 1983a). Accordingly, this study has also looked at some effects of *changes* in the wife's farming roles on the number of farm practices recently adopted. Role changes studied include the wife's increased involvement in farm work and farm decisions during the ten years prior to the study.

Tests of sixteen hypotheses appear to lend credence to the thesis of two patterns of wife influence, in support of the theory of gender power sharing in transition. Eight of the hypotheses use financial risk as a contextual control variable, in the economic domain of social action formation, to interact with wife and family factors to predict recent adoption. The other eight hypotheses use occupational commitment as a contextual control variable, in the personal/political domain of social action formation, to interact with wife and family factors to predict recent adoption.

Four of each set of eight hypotheses apply to traditional farm couples, as indicated by low husband-wife decision-sharing on farm matters, and especially to farm couples in phase II, the 'disrupted traditional' phase of family transition, indicated by increased involvement of the wife in farm work. The other four of each set apply to nontraditional couples, as indicated by high level of husband-wife decision-sharing on farm matters, especially to couples in phase III, the 'emerging nontraditional phase' of family transition, in which the wife, similarly, is increasingly involved in farm work.

An essential distinction between phases II and III is that the wife in phase II is a subordinate (in the personal/ political domain), since she is not highly involved in making farm decisions, whereas the wife in phase III is more of an equal partner with her husband in making farm decisions. Level of decision-sharing thus indicates a power-shift, since it distinguishes between indirect and direct wife influence on recent adoption, as measured by number of farm practices adopted within five years of the interview.

Accordingly, different, and generally opposite, patterns of wife influence on recent practice adoption were anticipated for traditional and nontraditional farm couples, and the analysis was separated on the power-shift indicator, level of decision-sharing, to test each pattern. The effects of four dimensions of the wife's farm role were tested for each subsample, traditional and nontraditional, interacting with two phases of family transition and with two levels of financial risk and two levels of occupational commitment (measures of the husband's farm role context) to predict extent of recent farm practice adoption.

Dimensions of the wife's farm role were selected from each of the four domains of social action formation identified in the theory of social action: the cultural and social as well as the economic and personal/political. All four role dimensions are regarded as farm resources, and as potential sources of wife influence on the adoption of innovative farm practices.

The findings suggest that in a traditional, subordinate role, the wife's influence on recent adoption is expressed indirectly, through moral support in the social domain and help with essential farm tasks in the economic domain. As gender roles coalesce, in a 'disrupted' phase of family transition, these influences appear to be positively associated with recent adoption, given a context of high risk or high occupational commitment. In the cultural and political domains, however, an influential but subordinate wife appears to refrain from offering suggestions and advice on a regular basis, unless or until her status is elevated to equal partner, in an 'emerging nontraditional' phase of family transition.

As equal partner, the nontraditional wife's influence is expressed directly, through sharing farm decisions in the political domain, as well as indirectly, as a source of new ideas in the cultural domain and as a help with essential farm tasks in the economic domain. Unlike the subordinate wife, her contribution to problem solving may cause friction in the social domain, resulting in the husband being less than completely satisfied with the way they make farm decisions and settle differences. For nontraditional couples, these effects appear to be favorable for recent adoption in an 'emerging' phase of family transition, where the wife's help with farm work is increasing, given either high financial risk or high occupational commitment.

Briefly, for each type of family, traditional and nontraditional, couples with specific combinations of wife roles, role changes, and role contexts appear to have higher mean levels of recent farm practice adoption than couples with alternative combinations of wife roles, role changes, and role contexts. Subjective assessments by the husband, in the cultural and social domains of social action formation, are included in defining the wife's farm roles.

Conclusions:

In support of the theory of power sharing in transition, and within a context of high financial risk or high occupational commitment, positive effects of traditional and nontraditional wife influence appear to be alike in facilitating adoption of new farm practices as wives are incorporated into the *instrumental role of task-sharing*, but different in their effects as wives are incorporated into the *leadership role of decision-sharing* (cf. Table 5, and Appendix B, Graphs 1 through 8).

Only where the wife shares in most farm decisions and her work role has increased, in the 'emerging nontraditional' phase of family transition, does an *assertive* wife role (decision role increase) appear to be positively associated with recent adoption. For couples where decision-sharing is low and the wife's work role has increased, in the 'disrupted traditional' phase of family transition, a *nonassertive* wife role seems to be positively associated with recent adoption.

These differences in patterns of wife influence are repeated in the cultural and social domains, where wives who are partners in decision-making in the 'emerging nontraditional' phase of family transition appear to facilitate farm improvements by contributing ideas but not moral support, and wives who are subordinate in decision-making in the 'disrupted traditional' phase appear to facilitate farm improvements by contributing moral support but not ideas.

The results seem to be more striking within a context of high *financial risk* (high farm debt with low net farm income) than high *occupational commitment* (the husband plans to continue farming to retirement, with no full-time work off the farm) possibly because the latter are the husband's responses, and do not measure the wife's commitment to farming as an occupation.

In general, the findings appear to demonstrate the value of study designs that include tests for statistical interactions, to identify pattern variables such as level of decision-sharing that confound (hide) primary relationships due to contingent, often disordinal effects.

The study also seems to demonstrate the value of looking at changes over time, in both the dependent and the independent variables, when seeking to draw causal inference. Where such measures of change are available, re-analysis of data from previous studies might show that they, too, support predictions of wife influence that helped to inspire studies of farm and home development beginning in the 1950s.

Finally, the analysis illustrates the use of broad-based theoretical frameworks for testing causal association, lends support to models that predict multiple as well as interactive patterns of effect, and appears to demonstrate the feasibility of testing formulas constructed from subjective theories of social action and social change.

Suggestions for Future Research :

The wife's decision-making involvement has been narrowly defined, for purposes of the study, as extent of (husband) reported wife participation in three types of farm decisions. Begging the question of how accurate this report might be (cf. Wilkening & Morrison, 1963; Bokemeier & Monroe, 1983; Rosenfeld, 1985; Claridge & Chamala, 1995), a more meaningful question might be to what extent this measure represents the full dynamic of the wife's decision-making role. A general framework is provided by Knop & Knop (1994:78) to assess, from interviews and observation, the normal and special circumstances in which the wife participates, publicly or privately, not only in various stages of the decision-making process, but in planning, implementation, and subsequent evaluation. To approximate a measure of this dynamic in large-scale survey designs poses a challenge, to weigh theoretical requirements against practical constraints within the limitations of self-report. Case studies suggest that inconsistencies in spousal report of decision-sharing are not unresolvable, and may shed light on public vs. private aspects of the decision-making process (Rocheleau, 1994). To accomplish this in survey research may require follow-up interviews.

"Over the long haul," what difference does it make to the farm operation, or to farming in general, for wives to be involved in farm work and farm decisions? Since the 1970s, the Farm Crisis of the 1980s and concerns for sustainable agriculture in the 1990s have increased the interest of researchers and policy makers in learning how family dynamics affect farm survival as well as restoration of the agricultural environment for future generations. Disenchanted with the costs, financial risks, and short-lived advantages of advanced technology (cf. Cochrane, 1979: the Technology Treadmill) and with expert advice that encouraged expansion, specialization, and high indebtedness, many farmers in the 1980s returned to a more conservative orientation for farm survival (Strange, 1988; Barlett, 1993). In this context, are these findings of wife influence on adoption of new farm practices in Wisconsin in the 1970s even relevant, or has "progressive farming" become obsolete?

The farm practices listed in the 1979 farm family survey (cf. Appendix A) were generally applicable to the farm units surveyed, were ecologically sound, and were not cost-prohibitive; however, in future research the applicability, feasibility, and cost-effectiveness of new technology for the individual units surveyed should be a research consideration. New methods of soil protection and improvement, ecologically-sound pest control, and more efficient use of water resources are among environmentally safe technologies of current interest, along with biotechnology and genetic engineering practices, some of which (e.g., bovine growth hormone to increase milk production) are opposed by some farmer groups.

Initial assessment of the models of interactive and multiple effects and theory of power sharing in transition are based on the logical consistency of the findings. As with all models and theories, further assessment must rely on replication of findings as well as application to related areas of research.

The correspondence of the data findings to expected results suggests the plausibility of application of the theories to other types of social action formation, under variable conditions and contexts of social system change. The ultimate goal of this research is to persuade other researchers that an interactive theoretical framework is applicable to many social science research questions of vital public concern.

As advised in the introduction to Part Two, such questions require a simultaneous analysis of social structure and social process, recognizing that social order and social change are separate continua, with structured propensity for change having implications for social stability along a different dimension: mode of resolving disparities to restore "order" within and between organizations, groups, societies, etc. Accordingly, adaptive behavior must be understood within an interactive framework capable of assessing both phenomena.

Postscript: This search for answers to critical societal concerns began in 1939, as the nation braced for the shock of World War II. It became focused in 1952, inspired by the leadership studies of Lewin, Lippitt & White, and evolved slowly, through academic study and research, during the remainder of the decade. In the intervening years, ways to communicate these special insights have included political correspondence and travel. Academic work resumed in 1975, was interrupted by further political involvement during the 1980s, and resumed again in recent years. The work is now complete and ready for review. The message has not changed over time, and is best expressed in the frontispiece to Hemingway's *For Whom the Bell Tolls:* "No man is an island..." (John Donne)

Appendix A

Survey of Wisconsin Farm Families

APPENDIX A: SURVEY OF WISCONSIN FARM FAMILIES

(v1) ADOPTION OF IMPROVED FARM PRACTICES *(H's Interview)*

Which of the following farm practices do you use on your farm?

    ____ ____ Soil test (total farm in past three years)
    ____ ____ High nitrogen side-dressing on corn
    ____ ____ Farm conservation plan (SCS or other)
    ____ ____ Minimum tillage
    ____ ____ Top-dressing alfalfa with potash after harvesting
    ____ ____ Crop-rotation to reduce insect problems
    ____ ____ Grassed waterways
    ____ ____ Contour farming
    ____ ____ Manure storage control facility
    ____ ____ Green chop feeding
    ____ ____ Haylage or wet corn storage
    ____ ____ Irrigation*
    ____ ____ Add extra protein to high producing cows
    ____ ____ Barn insulation

*[Irrigation was dropped from the index. It is largely inapplicable to the area and only 5 farmers were using this practice]

(v0) Which of these have you started using within the past five years?
(Check second column, above)
Have you tried any other new practices within the past five years?
____ Yes (If yes) What practices? _____ [Evaluated]

(v2) NET FARM INCOME *(Husband's Interview)*

Looking at the card, which number shows your approximate net farm income (after all farm expenses were paid) for 1978? _____
[The card showed increments of $5,000]
(If category 12) What was the approximate amount? _____
[If first category, interviewer asked if there was a loss.]

(v2 cont.) CHANGE IN NET FARM INCOME *(Husband's Interview)*

In the past five years (since 1973), has your net farm income (after farm expenses were paid) ____ increased ____ decreased ____ stayed about the same (____ not farming in 1973)
(If changed) Which number (on the card) shows the approximate amount of the (increase/decrease)? _____
[The card showed increments of $5,000]
(If category 12) What was the approximate amount? _____

(v3) TRACTOR HORSEPOWER *(Husband's Interview)*

How may tractors of what horsepower do you use on your farm?
#1 _____ , #2 _____ , #3 _____ , #4 _____ , #5 _____
[Interviewer recorded horsepower of each tractor]

(v3 cont.) CHANGE IN TRACTOR HORSEPOWER *(Husb's Interview)*

Compared to five years ago, has your total tractor horsepower
_____ increased _____ decreased _____ stayed about the same?

(If changed) By how much? _____ (CALCULATE)

(v4) HUSBAND/WIFE DECISION-SHARING *(H's Questionnaire)*

Families differ in the way decisions are made. We have listed some decisions that farm families make at some time or other. For each one, please look at the responses below and indicate which answer best describes how the decision is usually made in your family or how it would be made if the decision arose. [Five columns for responses]

Husband decides; seldom discusses with wife	Husband decides; usually discusses with wife	Both husband & wife decide equally	Wife decides usually discusses with husband	Wife decides; seldom discusses with husband

[Resource allocation]

    Whether to expand or reduce the farm business
    Whether to borrow money for the farm
    Whether to buy major farm equipment

[Operation change]

    Whether to try a new farm enterprise
    Whether the husband takes a job off the farm

[Operation management]

    What specific make of equipment to buy
    How much fertilizer to buy
    Whether to try out a new crop variety
    When to sell crops or livestock
    Whether to try a new farm practice

(v5) INCREASE IN THE W'S INVOLVEMENT IN FARM DECISIONS

(Wife's Interview)

Compared to ten years ago, do you and your husband talk over major farm purchases...
_____ more   _____ less   _____ about the same?

Compared to ten years ago, do you and your husband talk over other farm matters (day to day decisions)...
_____ more   _____ less   _____ about the same?

(v6) INCREASE IN THE WIFE'S INVOLVEMENT IN FARM WORK

(Wife's Interview)

Compared to 10 years ago, has your help with fieldwork...
_____ increased   _____ decreased   _____ stayed about the same?
(_____ never involved in fieldwork)

Compared to 10 years ago, has your help with farm chores...
_____ increased   _____ decreased   _____ stayed about the same?
(_____ never involved in doing farm chores)

Compared to 10 years ago, has your help with farm record keeping...
_____ increased   _____ decreased   _____ stayed about the same?
(_____ never kept farm books)

(v7) FAMILY LIFE CYCLE [based on age of oldest child living at home]

(W's Interview) _____ Wife's age _____ Age of oldest child living at home

1 Oldest child less than 14, or no children and wife less than 45
2 Oldest child 14, less than 18
3 Oldest child (at home) 18 or older
4 Children gone, or no children and wife age 45 or older

(v8) GOAL PRIORITY *(W's Questionnaire and H's Questionnaire)*

If you received an unexpected gift of one thousand dollars,

would you spend it on... _____ the farm enterprise

_____ the home   _____ the family

(If more than one answer, how would you spend most of it?
Double check that answer above)   [Multiple responses coded]

(v9) WIFE'S INVOLVEMENT IN FARM WORK *(H's Questionnaire)*

Now, we would like to know how you and your wife divide farm tasks

| Only the husband | Husband more than the wife | Husband & wife the same | Wife more than the husband | Only the wife |

[five columns provided for responses]

[Chores and field work]

> Farm chores such as milking, cleaning milking equipment, and feeding livestock.
> Driving the tractor and doing fieldwork

[Record keeping]

> Keeping the farm records and paying farm bills.
> Completing income tax forms.

[Information gathering]

> Obtaining information about farm matters from magazines, radio, and/or T.V.
> Obtaining information about farm matters through the extension service

[Three separate indices, not highly interrelated; only the 2nd was used]

(v10) WIFE'S PERCEPTION OF HER FARMING ROLE *(W's Interview)*

Do you see yourself...
_____ as a partner in the farm enterprise?
_____ as one who helps out regularly?
_____ as one who helps out occasionally?
_____ as not involved in farming?

(v11) HUSBAND'S ORIENTATION TO FARMING *(H's Questionnaire)*

We would like your opinion on some matters pertaining to farming and the family. (Please circle the response that best reflects your opinion.)

A = agree completely   ta = tend to agree   U = Uncertain
td = tend to disagree   D = disagree completely

Farming is primarily a profit making business rather than a way of life

    A   ta   U   td   D

(v12) HUSBAND'S OCCUPATIONAL COMMITMENT TO FARMING

Q. Do you plan to continue farming until retirement?
(1978 mail survey): _____ Full time _____ Part-time _____ Quit
Q. Do you plan to work off the farm?
(1978 mail survey) [_____ Yes, full-time]
Q. Do you consider yourself a full-time or part-time farmer?
(1979 H's interview)[_____ part-time, with full-time work off the farm]
Q. Do you plan to continue farming until retirement?
(1979 H's interview): _____ No _____ Undecided
_____ Yes, part-time _____ Yes, full-time

(v13) HUSBAND'S EDUCATION, TRAINING BEYOND HIGH SCHOOL

(1978 mail survey) [_____ One or more years of college]
[_____ Agricultural, vocational or technical training]

(v14) FARM DEBT *(1978 mail survey)*

___ none ___ less than $10,000 ____$10-19,999 ____$20-29,999
____$30-39,999 ____$40-44,999 ____$45-49,999 ____$50-54,999
____$55-59,999 ____$60-64,999 ____$65-69,999 ____$70,000+

(v15) NET FARM INCOME *(1977, from 1978 mail survey)*

_____ net loss _____ broke even _____ less than $2,500
_____$2,500, less than $5,000 _____$5,000, less than $10,000
_____$10,000, less than 20,000 _____$20,000 or more

(v16) HUSBAND'S AGE *(1978 mail survey)*
[_____ Husband's age, adjusted to 1979]

(v17) HUSBAND SATISFACTION WITH DECISION MAKING

(Husband's Questionnaire)

How satisfied are you with each of the following: [List provided]

The way you and your wife make farm decisions and settle differences?

[Seven choices provided: *completely satisfied, mostly satisfied, somewhat satisfied, neither satisfied nor dissatisfied, somewhat dissatisfied, mostly dissatisfied, completely dissatisfied*]

[_____ completely satisfied _____ all other responses]

(v18) WIFE AS SOURCE OF NEW IDEAS IN FARMING

(H's Questionnaire)

Which of the following is a source of new ideas in farming?

[Check list provided]   [_____ Wife]

(v19) HUSBAND/WIFE SOCIAL TIME TOGETHER

(Husband and Wife Questionnaires)

Which of the following describes you and your (spouse)?

[Check list provided]   [_____ Spent a recent evening just chatting]

(v20) HOW OFTEN WIFE AND HUSBAND DISAGREE RE: FARM

(Wife's Interview)

How often do you and your husband disagree on farm matters?

_____ often   _____ sometimes   _____ seldom
_____ never   _____ don't discuss

(v21) WHO WINS WHEN HUSBAND AND WIFE DISAGREE

(Wife's Interview)

Who mostly wins out when you disagree (on farm matters)?

_____ Husband   _____ compromise or win equally
_____ Wife

Appendix B

Graphs and Path Diagrams

List of Path Diagrams:

Path Diagram 1   Causal chain of interactive cultural, social, economic and personal/political latent variables necessary for social action formation   238

Path Diagram 2   Constellation of farm family variables that may interact to influence recent adoption of innovative farm practices   239

Path Diagram 3a Pattern of wife influence on recent adoption of farm practices given low decision-sharing on farm matters   240

Path Diagram 3b Pattern of wife influence on recent adoption of farm practices given high decision-sharing on farm matters   241

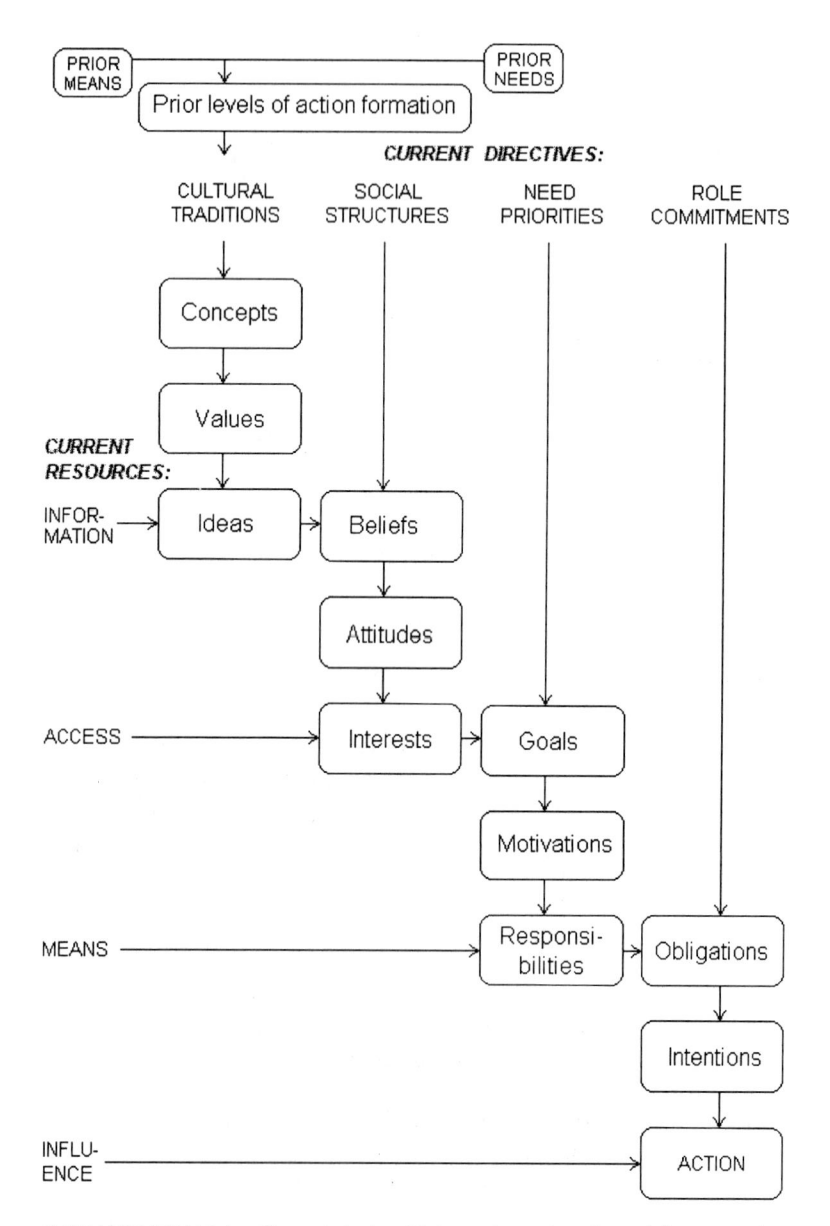

PATH DIAGRAM 1. Causal chain of interactive cultural, social, economic and personal/political latent variables necessary for social action formation

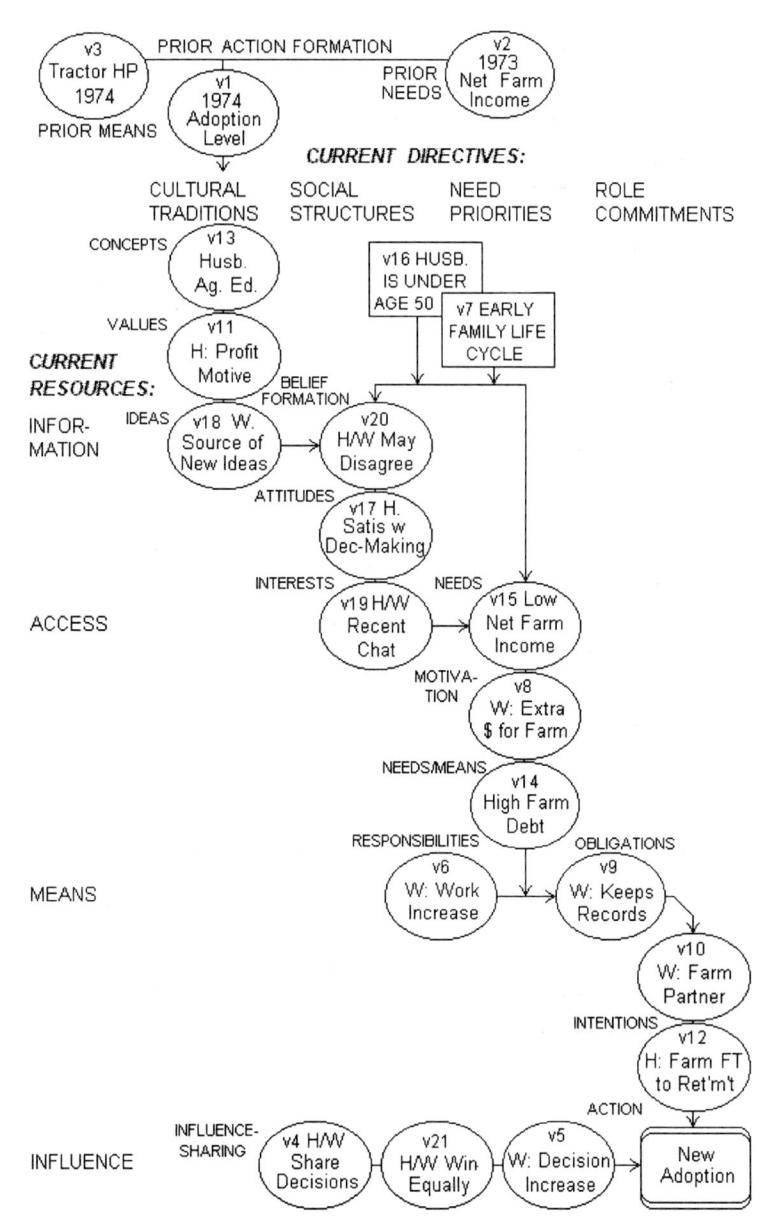

PATH DIAGRAM 2. Constellation of farm family variables that may interact to influence recent adoption of innovative farm practices

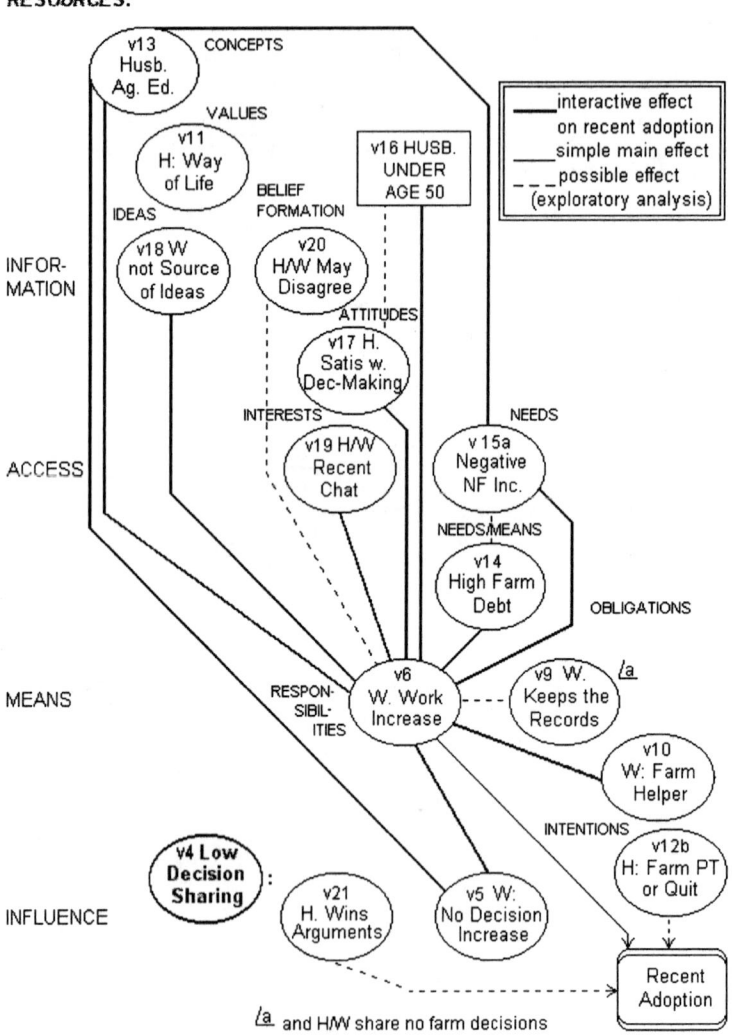

240

DIRECTIVES:

| CULTURAL | SOCIAL | NEED | ROLE |
| TRADITIONS | STRUCTURES | PRIORITIES | COMMITMENTS |

RESOURCES:

- v13 Husb. Ag. Ed. — CONCEPTS
- v11 H: Way of Life — VALUES
- v16 HUSB. UNDER AGE 50
- BELIEF FORMATION
- IDEAS
- v18 W not Source of Ideas
- v20 H/W May Disagree
- v17 H. Satis w. Dec-Making — ATTITUDES
- v19 H/W Recent Chat — INTERESTS
- v15a Negative NF Inc. — NEEDS
- v14 High Farm Debt — NEEDS/MEANS
- v6 W. Work Increase — RESPONSIBILITIES
- v9 W. Keeps the Records [a]
- v10 W: Farm Helper
- v12b H: Farm PT or Quit — INTENTIONS
- v4 Low Decision Sharing
- v21 H. Wins Arguments
- v5 W: No Decision Increase
- Recent Adoption

INFORMATION
ACCESS
MEANS
OBLIGATIONS
INFLUENCE

Legend:
— interactive effect on recent adoption
— simple main effect
- - - possible effect
(exploratory analysis)

[a] and H/W share no farm decisions

PATH DIAGRAM 3a. Pattern of wife influence on recent adoption of farm practices given low decision-sharing on farm matters

241

DIRECTIVES:

| CULTURAL | SOCIAL | NEED | ROLE |
| TRADITIONS | STRUCTURES | PRIORITIES | COMMITMENTS |

RESOURCES:

Legend:
— interactive effect on recent adoption
___ simple main effect
_ _ _ possible effect (exploratory analysis)

CONCEPTS
- v13 Husb. Ag. Ed.

VALUES
- v11 H: Profit Motive
- v16 HUSB. UNDER AGE 50

IDEAS / BELIEF FORMATION
- v18 W. Source of New Ideas
- v20 H/W May Disagree

INFORMATION

ATTITUDES
- v17 H. not Satis w. Dec-Making

INTERESTS
- v19 H/W no Recent Chat

NEEDS
- v15a (NF Inc. > $0 < $10k)

ACCESS

NEEDS/MEANS
- v14 High Farm Debt

RESPONSIBILITIES
- v6 W. Work Increase

OBLIGATIONS
- v9 W. Keeps the Records /a
- v10 W: Farm Partner

MEANS

INTENTIONS
- v12b H: Farm FT to Ret'm't

- v4 High Decision Sharing
- v21 H/W Win Equally
- v5 W: Decision Increase

INFLUENCE

SHARED-INFLUENCE

Recent Adoption

/a and H/W share all farm decisions

PATH DIAGRAM 3b. Pattern of wife influence on recent adoption of farm practices given high decision-sharing on farm matters

List of Graphs:

Graph 1   Average number of farm practices recently adopted by phase of family transition x financial risk x economic dimension of the wife's farm role   243

Graph 2   Average number of farm practices recently adopted by phase of family transition x financial risk x personal/political dimension of the wife's farm role   244

Graph 3   Average number of farm practices recently adopted by phase of family transition x financial risk x cultural dimension of the wife's farm role   245

Graph 4   Average number of farm practices recently adopted by phase of family transition x financial risk x social dimension of the wife's farm role   246

Graph 5   Average number of farm practices recently adopted by phase of family transition x occupational commitment x economic dimension of the wife's farm role   247

Graph 6   Average number of farm practices recently adopted by phase of family transition x occupational commitment x personal/political dimension of the wife's farm role   248

Graph 7   Average number of farm practices recently adopted by phase of family transition x occupational commitment x cultural dimension of the wife's farm role   249

Graph 8   Average number of farm practices recently adopted by phase of family transition x occupational commitment x social dimension of the wife's farm role   250

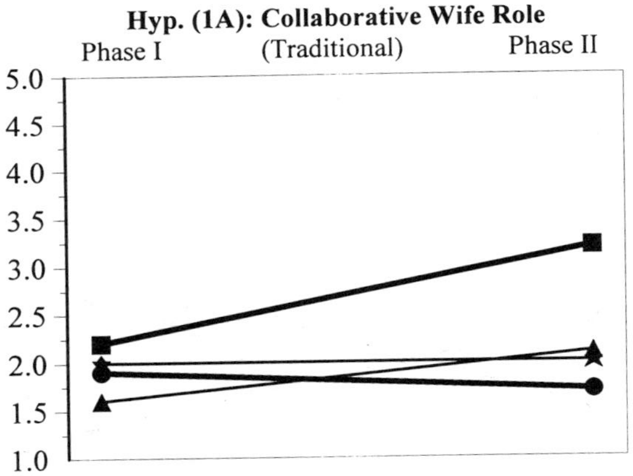

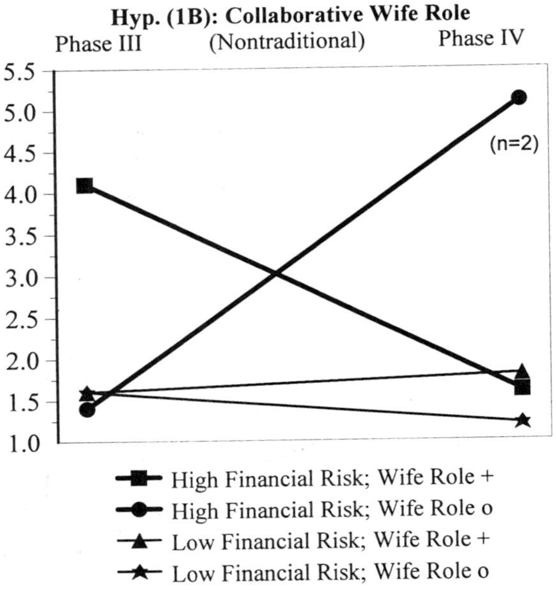

Graph 1: Average number of farm practices recently adopted, by phase of family transition, by financial risk, by economic dimension of the wife's farm role.

Hyp. (1A): Collaborative Wife Role (Traditional) — Phase I, Phase II

Hyp. (1B): Collaborative Wife Role (Nontraditional) — Phase III, Phase IV

Formula (1)
Recent adoption is a function of Phase x Financial Risk x Collaborative Wife Role.

— ■ — High Financial Risk; Wife Role +
— ● — High Financial Risk; Wife Role o
— ▲ — Low Financial Risk; Wife Role +
— ★ — Low Financial Risk; Wife Role o

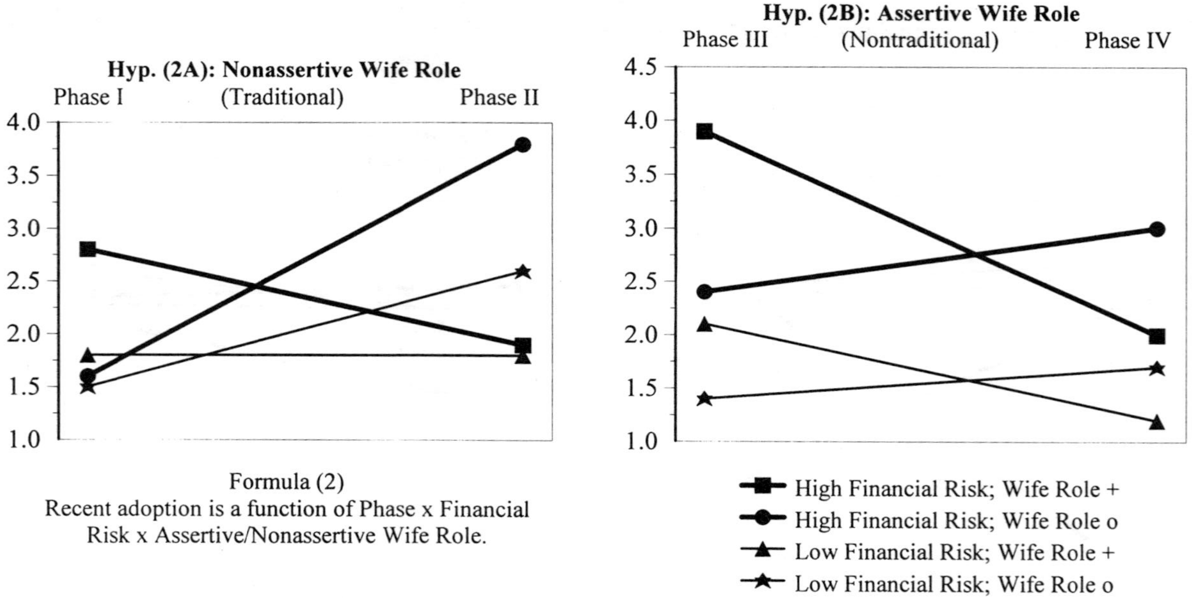

244   *Beyond Equilibrium Theory*

Hyp. (2A): Nonassertive Wife Role
(Traditional)

Hyp. (2B): Assertive Wife Role
(Nontraditional)

Formula (2)
Recent adoption is a function of Phase x Financial Risk x Assertive/Nonassertive Wife Role.

■ High Financial Risk; Wife Role +
● High Financial Risk; Wife Role o
▲ Low Financial Risk; Wife Role +
★ Low Financial Risk; Wife Role o

Graph 2: Average number of farm practices recently adopted, by phase of family transition, by financial risk, by personal/political dimension of the wife's farm role.

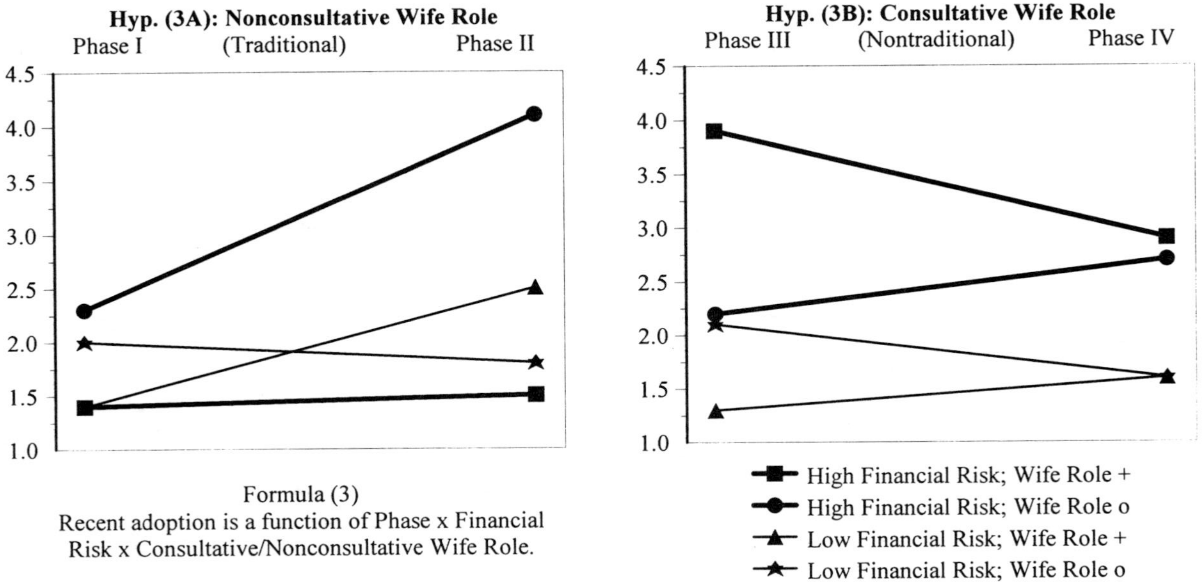

Hyp. (3A): Nonconsultative Wife Role
Phase I (Traditional) — Phase II

Hyp. (3B): Consultative Wife Role
Phase III — Phase IV (Nontraditional)

■ High Financial Risk; Wife Role +
● High Financial Risk; Wife Role o
▲ Low Financial Risk; Wife Role +
★ Low Financial Risk; Wife Role o

Formula (3)
Recent adoption is a function of Phase x Financial Risk x Consultative/Nonconsultative Wife Role.

Graph 3: Average number of farm practices recently adopted, by phase of family transition, by financial risk, by cultural dimension of the wife's farm role

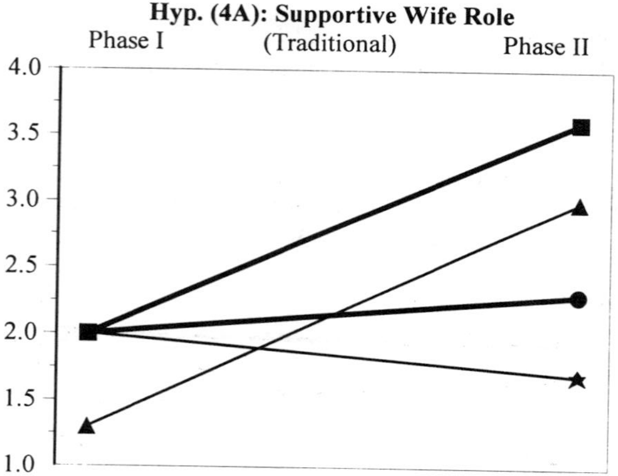

246 Beyond Equilibrium Theory

Hyp. (4A): Supportive Wife Role
(Traditional)

Phase I Phase II

Hyp. (4B): Nonsupportive Wife Role
(Nontraditional)

Phase III Phase IV

■ High Financial Risk; Wife Role +
● High Financial Risk; Wife Role o
◀ Low Financial Risk; Wife Role +
★ Low Financial Risk; Wife Role o

Formula (4)
Recent adoption is a function of Phase × Financial Risk × Supportive/Nonsupportive Wife Role.

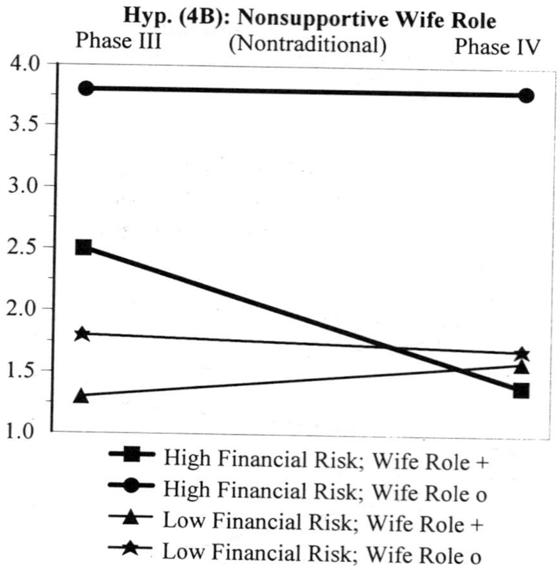

Graph 4: Average number of farm practices recently adopted, by phase of family transition, by financial risk, by social dimension of the wife's farm role

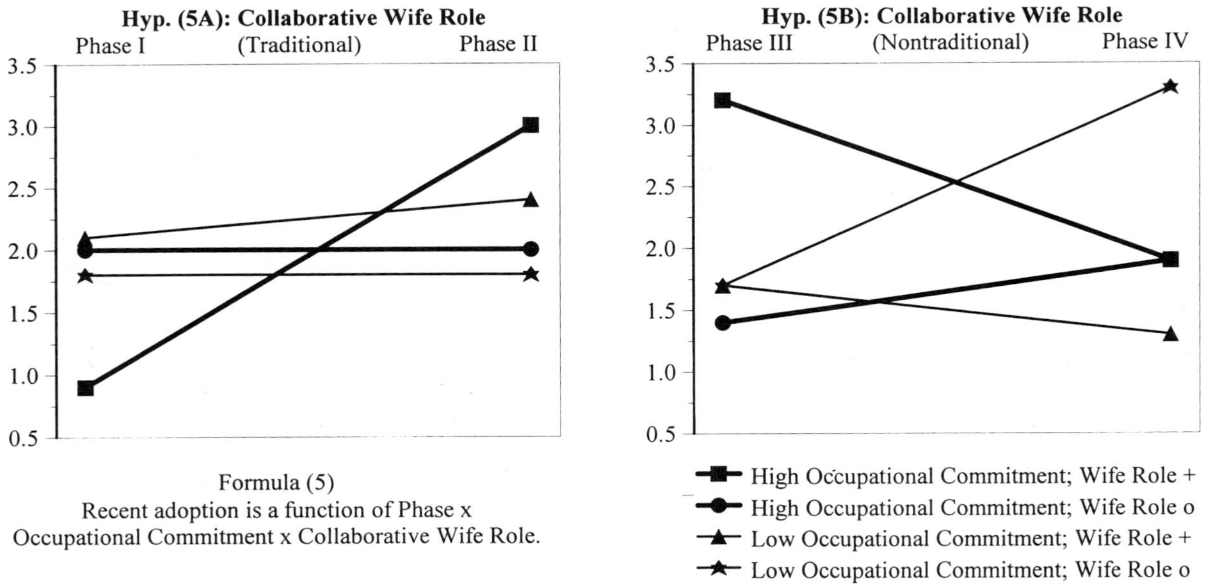

Beyond Equilibrium Theory 247

Hyp. (5A): Collaborative Wife Role
(Traditional)
Phase I — Phase II

Hyp. (5B): Collaborative Wife Role
(Nontraditional)
Phase III — Phase IV

Formula (5)
Recent adoption is a function of Phase x
Occupational Commitment x Collaborative Wife Role.

■ High Occupational Commitment; Wife Role +
● High Occupational Commitment; Wife Role o
◄ Low Occupational Commitment; Wife Role +
★ Low Occupational Commitment; Wife Role o

Graph 5. Average number of farm practices recently adopted, by phase of family transition, by occupational commitment, by economic dimension of the wife's farm role.

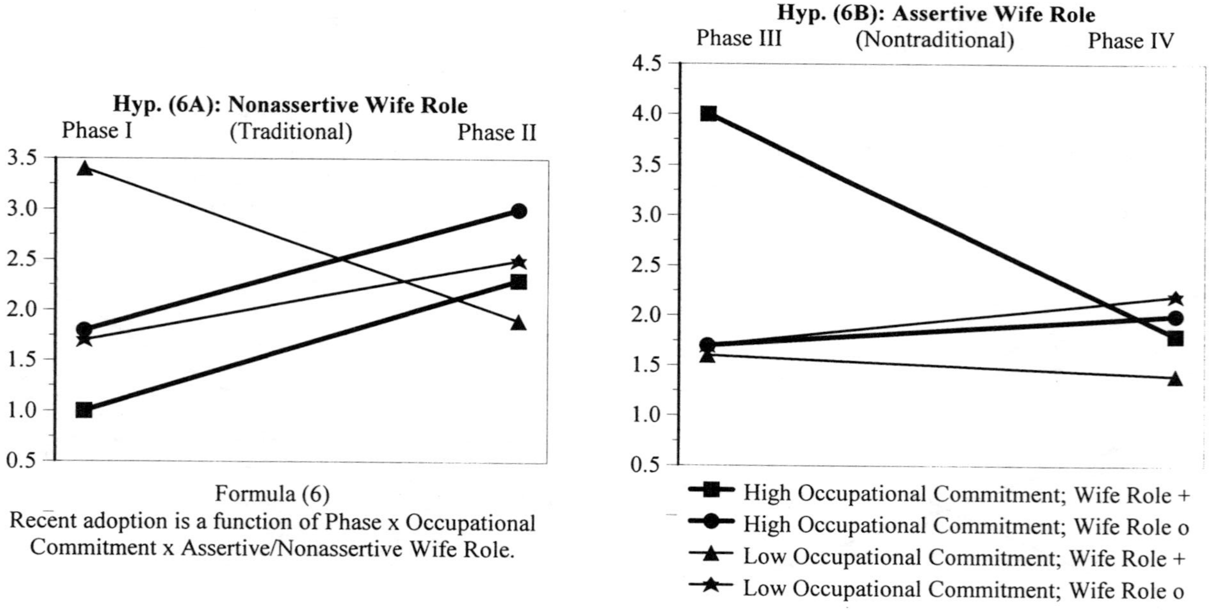

248 Beyond Equilibrium Theory

Graph 6. Average number of farm practices recently adopted, by phase of family transition, by occupational commitment, by personal/political dimension of the wife's farm role.

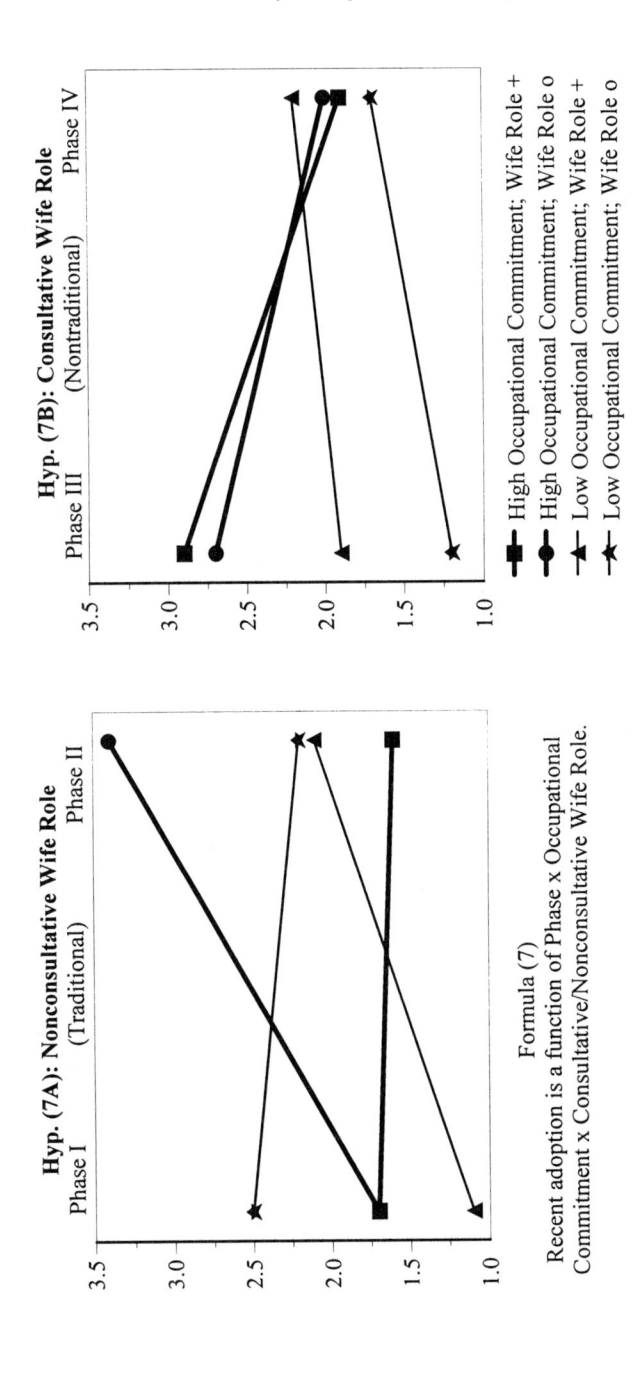

Beyond Equilibrium Theory 249

Hyp. (7A): Nonconsultative Wife Role
(Traditional)
Phase I   Phase II

Hyp. (7B): Consultative Wife Role
(Nontraditional)
Phase III   Phase IV

■ High Occupational Commitment; Wife Role +
● High Occupational Commitment; Wife Role o
▲ Low Occupational Commitment; Wife Role +
★ Low Occupational Commitment; Wife Role o

Formula (7)
Recent adoption is a function of Phase × Occupational Commitment × Consultative/Nonconsultative Wife Role.

Graph 7. Average number of farm practices recently adopted, by phase of family transition, by occupational commitment, by cultural dimension of the wife's farm role.

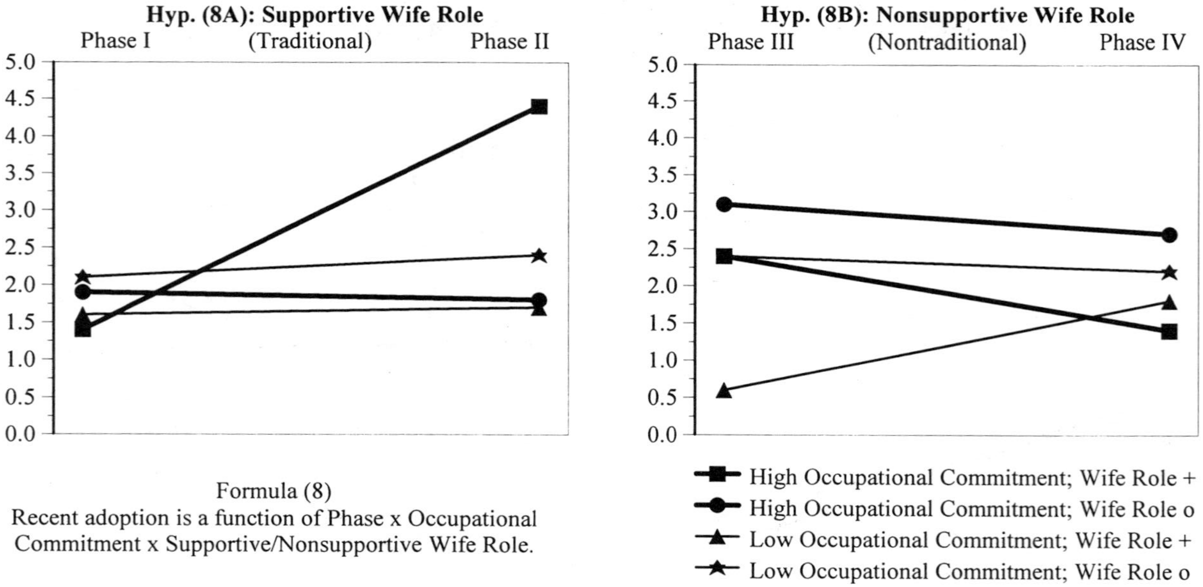

Hyp. (8A): Supportive Wife Role
(Traditional)

Hyp. (8B): Nonsupportive Wife Role
(Nontraditional)

Formula (8)
Recent adoption is a function of Phase x Occupational
Commitment x Supportive/Nonsupportive Wife Role.

■ High Occupational Commitment; Wife Role +
● High Occupational Commitment; Wife Role o
▲ Low Occupational Commitment; Wife Role +
★ Low Occupational Commitment; Wife Role o

Graph 8. Average number of farm practices recently adopted, by phase of family transition, by occupational commitment, by social dimension of the wife's farm role.

Appendix C

Reference Tables

List of Tables:

TABLE C-1 Analysis of wife influence on 1979 level of farm practice adoption (ANOVA)   253

TABLE C-2 Recent adoption by wife's farm role changes, wife's farm role, and husband's role context, by level of husband/wife decision-sharing (mean scores)   254

TABLE C-3 Recent adoption by additional farm role context of husband, by level of husband/wife decision-sharing (mean scores)   255

TABLE C-4 Recent adoption by couple's role interaction assessments, by level of husband/wife decision-sharing (mean scores)   256

TABLE C-1. Analysis of wife influence on 1979 level of farm practice adoption (ANOVA)

Source of variation:	SS	DF	MS	F	Sig. of F
Within + Residual	815.03	117	6.97		
Phase of family transition	15.27	3	5.09	.73	.536
Risk: high debt, low farm income	7.39	1	7.39	1.06	.305
Plan to continue farming	7.00	1	7.00	1.00	.318
Collaborative wife role	20.11	1	20.11	2.89	.092 +
Assertive wife role	.00	1	.00	.00	.996
Consultative wife role	14.55	1	14.55	2.09	.151
Supportive wife role	16.82	1	16.82	2.42	.123
Phase x Risk	9.38	3	3.13	.45	.719
Phase x Plan	52.31	3	17.44	2.50	.063 +
Phase x Collaborative	28.37	3	9.46	1.36	.259
Phase x Assertive	22.56	3	7.52	1.08	.361
Phase x Consultative	5.80	3	1.93	.28	.842
Phase x Supportive	17.56	3	5.85	.84	.475
Risk x Collaborative	5.79	1	5.79	.83	.364
Risk x Assertive	.55	1	.55	.08	.780
Risk x Consultative	.49	1	.49	.07	.791
Risk x Supportive	.75	1	.75	.11	.744
Plan x Collaborative	1.12	1	1.12	.16	.689
Plan x Assertive	1.02	1	1.02	.15	.703
Plan x Consultative	.00	1	.00	.00	.992
Plan x Supportive	8.94	1	8.94	1.28	.259
Phase x Risk x Collaborative	23.23	3	7.74	1.11	.347
Phase x Risk x Assertive	2.41	2	1.21	.17	.841
Phase x Risk x Consultative	42.24	3	14.08	2.02	.115
Phase x Risk x Supportive	56.16	3	18.72	2.69	.050 +
Phase x Plan x Collaborative	13.01	3	4.34	.62	.602
Phase x Plan x Assertive	30.45	3	10.15	1.46	.230
Phase x Plan x Consultative	10.58	3	3.53	.51	.679
Phase x Plan x Supportive	31.50	3	10.50	1.51	.216
(MODEL)	666.52	58	11.49	1.65	.011 *
(Total)	1481.55	175	8.47		

R^2 = .450*   Adjusted R^2 = .177*
NOTES: *P < .05   + P < .10

TABLE C-2. Recent adoption by wife's farm role changes, wife's farm role, and husband's role context, by level of husband/wife decision-sharing (**mean scores**).

Predictors	High dec.-sharing (n = 86) Percent	Mean	Low dec.-sharing (n = 87) Percent	Mean
TOTAL:	100%	**2.05**	100%	**2.14**
Wife's farm role changes:				
v5 Decision role increase	21	**3.44**	24	**2.24**
No increase	79	**1.68**	76	**2.11**
v6 Work role increase	48	**2.39**	39	**2.94**
No increase	52	**1.73**	61	**1.62**
Wife's farm role:				
v9 W equally or mostly keeps the farm records	60	**2.25**	45	**2.31**
H keeps the farm records	40	**1.74**	55	**2.00**
v10 W is partner in farming	65	**2.07**	47	**2.37**
W helps or is not involved	35	**2.00**	53	**1.93**
Husband's role context:				
v11 Farming is primarily a profit making business	44	**2.68**	46	**1.82**
Farming is a way of life	56	**1.54**	54	**2.41**
v12 Plan: farm full-time to retirement	51	**2.32**	44	**2.03**
Plan: farm part-time or quit	49	**1.76**	56	**2.23**

TABLE C-3. Recent adoption by additional farm role context of husband, by level of husband/wife decision-sharing (**mean scores**).

	High dec.-sharing (n = 86)		Low dec.-sharing (n = 87)	
Predictors	Percent	**Mean**	Percent	**Mean**
TOTAL:	100%	**2.05**	100%	**2.14**
Husband's role context (continued) [a]				
v12a Commitment to farming:				
Partnership or incorporated	13	**3.82**	24	**1.72**
Continue to retirement	70	**2.05**	62	**2.13**
Quit before retirement	17	**0.73**	14	**2.92**
v14 Farm indebtedness, 1977:				
$40,000 or less	55	**1.36**	53	**1.72**
Over $40,000	45	**2.87**	47	**2.61**
v15a Net farm income, 1977:				
Negative or broke even	31	**2.11**	25	**2.87**
Less than $10,000	53	**2.09**	51	**2.09**
$10,000 or more	15	**1.77**	24	**1.48**

NOTE: [a] See TABLE C-2 for v11, reason for farming, and v12, plan to continuefarming (v12 differentiates plan to continue full-time to retirement vs. part-time or quit.)

TABLE C-4. Recent adoption by couple's role interaction assessments, by level of husband/wife decision-sharing (**mean scores**).

Predictors	High dec.-sharing n = 86 Percent	**Mean**	Low dec.-sharing (n = 87) Percent	**Mean**
TOTAL	100%	**2.05**	100%	**2.14**
Husband's assessments:				
v17 H completely satisfied with way farm decisions made	47	**1.42**	33	**2.28**
H not completely satisfied	53	**2.59**	67	**2.07**
v18 W seen as source of new ideas in farming	65	**2.18**	37	**1.66**
W not seen as idea source	35	**1.80**	63	**2.42**
Wife's assessments:				
v19 H/W recently spent an evening "just chatting"	67	**2.14**	70	**2.21**
No recent evening chat	33	**1.86**	30	**1.96**
v20 H/W often or sometimes disagree on farm matters	28	**2.54**	26	**2.57**
Seldom disagree	53	**2.04**	50	**2.05**
Never disagree/don't discuss	19	**1.31**	24	**1.86**
v21 When disagree re: farm, H/W Compromise or win equally	69	**2.22**	55	**2.17**
One wins more	31	**1.67**	45	**2.11**

Notes for Part Two
(Arranged by author, see Bibliography for full citation)

Allport, F. H. (1962). A structuronomic conception of behavior: individual and collective. Structural theory and the master problem of social psychology.
   A retrospective account of the 'group mind' controversy of the 1920s, and an assessment of its "current status" (earlier objections reconsidered).

Bandura, A. (1996). *Self-efficacy: The exercise of control.*
   Self-efficacy belief systems embedded in broader socio-cognitive theory; subprocesses addressed at both the individual and collective level.

_____, (Ed.). (1995). *Self-efficacy in changing societies.*
   "To fully understand personal causation requires a comprehensive theory that explains, within a unified conceptual framework, the origins of beliefs of personal efficacy, their structure and function, the processes through which they operate, and their diverse effects" p. 2.

Blalock, H. M., Jr. (1986). Multiple causation, indirect measurement, and generalizability in the social sciences.
   '...continue to strive to achieve generalizability without sacrificing the complexity needed to construct realistic models of important social processes' p. 35.

Blood, R. 0. Jr., & Wolfe, D. M. (1960). *Husbands and wives.* (2nd ed., 1965, see also Wolfe, 1959)
   Found no differences between rural, urban, and immigrant couples in the power (of the wife) to make decisions, p. 24.

A Resource Theory interpretation of husband-wife relations: "...power to make decisions stems primarily from the resources which the individual can provide to meet the needs of his marriage partner and to upgrade his decision-making skill" p. 44; "...the relationship between husband and wife is affected by the way he plays his economic role..." p. 114.

Bokemeier, J. L., & Tait, J. L. (1980). Women as power actors: A comparative study of (two) rural communities.
    Describe two types: 'good companion' cf. Parsons, 1942, vs. 'resource' model, cf. Bozeman, et al., 1977.

Bott, E. (1971). *Family and social network: Roles, norms and external relationships in ordinary urban families.*
    Discussion in appendix B: independent, interdependent, and shared husband and wife activity.

Broderick, C. B., & Smith, J. (1979). The general systems approach to the family.
    Propositions derived from Wilkinson, 1977, e.g. 5A. 'It follows that the unit responsible for memory [e.g. record keeping] has greater access than other units to influence or power in the system' p. 128.

Burr, W. R. (1973). *Theory construction and the sociology of the family.*
    The nature of deductive theories, Ch. 1. Assessing the validity of deductive theories, Ch. 2. (Also see discussion of social exchange affected by norms.)

Buttel, F. H., Larson O. G. & Gillespie, G. W. Jr. (1990). *The sociology of agriculture.*
    Behaviorism and the social psychology of agriculture, pp. 43-72; Gender and agriculture pp. 115-125; Trends and gaps in the sociology of agriculture, pp. 171-186.

Campbell, B. K., & Barnlund, D. C. (1977). Communication patterns and problems of pregnancy.
    Measures of sensitivity, directness, control, empathy, and clarity in interpersonal communication skills.

Christensen, R. (1996). *Plane answers to complex questions: The theory of linear models.*
    Tukey's method depends on knowing the distribution of the studentized range.. [and].. provides a competitor to the usual analysis of variance F test..." pp. 102-103.

Cohen, J., & Cohen, P. (1983). *Applied multiple regression/correlation analysis for the behavioral sciences.*
Discussions of family-wise error and experiment-wise error.

Collins, B. E., & Raven, B. H. (1968). Group structure: Attraction, coalitions, communication, and power, pp. 168-185.
Empirical studies of power, influence, and change in small groups.

Cowan, P. A. (1991). Individual and family life transitions: A proposal for a new definition.
Presents a structural and process model of transitions, pp. 12-19.

Di Tomaso, N. (1982). Sociological reductionism from Parsons to Althusser: Linking action and structure in social theory.
Suggests incorporating choice in theories of the social in order to explain social change.

Emerson, R. M. (1972). Exchange theory, part I: A psychological basis for exchange; part II: Exchange relations and network structures.

Ferber, R. (1973). Family decision making and economic behavior: a review, with introduction by R. Hill and D. Klein, pp. 27-28.
List of empirical generalizations, e.g. 'Role allocation in family decision making is determined in part by the culture-specific power resources and perceptions of family members' p. 28.

Flora, C. B. & Flora, J. L. (1988). Structure of agriculture and women's culture in the Great Plains.
Contrast women's roles in two ethnic groups: U. S.-born entrepreneurial farmers and German-born yeoman farmers, pp. 195-205.

French, J. R. P., Jr., & Raven B. H. (1959). The bases of social power.
Reward, coercive, legitimate, information, referent, and expert power, pp. 155-164. (See also Collins & Raven, 1968.)

Gasson, R., et al. (1988). The farm as a family business: A review, pp. 1-41.
Conclusion: family relationships in the UK may have become less relevant in the case of smaller farms, but more relevant to the conduct of a successful large farm business.

Gray, I, Dunn, T., & Phillips, E. (1997). Power, interests, and the extension of sustainable agriculture, pp. 97-113.
Economic treadmills preventing progress, p. 110.

Gullotta, T. P., Adams, G. R., & Alexander, S. J. (1986). *Today's marriages and families.*
Theoretical frameworks, pp. 27-35; Relationship enhancement and perceived power, pp. 160- 16; Decision-making power, pp. 183-185.

Hall, R. H. (1991). *Organizations: Structures, processes, and outcomes.*
The interdependent nature of power relations in organizations, p. 123.

Harding, S. (Ed.). (1993). *The "racial" economy of science: Toward a democratic future.*
Race and gender, the role of analogy in science, pp 359-376.

Hassard, J., & Pym, D. (Eds.). (1990). *The theory and philosophy of organizations: Critical issues and new perspectives.*
Paradigm diversity in organizational research, G. Morgan, pp. 13-29.

Hill, R., et al. (1970). *Family development in three generations.*
A longitudinal study of changing patterns of planning and achievement over the family life cycle. Differences in observer and self-reported ratings of couple interaction in reaching consensus: *both* spouses rated influence of self below observer ratings. Authority patterns in husband-wife relations: younger wives seen as less influential than older wives, Table 2.14, p. 48 .

Hobbes, T. (1962). *Leviathan*, elements in human nature.
Uses of power, cit. in Wrong, Ch. 4 , 1994.

Huber, J. (Ed.). (1991). *Macro-Micro Linkages in Sociology.*
From exchange to structure, M. Hechter, pp. 46-50. Historical change and the ritual production of gender, R. Collins, pp. 109-120.

Iannello, K. P. (1992). *Decisions without hierarchy: Feminist interventions in organization theory and practice.*
Webster's dictionary and feminist definitions of power differ from dominant definitions, p. 43. "Power, defined as domination, supports hierarchical arrangements in organizations," cit. R. M. Kanter, 1977.

Kemper, T. D. (1973). The fundamental dimensions of social relationship.
Two explanations of compliance: power relations [control] and status relations [affection]; use of factor analysis; cit. Bierstedt, 1950, pp. 41-57.

Kenkel, W. F. & Hoffman, D. K. (1956). Real and conceived roles in family decision making.
"inability of husbands and wives to recognize their roles" in a study of 25 college student, married pairs, pp. 311-316.

Keppel, G., & Zedeck, S. (1989). *Data analysis for research designs: Analysis of variance and multiple regression/correlation approaches.*
Correction for (single-df) multiple comparisons, pp. 169-181. Analysis of interaction comparisons: the interaction contrast, pp. 239-260.

Kohl, S. B. (1977). Women's participation in the North American family farm, in a sparsely populated region of southwestern Saskatchewan.
"...virtually all women were important participants in the ongoing managerial decisions concerning the enterprise."

Komarovsky, M. (1973). Presidential address: Some problems in role analysis.
Two challenges: specify more precisely the interplay of psychological and structural variables, explore (role aspects of) conflict, deviation, malintegration and social change, pp. 649-662.

Lewin, K. (1947). Group decision and social change, pp. 330-344.
Conclusion: "...certain methods of group decision prove to be superior to lecturing and individual treatment as means of changing social conduct." (See also Pelz, 1958.)

Lippitt, R., & White, R. K. (1947). An experimental study of leadership and group life.
Contrast of democratic, authoritarian, and laissez-faire leadership styles, pp. 315-330.

Liska, A. (1984). A critical examination of the causal structure of the Fishbein-Ajzen attitude-behavior model.
Methods questioned.

Lorenz, K. (1994). Competition and cooperation: Are they antagonistic or complementary?
A reflexive process which "leads to both individuation and socialization" p 24.

Lyson, T. A. (1985). Husband and wife work roles and the organization and operation of family farms.
Adoption and decision sharing, Tables 3 and 4, pp. 762-763 .

Maman, M. & Tate, T. H. (1996). *Women in agriculture: A guide to research.*
Decision-making on the farm, pp. 151-160.

Meeker, B. F., & Weitzel-O'Neill, P. A. (1985). Sex roles and interpersonal behavior in task-oriented groups.

Sex role differentiation hypothesis of Bales et al. challenged by alternative hypotheses: 'women must prove that they are both competent and well intentioned before either they or others expect or accept high levels of task behavior from them...' and 'relatively high rates of positive social behavior that have been observed for women are also related to the necessity of proving good intentions' pp. 389-390.

Moore, K. M. (1989). Agrarian or non-agrarian identities of farm spouses.
Types of farming orientation: agrarian, profit maximization, and non-farm lifestyle, pp. 74-82.

Moreno, J. L. (1934). *Who shall survive?*
Report of experience with the sociometric test, which provides quantifiable data on patterns of attraction and repulsion in groups, and with psychodrama and sociodrama techniques of role-playing.

Mouzelis, N. (1995). *Sociological theory: What went wrong? Diagnosis and remedies,.*
Two ways to assess new concepts or conceptual frameworks: one is 'direct relevance to empirical research' the other is '...tackling ...persistent theoretical puzzles and misconceptions' p.127.

Murstein, B., Ceretto, M., & MacDonald, M. G. (1977). A theory and investigation of the effect of exchange-orientation on marriage and friendship.
'...an exchange-orientation is negatively associated with marital adjustment for men' p.548.

Office of Technology Assessment. (1986). *Technology, public policy, and the changing structure of American agriculture: A special report for the 1985 farm bill.*
Bleak forecasts for new farm enterprises not already capitalized, and for farms already heavily in debt, especially midsized, even with government supports.

O'Keefe, G. F. Jr. (1973). Coorientation variables in family study, pp. 513-536
Use of mass media as sources of information; exchange of information with others; social integration and social power concepts "not appropriate."

Osmond, M. W., & Martin, P. Y. (1978). A contingency model of marital organization in low income families, using automatic interaction detector, AID, pp. 315-329.
Key findings: conjoint decision-making explains intactness, and, by family type, different patterns of variables explain intactness.

Measures include topics of disagreement and methods of conflict resolution.

Family typology: democratic, semi-democratic, semi-autocratic, and autocratic, based on mode of decision-making, strategies of conflict resolution.

Orkin, M. (1987). Ideology and the interpretative foundation of science.
Argues for critical social inquiry and reflexive theory, pp. 80-107.

Parsons, T. (1963). On the concept of influence.
Four types, corresponding roughly to political, economic, social, and cultural.

Pelz, E. B. (1958). Some factors in 'group decision.'
Defines 'group decision' to mean "decision about individual goals in a setting of shared norms re: such goals;"
Finds that process of making a decision in combination with degree to which group consensus is obtained and perceived generates differences as great as those found previously by Lewin, Lippitt and White;
Suggests that leadership technique, salience of subject, and group cohesiveness probably affects influence of these factors on subsequent action, p. 218.

Popper, K. R. (1963). *Conjectures and refutations: The growth of scientific knowledge*, cf. :
Problems of induction and demarcation, p. 254; testability and meaning, pp. 273-292; demarcation between science and metaphysics, Ch. 11.

Posner, M. I. (Ed.). (1989). *Foundations of cognitive science*.
Role of culture in directing the thought processes, Ch. 20; how the brain creates and contains subjective experience, Ch. 21.

Rasmussen, W. D. (1985). *Historian makes chilling comparison.*
Sixty-year comparison on farm situation, current seesaw in commodity prices and land prices, (see also Brewster, 1983.)

Rathge, R. W., Leistritz, F. L., & Goreham, G. A. (1988). Farmers displaced in economically depressed times, p. 354:
"...those who were the more astute managers (i.e. the adopters) in the 1970s were probably those most at risk to financial tragedy in the 1980s."

Reinhardt, N. & Barlett, P. (1989). The persistence of family farms in U. S. agriculture...
"...despite the weight of all the policies operating against it..." p. 221.

Sachs, C. E. (1983) The invisible farmers: Women in agricultural production. Historical perspective on decision making and the sexual division of labor on family farms, pp 29-34.

Saville, D. J. (1990). Multiple comparison procedures: The practical solution. Scheffe is excessively conservative; use unrestricted LSDs for .10, .05, .01 & .001 to determine strength of evidence for each difference, and distinguish between confirming hypotheses and generating hypothesis for further study, pp 174-180.

Saville, D. J., & Wood, G. R. (1991). *Statistical methods: The geometric approach.*
Use planned comparisons to confirm hypotheses, unplanned comparisons to generate hypotheses, p. 290.

Scanzoni, J., & Szinovacz, M. (1980). *Family decision-making: A developmental sex role model.*
Impact of family life cycle events and sociocultural influences on marital and familial decision-making processes.

Selig, A. L. (1976). The myth of the multi-problem family, article on crisis theory and family types, pp. 526-532.
Summary: Role transitions... "create hazards for meeting basic needs"... increasing problem of either interpersonal disturbance or new adaptations and increased functional capacity, i.e. role transitions render family "at risk" - with potential for "post crisis resolution of deteriorated, status quo, or enhanced functioning."
Family types identified: "maximal-distant" vs. "undifferentiated family ego mass" (intense emotional closeness: calm or hostile rejection).

Sewell, W. H. Jr. (1987). Theory of action, dialectic, and history: Comment on Coleman.
Raises the "question of how structurally constituted actors act in such a way that the combined effect of their actions changes the very structures that constituted them" cit. A. Giddens, 1979.

Slocum, W. L. (1962). *Agricultural sociology: A study of sociological aspects of American farm life.*
1956 report: 70% to 84% of commercial farmers under age 45 in the state of Washington discussed farm decisions (crops, farm changes, and machinery purchases) with their wives, and 27% to 47% made farm decisions jointly with their wives, p. 254.

Sprecher, S. (1985). Sex differences in bases of power in dating relationships.
"...significant negative correlation between contributions of resources and perceived power for females" p.107.

Tannenbaum, A. S., & Allport, F. H. (1956). Personality structure and group structure: An interpretive study of their relationship through an event-structure hypothesis.
Motive-strength and perceived goal relevance as alternative explanations of findings, p. 280. (See also Allport, 1954, 1955).

Turner, J. H. (1985). The concept of 'action' in sociological analysis.
Definition of social action: action that is constrained or circumscribed by the behavior of others, p. 83.

U. S. Dept. of Agriculture. (1985). Role of women in survival of family farms.
Finding: 13.7% of midsized commercial farms approaching insolvency, an unpublished report.

Walker, H. A., & Cohen, B. P. (1985). Scope statements: imperatives for evaluating theory, pp. 288-301.
A strategy for making sociological theories conditional, compared with other strategies such as adding more variables.

Whatmore, S. (1991). *Farming women: Gender, work and family enterprise.*
Patriarchal gender relations in a study of family farming in England: 46% of women who have partnership status declared that they had never participated in decision-making.

Wilcox, R. R. (1987). *New statistical procedures for the social sciences: Modern solutions to basic problems.*
Multiple comparisons, pp. 173-203. Two-way anova, multiple comparisons, interactions, pp. 220-227. The multivariate studentized range distribution, Table A13, pp. 376-385. (See also Edwards, 1983.)

Wilson, T. P. (1970a). Conceptions of interaction and forms of sociological explanation.
Social interaction as an interpretive process, p. 697; "...if interaction is essentially interpretive, then descriptions of interaction cannot satisfy the requirements of literal description imposed by the logic of deductive explanation" p. 707.

Wrong, D. (1988). *Power, its forms, bases, and uses.*
Different forms of power and their combinations, pp. 21-83.

_____. (1994). *The problem of order: What unites and divides society?*
Distinguishes 'power over' others in social relations as a special case of 'power to' produce intended consequences, cits. T. Hobbes, 1962 and B. Russell, 1938.
Does not address social change.

Yamagishi, T., & Cook, K. S. (1990). Power relations in exchange networks: A comment on 'network exchange theory.'
Remarks re: merging of power-dependence notions with network exchange concepts, pp. 297-300.

Yandell, B. S. (1997). *Practical data analysis for designed experiments.*
"...advisable to use a combination of univariate and multivariate approaches when there are multiple responses of interest" p. 275.
"Once the important responses have been identified, multiple comparisons can be addressed either on individual responses or on linear combinations suggested by the analysis" p. 276.

Bibliography

Abd-Ella, M. M., Hoiberg, E. 0., & Warren, R. D. (1981). Adoption behavior in farm family systems: An Iowa study. *Rural Sociology, 46,* 42-61.

Abell, H. C. (1961). Decision-making on the farm. *The Economic Annalist, 31.*

Abelson, R. P., et al. (Eds.). (1968). *Theories of cognitive consistency: A source book.* Chicago: Rand McNally.

Adams, B. N. (1966). Coercion and consensus theories: Some unresolved issues. *AJS, 71:* 714-717. (Also in *The sociology of knowledge,* in 1970. J. E. Curtis & J. W. Petras, eds. New York: Praeger).

_____. (1967). Interaction theory and the social network. *Sociometry, 30.*

_____. (1980). *The American family: A sociological interpretation* (3rd ed.). Chicago: Rand McNally.

Adams, B. N., & Campbell, J. L. (1984). *Framing the family: Contemporary portraits.* Prospect Heights, IL: Waveland Press.

Adams, J. S. (1965). Inequity in social exchange. In *Advances in experimental social psychology* (Vol. 2). L. Berkowitz, ed. NYC: Academic Press.

Adams, J. S., & Freeman, S. (1976). Equity theory revisited. In *Advances in experimental social psychology* (Vol. 9). L. Berkowitz, ed. New York: Academic Press.

Ajzen, I., & Fishbein, M. (1980). *Understanding attitudes and predicting social behavior.* Englewood Cliffs, NJ: Prentice-Hall.

Ajzen, I., & Madden, T. J. (1986). Prediction of goal-directed behavior: Attitudes, intentions, and perceived behavioral control. *Journal of Experimental Social Psychology, 22,* 453-474.

Alexander, J. C. (1988). The new theoretical movement. In *Handbook of sociology.* N. J. Smelser, ed. Newbury Park, CA: Sage.

_____. (1988). *Action and its environments: Toward a new synthesis.* New York: Columbia Univ. Press.

Alexander, J. C., & Columy, P. (Eds.). (1990). *Differentiation theory and social change.* New York: Columbia Univ. Press.

Alexander, J. C., & Sztompka, P. (Eds.). (1990). *Rethinking progress: Movements, forces, and ideas.* Boston: Unwin Hyman.

Allport, F. H. (1954). The structuring of events: Outline of a general theory with applications to psychology. *Psychological Review, 61,* 281-303.

_____. (1955). *Theories of perception and the concept of structure.* New York: Wiley.

_____. (1962). A structuronomic conception of behavior: Individual and collective. I. Structural theory and the master problem of social psychology. *Journal of Abnormal and Social Psychology, 64,* 3-30.

Anthias, F., & Kelly, M. P. (Eds.). (1995). *Sociological debates: Thinking about 'the social.'* Dartford, UK: Greenwich Univ. Press.

Bahr, S. J. (1976). Role competence, role norms, and marital control. In *Role structure and analysis of the family* (Part III: Family roles as social exchange) F. I. Nye, ed. Beverly Hills, CA: Sage.

Bales, R. F. (1950). *Interaction process analysis: A method for the study of small groups.* Reading, MA: Addison-Wesley.

Bales, R. F., & Slater, P. E. (1955). Role differentiation in small decision-making groups. In *Family, socialization and interaction process.* T. Parsons & R. F. Bales, et al., eds. New York: Free Press.

Bandura, A. (1986). *Social foundations of thought and action: A social cognitive theory*. Englewood Cliffs, NJ: Prentice-Hall.

_____. (1996). *Self-efficacy: The exercise of control*. NYC: Freeman

_____, (Ed.). (1995). *Self-efficacy in changing societies*. New York: Cambridge Univ. Press.

Barlett, P. F. (1987). The crisis in family farming: Who will survive? In *Farm work and fieldwork*. M Chibnik, ed. Ithaca, NY: Cornell Univ. Press.

_____. (1993). *American dreams, rural realities: Family farms in crisis*. Chapel Hill: Univ. of North Carolina Press.

Barnett, H. G. (1953). *Innovation: The basis of cultural change*. New York: McGraw-Hill.

Barnes, B. (1988). *The nature of power*. Chicago: Univ. of Illinois Press.

Baron, R. M., & Kenny, D. A. (1986). The moderator-mediator variable distinction in social psychological research: Conceptual, strategic, and statistical considerations. *Jn. of Personality and Social Psychology, 51*.

Bates, F. (1974). Alternative models for the future of society. *Social Forces, 53*

Bauer, R. A. (1963). Communication as a transaction: A comment on (Parsons') 'On the concept of influence.' *Public Opinion Quarterly, 27*.

Beal, G. M., & Bohlen, J. M. (1957). *The diffusion process* (Special Report No. 18). Ames: Iowa Agricultural Extension Service.

Becker, B. J. (1986). Influence again: Another look at studies of gender differences in social influence. In *The psychology of gender: Advances through meta-analysis*. J. S. Hyde & M. C. Linn, eds. Baltimore, MD: Johns Hopkins Univ. Press.

Becker, H. P. (1950). *Through values to social interpretation*, p. 254 ff. Durham, NC: Duke Univ. Press.

Beers, H. W. (1935). *Measurements of family relationships in farm families of central New York*. (Memoir 163, cf. Table 12). Ithaca, NY: Agricultural Experiment Station (AES), Cornell University.

_____. (1937). A portrait of the farm family in central New York state. *ASR, 2*, 591-600.

Bem, D. J. (1972). Self-perception theory. In *Advances in experimental social psychology* (Vol. 6). L. Berkowitz, ed. New York: Academic Press.

Benedict, R. (1935). *Patterns of culture*. London: Routledge & Kegan Paul.

Bennett, J. W., with Kohl, S. B., & Binion, G. (1982). *Of time and enterprise: North American family farm management in a context of resource marginality*. Minneapolis: Univ. of Minnesota Press.

Benson, J. K. (1977). Organizations: A dialectical view. *ASQ, March.*

Bentley, S. E. (1992). *Characteristics of farms with sales of $40,000 or more, 1987-89*. Wash., DC: USDA, Economic Research Services, Agriculture and Rural Economy Division.

Bentley, S. E., & Sachs, C. (1984). *Farm women in the U. S.: An updated literature review and annotated bibliography*. University Park, PA: Center for Rural Women, AES, Pennsylvania State University.

Berardi, G. M. (1981). Socioeconomic consequences of agricultural mechanization in the United States: Needed redirection for mechanization research. *Rural Sociology, 46*, 483-504.

Berardi, G. M., & Geisler, C. C. (Eds.). (1984). *The social consequences and challenges of new agricultural technologies*. Boulder, CO: Westview.

Berger, J., & Zelditch, M., Jr. (Eds.). (1985). *Status, rewards and influence: How expectations organize behavior*. San Francisco, CA: Jossey-Bass.

Berger, J., & Zelditch, M., Jr. (Eds.). (1993). *Theoretical research programs: Studies in the growth of theory*. Stanford: Stanford Univ. Press.

Berger, J., Zelditch, M., Jr., & Anderson, B. (Eds.). (1972). *Sociological theories in progress* (Vol. II). Boston: Houghton Mifflin.

Berger, J., Zelditch, M., Jr., & Anderson, B. (Eds.). (1989). *Sociological theories in progress* (Vol.III). Newbury Park, CA: Sage.

Berger, P. L., & Luckman, T. (1971). *The social construction of reality* (first published in 1966, Garden City, NY: Doubleday). Harmondsworth, UK: Allen Lane.

Berger, P. L., Wagner, D. G., & Zelditch, M. Jr. (1992). A working strategy for constructing theories. In *Studies in metatheorizing in sociology.* G. Ritzer, ed. Newbury Park, CA: Sage.

Bergon-Larson, M. (1982). In *Scientific-technological change and the role of women in development.* P. M. D'Onofrio-Flores & S. M. Pfafflin, eds. Boulder, CO: Westview.

Berlan-Darque, M. (1988). The division of labour and decision-making in farming couples: Power and negotiation. *Sociologia Ruralis, 28.*

Berkowitz, L. (1954). Group standards, cohesiveness, and productivity. *Human Relations, 7,* 509-519.

_____, (Ed.). (1978). *Group processes.* New York: Academic Press.

Bernard, J. (1942). *American family behavior.* New York: Harper.

Bertrand, A. L. (1958). *Rural sociology.* New York: McGraw-Hill.

Bianchi, S. M. & Spain, D. (1983). *American women: Three decades of change* (DCS-80-8) Washington, DC: U. S. Bureau of the Census.

Bienvenu, M. J., Sr. (1970). Measurement of marital communication. *Family Coordinator, 19,* 26-31.

_____. (1971). An interpersonal communication inventory. *The Journal of Communication, 21,* 381-388.

Bierstedt, R. (1976). An analysis of social power. In *Sociological theory,* pp. 136-147. L. Coser & B. Rosenberg, eds. New York: Macmillan.

Blalock, H. M., Jr. (1969). *Theory construction: From verbal to mathematical formulations.* Englewood Cliffs, NJ: Prentice-Hall.

_____. (1970). The formalization of sociological theory. In *Theoretical sociology.* J. C. McKinney & E. A. Tiryakian, eds. New York: Appleton-Century-Croft.

_____. (1974). *Measurement in the social sciences: Theories and strategies.* Chicago: Aldine.

_____. (1982). *Conceptualization and measurement in the social sciences.* Beverly Hills, CA: Sage.

_____. (1984). *Basic dilemmas in the social sciences.* Beverly Hills, CA: Sage.

_____. (1986). Multiple causation, indirect measurement, and generalizability in the social sciences. *Synthese, 68,* 13-36.

_____. (1989a). *Power and conflict: Toward a general theory.* Newbury Park, CA: Sage.

_____. (1989b). The real and unrealized contributions of quantitative sociology. *ASR, 54,* 447-460.

_____. (1991). *Understanding social inequality: Modeling allocation processes.* Newbury Park, CA: Sage.

Blalock, H. M., Jr. (Ed.). (1971). *Causal models in the social sciences.* Chicago: Aldine.

_____, (Ed.). (1980). *Sociological theory and research: A critical appraisal.* New York: Free Press.

_____, (Ed.). (1985). *Causal models in the social sciences* (2nd. ed.). Chicago: Aldine.

Blalock, H. M., Jr., & Wilken, P. H. (1979). *Intergroup processes: A micro-macro perspective.* New York: Free Press.

Blau, P. M. (1964). *Exchange and power in social life.* New York: Wiley.

_____. (1977). *Inequality and heterogeneity.* New York: Free Press.

_____. (1987). Microprocesses and macrostructures. In *Social exchange theory.* K. S. Cook, ed. London: Sage.

Bleir, R. (Ed.). (1986). *Feminist approaches to science.* New York: Pergamon.

Blood, R. 0. Jr. (1958). The division of labor in city and farm families. *JMF, 20,* 170-174.

Blood, R. 0. Jr., & Wolfe, D. M. (1960). *Husbands and wives.* Glencoe, IL: Free Press.

Blumberg, R. L. (1984). A general theory of gender stratification. In *Sociological theory.* R. Collins, ed. San Francisco, CA: Jossey-Bass.

Blumer, H. (1962). Society as symbolic interaction. In *Human behavior and social processes.* A. Rose, ed. Boston: Houghton Mifflin.

_____. (1966). Sociological implications of the thought of George Herbert Mead. *AJS, 71*: 535-547.

_____. (1969). *Symbolic interaction: Perspective and method.* New York: Prentice-Hall.

_____. (1970). An essay on the nature of social theory. In *Sociological methods*, pp. 84-95. N. K. Denzin, ed. Chicago: Aldine.

_____. (1972a). Society as symbolic interaction. In *Symbolic interaction: A reader in social psychology.* J. G. Manis & B. M. Meltzer, eds. Boston: Allyn & Bacon.

_____. (1972b). Action vs. interaction. *Society, 20* (April).

Bohlen, J. M. (1964). The adoption and diffusion of ideas in agriculture. In *Our changing rural society.* J. H. Copp, ed. Ames: IA State Univ. Press.

Bokemeier, J. L., & Coughenour, C. M. (1980). Men and women in four types of farm families: work and attitudes. Paper presented at the RSS annual meeting, Cornell University.

Bokemeier, J. L., & Garkovich, L. (1987). Assessing the influence of farm women's self-identity on task allocation and decision making. *Rural Sociology, 52*, 13-36.

Bokemeier, J. & Monroe, P. (1983). Continued reliance on one respondent in family decision-making studies: A content analysis. *JMF, 45*, 645-652.

Bokemeier, J. L., & Tait, J. L. (1980). Women as power actors: A comparative study of rural communities. *Rural Sociology, 45*, 238-255.

Boskoff, A. (1972). *The mosaic of sociological theory.* New York: Crowell.

Bott, E. (1957). *Family and social networks.* London: Tavistock.

_____. (1971). *Family and social network: Roles, norms and external relationships in ordinary urban families* (2nd ed.). NYC: Free Press.

Boulding, K. E. (1967). An economist looks at the future of sociology. *Et al., 1*

_____. (1973). The microtheory of grants and granting behavior. In *The economy of love and fear*. Belmont, CA: Wadsworth.

_____. (1978). Societal evolution: Movement from threat to exchange to integration. *Ecodynamics: A new theory of societal evolution*. Beverly Hills, CA: Sage.

_____. (1989). *Three faces of power*. Newbury Park, CA: Sage.

Bourdieu, P. (1977). *Outline of a theory of action*. Cambridge: Cambridge Univ. Press.

_____. (1990) *In other words: Essays toward a reflexive sociology*. Stanford: Stanford Univ. Press.

Bourdieu, P., & Wacquant, L. J. D. (1992). *An invitation to reflexive sociology*. Cambridge: Polity.

Bowen, G. L., & Pittman, J. F. (Eds.). (1995). *The work and family interface: Toward a contextual effects perspective*. Minneapolis, MN: NCFR.

Boyd, J. P. (1980). Three orthogonal models of the adoption of agricultural innovation. *Rural Sociology, 45*, 309-324.

Bozeman, B., Thornton, S., & McKinney, M. (1977). Continuity and change in opinions about sex roles. In *A portrait of marginality: The political behavior of the American woman*, pp. 38-65. M. Githens & J. L. Prestage, eds. New York: D. McKay.

Braithwaite, R. B. (1964). *Scientific explanation: A study of the function of theory, probability and law in science* (based on Tarner lectures, 1946). London: Cambridge Univ. Press.

Brandstatter, H., Davis, J. H., & Stocker-Kreichgauer, G. (Eds.). (1982). *Group decision making*. New York: Academic Press.

Brewster, D. E., Rasmussen, W. D., & Youngberg, G. (Eds.). (1983). *Farms in transition: Interdisciplinary perspectives on farm structure*. Ames: Iowa State Univ. Press.

Broderick, C. B. (1993). *Understanding family process: Basics of family systems theory*. Newbury Park, CA: Sage.

Broderick, C. B., & Smith, J. (1979). The general systems approach to the family. In W. R. Burr, et al., *Contemporary theories about the family* (Vol. II). New York: Free Press.

Brown, L. A. (1981). *Innovation diffusion: A new perspective.* NYC: Methuen.

Brown, L. A., Malecki, E. J., & Spector, A. N. (1976). Adopter categories in a spatial context: Alternative explanations for an empirical regularity. *Rural Sociology, 41*, 99-118.

Browne, W. P. (1987). *Private interests, public policy, and American agriculture.* Lawrence, KS: Univ. of Kansas Press.

Bruce, S., & Wallis, R. (1983). Rescuing motives. *The British Journal of Sociology, 34*, 61-72.

Bruce, S., & Wallis, R. (1985). 'Rescuing motives' rescued: A reply to Sharrock and Watson. *The British Journal of Sociology, 36*, 467-470.

Buckley, W. (1967). *Sociology and modern systems theory.* Englewood Cliffs, NJ: Prentice-Hall.

Burger, T. (1977). Talcott Parsons, The problem of order in society, and the program of an analytical sociology. *AJS, 83*: 320-334. (See also: Parsons' Comment on Burger's critique: 335-339, and Burger's Reply: 983-986)

Burgess, R. L., & Bushell, D. Jr. (Eds.). (1969). *Behavioral sociology: The experimental analysis of social process.* NYC: Columbia Univ. Press.

Burke, P. J. (1967). The development of task and social-emotional role differentiation. *Sociometry, 30*, 379-392.

Burr, W. R. (1973). *Theory construction and the sociology of the family.* New York: Wiley.

_____. (1994). *Reexamining family stress: New theories and research.* Newbury Park, CA: Sage.

Burr, W., Hill, R., Nye, I. F., & Reiss, I. L. (Eds.). (1979). *Contemporary theories about the family.* (Vol. 1: Research-based). NYC: Free Press.

Burrell, G., & Morgan, G. (1979). *Sociological paradigms and organizational analysis.* Exeter, NH: Heinemann.

Bush, C. G. (1982). The barn is his, the house is mine: Agricultural technology and sex roles. In *Energy and transport: Historical perspectives on policy issues*, pp 235-259. G. H. Daniels & M. H. Rose, eds. Beverly Hills: Sage

Buttel, F. H. (1982). The political economy of agriculture in advanced industrial societies: Some observations on theory and method. In *Current perspectives on social theory* (Vol. 3), pp. 27-55. S. G. McNall, ed. Greenwich, CT: JAI Press.

_____. (1983). Beyond the family farm. In *Technology and social change in rural areas*, pp. 87-107. G. F. Summers, ed. Boulder, CO: Westview.

Buttel, F. H. (1985). The land-grant system: A sociological perspective on value conflicts and ethical issues. *Agriculture and Human Values, 2.*

_____. (1989). The U.S. farm crisis and the restructuring of American agriculture: Domestic and international dimensions. In *The international farm crisis.* D. Goodman & M. Redclift, eds. New York: St. Martin's.

Buttel, F. H., Cowan, J. T., Kenney, M., & Kloppenburg, J. Jr. (1984). Biotechnology in agriculture: The political economy of agribusiness reorganization and industry-university relationships. *Research in Rural Sociology and Development, 1,* 315-343.

Buttel, F. H., & Gertler, M. E. (1982). Small farm businesses: A typology of farm, operator, and family characteristics with implications for public research and extension policy. *Journal of the Northeastern Agricultural Economics Council, 11,* 35-44.

Buttel, F. H., & Gillespie, G. W. Jr. (1984). The sexual division of farm household labor: An exploratory study of the structure of on-farm and off-farm labor allocation among farm men and women. *Rur. Soc., 49.*

Buttel, F. H., Larson O. G. & Gillespie, G. W. Jr. (1990). *The sociology of agriculture.* New York: Greenwood.

Camilleri, S. F. (1970). An essay on the nature of social theory. In *Sociological methods*, pp. 70-83. N. K. Denzin, ed. Chicago: Aldine.

Campbell, B. K., & Barnlund, D. C. (1977). Communication patterns and problems of pregnancy. *American Journal of Orthopsychiatry, 47* (1).

Campbell, C. (1991). Reexamining Mills on motive: A character vocabulary approach. *Sociological Analysis, 52,* 89-98.

_____. (1992). In defense of the traditional concept of action in sociology. *Journal for the Theory of Social Behavior, 22,* 1-23.

_____. (1996). *The myth of social action.* NYC: Cambridge Univ. Press.

Campbell, N. R. (1921). *What is science?* New York: Dover.

Campbell, R. R., Heffernan, W. D., & Giles, J. L. (1984). Farm operator cycles and farm debts: An accident of timing. *The Rural Sociologist, 4,* 404-408.

Cancian, F. (1967). Stratification and risk-taking: A theory tested on agricultural innovation. *ASR, 32,* 912-927.

_____. (1975). *What are norms?* London: Cambridge Univ. Press.

Carlson, C. (1990). *Perspectives on the family: History, class, and feminism.* Belmont, CA: Wadsworth.

Carlson, J. E., & Dillman, D. A. (1983). Influence of kinship arrangements on farmers' innovativeness. *Rural Sociology, 48,* 183-200.

Carstensen, F. V., Rothstein, M., & Swanson, J. A. (1993). *Outstanding in his field: Perspectives on American agriculture in honor of Wayne D. Rasmussen.* Ames, IA: Iowa State Univ. Press.

Cartwright, D. (1959). *Studies in social power.* Ann Arbor, MI: Institute for Social Research.

_____. (1971). Risk taking by individuals and groups: An assessment of research employing choice dilemmas. *Journal of Personality and Social Psychology, 20,* 361-378.

Cartwright, D., & Harary, F. (1956). Structural balance: A generalization of Heider's theory. *Psychological Review, 63*: 277-293.

Cartwright, D., & Zander, A. (Eds.). (1968). *Group dynamics: Research and theory* (3rd ed.). New York: Harper & Row.

Cell, C. P., & Johnson, D. E. (1979). *Wisconsin farmers in 1977: A regional profile.* Population Notes, No. 9. Madison, WI: Univ. of Wis., Ag. Ext.

Chafetz, J. S. (1978). *A primer on the construction and testing of theories in sociology.* Itasca, IL: Peacock.

_____. (1988). *Feminist sociology: An overview of contemporary theories.* Itasca, IL: Peacock.

_____. (1990). *Gender equity: A theory of stability and change.* Newbury Park, CA: Sage.

Chaffee, S. H., & McLeod, J. M. (1970). Coorientation and the structure of family communication. Paper presented to the International Communication Assn., Minneapolis, MN.

Chaliand, G. (1977). *Revolution in the third world, Myths and prospects.* New York: Viking Press.

Chapman, M. (Ed.). (1984). Intentional action as a paradigm for developmental psychology: A symposium. *Human Development, 27,* 113-144.

Chapin, F. S. (1928). *Cultural change.* New York: Century.

Chew, V. (1980). Testing differences among means: Correct interpretation and some alternatives. *HortScience, 15,* 467-470.

Christensen, R. (1996). *Plane answers to complex questions: The theory of linear models* (2nd. ed.). New York: Springer.

Christenson, J. A., & Garkovich, L.E. (1985). Fifty years of *Rural Sociology*: Status, trends, and impressions. *Rural Sociology, 50,* 503-522.

Cicourel, A. V. (1972). Basic & normative rules in the negotiation of status and role. In *Studies of social interaction.* D. Sudnow, ed. NYC: Free Press.

_____, (Ed.). (1973). *Cognitive sociology.* Harmondsworth: Penguin.

Claridge, C. L. & Chamala, S. (1995). Role of women in Australian agriculture and natural resource management: Issues of empowerment and leadership. In *Women in agriculture: Perspective, issues and experiences,* pp. 25-66. R. K. Samata, ed. New Delhi: M. D. Publications.

Clegg, S. (1975). *Power, rule, and domination* (in sociological theory and organizational life). Boston: Routledge & Kegan Paul.

Clifford, J. (1988). *The predicament of culture.* Cambridge: Harvard Press.

Cochrane, W. W. (1979). *The development of American agriculture: A historical analysis.* Minneapolis: Univ. of Minnesota Press.

Cohen, B. P. (1989). *Developing sociological knowledge: Theory and method* (2nd ed.). Chicago: Nelson-Hall.

Cohen, J. (1988). *Statistical power analysis for the behavioral sciences* (2nd ed.). Hillsdale, NJ: L. Erlbaum.

Cohen, J., & Cohen, P. (1983). *Applied multiple regression/ correlation analysis for the behavioral sciences* (2nd. ed.). Hillsdale, NJ: L. Erlbaum.

Coleman, J. S. (1963). Comment on (Parsons') 'On the concept of influence.' *Public Opinion Quarterly, 27*, 63-82.

_____. (1970). Properties of collectivities. In *Macrosociology*. J. S. Coleman, A. Etzioni & J. Porter, eds. Boston: Allyn & Bacon.

_____. (1986). Social theory, social research, and a theory of action. *AJS, 91* (6).

_____. (1987). Actors and action in social history and social theory: Reply to Sewell. *AJS, 93*, 172-175.

_____. (1990). *Foundations of social theory*. Cambridge, MA: Harvard Univ. Press.

_____. (1993). The rational reconstruction of society. *ASR, 58*, 1-15.

Coleman, J. S., & Fararo, T. J. (Eds.). (1992). *Rational choice theory: Advocacy and critique*. London: Sage.

Coleman, J. S., Katz, E., & Menzel, H. (1966). *Medical innovation: A diffusion study*. New York: Bobbs-Merrrill.

Collins, B. E., & Raven, B. H. (1968). Group structure: Attraction, coalitions, communication and power. In *Handbook of social psychology*. G. Lindzey & E. Aronson, eds. Reading, MA: Addison-Wesley.

Collins, R. (1975). *Conflict sociology: Toward an explanatory science*. New York: Academy Press.

_____. (1986). Death of sociology in the 1980s, *AJS, 91*, 1336-1355.

_____. (1987). Reply to N. K. Denzin (emotions vs. cognitions), *AJS, 93*.

_____. (1988). *Theoretical sociology*. San Diego, CA: Harcourt Brace & Jovanovich.

_____. (1994). *Four sociological traditions*. NYC: Oxford Univ. Press.

Comte, A. (1875-1877). *The positive philosophy of Auguste Comte*, 3 Vols. (H. Martineau, Tran.). London: G. Bell. (First published 1830-1842).

_____. (1875-1877). *System of positive polity*. 4 Vols. (H .H. Bridges, F. Harrison, E. S. Beasly, et al., R. Congreve, Trans.). London: George Bell. (First published 1851 to 1854).

_____. (1974). *The crisis of industrial civilization: The early essays of Auguste Comte*. (H. D. Hutton, Tran., F. Fletcher, Ed. & Intro.). London: Heineman.

_____. (1975). *Auguste Comte and positivism: The essential writings*. (G. Lenzer, Ed. & Intro.). (Writings from 1819, 1822, 1830-1842, 1851-1854). New York: Harper & Row.

Conger, R. D. & Elder, G. H., Jr. (Eds.). (1994). *Families in troubled times: Adapting to change in rural America*. Hawthorne, NY: Aldine DeGruyter.

Cook, K. S. (1987). *Social exchange theory* (tribute to R. M. Emerson). London: Sage.

Cook, K. S., & Emerson, R. M. (1978). Power, equity, and commitment in exchange networks. *ASR, 43,* 721-739.

Cook, K. S., O'Brien, J., & Kollock, P. (1990). Exchange theory: A blueprint for structure and process. In *Frontiers of social theory: The new syntheses*. Ritzer, G., ed. New York: Columbia Univ. Press.

Cook, K. S., & Whitmeyer, J. M. (1992). Two approaches to social structure: Exchange theory and network analysis. *Annual Review of Sociology, 18.*

Cooley, C. H. (1902). *Human nature and the social order*. New Y.: Scribner.

_____. (1908). A study of the early use of self-words by a child. *Psychological Review, 15,* 339-357.

Copp, J. H. (1964). *Our changing rural society*. Ames: Iowa State Univ. Press.

_____. (1983). *Agricultural mechanization* (CAST Report No. 96). Ames, IA: Council for Agricultural Science & Technology.

_____. (1984). Agricultural mechanization: Physical and societal effects and implications for policy development. In *The social consequences and challenges of new agricultural technologies*. G. M. Berardi & C. C. Geisler, eds. Boulder, CO: Westview.

Copp, J. H., Sill, M. L., & Brown, E. J. (1958). The function of information sources in the farm practice adoption process. *Rural Soc., 23*, 146-157.

Coser, L. A. (1956). *The functions of social conflict*. New York: Free Press.

_____. (1967). *Continuities in the study of social conflict*. NYC: Free Press.

_____. (1977). *Masters of sociological thought, Ideas in historical and social context*, 2nd ed. New York: Harcourt Brace & Jovanovich.

Coughenour, C. M. (1965). The problem of reliability of adoption data in survey research. *Rural Sociology, 30*, 184-203.

_____. (1984). Farmers and farm workers: Perspectives on occupational complexity and change. *Research in Rural Sociology and Development, 1*, 1-35.

Cowan, P. A. (1991). Individual and family life transitions: A proposal for a new definition. In *Family transitions*. P. A. Cowan & M. Hetherington, eds. Hillsdale, NJ: L. Erlbaum.

Cowan, P. A., & Hetherington, M. (1991). *Family transitions*. Family Research Consortium: Advances in Family Research. Hillsdale, NJ: L. Erlbaum.

Coward, R. T., & Smith, W. M. Jr. (Eds.), (1981). *The family in rural society*. Boulder, CO: Westview.

Cromwell, R. E., & Olson, D. H. (Eds.). (1975). *Power in families*. Beverly Hills, CA: Sage.

Cross, J. G. (1983). *A theory of adaptive economic behavior* (psychological aspects). New York: Cambridge Univ. Press.

Crozier, M. (1971). The relationship between micro and macro-sociology. *HR, 25*, 239-251.

Curtis, J. E. & Petras, J. W., (Eds). (1970). *The sociology of knowledge*. New York: Praeger.

Dahl, R. (1957). The concept of power. *Behavioral Science, 2*, 201-218.

Dahlberg, K. A. (Ed.). (1986). *New directions for agriculture and agricultural research: Neglected dimensions and emerging alternatives*. Totowa, NJ: Rowman & Allanheld.

Dahrendorf, R. (1959). *Class and conflict in industrial society*. Stanford: Stanford Univ. Press.

Daloz, L. A. P., Keen, C. H., Keen, J. P., & Parks, S. D. (1996). *Common fire: Lives of commitment in a complex world*. Boston: Beacon Press.

Davis, J. A. (1963). Structural balance, mechanical solidarity, and interpersonal relations. *AJS, 68*: 444-462.

Davis, K. (1959). The myth of functional analysis as a special method in sociology and anthropology. *ASR, 24*, 757-772.

Deming, W. E. (1944). On errors in surveys. *ASR, 9*, 359-369.

Demos, J. (1986). *Past, present, and personal: The family and the life course in American history*. New York: Oxford Univ. Press.

Denzin, N. K. (1986). Postmodern social theory. *Sociological Theory, 4*.

Dewey, J. (1938). *Logic: The theory of inquiry*. New York: Holt.

DeWitt, M. R. (1967). A conversion technique for controlling analyses of population change (from M. S. thesis, Univ. of Wisconsin-Madison). Paper presented at annual mtg. of Population Assn. of America, Chicago.

_____. (1981). 'Conferred exchange' - An expansion of social exchange theory. Paper presented at the Theory and Methods Pre-conference Workshop, NCFR annual conference, Milwaukee, WI.

Dienstbier, R. A. (Ed.). (1991). *Perspectives on motivation: Nebraska symposium on motivation*. Lincoln: Univ. of Nebraska Press.

Dijkstra, W. & Van der Zouwen, J. (Eds.). (1982). *Response behavior in the survey interview*. London: Academic Press.

Dillman, D. A., & Hobbs, D. J. (Eds.). (1982). *Rural society in the U.S.: Issues for the 1980s.* Boulder, CO: Westview.

Di Tomaso, N. (1982). Sociological reductionism from Parsons to Althusser: Linking action and structure in social theory. *ASR, 47,* 14-28.

Dix, L. C. (1957). 'Decision-making in the farm family.' Masters thesis, Cornell University, Ithaca, NY (Unpublished).

Dixon, V. (1976). World views and research methodology. In *African philosophy: Assumptions and paradigms for research on Black persons.* L. M. King, V. Dixon, & W. W. Nobles, eds. Los Angeles: Fanon Center, C. R. Drew Postgraduate School.

Donaldson, L. (1994). The liberal revolution and organization theory. In *Towards a new theory of organizations.* J. Hassard & M. Parker, eds. London: Routledge.

Donovan, J. (1986). *Feminist theory.* New York: Ungar.

Dorner, P. (1955). An extension philosophy for farm and home development work. *Journal of Farm Economics, 37,* 493-505.

_____. (1956). What's ahead for families on small farms? *Economic Information for Wisconsin Farmers, 27,* No. 1. Madison, WI: Univ. of Wisconsin, College of Agriculture, Extension Service.

_____. (1981). *Economic and social changes on Wisconsin family farms.* Research Bulletin R3105. Madison, WI: Univ. of Wis. Research Division of the College of Agricultural and Life Sciences (CAL).

Dorner, P., & Marquardt, M. (1977). *Economic changes in a sample of Wisconsin farms: 1950-1975.* Madison, WI: Univ. of Wis. Agricultural Economics Staff paper Series, No. 135.

Dorner, P., & Marquardt, M. (1978). *Land transfers and funds needed to start farming: A sample of Wisconsin Farms 1950-1975.* Madison, WI: Univ. of Wis. Agricultural Economics Staff paper Series, No. 148.

Dorner, P., & Marquardt, M. (1979). *The family's role in the Wisconsin family farm.* Madison, WI: Univ. of Wis. Ag. Econ. Staff paper Series, No. 171.

Douglass, G. K., (Ed.). (1984) *Agricultural sustainability in a changing world order.* Boulder, CO: Westview.

Draper, T. W., & Marcos, A. C. (Eds.). (1990). *Family variables: Conceptualization, measurement, and use.* Newbury Park, CA: Sage.

Dubin, R. (1978) *Theory building* (first published in 1969). NYC: Free Press.

Duncan, D. B. (1955). Multiple range and multiple F tests. *Biometrics, 11.*

Duncan, O. D. (1966). Path analysis: Sociological examples. *AJS, 72,* 1-16

Duncan, R. B. (1972). Characteristics of organizational environments and perceived environmental uncertainty. *Admin. Science Quarterly, 17.*

Dunn, E. S., Jr. (1971). The emerging social science paradigm: Optional portals. In E. S. Dunn, Jr., *Economic and social development.* Baltimore, MD: Johns Hopkins Press.

Dunn, O. (1961). Multiple comparisons among means. *JASA, 56,* 52-64.

_____. (1974). On multiple tests and confidence intervals. *Communications in Statistics, 3,* 101-103.

Dunnett, C. (1955). A multiple comparison procedure for comparing several treatments with a control. *JASA, 50,* 1096-1121.

_____. (1982). Robust multiple comparisons. *Communications in Statistics -Theory and Methods, 11,* 2611-2629.

Durkheim, E. (1966). *Suicide: A study in sociology* (J. A. Spaulding & G. Simpson, Trans.). Glencoe, IL: Free Press. (First published in 1897).

_____. (1982). *The rules of sociological method.* (W. D. Halls, Tran.). New York: Free Press. (First published in 1895).

_____. (1984). *The division of labor in society.* (W. D. Halls, Trans.; introduction by L. A. Coser). NYC: Free Press. (First published in 1893).

_____. (1915). *Elementary forms of the religious life.* (K. E. Fields, Tran.) NYC: Free Press. (First published in 1912, reissued 1965, 1995).

DuVall, E. (1971). *Family development* (4th ed.). Philadelphia: Lippincott.

_____. (1977). *Marriage and family development* (5th ed.). Philadelphia: Lippincott.

Dyer, W. G. & Urban, D. (1958). The institutionalization of egalitarian family norms. *Marriage and Family Living (now JMF), 20*, 53-58.

Edwards, A. L. (1985). *Multiple regression and the analysis of variance and covariance* (2nd. ed.). New York: Freeman.

Edwards, G. (1979). Familiar groups as molecules of society. In *The family in post-industrial America*, Selected AAAS symposium No. 32, pp. 89-93. D. P. Snyder, ed. Boulder, CO: Westview.

Edwards, J. N. (1969a). Familial behavior as social exchange. *JMF, 31*.

_____, (Ed.). (1969b). *The family and change*. New York: A. Knopf.

Edwards, W. (1954). The theory of decision-making. *Psych. Bulletin, 51*.

Eisenstadt, S. (1978). *Revolution and the transformation of societies*. New York: Free Press.

Ekeh, P. (1974). *Social exchange theory*. London: Heineman.

Elder, G. H. Jr. (1978). Approaches to social change and the family. In *Turning points*. S. Boocock & J. Demos, eds. Chicago: Univ. of Chicago Press *(published as AJS, 84)*.

_____. (1981). History and the family: The discovery of complexity. *JMF, 43*, 489-519.

_____. (1987). Families and lives: Developments in life course studies. *Journal of Family History, 12*, 179-199.

_____. (1991). Family transitions, cycles, and social change. In *Family transitions*. P. A. Cowan & M. Hetherington, eds. Hillsdale, NJ: L. Erlbaum.

Elder, J. W. (1972). Social and cultural factors in agricultural development. In *The political economy of development: Theoretical and empirical contributions*. N. T. Uphoff, & W.F. Ilchman, eds. Berkeley: Univ. of California Press.

Ellis, D. (1971). The Hobbesian problem of order. *ASR, 36*, 692-703.

Elster, J. (Ed.). (1986). *Rational choice*. New York: New York Univ. Press.

Emerson, R. M. (1972). Exchange theory, part I: A psychological basis for exchange: part II: Exchange relations and network structures. In *Sociological theories in progress* (Vol. 2). J. Berger, M Zelditch, Jr., & B. Anderson, eds. New York: Houghton-Mifflin.

_____. (1976). Social exchange theory. *Annual Review of Sociology, 2*, pp. 335-362. Palo Alto, CA: Annual Reviews, Inc.

_____. (1981). Social exchange theory. In *Social psychology: Sociological perspectives*. M. Rosenburg & R. H. Turner, eds. New York: Basic Books.

Etzioni, A. (1970). Toward a macrosociology. In *Macrosociology*. J. S. Coleman, A. Etzioni & J. Porter, eds. Boston: Allyn & Bacon.

Evans, N. J., & Jarvis, P. A. (1980). Group cohesion: A review and reevaluation. *Small Group Behavior, 11*, 359-370.

Fararo, T. J. (1989a). *The meaning of general theoretical sociology: Tradition and formalization*, ASA Rose Monograph. NYC: Cambridge Univ. Press.

_____. (1989b). The spirit of unification in sociological theory. *Sociological Theory, 7*

_____, (Ed.). (1984). *Mathematical ideas and sociological theory*. New York: Gordon & Breach.

Fararo, T. J., & Skvoretz, J. (1989). Theoretical integration: Methods and problems. Paper presented at the Stanford Conference on Theory Growth and the Study of Group Process, August.

Farber, B. (1964). *Family organization and interaction*. San Francisco: Chandler.

Farrington, K. & Foss, G. E. (1981). In F. I. Nye, *Emerging conceptual frameworks* (2nd ed.). New York: Praeger.

Fassinger, P. A., & Schwarzweller, H. K. (1984). The work of farm women: A Midwestern study. *Research in Rural Sociology and Development, 1*.

Fausto-Sterling, A. (1992). *Myths of gender: Biological theories about women and men* (first published in 1985). New York: Basic Books.

Ferber, R. (1973). Family decision making and economic behavior: A review (intro. by R. Hill & D. Klein). In *Family economic behavior: Problems and prospects*, pp. 25-61. E. B. Sheldon, ed. Philadelphia: Lippincott.

Festinger, L. A. (1957). *A theory of cognitive dissonance*. Evanston, IL: Row, Peterson.

Fiedler, F. E. (1966). The effect of leadership and cultural heterogeneity on group performance: A test of the contingency model. *Journal of Experimental Social Psychology, 2*, 237-264.

_____. (1967). *A theory of leadership effectiveness*. NYC: McGraw-Hill.

_____. (1978). Recent developments in research on the contingency model. In *Group processes*. L. Berkowitz, ed. NYC: Academic Press.

_____. (1981). Leadership effectiveness. *American Behavioral Scientist, 24*, 619-632.

Fielding, N. C. (Ed.). (1988). *Actions and structure: Research methods and social theory*. London: Sage.

Finch, J. (1993). *Negotiating family responsibilities*. NYC: Tavistock/Routledge.

Fishbein, M. (1967). Attitude and the prediction of behavior. In *Readings in attitude theory and measurement*, pp. 477-492. M. Fishbein, ed. New York: Wiley.

Fishbein, M., & Ajzen I. (1975). *Belief, attitude, intention and behavior, An introduction to theory and research*. Reading, MA.: Addison-Wesley.

Fisher, R. (1949). *The design of experiments*. Edinburgh, UK: Oliver & Boyd.

Fliegel, F. C. (1956). A multiple correlation analysis of factors associated with adoption of farm practices. *Rural Sociology, 21*, 284-292.

_____. (1957). Farm income and the adoption of farm practices. *Rural Sociology, 22*, 159-162.

_____. (1962). Traditionalism in the farm family and technological change. *Rural Sociology, 27*, 70-76.

_____. (1993). *Diffusion research in rural sociology: The record and prospects for the future.* (Foreword by J. J. Zuiches). Westport, CT: Greenwood.

Fliegel, F. C., & van Es, J. C. (1983). The diffusion-adoption process in agriculture: Changes in technology and changing paradigms. In *Technology and social change in rural areas*, pp. 13-28. G. F. Summers, ed. Boulder: Westview.

Flora, C. B. & Flora, J. L. (1988). Structure of agriculture and women's culture in the Great Plains. *Great Plains Quarterly, 8*, 195-205.

Flora, C. B., & Johnson, S. (1978). Discarding the distaff: New roles for rural women. In *Rural U.S.A.: Persistence and Change*, pp. 168-181. T. R. Ford, ed. Ames, IA: Iowa State Univ. Press.

Flora, C. B., & Stitz, J. M. (1984). Land tenure, patriarchy, and the family farm: Changes and continuities in dryland agriculture in Western Kansas. Paper presented at the American Farm Women in Historical Perspective Conference, New Mexico State University, Las Cruces, 2-4 February.

Foote, N. N. (1951). Identification as the basis for a theory of motives. *ASR, 16.*

_____, (Ed.). (1961). *Household decision-making*, p 260. New York: New York Univ. Press.

Freese, L. (Ed.). (1980). *Theoretical methods in sociology.* Pittsburgh: Univ. of Pittsburgh Press.

French, J. R. P., Jr. (1956). A formal theory of social power. *Psych. Review, 63*, 181-194

French, J. R. P., Jr., & Raven B. H. (1959). The bases of social power. In *Studies in social power.* D. Cartwright, ed. Ann Arbor, MI: Institute for Social Research.

French, J. R. P., Jr., & Snyder, R. (1959). Leadership and interpersonal power. In *Studies in social power.* D. Cartwright, ed. Ann Arbor, MI: Institute for Social Research.

Freud, S. (1959). Formulas regarding the two principles in mental functioning. In *General psychological theory* from *Collected papers* (Vol. 4). New York: Basic Books. (First published 1911)

_____. (1961). *Beyond the pleasure principle* (revised ed.). (J. Strachey, Tran.). London: Hogarth. (First published 1920).

_____. (1963). *Character and culture*. (P. Rieff, Ed. & Intro.) New York: Collier Books. (First published 1915 to 1932)

Friedland, Wm. H. et al. (Eds.). (1991). *Towards a new political economy of agriculture*. Boulder, CO: Westview.

Friedmann, H. (1982). The political economy of food: The rise and fall of the postwar international food order. *AJS, 88 (Supplement)*, S248-286.

Friedmann, H., & McMichael, P. (1989). The world-historical development of agriculture: Western agriculture in comparative perspective. *Sociologia Ruralis, 29*.

Galeski, B. (1972). *Basic concepts in rural sociology*. Manchester: Univ. of Manchester Press.

Galjart, B. (1971) Rural development and sociological concepts: A critique. *Rural Sociology, 36*, 31-41.

Garcia-Ramon, M. D. & Canoves, G. (1988). The role of women on the family farm. *Sociologia Ruralis, 28*, 263-270.

Gardner, G. (1996). Preserving agricultural resources. In L. R. Brown, et al., *State of the world: A Worldwatch Institute report on progress toward a sustainable society*, pp. 78-94. New York: W. W. Norton.

Garfinkel, H. (1984). *Studies in ethnomethodology* (first published in 1967, Englewood Cliffs, NJ: Prentice-Hall). Cambridge: Polity Press.

Garrett, P., & Schulman, M. D. (1989). Family division of labor and decision-making among smallholders. *Sociology & Social Research, 74*.

Gartrell, C. D, & Gartrell, J. W. (1985). Social status and agricultural innovation: A meta-analysis. *Rural Sociology, 50*, 38-50.

Gasson, R. (1988). Changing gender roles: A workshop report. *Sociologia Ruralis, 28*, 300-305.

_____. (1992). Farm wives: Their contribution to the farm business. *Journal of Agricultural Economics, 43*, 74-87.

Gasson, R., et al. (1988). The farm as a family business: A review. *Journal of Agricultural Economics, 39*, 1-41.

Gatlin, R. (1987). *American women since 1945.* Jackson, MS: Univ. Press of Mississippi.

Gaventa, J. (1980). *Power and powerlessness.* Urbana: Univ. of Illinois Press.

Gergen, K. J. (1992). Organization theory in the postmodern era. In *Rethinking organization: New directions in organization theory & analysis.* M. Reed & M. Hughes, eds. London: Sage.

_____. (1994). *Realities and relationships: Soundings in social construction.* Cambridge, MA: Harvard Univ. Press.

_____. (1995). Relational theory and the discourses of power. In *Management and organization: Relational alternatives to individualism.* D-M. Hosking, et al., eds. Brookfield, VT: Ashgate.

Gibbs, J. (1972). *Sociological theory construction.* Hinsdale, IL: Dryden Press.

_____. (1982). Evidence of causation. *Current Perspectives in Social Theory, 3,* 93-127.

_____. (1989). *Control: Sociology's central notion.* Urbana, IL: Univ. of Illinois Press.

_____. (1990). The notion of a theory in sociology. *National Journal of Sociology, 4,* 1-30.

_____. (1994). *A theory about control.* Boulder, CO: Westview.

Giddens, A. (1971). Fundamental concepts of sociology. In *Capitalism and modern social theory: An analysis of the writings of Marx, Durkheim and Max Weber.* A. Giddens, ed. Cambridge: Cambridge Univ. Press.

_____. (1976). *New rules of sociological method: A positive critique of interpretive sociologies.* New York: Basic Books.

_____. (1979). *Central problems in social theory: Action, structure and contradiction in social analysis.* Berkeley: Univ. of California Press.

_____. (1987). *Social theory and modern sociology.* Cambridge: Polity Press.

Giddens, A., & Turner, J. H. (Eds.). (1987). *Social theory today.* Stanford, CA: Stanford Univ. Press.

Giere, R. N. (Ed.). *Cognitive models of science.* Minneapolis: U. of MN Press.

Gilbert, J. (1982). Rural theory: The grounding of rural sociology. *Rural Sociology, 47,* 609-633.

Gilbert, J., & Akor, R. (1988). Increasing structural divergence in U.S. dairying: California and Wisconsin since 1950. *Rural Soc., 53,* 56-72.

Gilbert, J. & Barnes, F. (1988). Reproduction or transformation of family farming?: An empirical analysis of Wisconsin farms, 1950-1975. Paper presented at the RSS annual meeting, Athens, GA, August.

Gilespie, D. (1984). 'Who has the power?' In B. N. Adams & J. L. Campbell, *Framing the family: Contemporary portraits.* Prospect Heights, IL: Waveland Press.

Gillette, J. M. (1913). *Constructive rural sociology.* NYC: Sturgis & Walton.

Gilligan, C. (1982). *In a different voice.* Cambridge, MA: Harvard Univ. Press.

Gladwin, C. H. (1985). Changes in women's roles on the farm: A response to the intensification or capitalization of agriculture? Paper presented at the Center for Rural Women, Pennsylvania State University, March.

_____. (1993). Women and structural adjustment in a global economy. In *The women and international development annual* (Vol. 3). R. S. Gallin, A. Ferguson, & J. Harper, eds. Boulder, CO: Westview.

Glaser, B. G., & Strauss, A. L. (1967). *The discovery of grounded theory.* Chicago: Aldine.

Glen, E. N. (1987). Gender and the family. In *Analyzing gender: A handbook of social science research.* B. B. Hess & M. M. Ferree, eds. Newbury Park, CA: Sage.

Goffman, E. (1972). *The presentation of self in everyday life* (first published: 1959, Garden City, NJ: Doubleday). Harmondsworth: Penguin.

_____. (1974). *Frame analysis: An essay on the organization of experience.* Cambridge: Harvard Univ. Press; also NYC: Harper & Row.

_____. (1983). The interaction order. *ASR, 48*, 1-17.

Goldman, E. (1970). *The traffic in women and other essays on feminism.* New York: Times Change Press. (First published in 1917.)

Goldschmidt, W. (1978). Large-scale farming and the rural social structure. *Rural Sociology, 43*, 362-366.

Gollwitzer, P. M. (1993). Goal achievement: The role of intentions. In *European review of social psychology, Vol. 4*, pp. 141-185. M. Hewstone & W. Stroebe, eds. Chichester, England: Wiley.

Goode, W. J. (1963). *World revolutions and family patterns.* NYC: Free Press.

_____. (1968). The theory and measurement of family change. In *Indicators of social change: Concepts and measurement*, pp. 295-256. E. B. Sheldon & W. E. Moore, eds. New York: Sage.

Goodman, D., & Redclift, M., (Eds.). (1989). *The international farm crisis.* London: Macmillan.

Goss, K. F. (1979). Consequences of diffusion of innovations. *Rural Sociology, 44*, 802-806.

Gouldner, A. W. (1960). The norm of reciprocity: A preliminary statement. *ASR, 25*, 161-178.

_____. (1970). *The coming crisis of western sociology.* New York: Basic Books.

Gray, I., Dunn, T., & Phillips, E. (1997). Power, interests, and the extension of sustainable agriculture. *Sociologia Ruralis, 37*, 97-113.

Gray, L. N., & Griffith, W. I. (1984). On differentiation in small group power relations. *Social Psychology Quarterly, 47*, 391-396.

Gray, L. N., Mayhew, B. H. Jr., & Campbell, R. (1974). Communication and three dimensions of power: An experiment and a simulation. *Small Group Behavior, 5*, 289-320.

Gray, L. N., Richardson, J. T., & Mayhew, B. H. Jr. (1968). Influence attempts and effective power: A reexamination of an unsubstantiated hypothesis. *Sociometry, 31*, 245-258.

Gray, L. N., & Stafford, M. C. (1988). On choice behavior in individual and social situations. *Social Psychology Quarterly, 51*, 58-65.

Gray, P. G. (1955). The memory factor in social surveys. *JASA, 55*, 344-363.

Green, G. P. (1987). *Finance capital and uneven development* (in agriculture). Boulder, CO: Westview.

Gross, N. C. (1949). The differential characteristics of acceptors and non-acceptors of an approved agricultural technological practice. *Rural Sociology, 14*, 148-158.

Gross, N. C., & Taves, M. J. (1952). Characteristics associated with acceptance of recommended farm practices. *Rural Sociology, 17*, 321-327.

Gullotta, T. P., Adams, G. R., & Alexander, S. J. (1986). *Today's marriages and families*. Monterey, CA: Brooks/Cole.

Gusfield, J. R. (1967). Tradition and modernity: Misplaced polarities in the study of social change. *AJS, 72*, 351-362.

Habermas, J. (1967). *On the logic of the social sciences*. Cambridge: Polity Press.

_____. (1981a). Talcott Parsons: Problems of theory construction. *Sociological Inquiry, 51*, 173-196.

_____. (1981b). *The theory of communicative action*, (Vol. I): *Reason and the rationalization of society*. London: Heinemann.

_____. (1981c). *The theory of communicative action*, (Vol. II): *The critique of functionalist reason*. London: Heinemann.

Hadwiger, D. F. (1982). *The politics of agricultural research*. Lincoln: Univ. of Nebraska Press.

Hage, J. (1972). *Techniques and problems of theory construction in sociology*. New York: Wiley.

_____, (Ed.). (1994). *Formal theory in sociology: Opportunity or pitfall?* Albany: SUNY Press.

Hage, J., & Meeker, B. F. (1988). *Social causality*. Boston: Unwin Hyman.

Hage, J., & Powers, C. H. (1992). *Post-industrial lives: Roles and relationships in the 21st century*. Newbury Park, CA: Sage.

Hall, R. H. (1991). *Organizations: Structures, processes, and outcomes* (5th ed.). Englewood Cliffs, NJ: Prentice-Hall.

Hamblin, R. L., & Kunkel, J. H. (Eds.). (1977). *Behavioral theory in sociology*. New Brunswick, NJ: Transaction Books.

Handel, W. (1979). Convergence of structural and interactionist views. *AJS, 84*, 855-885.

Haney, W. G. (1983). Farm family and the role of women. In *Technology and social change in rural areas*. G. F. Summers, ed. Boulder, CO: Westview.

Haney, W. G., & Knowles, J. B., (Eds.). (1988). *Women and farming: changing roles, changing structures*. Boulder, CO: Westview.

Hannan, D. F., & Katsiaouni, L. A. (1977). *Traditional families? From culturally prescribed to negotiated roles in farm families*. Dublin: Economic and Social Research Institute.

Harding, S. (1986). *The science question in feminism*. Ithaca: Cornell Univ. Press.

_____, (Ed.). (1993). *The "racial" economy of science: Toward a democratic future*. Bloomington, IN: Indiana Univ. Press.

Hare, A. P., Borgatta, E. F., & Bales, R F. (Eds.). *Small groups: Studies in social interaction*. New York: A. Knopf.

Hareven, T. K. (1978). *Transitions: The family and the life course in historical perspective*. New York: Academic Press.

_____. (1996). The impact of the historical study of the family and the life course paradigm on sociology. In *Normative social action*. D. Sciulli, ed. Greenwich, CT: JAI Press.

Harris, C. K., & Gilbert, J. (1982). Large-scale farming, rural income, and Goldschmidt's agrarian thesis. *Rural Sociology, 47* pp 449-458.

Hartsock, N. (1985). *Money, sex and power*. Boston: Northeastern Univ. Press.

_____. (1990). Foucault on power: A theory for women? In *Feminism/Postmodernism*. L. J. Nicholson, ed. New York: Routledge.

Harvey, O. J. (1963). *Motivation and social interaction, Cognitive determinants*. New York: Ronald Press.

Hassard, J. (1993). *Sociology and organizational theory: Positivism, paradigms and post-modernity*. New York: Cambridge Univ. Press.

Hassard, J., & Parker, M. (Eds.). (1994). *Towards a new theory of organizations*. New York: Routledge.

Hassard, J., & Pym, D. (Eds.). (1990). *The theory and philosophy of organizations: Critical issues and new perspectives*. NYC: Routledge.

Hatfield (Walster), E., Walster, G. W., & Berscheid, E. (1978). *Equity*. Boston: Allyn & Bacon.

Haugaard, M. (1992). *Structures, restructuration and social power*. Brookfield, VT: Ashgate.

Havens, A. E., et al., (Eds.). (1986). *Studies in the transformation of U. S. agriculture*. Boulder, CO: Westview.

Hays, W. L. (1981). *Statistics* (3rd ed.). New York: Holt Rinehart & Winston.

_____. (1988). *Statistics* (4th ed.) New York: Holt Rinehart & Winston.

Hayter, A. (1986). The maximum family-wise error rate of Fisher's least significant difference test. *JASA, 81*, 1000-1004.

Heath, A. (1976). *Rational choice and social exchange A critique of exchange theory*. Cambridge: Cambridge Univ. Press.

Heffernan, W. D., & Heffernan, J. B. (1986). Impact of the farm crisis on rural families and communities. *The Rural Sociologist, 6*, 160-170.

Heider, F. (1944). Social perception and phenomenal causality. *Psychological Review, 51*, 258-274.

_____. (1946). Attitudes and cognitive organization. *Journal of Psychology, 21*, 107-112.

_____. (1958). *The psychology of interpersonal relations*. NYC: Wiley.

Heise, D. (1975). *Causal analysis*. New York: Wiley.

_____. (1979). *Understanding events: Affect and the construction of social action*. New York: Cambridge Univ. Press.

Heise, D., & Lewis, E. (1988). *Introduction to INTERACT*. Durham, NC: National Collegiate Software Clearinghouse, Duke Univ. Press.

Hempel, C. G. (1965). *Aspects of scientific explanation*. New York: Free Press.

Henderson, A. H. (1981). *Social power: Social psychological models and theories*. New York: Praeger.

Herschberger, R. (1970). *Adam's rib* (First published in 1948). New York: Harper & Row.

Hill, R. (1965). Decision making and the family life cycle. In *Social structure and the family: Generational relations*. E. Shanas & G. Streib, eds. Englewood Cliffs, NJ: Prentice-Hall.

Hill, R., et al. (1970). *Family development in three generations*. Cambridge, MA: Schenkman.

Hill, R., & Rodgers, R. H. (1964). The developmental approach. In *Handbook of marriage and the family*, pp. 171-209. H. T. Christensen, ed. Chicago: Rand McNally.

Hiller, D. V. & Philliber, W. W. (1986). The division of labor in contemporary marriage: Expectations, perceptions, and performance. *Social Problems, 33*, 191-201.

Hinkle, R. C. (1963). Antecedents of the action orientation in American sociology before 1935. *ASR, 28*, 705-715.

Hobbes, T. (1962). *Leviathan* (elements in human nature: uses of power). Harmondsworth, UK: Penguin Books. (First published 1651).

Hochschild, A. (1975). Sociology of emotions and feelings. In M. Millman & R. M. Kantor, *Another voice*. New York: Doubleday.

_____. (1989). *The second shift: Working parents and the revolution at home*. New York: Viking.

Hoffer, C. M., & Stangland, D. (1958). Farmers' attitudes and values in relation to adoption of approved practices in corn growing. *Rural Sociology, 23*, 112-120.

Hoffman, L. R. (1965). Group problem solving. In *Advances in experimental social psychology* (Vol. 2). L. Berkowitz, ed. NYC: Academic Press.

_____, (Ed.). (1979). *The group problem solving process: Studies of a valence model.* New York: Praeger.

Hogarth, R. M., & Reder, M. W. (Eds.). (1986). *Rational choice: The contrast between economics and psychology.* Chicago: Univ. of Chicago Press.

Hollander, E. P., & Julian, J. W. (1970). Studies in leader legitimacy, influence, and innovation. In *Advances in experimental social psychology* (Vol. 5). L. Berkowitz, ed. New York: Academic Press.

Homans, G. C. (1950). *The human group.* New York: Harcourt Brace.

_____. (1958). Social behavior as exchange. *AJS, 63*, 597-606.

_____. (1961). *Social behavior: Its elementary forms.* New York: Harcourt Brace & World.

_____. (1970). An essay on the nature of social theory. In *Sociological methods*, pp. 51-69. N. K. Denzin, ed. Chicago: Aldine.

Hooks, G. M., Napier, T. L., & Carter, M. V. (1983). Correlates of adoption behaviors: The case of farm technologies. *Rural Sociology, 48*, 308-323.

Hosking, D-M., Dachler, H. P., & Gergen, K. J. (Eds.). (1995). *Management and organization: Relational alternatives to individualism.* Brookfield, VT: Ashgate.

Huber, J. (1988). A theory of family, economy, and gender. *Journal of Family Issues, 9* (1).

_____, (Ed.). (1991). *Macro-Micro Linkages in Sociology.* Newbury Park, CA: Sage.

Hughes, H. S. (1958). *Consciousness and society: The reorientation of European social thought, 1890-1930.* New York: Vintage Books.

Hussain, M. Y. (1983). *Farm wives involved in decision making in Malaysia.* Doctoral dissertation, Univ. of Wisconsin, Madison, WI (unpublished).

Hymans, H. H. (1968). Reference groups. In *International Encyclopedia of the Social Sciences, 13,* 353-361. D. L. Sills, ed. New York: Macmillan.

Iannello, K. P. (1992). *Decisions without hierarchy: Feminist interventions in organization theory and practice.* New York: Routledge.

Irigaray, L. (1985). Is the subject of science sexed? *Cultural Critique, 1,* 73-88.

Jaccard, J., & Wan, C. K. (1996). *LISREL approaches to interaction effects in multiple regression.* Thousand Oaks, CA: Sage.

Jaccard, J., & Brinberg, D. (Eds.). (1989). *Dyadic decision-making.* New York: Springer-Verlag.

Jackson, J. E. (Ed.). (1990). *Institutions in American society: Essays in market, political and social organizations.* Ann Arbor, MI: Univ. of Mich. Press.

Jaeger, C. M., & Pennock, J. L. (1961). An analysis of consistency of response in household surveys. *JASA, 56,* 320-327.

James, W. (1952). *The principles of psychology.* Chicago: Britannica. (First published 1891).

Jasso, G. (1988). Principles of theoretical analysis. *Sociological Theory, 6.*

Jellison, K. K. (1991). Entitled to power: Farm women and technology, 1913-1963. Doctoral dissertation, University of Iowa. Ann Arbor, MI: University Microfilms International.

Jensen, J. (1981). *With these hands: Women working on the land.* Old Westbury, New York: Feminist Press.

Johnson, D. W., Maruyama, G., Johnson, R., Nelson, D., & Skon, L. (1981). Effects of cooperative, competitive, and individualistic goal structures on achievement: A meta-analysis. *Psychological Bulletin, 89,* 47-62.

Johnston, C. (1992). *Sexual power: Feminism and the family in America.* Tuscaloosa: Univ. of Alabama Press.

Jones, C. C., & Rosenfeld, R. A. with L. Olson. (1981) *American farm women: Findings from a national survey* (NORC Report No. 130). Chicago, IL: National Opinion Research Center.

Jones, E. H. & Gerard, H. H. (1967). *Foundations of social psychology.* New York: Wiley.

Judson, D. H., & Gray, L. N. (1990). Modifying power asymmetry in dyads via environmental reinforcement contingencies. *Small Group Research, 21.*

Kahn, R. L., & Zald, M. N. (Eds.). (1990). *Organizations and nation-states: New perspectives on conflict and cooperation.* San Francisco: Jossey-Bass

Kanter, R. M. (1977). *Men and women of the corporation.* NYC: Basic Books.

Kaplan, M. F. (1987). The influencing process in group decision making. In *Group processes.* C. Hendrick, ed. Newbury Park, CA: Sage.

Kaplan, M. F., & Miller, C. E. (1987). Group decision making and normative vs. informational influence: Effects of type of issue and assigned decision rule. *Journal of Personality and Social Psychology, 53*, 306-313.

Karpik, L. (1972). "Les politiques de les logiques d'action de la grande entreprise industrielle." *Sociologie du Travail, 13 (Jan.-Mar.):* 82-105.

Katz, D. & Kahn, R. L. (1978). *The social psychology of organizations.* New York: Wiley.

Katz, D., Kahn, R. L., & Adams, J. S. (1980). *The study of organizations: Findings from field and laboratory.* San Francisco: Jossey-Bass.

Katz, E., & Lazarsfeld, P. (1955). *Personal influence: The part played by people in mass communications.* Glencoe: Free Press.

Katz, E., Levin, M. L., & Hamilton, H. (1972). Traditions of research on the diffusion of innovations. In *Creating social change.* G. Zaltman, P. Kotler & I. Kaufman, eds. New York: Holt Rinehart & Winston.

Keller, E. F. (1985). *Reflections on gender and science.* New Haven, CT: Yale Univ. Press.

Kelley, H. H., & Thibaut, J. W. (1968). Group problem solving. In *Handbook of social psychology.* G. Lindzey & E. Aronson, eds. Reading, MA: Addison-Wesley.

Kelley, H. H., & Thibaut, J. W. (1978). *Interpersonal relations: A theory of interdependence*. New York: Wiley.

Kemper, T. D. (1973). The fundamental dimensions of social relationship. *Acta Sociologica, 16*, 41-57.

_____. (1978). *A social interactional theory of emotions*. NYC: Wiley.

_____, (Ed.). (1990). *Research agendas in the sociology of emotions*. Albany, NY: SUNY Press.

Kenkel, W. F. (1957). Influence differentiation in family decision-making. *Sociology and Social Research, 42*, 18-25.

Kenkel, W. F. & Hoffman, D. K. (1956). Real and conceived roles in family decision making. *Marriage and Family Living (now JMF), 18*, 311-316.

Kennedy, J. J., & Bush, A. J. (1985). *An introduction to the design and analysis of experiments in behavioral research*. New York: University Press of America.

Kenney M. F. (1986). *Biotechnology: The university-industrial complex*. New Haven, CT: Yale Univ. Press.

Keppel, G., & Zedeck, S. (1989). *Data analysis for research designs: Analysis of variance and multiple regression/ correlation approaches*. New York: Freeman.

Kirk, R. E. (1982). *Experimental design: Procedures for the behavioral sciences* (2nd ed.). Monterey, CA: Brooks/Cole.

Kirkpatrick, E. L., Tough, R., & Cowles, M. L. (1934). *The life cycle of the farm family*. Wis. AES Res. Bull. 121. Madison, WI: Coll. of Agriculture.

Klonglan, G. E., Beal, G. M., Bohlen, J. M. , & Coward, W. Jr. (1971). Conceptualizing and measuring the diffusion of innovations. *Sociologia Ruralis, 11*, 36-48.

Knop, E. & Knop, S. (1994). Addressing full-family dynamics in rural development. In *Tools for the Field: Methodologies handbook for gender analysis in agriculture*, pp. 73-79. H. S. Feldstein & J. Jiggins, eds. West Hartford, CT: Kumarian.

Knorr-Cetina, K., & Cicourel, A. V. (1981). *Advances in social theory and methodology: Towards an integration of micro- and macro-sociologies.* Boston: Routledge & Kegan Paul.

Kockelmans, J. J. (1966). *Phenomenology and physical science.* Pittsburgh, Pa.: Duquesne Univ. Press.

_____, (Ed.). (1967). *Phenomenology, The philosophy of Edmund Husserl and its interpretation.* Garden City, NY: Doubleday (Anchor).

Kogan, N., & Wallach, M. A. (1964). *Risk taking: A study in cognition and personality.* New York: Holt Rinehart & Winston.

Kohl, S. B. (1977). Women's participation in the North American family farm. *Women's Studies International Quarterly, 1,* 47-54.

Kohlberg. L. (1969). Stage and sequence: The cognitive-developmental approach to socialization. In *Handbook of socialization theory and research.* D. Goslin, ed. Chicago: Rand McNally.

Komarovsky, M. (1953). *Women in the modern world: Their education and their dilemmas.* Boston: Little, Brown.

_____. (1973). Some problems in role analysis (ASA Presidential address). *ASR, 38,* 649-662.

_____. (1988). The new feminist scholarship: Some precursors and polemics. *JMF, 50,* 585-593.

Krishnan-Namboodiri, N., Carter, L. F., & Blalock, H. M., Jr. (1975). *Applied multivariate analysis and experimental designs.* NYC: McGraw-Hill.

Kroeber, A. L. & Kluckhohn, C. (1963). *Culture: A critical review of concepts and definitions.* New York: Vintage Books.

Krohn, G. M. (1969). Power in family decision-making: Perceptual differences of husbands and wives. MBA thesis, Univ. of Wisconsin, School of Business. (Unpublished).

Kuhl, J., & Beckmann, J. (Eds.). (1994). *Volition and Personality: Action versus state orientation.* Gottingen, Germany: Hogrefe.

Kuhn, T. S. (1966). *The structure of scientific revolutions* (first published in 1962, in the *International Encyclopedia of Unified Science, 2)*. Chicago: Univ. of Chicago Press.

Lackey, A. S. & Larson, O. F. (1959). Turnover and changing characteristics of the farm operator population. *Canadian Jn. of Ag. Economics, 7*, 70-85.

Lakatos, I., & Musgrave, A. (Eds.). (1970). *Criticism and the growth of knowledge*. Cambridge: Cambridge Univ. Press.

Lantz, H. R. (1984). Continuities and discontinuities in American sociology. *The Sociological Quarterly, 25*, 581-596.

Larkin, J. A., & Simon, H. A. (1987). Why a diagram is (sometimes) worth 10,000 words. *Cognitive Science, 11*, 65-100.

Latour, B. (1987). *Science in action*. Cambridge, MA: Harvard Univ. Press.

Lawler, E. J. (Ed.). (1986). *Advances in group processes* (Vol. 3). Greenwich, CT: JAI Press.

Lawler, E. J., & Markovsky, B. (Eds.). (1987). *Advances in group processes* (Vol. 4). Greenwich, CT: JAI Press

Lawrence, P. R., & Lorsch, J. W. (1967). *Organization and environment: Managing differentiation and integration*. Cambridge, MA: Harvard Graduate School of Business Admin.

Lazarsfeld, P. F. (1972). *Qualitative analysis: History and critical essays*. Boston: Allyn & Bacon.

Leik, R. K. (1963). Instrumentality and emotionality in family interaction. *Sociometry, 26*, 131-145.

LeMasters, E. E. (1975). *Blue-collar aristocrats: Lifestyles in a working-class tavern*. Madison: Univ. of Wisconsin Press.

Lenski, G. (1988). Rethinking macrosociological theory. *ASR, 53*, 163-171.

Leventhal, H. (1980). Toward a comprehensive theory of emotion. In *Advances in experimental social psychology* (Vol. 13). L. Berkowitz, ed. New York: Academic Press.

Levine, D. (1989). 'Parsons' structure (and Simmel) revisited. *Sociological Theory, 7*.

Levine, J. M., & Russo, E. M. (1987). Majority and minority influence. In *Group processes.* C. Hendrick, ed. Newbury Park, CA: Sage.

Lewin, K. (1938). *The conceptual representation and the measurement of psychological forces.* Durham, NC: Duke Univ. Press.

———. (1946). Behavior and development as a function of the total situation. In *Manual of child psychology.* L. Carmichael, ed. NYC: Wiley

———. (1947). Group decision and social change. In *Readings in social psychology* (1st ed.). T. Newcomb & E. L. Hartley, eds. New York: Holt.

———. (1951). *Field theory in social science.* New York: Harper & Row.

———. (1958). *Resolving social conflicts: Selected papers on group dynamics: 1935-1946.* (G. W. Lewin, Ed.; first published in 1948). New York: Harper.

Lewin, K., Lippitt, R., & White, R. K. (1939). Patterns of aggressive behavior in experimentally created 'social climates.' *Jn. of Social Psychology, 10.*

Lewis, G. H. (1972). Role differentiation. *ASR, 37,* 424-434.

Linn, J. G. (1983). Task performance and decision-making as related to marital satisfaction in Wis. farm families. Doctoral diss., Univ. of Wis-Madison.

Lionberger, H. F. (1960). *Adoption of new ideas and practices.* Ames, IA: Iowa State Univ. Press.

Lippitt, R., Polansky, N., Redl, F., & Rosen, S. (1958). The dynamics of power: A field study of social influence in groups of children. In *Readings in social psychology* (3rd. ed.) E. E. Maccoby, T. M. Newcomb, & E. L. Hartley, eds. New York: Holt Rinehart & Winston. (First published in 1953 in *Group dynamics.* D. Cartwright & A. Zander, eds. Evanston, IL: Row Peterson).

Lippitt, R., & White, R. K. (1947). An experimental study of leadership and group life. In *Readings in social psychology.* T. M. Newcomb, & E. L. Hartley, eds. New York: Holt.

Liska, A. (1984). A critical examination of the causal structure of the Fishbein-Ajzen attitude-behavior model. *Social Psychology Quarterly, 47,* 61-74.

Lockheed, M. E. (1985). Sex and social influence: A meta-analysis guided by theory. In *Status, rewards, and influence.* J. Berger & M. Zelditch, Jr., eds. San Francisco: Jossey-Bass.

Long, N. (Ed.). (1984). *Family and work in rural societies: Perspectives on non-wage labour.* London: Tavistock.

Loomis, C. P., & Beegle, J. A. (1957). *Rural sociology.* Englewood Cliffs, NJ: Prentice-Hall.

Lorenz, K. (1994). Competition and cooperation: Are they antagonistic or complementary? In *Sociogenesis reexamined.* W. de Graaf & R. Maier, eds. New York: Springer-Verlag.

Lorsch, J. W., & Morse, J. J. (1974). *Organizations and their members: A contingency approach.* New York: Harper & Row.

Luhmann, N. (1982). *The differentiation of society.* NYC: Columbia U. Press.

Lyson, T. A. (1985). Husband and wife work roles and the organization and operation of family farms. *JMF, 47* 759-764.

Macaulay, J., & Berkowitz, L. (1970). *Altruism and helping behavior.* NYC: Academic Press.

McClelland, D., & Winter, D. (1969). *Motivating economic achievement.* New York: Free Press.

McDonald, G. W. (1980). Family power: The assessment of a decade of theory and research, 1970-1979. *JMF, 42,* 841-854.

McDonald, G. W. & Osmond, M. W. (1980). Jealousy and trust, Unexplored dimensions of social exchange dynamics. *NCFR Theory and Methods Pre-Conference Workshop, NCFR annual mtgs.*

McKinney, J. C., & Tiriakian, E. A. (Eds.). (1970). *Theoretical sociology: Perspectives and developments.* New York: Appleton-Century-Crofts.

MacKinnon, N. J. (1994). *Symbolic interactionism as affect control.* Albany: SUNY Press.

McLeod, J. M., & Chaffee, S. H. (1972). The construction of social reality. In *The social influence processes.* J. T. Tedeschi, ed. Chicago: Aldine.

Maman, M. & Tate, T. H. (1996). *Women in agriculture: A guide to research.* New York: Garland.

Mann, M. (1986). *The sources of social power* (Vol. 1) *A history of power: From the beginning to A. D. 1756.* Cambridge: Cambridge Univ. Press.

Mannheim, K. (1936). *Ideology and utopia.* New York: Harvest Books.

March, J. G. (1953). Political issues and husband-and-wife interaction. *Public Opinion Quarterly, 17,* 461-470.

Markovski, B., Willer, D., & Patton, T. (1988). Power relations in exchange networks. *ASR, 53,* 220-236.

Markovski, B., Willer, D., & Patton, T. (1990). Theory, evidence, and intuition. *ASR, 55,* 300-305.

Marsh, C. P., & Coleman, A. L. (1955). The relation of farmer characteristics to the adoption of recommended farm practices. *Rural Sociology, 20.*

Martindale, D. (1960). *The nature and types of sociological theory.* Boston: Houghton Mifflin.

Marwell, G. (1975). *Cooperation.* New York: Academic Press.

_____. (1993). *The critical mass in collective action: a micro-macro social theory.* New York: Cambridge Univ. Press.

Marwell, G. & Schmitt, D. R. (1972). Cooperation and interpersonal risk. *Journal of Experimental Social Psychology, 8,* 594-599.

Marx, K. (1964a). *Economic and philosophical manuscripts.* (M. Milligan, Tran.; Introduction by J. Struik, Ed.). New York: International Publishers. (First published 1844).

_____. (1964b). *Selected writings in sociology and social philosophy.* (T. B. Bottomore, Ed. & Tran., Foreword by E. Fromm). New York: McGraw-Hill. (First published 1859).

_____. (1967). *Capital* (Vol. I). (S. Moore & S. Aveling, Trans.). New York: International Publishers. (First published 1867).

_____. (1976). *Capital: A critique of political economy* (3 Vols.) (B. Fowkes, Tran.; Intro. by E. Mandel). Harmondswork, UK: Penguin. (First published 1867 to 1895).

Marx, K. & Engels, F. (1970). Concerning the production of consciousness. In *The sociology of knowledge*. J. H. Curtis & J. W. Petras, eds. New York: Praeger.

Marx, K., & Engels, F. (1983). *Letters on 'Capital.'* (A. Drummond, Tran.) Detroit MI: Labor Publications.

Mead, G. H. (1934). *Mind, self and society*. Chicago: Univ. of Chicago Press.

_____. (1938). *The philosophy of the act*. Chicago: U. of Chicago Press.

_____. (1964). The genesis of the self and social control. In *Selected writings*, pp 267-293. A. Reck, ed. Indianapolis: Bobbs-Merrill.

Mead, M. (1967). The life cycle and its variations: The division of roles. *Daedalus, 96*, 871-875.

_____. (1976). A comment on the role of women in agriculture. In I. Tinker & M. B. Bramsen, *Women and world development*. Washington, D. C.: Overseas Development Council.

_____, (Ed.). (1937). *Cooperation and competition among primitive peoples*. New York: Macmillan.

Meeker, B. F., & Hornung, C. A. (1976). Strategies of interaction. *Social Science Research, 5*, 153-172.

Meeker, B. F., & Weitzel-O'Neill, P. A. (1985). Sex roles and interpersonal behavior in task-oriented groups. In *Status, rewards, and influence*. J. Berger & M. Zelditch, Jr., eds. San Francisco: Jossey-Bass.

Menzel, H. (1957). Public and private conformity under different conditions of acceptance in the group. *Journal of Abnormal and Social Psychology, 55*, 398-402.

Merchant, C. (1980). *The death of nature: Women, ecology, and the scientific revolution*. New York: Harper & Row.

Merk, F. (1978). *History of the westward movement*. New York: A. Knopf.

Merton, R. K. (1948). The self-fulfilling prophecy. *Antioch Review, 8*.

_____. (1949). Patterns of influence: A study of interpersonal influence and communication behavior in a local community. In *Community research, 1948-1949*. P. F. Lazarsfeld & F. N. Stanton, eds. New York: Harper & Row.

_____. (1968). *Social theory and social structure* (3rd ed.) New York: Free Press. (First published in 1947, 2nd ed. in 1957).

_____. (1996). *On social structure and science*. Chicago: Univ. of Chicago Press.

Merton, R. K., Broom, L., & Cottrell, L. (Eds.). (1959). *Sociology today*. New York: Basic Books.

Michener, H. A. & Burt, M. R. (1974). Legitimacy as a base of social influence. In *Perspectives on social power*. J. T. Tedeschi, ed. Chicago: Aldine Atherton.

Michener, H. A. & Burt, M. R. (1975). Use of social influence under varying conditions of legitimacy. *Jn. of Personality and Social Psychology, 32*.

Michener, H. A. & Lawler, E. J. (1975). Endorsement of formal leaders: An integrative model. *Jn of Personality and Social Psychology, 31*, 216-223.

Mills, C. W. (1940). Situated action and the vocabulary of motives. *ASR, 5*.

_____. (1959). *The sociological imagination*. NYC: Oxford Univ. Press.

_____. (1967). On knowledge and power. In *Power, politics, and people: The collected essays of C. Wright Mills*. I. L. Horowitz, ed. London: Oxford Univ. Press.

Molm, L. D. (1981). Power use in the dyad: The effects of structure, knowledge and interaction history. *Social Psychology Quarterly, 44*.

_____. (1989). Structure, action, and outcomes: A multilevel analysis of power. Paper presented at the ASA annual meeting, San Francisco, Aug.

Molm, L. D., & Wiggins, J. A. (1979). A behavioral analysis of the dynamics of social exchange in the dyad. *Social Forces, 57*, 1157-1179.

Molnar, J. J. (1986). *Agricultural change*. Boulder, CO: Westview.

Molnar, J. J., & Kinnucan, J. (Eds.). (1989). *Biotechnology and the new agricultural revolution.* Boulder, CO: Westview.

Moodie, T. D. (1976). Social order as social change. In *Social change: Explorations, diagnoses, and conjectures.* G. K. Zollschan & W. Hirsch, eds. New York: Wiley.

Mooney, P. H. (1987). Sociology and the farm crisis. *Mid-American Review of Sociology, 12*, 3-14.

_____. (1988). *My own boss? Class, rationality and the family farm.* Boulder, CO: Westview.

Moore, B. (1966). *The social origins of dictatorship and democracy.* Boston: Beacon Press.

Moore, J. C. Jr. (1968). Status and influence in small group interaction. *Sociometry, 31*, 47-63.

Moore, K. M. (1989). Agrarian or non-agrarian identities of farm spouses. *Rural Sociology, 54*, 74-82.

Moreno, J. L. (1934). *Who shall survive?* Washington, D. C.: Nervous and Mental Diseases Publishing Co.

Morgan, R., & Heise, D. (1988). Structure of emotions. *Social Psychology Quarterly, 51*, 19-31.

Morgenthau, H. (1949). *Politics among the nations.* New York: A. Knopf.

Morrione, T. J. (1975). Symbolic interactionism and social action theory. *Sociology and Social Research, 59*, 201-218.

Morrison, D. E., Kumar, K, Rogers, E. M. & Fliegel, F. C. (1976). Stratification and risk-taking: A further negative replication of Cancian's theory. *ASR, 41*, 912-919.

Moscovici, S. (1985). Innovation and minority influence. In *Perspectives on minority influence.* S. Moscovici, G. Mugny, & E. Van Avermaet, eds. Cambridge: Cambridge Univ. Press.

Mouzelis, N. (1976). Capitalism and the development of agriculture. *Journal of Peasant Studies, 3*, 483-492.

_____. (1990). *Back to sociological theory: The construction of social orders*. London: Macmillan.

_____. (1991). The interaction order and the micro-macro distinction. *Sociological Theory, 9,* (2) (Nov.).

_____. (1995). *Sociological theory: What went wrong? Diagnosis and remedies.* New York: Routledge.

Munch, R. (1987). *The theory of action: Towards a new synthesis going beyond Parsons.* New York: Routledge & Kegan Paul.

Murdock, S. H., et al. (1986). The farm crisis in the Great Plains: Implications for theory and policy development. *Rural Sociology, 51,* 406-435.

Murdock, S. H. & Leistritz, F. L., (Eds.). (1988). *The farm financial crisis: Socioeconomic dimensions and implications for producers and rural areas.* Boulder, CO: Westview.

Murray, H. A. (1951). Toward a classification of interactions. In *Toward a general theory of social action.* T. Parsons & E. A. Shils, ed. Cambridge, MA: Harvard Univ. Press.

Murstein, B., Ceretto, M., & MacDonald, M. G. (1977). A theory and investigation of the effect of exchange-orientation on marriage and friendship. *JMF, 39* 543-548.

Nagel, E. (1961). *The structure of science.* NYC: Harcourt Brace & World.

Namboodiri, K. (1994). *Methods of macrosociological research.* San Diego: Academic Press.

Namboodiri, K., & Corwin, R. G. (1993). *Organizational networks and interorganization relations.* Greenwich, CT: JAI Press.

Napier, T. L., Thraen, C., Gore, A., & Gore, W. (1984). Factors affecting the adoption of conventional and conservation practices in Ohio. *Journal of Soil and Water Conservation, 39,* 205-208.

Nelson, L. (1969). *Rural sociology.* Minneapolis: Univ. of Minnesota Press.

Newby, H. (1983). The sociology of agriculture: Toward a new rural sociology. *Annual Review of Sociology, 9,* 67-81.

Newby, H., Bell, C., Rose, D., & Saunders, P. (1978). *Property, paternalism, and power*. London: Hutchinson.

Newell, A. & Simon, H. A. (1972). *Human problem solving*. Englewood Cliffs, NJ: Prentice-Hall.

Norris, P. E., & Batie, S. S. (1985). Factors influencing the adoption of soil conservation practices: A Virginia case study. Paper presented at the RSS annual meeting, Virginia Polytechnic Inst. and State University, August.

North Central Rural Sociology Committee. (1955). *How farm people accept new ideas* (Publication No. 1). Ames: Iowa State Coll., Ag. Ext. Service. (1956). *Bibliography of research on: Social factors in the adoption of farm practices* (supplement to Publication No. 1). Ames: Iowa State College, Agricultural Extension Service.

_____. (1961). *Adopters of new farm ideas: Characteristics and communications behavior* (Publication No. 13). East Lansing, MI: Michigan State University, Cooperative Ext. Service.

Nowak, P. J. (1984). Adoption and diffusion of soil and water conservation practices. In *Future agricultural technology and resource conservation*, pp. 214-237. B. C. English, et al., eds. Ames: Iowa State Univ. Press.

_____. (1987). The adoption of agricultural conservation technologies: Economic and diffusion explanations. *Rural Sociology, 52*, 208-220.

Nozick, R. (1993). *The nature of rationality*. Princeton, NJ: Princeton U. Press.

Nye, F. I. (1978). Is choice and exchange theory the key? *JMF, 40* (May).

_____. (1982). *Family relationships: Rewards and costs*. Beverly Hills: Sage

Nye, F. I., with Bahr, H. M., et al. (1976). *Role structure and analysis of the family*. Beverly Hills, CA: Sage.

Nye, F. I., & Berardo, F. (1966). *Emerging conceptual frameworks in family analysis* (1st ed.). New York: Macmillan.

Nye, F. I., & Berardo, F. (1973). *The family: Its structure and interaction*. New York: Macmillan.

Nye, F. I., & Berardo, F. (Eds.). (1981). *Emerging conceptual frameworks in family analysis* (2nd ed.). New York: Praeger.

Österberg, D. (1988). *Metasociology: An inquiry into the origins and validity of social thought*. London: Oxford Univ. Press.

Office of Technology Assessment. (1986). *Technology, public policy, and the changing structure of American agriculture: A special report for the 1985 farm bill*. Washington, D.C.: U. S. Congress.

Ogburn, W. F. (1922). *Social change with respect to culture and original nature*. New York: B. W. Huebsch.

_____. (1957). Cultural lag as theory. *Sociology and Social Research, 41*, 167-174.

O'Hara, P. (1994). Out of the shadows: Women on family farms and their contribution to agriculture and rural development. In *Rural gender studies in Europe*. L. van der Plas & M Fonte, eds. Assen, Netherlands: Van Gorcum.

O'Keefe, G. F. Jr. (1973). Coorientation variables in family study. *American Behavioral Scientist, 16*, 513-536.

Orkin, M. (1987). Ideology and the interpretative foundation of science. In *Ideological beliefs in the social sciences*, pp. 80-107. Z. van Straaten, ed. Pretoria: Human Sciences Research Council (HSRC).

Osgood, C. F. & Tannenbaum, P. H. (1955). The principle of congruity in the prediction of attitude change. *Psychological Review, 62*: 42-55.

Osmond, M. W., & Martin, P. Y. (1978). A contingency model of marital organization in low income families. *JMF, 40*, 315-329.

Overington, M. A. & Zollschan, G. K. (1976). Goal formation. In *Social change: Explorations, diagnoses, and conjectures*. G. K. Zollschan & W. Hirsch, eds. New York: Wiley.

Pampel, F. Jr., & van Es, J. C. (1977). Environmental quality and issues of adoption research. *Rural Sociology, 42*, 57-71.

Parke, F. J. & Glick, P. C. (1967). Prospective changes in marriage and the family. *JMF, 29*, 249-256.

Parsons, T. (1937). *The structure of social action.* New York: McGraw-Hill. (Also published in 1948 and 1961 by the Free Press).

_____. (1940). The motivation of economic activities. In T. Parsons, *Essays in sociological theory,* pp. 50-68. Glencoe: Free Press.

_____. (1942). 'Good companion' role of women. *ASR, 7,* 604-616.

_____. (1949). The social structure of the family. In *The family: Its function and destiny,* pp. 173-201. R. N. Anshen, ed. New York: Harper & Row.

_____. (1951). *The social system.* Glencoe: Free Press.

_____. (1960). *Structure and process in modern society.* NYC: Free Press.

_____. (1961). *The structure of social action.* New York: Free Press. (Also published in 1948) (First published in 1937 by McGraw-Hill).

_____. (1963). On the concept of influence. *Public Opinion Quarterly, 27,* 55-62. (Also see his rejoinder to Bauer & Coleman comments, pp. 87-92)

_____. (1964). The prospects of sociological theory. In *Essays in sociological theory* (Rev. ed.), pp. 348-369. T. Parsons, ed. NYC: Free Press.

_____. (1969). On the concept of political power. In *Political power: A reader in theory and research,* pp. 251-284. R. Bell, D. Edwards, & R. Wagner, eds. New York: Free Press.

_____. (1970). An approach to the sociology of knowledge. In *The sociology of knowledge.* J. E. Curtis & J. W. Petras, eds. New York: Praeger.

_____. (1977). *Social systems and the evolution of action theory.* New York: Free Press.

Parsons, T., Bales, R. F., et al. (1955). *Family, socialization and interaction process.* New York: Free Press.

Parsons, T., & Shils, E. (Eds.). (1951). *Toward a general theory of social action.* Cambridge, MA: Harvard Univ. Press.

Parsons, T., Shils, E., & Bales, R. F. (Eds.). (1953). *Working papers in the theory of action.* Glencoe, IL: Free Press.

Parsons, T., Shils, E., et al. (Eds.). (1965). *Theories of society: Foundations of modern sociological theory*. New York: Free Press.

Parsons, T., & Smelser, N. (1956). *Economy and society*. Glencoe: Free Press.

Paulus, P. B. (Ed.). (1983). *Basic group processes*. New York: Springer-Verlag.

Pavlov, I. P. (1927). *Conditioned reflexes: An investigation of the physiological activity of the cerebral cortex* (1928 in U.S.; W. H. Gantt, Trans.; New York: International Publishers). Trans. by H. Milford. London: Oxford Univ. Press. (First published in 1926).

Pelz, E. B. (1958). Some factors in 'group decision.' In *Readings in social psychology* (3rd ed.). E. E. Maccoby, T. M. Newcomb & E. L. Hartley, eds. New York: Holt Rinehart & Winston.

Peotrkowski, C. S. (1979). *Work and the family system*. New York: Free Press.

Peters, R. S. (1958). *The concept of motivation*. London: Routledge & Kegan Paul.

Pfeffer, M. J. (1983). Social origins of three systems of farm production in the United states. *Rural Sociology, 48*, 540-562.

Photiadis, J. D. (1962). Motivation, contacts, and technological change. *Rural Sociology, 48*, 540-562.

Piattelli-Palmarini, M. (1994). *Inevitable illusions: How mistakes of reason rule our minds*. (M. Piattelli-Palmarini & K. Botsford, Trans.). New York: Wiley.

Pogrebin, L. C. (1983). *Family politics: Love and power on an intimate frontier*. New York: McGraw Hill.

Pope, W., Cohen, J., & Hazelrigg, L. E. (1975). On the divergence of Weber and Durkheim: A critique of Parsons' convergence thesis. *ASR, 40*.

Popper, K. R. (1959). *The logic of scientific discovery*. New York: Basic Books. (First published in 1934).

_____. (1963). *Conjectures and refutations: The growth of scientific knowledge*. London: Routledge & Kegan Paul. (First published in 1940, and in 1962 by Basic Books).

Porter, J. H., & Hamm, R. J. (1986). *Statistics: Applications for the behavioral sciences*. Monterey, CA: Brooks/Cole.

Posner, M. I. (Ed.). (1989). *Foundations of cognitive science*. Cambridge, MA: The MIT Press.

Poster, M. (1978). *Critical theory of the family*. New York: Seabury Press.

Presser, H. A. (1969). Measuring innovativeness rather than adoption. *Rural Sociology, 34*, 510-527.

Rainwater, L. (1965) *Family design*. Chicago: Aldine.

Ramsey, C. E., Polson, R. A., & Spencer, G. E. (1959). Values and the adoption of practices. *Rural Sociology, 24*, 35-47.

Rasmussen, W. D. (Ed.). (1975). *Agriculture in the U. S.: A documentary history*. New York: Random House.

_____. (1985). *Historian makes chilling comparison* (60-year comparison on farm situation), D. Kendall, March 21, Wash. DC: AP.

_____. (1989). *Taking the university to the people: Seventy five years of cooperative extension*. Ames: Iowa State Univ. Press.

_____. (1991). *Farmers, cooperatives, and USDA: A history of the Agricultural Cooperative Service*. Wash., DC: USDA.

Rasmussen, W. D., & Baker, G. L. (1979). *Price-support and adjustment programs from 1933 through 1978: A short history*. Wash., DC: USDA, Economics Statistics and Cooperative Service.

Rasmussen, W. D., Baker, G. L., & Ward, J. (1976). *A short history of agricultural adjustment, 1933-1975*. Wash., DC: USDA, Econ. Res. Serv.

Rathge, R. W., Leistritz, F. L., & Goreham, G. A. (1988). Farmers displaced in economically depressed times. *Rural Sociology, 53*, 346-356.

Redclift, M. (1986). Survival strategies in rural Europe: Continuity and change. *Sociologia Ruralis, 26*, 218-227.

_____. (1987). *Sustainable development*. London: Methuen.

Reed, M. (1985). *Redirections in organizational analysis*. London: Tavistock.

Reed, M., & Hughes, M. (Eds.). (1992). *Rethinking organizations: New directions in organization theory and analysis.* London: Sage.

Reimer, B. (1986) Women as farm labor. *Rural Sociology, 51,* 143-155.

Reinhardt, N. & Barlett, P. (1989). The persistence of family farms in U. S. agriculture. *Sociologia Ruralis, 29,* 203-225.

Rex, J. (1962). *Key problems of sociological theory.* London: Routledge & Kegan Paul.

Richardson, J. L., & Larson, O. F. (1976). Small community trends: A 50-year perspective on social-economic change in 13 New York communities. *Rural Sociology, 41,* 45-59.

Richardson, J. T., Dugan, J. R., Gray, L. N. & Mayhew, B. H. Jr. (1973). Expert power: A behavioral interpretation. *Sociometry, 36,* 302-324.

Rickson, S. T. (1995). Women and management of resources: Decision-making on the family farm. Paper presented at the RSS annual mtg., Wash., D. C.

_____. (1997). Outstanding in their field: Women in agriculture. *Current sociology, 45,* 91-133.

Riesman, D., et al. (1966). *The lonely crowd: A study in the changing American character.* New York: Doubleday.

Ringland, J. (1983). Robust multiple comparisons. *JASA, 78,* 145-151.

Ritzer, G. (1980). Social facts, social definitions, and social behavior. In *Sociology: A multiple paradigm science.* Boston: Allyn & Bacon.

_____. (1990). The current status of sociological theory: The new syntheses. In *Frontiers of social theory.* G. Ritzer, ed. NYC: Columbia Univ. Press.

_____. (1991). *Metatheorizing in sociology.* Lexington, MA: Lexington Books.

_____, (Ed.). (1992). *Metatheorizing.* Newbury Park, CA: Sage.

Rocheleau, D. E. (1994). Investigating contradictions and mysteries. In *Tools for the Field: Methodologies handbook for gender analysis in agriculture,* H. S. Feldstein & J. Jiggins, eds. West Hartford, CT: Kumarian.

Rodefeld, R. D. (1980). Farm structural characteristics: Recent trends, causes, implications, and research needs. In *Structure of agriculture and information needs regarding small farms*. L. Tweeten, et al., eds. Wash., DC: National Rural Center

Rodefeld, R. D. et al. (Eds.). (1978). *Change in rural America: Causes, consequences and alternatives*. St. Louis: C. B. Mosby.

Rodgers, R. H. (1973). *Family interaction and transaction*. Englewood Cliffs, NJ: Prentice-Hall.

_____. (1957). Personality correlates of the adoption of technological practices. *Rural Sociology, 22,* 267-268.

_____. (1958a). A conceptual variable analysis of technological change. *Rural Sociology, 23,* 136-145.

_____. (1958b). Categorizing the adopters of agricultural practices. *Rural Sociology, 23,* 345-354.

_____. (1962). Stages in the adoption process. In E. M. Rogers, *Diffusion of innovations*. New York: Free Press.

_____. (1976). Communication and development: The passing of a dominant paradigm. *Communications Research, 3,* 213-240.

_____. (1983). *Diffusion of innovations* (3rd ed.). NYC: Free Press.

Rogers, E. M., & Beal, G. M. (1958). The importance of personal influence in the adoption of technological changes. *Social Forces* (May).

Rogers, E. M., & Rogers, L. E. (1961). A methodological analysis of adoption scales. *Rural Sociology, 26,* 325-336.

Rogers, E. M. with Shoemaker, F. F. (1971). *Communication of innovations: A cross-cultural approach*. New York: Free Press.

Rogers, S. C. (1975). Female forms of power and the myth of male dominance: A model of female/male interaction in peasant society. *American Ethnologist, 2,* 727-756.

_____. (1982). The Illinois family farm project. Paper presented at the Wingspread Seminar on women's roles on North American farms. Racine, WI, 7-9 July.

Rodrigues, A., Centers, R., & Raven, B. H. (1971). Conjugal power structure: A re-examination. *ASR, 36,* 2: 264-277.

Rosenblatt, P. C. (1990). *Farming is in our blood: Farm families in economic crisis.* Ames, IA: Iowa State Univ. Press.

Rosenfeld, R. A. (1982). U. S. farm women: Their work and self-perceptions. Paper presented at Southern Sociological Society annual mtg, Memphis.

_____. (1985). *Farm women: Work, farm and family in the United States.* Chapel Hill: Univ. of North Carolina Press.

_____. (1986). U. S. farm women: Their part in farm work and decision making. *Work and Occupations, 13,* 179-202.

Ross, P. J. (1985). A commentary on research on American farm women. *Agriculture and Human Values, 2,* 19-30.

Rotter, J. B. (1967). Beliefs, Social Attitudes, and Behavior. In *Cognition, personality, and clinical psychology.* R. Jessor & S. Feshbach, eds. San Francisco: Jossey-Bass.

Ruesch, J., Block, J., & Bennett, L. (1953). The assessment of communication: A method for the analysis of social interaction. *The Jn. of Psychology, 35.*

Russell, B. (1938). *Power: A new social analysis.* London: Allen & Unwin.

Ryan, B. (1948). A study in technological diffusion. *Rural Sociology, 13.*

Ryan, B., & Gross, N. C. (1943). The diffusion of hybrid seed corn in two Iowa communities. *Rural Sociology, 8,* 15-24.

Sachs, C. E. (1983) *The invisible farmers: Women in agricultural production.* Totowa, NJ: Rowman & Allanheld.

Safillios-Rothschild, C. (1970). The study of family power structure: A review 1960-1969. *JMF, 32,* 539-552.

Sahlins, M. D. (1972). *Stone age economics.* Chicago: Aldine.

_____. (1976). *Culture and practical reason.* Chicago: U. of Chicago Press.

Saint, W. S., & Coward, E. W. (1977). Agriculture and behavioral science: Emerging orientations. *Science, 197,* 733-737.

Salamon, S. (1992). *Prairie patrimony: Family, farming, and community in the Midwest.* Chapel Hill: Univ. of North Carolina Press.

Salamon, S., & Davis-Brown, K. (1986). Middle-range farmers persisting through the agricultural crisis. *Rural Sociology, 51,* 503-512.

Salant, P. (1983). *Farm women: Contribution to farm and family.* (Ag. econ. research report No. 140). Wash., DC: Econ. Res. Serv., USDA.

Salant, P. & Waller, A. J. (1995). *Guide to rural data.* Wash., DC: Island Press.

Saltzer, E. B. (1981). Cognitive moderation of the relationship between behavioral intentions and behavior. *Journal of Personality and Social Psychology, 41,* 260-271.

Saville, D. J. (1990). Multiple comparison procedures: The practical solution. *American Statistician, 44,* 174-180.

Saville, D. J., & Wood, G. R. (1991). *Statistical methods: The geometric approach.* New York: Springer-Verlag.

Sawer, B. J. (1973). Predictors of the farm wife's involvement in general management and adoption decisions. *Rural Sociology, 38,* 412-426.

Scanzoni, J. (1975). *Sex roles, life styles and child rearing: Changing patterns in marriage and the family.* New York: Free Press.

_____. (1978). *Sex roles, women's work, and marital conflict: A study of family change.* Lexington, MA: Lexington Books.

_____. (1979). Social processes and power in families. In *Contemporary theories about the family* (Vol. 1). W. Burr, R. Hill, F. Nye, & I. Reiss, eds. New York: Free Press.

_____. (1982). *Sexual bargaining: Power politics in the American marriage* (2nd ed.). Englewood Cliffs, NJ: Prentice-Hall.

_____. (1983). *Shaping tomorrow's family: Theory and policy for the 21st century.* Beverly Hills: Sage.

_____. (2000). *Designing families: The search for self and community in the information age*. Pine Forge: Sage.

Scanzoni, J., et al. (1989). *The sexual bond: Rethinking families and close relationships*. Beverly Hills, CA: Sage.

Scanzoni, J., & Szinovacz, M. (1980). *Family decision-making: A developmental sex role model*. Beverly Hills, CA: Sage.

Scheff, T. (1968). Negotiating reality: Notes on power in the assessment of responsibility. *Social Problems, 16*, 3-17.

Scheffe, H. A. (1953). A method for judging all possible contrasts in the analysis of variance. *Biometrika, 40*, 87-104.

_____. (1959). *The analysis of variance*. New York: Wiley.

Schindler-Rainman, E., & Lippitt, R. (1980). *Building the collaborative community: Mobilizing citizens for action*. Riverside, CA: U. of CA Ext.

Schroeder, E. H., Fliegel, F. C., & van Es, J. C. (1985). Measurement of the lifestyle dimensions of farming for small-scale farmers. *Rur. Soc., 50*.

Schultz, T. W. (1964). *Transforming traditional agriculture*. New Haven: Yale Univ. Press.

Schutz, A. (1965). An essay on social action theory. In *Philosophical problems of the social sciences*, pp. 53-67. D. Baybrooke, ed. NYC: MacMillan

_____. (1967a). Phenomenology and the social sciences. In *Phenomenology, The philosophy of Edmund Husserl and its interpretation*, pp. 450-472. J. J. Kockelmans, ed. Garden City, NY: Doubleday.

_____. (1967b). *The phenomenology of the social world* (G. Walsh & F. Lehnert, Trans.; Intro. by G. Walsh). Evanston, IL: Northwestern Univ. Press. (First published in 1932).

_____. (1973). Collected papers: (Vol. I) *The problem of social reality*, (Vol. II) *Studies in social theory* (M. Natanson, Ed. and Introduction). The Hague: M. Nijhoff. (First published 1932-1958).

_____. (1978). *The theory of social action: The correspondence of A. Schutz and T. Parsons* (R. Grathoff, Ed.). Bloomington, IN: Indiana Univ. Press.

Schutz, A. & Luckman, T. (1973). *The structures of the life-world* (Vol. I) (R. M. Zaner & H. T. Engelhardt, Jr., Trans.). Evanston, IL: Northwestern Univ. Press.

Schutz, A. & Luckman, T. (1989). *The structures of the life-world* (Vol. II) (R. M. Zaner & H. T. Engelhardt, Jr., Trans.). Evanston, IL: Northwestern Univ. Press.

Sciulli, D. (Ed.). (1996a). *Normative social action*. Greenwich, CT: JAI Press.

_____, (Ed.). (1996b). *Macro socio-economics: From theory to activism (a Festschrift for A. Etzioni)*. Armonk, NY: M. E. Sharpe.

Sciulli, D. & Gerstein, D. (1985). Social theory and Talcott Parsons in the 1980s. *Annual Review of Sociology, 11*, 369-387.

Scott, J., (1995). *Sociological theory: Contemporary debates*. Brookfield, VT: E. Elgar.

Searle, J. R. (1980). The intentionality of intention and action. *Cognitive Science, 4*, 47-70.

Selig, A. L. (1975). Socio-cultural intervention techniques. In *Mental health: The public health challenge*. E. J. Lieberman, ed. Washington, DC: American Public Health Assn.

_____. (1976). The myth of the multi-problem family. *American Journal. of Orthopsychiatry: A Journal of Human Behavior, 46*, 526-532.

_____. (1977). *Making things happen in communities*. San Francisco: R & E Research Associates.

Sewell, W. H. Jr. (1987). Theory of action, dialectic, and history: Comment on Coleman. *AJS, 93*, 166-172.

Shaffer, J. P. (1977). Multiple comparisons emphasizing selected contrasts: An extension and generalization of Dunnett's procedure. *Biometrics, 33*.

Sharrock, W. W., & Watson, D. R. (1984). What's the point of 'rescuing motives?' *British Journal of Sociology, 35*, 435-451.

Sharrock, W. W., & Watson, D. R. (1986). Relocating motives. *British Journal of Sociology, 37*, 581-583.

Shaw, M. E. (1955). A comparison of two types of leadership in various communication nets. *Journal of Abnormal and Social Psychology, 50*.

Shaw, M. & Costanzo, P. (1982). *Theories of social psychology* (2nd Ed.). New York: McGraw-Hill.

Sheldon, E. B. (Ed.). (1973). *Family economic behavior: Problems and prospects*. Philadelphia: J. B. Lippincott.

Sherman, S. J., Judd, C. M., & Park, B. (1989). Social cognition. *Annual Review of Psychology, 40*, 281-326.

Shibutani, T. (1966). *Improvised news: A sociological study of rumor*. Indianapolis: Bobbs-Merrill.

_____. (1970). On the personification of adversaries. In *Human nature and collective behavior: Papers in honor of Herbert Blumer*, pp. 223-233. T. Shibutani, ed. New Brunswick, NJ: Transaction.

Shiflett, S. C. (1973). The contingency model of leadership effectiveness: Some implications of its statistical and methodological properties. *Behavioral Science, 18*, 429-440.

Shoemaker, P. K. & Thorpe, A. C. (1963). Financial decision-making as reported by (100) farm families in Michigan. *Quarterly Bulletin, 46*, (November) (Michigan State University).

Shorter, E. (1975). *The making of the modern family*. New York: Basic Books.

Simmel, G. (1910). How is society possible? *AJS, 16*, 372-391.

_____. (1950). *The sociology of Georg Simmel* (K. H. Wolff, Ed., Tran., & Intro.). Glencoe, IL: Free Press. (First published 1908).

_____. (1964). *Conflict; The web of group-affiliations*. (K. H. Wolff & R. Bendix, Trans.) NYC: Free Press. (First published 1908, 1922 &1923).

_____. (1968). *The conflict in modern culture, and other essays* (K. P. Etzkorn, Tran.). NYC: Teachers Coll. Press. (First published 1909-1918)

_____. (1971). *On individuality and social forms; selected writings* (D. N. Levine, Ed.; D. N. Levine, et al. Trans). Chicago: Univ. of Chicago Press. (First published 1903 to 1918 and posthumously).

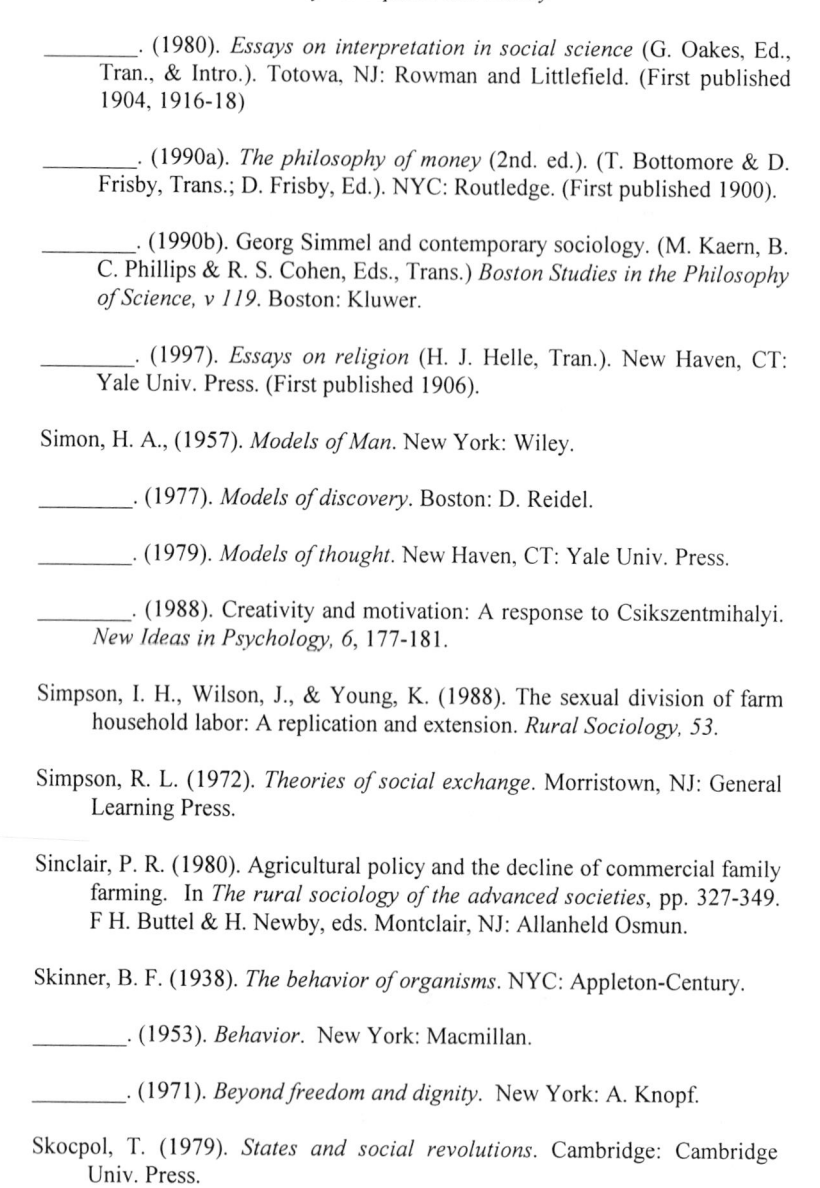

_____. (1980). *Essays on interpretation in social science* (G. Oakes, Ed., Tran., & Intro.). Totowa, NJ: Rowman and Littlefield. (First published 1904, 1916-18)

_____. (1990a). *The philosophy of money* (2nd. ed.). (T. Bottomore & D. Frisby, Trans.; D. Frisby, Ed.). NYC: Routledge. (First published 1900).

_____. (1990b). Georg Simmel and contemporary sociology. (M. Kaern, B. C. Phillips & R. S. Cohen, Eds., Trans.) *Boston Studies in the Philosophy of Science, v 119.* Boston: Kluwer.

_____. (1997). *Essays on religion* (H. J. Helle, Tran.). New Haven, CT: Yale Univ. Press. (First published 1906).

Simon, H. A., (1957). *Models of Man.* New York: Wiley.

_____. (1977). *Models of discovery.* Boston: D. Reidel.

_____. (1979). *Models of thought.* New Haven, CT: Yale Univ. Press.

_____. (1988). Creativity and motivation: A response to Csikszentmihalyi. *New Ideas in Psychology, 6,* 177-181.

Simpson, I. H., Wilson, J., & Young, K. (1988). The sexual division of farm household labor: A replication and extension. *Rural Sociology, 53.*

Simpson, R. L. (1972). *Theories of social exchange.* Morristown, NJ: General Learning Press.

Sinclair, P. R. (1980). Agricultural policy and the decline of commercial family farming. In *The rural sociology of the advanced societies,* pp. 327-349. F H. Buttel & H. Newby, eds. Montclair, NJ: Allanheld Osmun.

Skinner, B. F. (1938). *The behavior of organisms.* NYC: Appleton-Century.

_____. (1953). *Behavior.* New York: Macmillan.

_____. (1971). *Beyond freedom and dignity.* New York: A. Knopf.

Skocpol, T. (1979). *States and social revolutions.* Cambridge: Cambridge Univ. Press.

_____. (1976). Explaining revolutions: In quest of a social-structural approach. In *The uses of controversy in sociology*, pp. 155-175. L. Coser & O. N. Larsen, eds. New York: Free Press.

Skocpol, T., & Finegold, K. (1982). State capacity and economic intervention in the early New Deal. *Political Science Quarterly, 97*, 255-278.

Skolnick, A. S. (1973). *The intimate environment.* Boston: Little, Brown.

Skolnick, A. S. & Skolnick, J. H. (Eds.). (1971). *Family in transiiton.* Boston: Little, Brown.

Skvoretz, J., & Fararo, T. J. (1989). Action structures and sociological action theory. *Journal of Mathematical Sociology, 14*, 111-137.

Skvoretz, J., Willer, J. D., & Fararo, T. J. (1993). Towards models of power development in exchange networks. *Sociological Perspectives, 36* (2).

Slocum, W. L. (1962). *Agricultural sociology: A study of sociological aspects of American farm life.* New York: Harper.

Slocum, W. L., & Brough, O. L. (1961). *Family and farm changes associated with farm and home planning in Washington* A report to the W. K. Kellogg Foundation, Washington State University, August 30.

Smale, M., Saupe, W. E., & Salant, P. (1986). Farm family characteristics and the viability of farm households in Wisconsin, Mississippi, and Tennessee. *Agricultural Economic Research, 38*, 11-27.

Small Farm Viability Project. (1977). *The family farm in California.* Sacramento: Small Farm Viability Project.

Small, M. (Ed.). (1984). *Female primates: Studies by women primatologists.* New York: A. Liss.

Smith, D. E. (1989). Sociological theory: Methods of writing patriarchy. In *Feminism and sociological theory.* R. Wallace, ed. Newbury, CA: Sage.

Smith, J. P. (1987). The social and ecological correlates of bankruptcy during the fiscal crisis, 1970-1987. *Mid-American Review of Sociology, 12*.

Sorokin, P. A, & Zimmerman, C. C. (1929). *Principles of rural-urban sociology.* New York: Holt.

Spencer, H. (1969). *The principles of sociology.* (S. Andreski, Ed.). Hamden, CT: Archon. (First published in 1874).

Sperber, I. (1990) *Fashions in science: Opinion leaders and collective behavior in the social sciences.* Minneapolis: Univ. of Minnesota Press.

Sprecher, S. (1985). Sex differences in bases of power in dating relationships. *Sex Roles, 12,* 449-462.

Sprey, J. (1975). Family power and process. In *Power in families,* pp. 61-79. R. E. Cromwell & D. H. Olson, eds. New York: Wiley.

_____, (Ed.). (1990). *Fashioning family theory: New approaches.* Newbury Park, CA: Sage.

Stacey, J. & Thorne, B. (1985). The missing feminist revolution in sociology. *Social Problems, 32,* 301-316.

Stinchcombe, A. L. (1968). *Constructing social theories.* NYC: Harcourt Brace.

Stockdale, J. D. (1977). Technology and change in United States agriculture: Model or warning? *Sociologia Ruralis, 17,* 43-58.

Stokes, C. S, & Miller, M. K. (1985). A methodological review of fifty years of research in *Rural Sociology. Rural Sociology, 50,* 539-560.

Stouffer, S. A., et al. (1949). *The American soldier: Studies in social psychology in W. W. II* (2 vols.). Princeton, NJ: Princeton Univ. Press.

Strange, M. (1988). *Family farming: A new economic vision.* Lincoln, NB: Univ. of Nebraska Press.

Stratigaki, M. (1988). Agricultural modernization and gender division of labor. *Sociologia Ruralis, 28,* 248-262.

Straus, M. A. (1958). The role of the wife in the settlement of the Columbia Basin project. *Journal of Marriage and Family Living, 20,* 59-64.

_____. (1960). Family role differentiation and technological change in farming. *Rural Sociology, 25,* 219-228.

Strauss, A. (1978). *Negotiations: Varieties, contexts, processes, and social order.* San Francisco: Jossey-Bass.

Strodtbeck, F. (1951). Husband-wife interaction over revealed differences. *ASR, 18,* 141-145.

Stryker, S. (1980). *Symbolic interactionism: A social structural version.* Menlo Park, CA: Benjamin-Cummings.

Stryker, S., & Statham, A. (1985). Symbolic interaction and role theory. In *Handbook of social psychology* (Vol. 1). G. Lindzey & E. Aronson, eds. New York: Random House.

Subcommittee of the RSS. (1952). *Sociological research on diffusion and adoption of farm practices.* (Bulletin RS-2). Lexington: Kentucky AES.

Subcommittee for the Study of Diffusion of Farm Practices. North Central Rural Sociology Committee. (1955). *How farm people accept new ideas.* (Special report 15). Ames, IA: Iowa Ag. Ext. Service.

Sudnow, D. (Ed.). (1972). *Studies of social interaction.* New York: Free Press.

Summers, G. F. (1983a). The future of rural sociology: An introduction. *The Rural Sociologist, 3,* 312-314.

_____, (Ed.). (1983b). *Technology and social change in rural areas: A festschrift for E. A. Wilkening.* Boulder, CO: Westview.

Suppe, F. (1977). *The structure of scientific theories* (2nd ed.). Urbana, IL: Univ. of Illinois Press.

Swanson, Guy E. (1978). Travels through inner space: Family structure and openness to absorbing experiences. *AJS, 83,* 890-919.

Swanson, L. E. (Ed.). (1988). *Agriculture and community change in the U. S.* Boulder, CO: Westview.

Szinovacz, M. E. (1987). Family power. In *Handbook of marriage and the family.* M. B. Sussman & S. K. Steinmetz, eds. New York: Plenum.

Sztompka, P. (1979). *Sociological dilemmas: Toward a dialectic paradigm.* New York: Academic Press.

_____. (1983). Social development: The dialectics of theory and action. *Reports on Philosophy, 7,* 79-98.

_____. (1984). The global crisis and the reflexiveness of the social system. *International Journal of Comparative Sociology, 25*, 45-58.

_____, (Ed.). (1991). *Society in action: The theory of social becoming.* Chicago, IL: Univ. of Chicago Press.

_____, (Ed.). (1994a). *Agency and structure: Reorienting social theory* (from presentation in Madrid, 1990). Langhorne, PA: Gordon & Breach.

_____, (Ed.). (1994b). *The sociology of social change.* Cambridge, MA: Blackwell.

Taeuber, I. B. (1969). Change and transition in family structure. In *The family in transition,* Fogarty Int'l. Ctr. Proceedings No. 3. Bethesda, MD: NIH.

Tallman, I., & Miller, G. (1974). Class differences in family problem solving: The effects of verbal ability, hierarchical structure, and role expectations. *Sociometry, 37,* 13-37.

Tannenbaum, A. S., & Allport, F. H. (1956). Personality structure and group structure: An interpretive study of their relationship through an event-structure hypothesis. *Journal of Abnormal Social Psychology, 53.*

Tannenbaum, A. S., et al. (1974) *Hierarchy in organizations* (an international comparison). San Francisco: Jossey-Bass.

Tannenbaum, A. S., & Rozgonyi, T. (1986) *Authority and rewards in organizations.* Ann Arbor, MI: Survey Res. Ctr, Inst. for Social Research.

Taylor, C. C. et al. (1949). *Rural life in the United States.* NYC: A. Knopf.

Taylor, G. W. (1962). An analysis of certain social and psychological factors differentiating successful from unsuccessful farm families. *Rur. Soc., 27.*

Tedeschi, J. T. (Ed.). (1972). The *social influence processes.* Chicago: Aldine.

_____, (Ed.). (1974). *Perspectives on social power* (Albany symposium on power and influence, 1971). Chicago: Aldine.

Tedeschi, J. T., & Felson, R. B. (1994). *Violence, aggression, coercive actions.* Hyattsville, MD: American Psychological Association.

Tedeschi, J. T., & Lindskold, S. (1976). *Social psychology: Interdependence, interaction and influence.* New York: Wiley.

Thibaut, J. W., & Kelley, H. H. (1959). *The social psychology of groups.* New York: Wiley.

Thomas, R. J. (1985). *Citizenship, gender, and work: Social organization of industrial agriculture.* Berkeley: Univ. of California Press.

Thomas, W. I. (1927). The behavior pattern and the situation. *ASA Publications, 22,* 1-13.

Tigges, L. M., & Rosenfeld, R. A. (1987). Independent farming: Correlates and consequences for women and men. *Rural Sociology, 52,* 345-364.

Tilly, L. A. & Scott, J. W. (1987). *Women, work, and family.* NYC: Routledge.

Tönnies, F. (1963). *Community and society (Gemeinschaft und Gesellschaft).* (C. P. Loomis, Ed. & Tran.) NYC: Harper & Row. (First published 1889).

Tong, R. (1989). *Feminist thought.* Boulder, CO: Westview.

Tukey, J. W. (1949). Comparing individual means in the analysis of variance. *Biometrics, 5,* 99-114.

_____. (1977). *Exploratory data analysis.* Reading, MA: Addison-Wesley.

Turner, J. H. (1983). Theoretical strategies for linking micro and macro processes: An evaluation of seven approaches. *Western Sociological Review, 14,* 4-15.

_____. (1985). The concept of 'action' in sociological analysis. In *Social Action.* G. Seebass & R. Tuomela, eds. Dordrecht: D. Reidel.

_____. (1987a). Analytical theorizing. In *Social theory today,* pp. 156-194. A. Giddens & J. H. Turner, eds. Stanford: Stanford Univ. Press.

_____. (1987b). Toward a sociological theory of motivation. *ASR, 52.*

_____. (1988). *A theory of social interaction.* Stanford: Stan. Univ. Press.

_____. (1989a). The disintegration of American sociology. *Sociological Perspectives, 32,* 419-433.

_____. (1990). The misuse and use of metatheory. *Sociological Forum, 5.*

_____. (1991). *The structure of sociological theory* (5th ed.). Belmont, CA: Wadsworth.

_____, (Ed.). (1989b). *Theory building in sociology: Assessing theoretical cumulation*. Newbury Park, CA: Sage.

Turner, R. H. (1962). Role-taking: Process vs. conformity. In *Human behavior and social process*. A. Rose, ed. Boston: Houghton Mifflin.

_____. (1978). The role and the person. *AJS, 84*, 1-23.

Turner, S. P., & Turner, J. H. (1990). *The impossible science: An institutional analysis of American sociology*. Newbury Park, CA: Sage.

U. S. Dept. of Agriculture. (1958). *Federal grant research at the state agricultural experiment stations: Projects on rural life studies, Part 20*. Wash., DC: Ag. Research Service, USDA.

_____. (1979). *Structure issues of American agriculture*. Wash., DC: Economics, Statistics, and Cooperatives Service, USDA.

_____. (1981). *A time to choose*. Washington, DC: USDA.

_____. (1985). *Family economics review*. Washington, DC: Economic Research Service, USDA.

_____. (1987). *The U. S. farm sector: How is it weathering the 1980s?* Ag. information bulletin No. 506. Wash., DC: U.S. Govt. Printing Office.

Vail, D. (1982). Exploring the rural political economy of the United States: family farms in the web of community. *Antipode, 14*, 26-38.

Valkonen, T. (1970). On the theory of diffusion of innovations. *Sociologia Ruralis, 10*, 162-179.

Van Den Berghe, P. L. (1963). Dialectic and functionalism: Toward a theoretical synthesis. *ASR, 28*: 695-705.

van Es, J. C., & Tsoukalas, T. (1987). Kinship arrangements and innovativeness: A comparison of Palouse and Prairie findings. *Rural Sociology, 52*.

Vogeler, I. (1981). The case for agrarian democracy. In *The myth of the family farm: Agribusiness domination of U. S. agriculture*. Boulder, CO: Westview.

Wagner, D. G. (1984). *The growth of sociological theories.* Beverly Hills: Sage

Walker, H. A., & Cohen, B. P. (1985). Scope statements: Imperatives for evaluating theory. *ASR, 50,* 288-301.

Wallace, R. (Ed.). (1989). *Feminism and sociological theory* (Key issues in sociological theory, No. 4). Newbury Park, CA: Sage.

Walster, E. (see Hatfield).

Warner, R. S. (1978). Toward a redefinition of action theory: Paying the cognitive element its due. *AJS, 83,* 1317-1349, (with commentaries by T. Parsons, pp. 1350-1358, and W. Pope & J. Cohen, pp. 1359-1367).

Warner, W. L. (1953). *American life: Dream and reality.* Chicago: Univ. of Chicago Press.

Wayland, S. R. (1951). *Social patterns of farming.* New York: Seminar on Rural Life, Columbia University.

Weber, M. (1946). *From Max Weber: Essays in sociology* (reprinted 1958) (H. Gerth & C. W. Mills, Trans.). New York: Oxford Univ. Press. (First published 1918).

_____. (1947). *The theory of social and economic organization* (A. M. Henderson & T. Parsons, Trans.; T. Parsons, Ed.). New York: Simon & Schuster. (First published 1922, & as Vol. 3 of *Grundusa & Soziaoekonimik,* in collaboration with others).

_____. (1949). *The methodology of the social sciences* (E. A. Shils & H. A. Finch, Trans.). NYC: Free Press. (First published 1904, 1905, & 1917).

_____. (1968a). The economy and the arena of normative and defacto powers. In *Economy and society: An outline of interpretive sociology* (E. Fischoff, et al., Trans.; G. Roth & C. Wittich, Eds.). New York: Bedminster Press. (First published 1914).

_____. (1968b). Conceptual exposition. In *Economy and society: An outline of interpretive sociology* (E. Fischoff et al., Trans.; G. Roth & C. Wittich, Eds.). New York: Bedminster Press. (First published 1920).

_____. (1969). *Basic concepts in sociology* (H. P. Secher, Intro. & Tran.) NYC: Citadel Press. (First published 1922, in Wirtschaft & Gesellschaft).

_____. (1976). *The Protestant ethic and the spirit of capitalism* (2nd. ed.) (T. Parsons, Tran.; A. Giddens, Intro.). London: Allen & Unwin. (First published 1905).

_____. (1983). *Max Weber on capitalism, bureaucracy, and religion* (S. Andreski, Ed. & Tran.). (First published 1921) Boston: Allen & Unwin.

Wells, R. H., & Picou, J. S. (1982). *American sociology: Theoretical and methodological structure*. Washington, D. C.: Univ. Press of America.

Wenger, M. G., & Buck, P. D. (1988). Farms, families, and super-exploitation: An integrative reappraisal. *Rural Sociology, 53*, 460-472.

Wexler, P. (1977). Comment on R. Turner's 'The real self: from institution to impulse.' *AJS, 83*, July: 178-184.

Whatmore, S. (1988). From women's roles to gender relations: Developing perspectives in the analysis of farm women. *Sociologia Ruralis, 28*.

_____. (1991). *Farming women: Gender, work and family enterprise*. London: Macmillan.

_____. (1994). Theoretical achievements and challenges in European rural gender studies. In *Rural gender studies in Europe*. L. van der Plas & M. Fonte, eds. Assen, Netherlands: Van Gorcum.

White, R. K., & Lippitt, R. (1960). *Autocracy and democracy, An experimental inquiry*. New York: Harper.

Whyte, W. F. (1943). *Street corner society*. Chicago: Univ. of Chicago Press.

Wilcox, R. R. (1987). *New statistical procedures for the social sciences: Modern solutions to basic problems*. Hillsdale, NJ: L. Erlbaum.

Williams, T. T., (Ed.). (1985). *Strategy for the survival of small farmers*. Tuskegee, AL: Human Resources Development Center, Tuskegee Inst.

Wilkening, E. A. (1949). A sociopsychological study of the adoption of improved farming practices. *Rural Sociology, 14*, 68-69.

_____. (1950). A sociopsychological approach to the study of the acceptance of innovations in farming. *Rural Sociology, 15*, 352-364.

_____. (1953). *Adoption of improved farm practices as related to family factors*. AES Research Bulletin 183. Madison, WI: Univ. of Wis.

_____. (1954). Change in farm technology as related to familism, family decision-making, and family integration. *ASR, 19,* 29-37.

_____. (1958a). Joint decision-making in farm families as a function of status and role. *ASR, 23,* 187-192.

_____. (1958b). An introductory note on the social aspects of practice adoption. *Rural Sociology, 23,* 97-102.

_____. (1981a). *Farm husbands and wives in Wisconsin: Work roles, decision-making, and satisfactions, 1962 and 1979*. Research report R3147. Madison, WI: AES, CAL, University of Wisconsin.

_____. (1981b). Farm families and family farming. In *The family in rural society*, pp. 27-37. R. T. Coward & W. M. Smith, Jr., eds. Boulder, CO: Westview.

Wilkening, E. A., & Ahrens, N. (1979). Involvement of wives in farm tasks as related to characteristics of the farm, the family, and work off the farm. Paper presented at the RSS annual meeting, Burlington, VT, Aug.

Wilkening, E. A., & Bharadwaj, L. K. (1967). Dimensions of aspirations, work roles, and decision-making among farm husbands and wives in Wisconsin. *JMF, 29,* 703-711.

Wilkening, E. A., & Bharadwaj, L. K. (1968). Aspirations and task involvement as related to decision-making among farm husbands and wives. *Rural Sociology, 33,* 30-45.

Wilkening, E. A., & Galeski, B. (Eds.). (1987). *Family farming in Europe and America*. Boulder, CO: Westview.

Wilkening, E. A., & Guerrero, S. (1969). Consensus in aspirations for farm improvements and adoption of farm practices. *Rural Soc., 34,* 182-196.

Wilkening, E. A., Tully, J. & Presser, H. (1962). Communication and acceptance of recommended farm practices among dairy farmers in Northern Victoria. *Rural Sociology, 27,* 116-197.

Wilkinson, M. L. (1977). Yes Virginia, propositions can be derived from systems theory. Paper presented at NCFR theory construction workshop, annual NCFR meetings, San Diego, CA.

Willer, D. (1967). *Scientific sociology: Theory and method.* Englewood Clliffs, NJ: Prentice-Hall.

_____. (1984). Analysis and composition as theoretic procedures. *Journal of Mathematical Sociology, 10,* 241-270.

_____. (1987). *Theory and experimental investigation of social structure.* New York: Gordon & Breach.

Willer, D., & Brennan, J. S. (1981). Can formal theory integrate experimental and historical research? Paper presented at ASA annual mtg., Toronto.

Willer, D., & Webster, Jr., M. (1970). Theoretical concepts and observables. *ASR, 35,* 748-757.

Williams, B. O. (1939). The impact of mechanization of agriculture on the farm population of the South. *Rural Sociology, 4,* 300-311.

Wilson, J. (Ed.). (1987). *Current perspectives in social theory* (Vol. 8). Greenwich, CT: JAI Press.

Wilson, T. P. (1970a). Conceptions of interaction and forms of sociological explanation. *ASR, 35,* 697-710.

_____. (1970b). Normative and interpretative paradigms in sociology. In *Understanding everyday life: Toward the reconstruction of sociological knowledge,* pp. 64-83. J. D. Douglas, ed. Chicago: Aldine.

Wilson, W H. (1912). *The evolution of the country community.* Boston: Pilgrim Press.

Wimberley, R. C. (1987). Dimensions of U. S. agristructure: 1969-1982. *Rural Sociology, 52,* 445-461.

Winch, R. F. (1977). Is influence based on altruism or exchange? In R. W. Winch, *Familial organization: A quest for determinants.* NYC: Free Press.

Winer, B. J. (1971). *Statistical principles in experimental design (2nd* ed.) New York: McGraw-Hill.

Wolf, S. (1985). Manifest and latent influence of majorities and minorities. *Journal of Personality and Social Psychology, 48,* 899-908.

Wolfe, D. M. (1959). Power and authority in the family. In *Studies in social power*, pp. 99-117. D. Cartwright, ed. Ann Arbor, MI: Inst. for Soc. Res.

Wolff, K. H. (1970). The Sociology of knowledge and sociological theory. In *The sociology of knowledge.* J. E. Curtis & J. W. Petras, eds. NYC: Praeger.

Wollstonecraft, M. (1975). *Vindication of the rights of woman.* Baltimore, MD: Penguin Books. (First published in 1792.)

Wood, R., & Bandura, A. (1989). Social cognitive theory of organizational management. *Academy of Management Review, 14,* 361-384.

Woodward, J. (1958). *Management and technology.* London: HMSO.

_____. (1965). *Industrial organizations: Theory and practice.* New York: Oxford Univ. Press.

Wright, E. O. (1978). *Class, crisis, and the state.* London: New Left Books.

_____. (1997). *Class counts: Comparative studies in class analysis.* In series: *Studies in Marxism & social theory.* NYC: Cambridge Univ. Press.

_____, (Ed.). (1998). *Recasting egalitarianism: New rules for communities, states and markets,* by S. Bowles & H. Gintis. NYC: Verso.

Wrong, D. (1961). The oversocialized conception of man in modern society. *ASR, 26,* 187-193.

_____. (1979). *Power, its forms, bases, and uses.* NYC: Harper & Row.

_____. (1988). *Power, its forms, bases, and uses* (2nd ed.). Chicago: University of Chicago Press.

_____. (1994). *The problem of order: What unites and divides society?* New York: Free Press.

Yamagishi, T., & Cook, K. S. (1990). Power relations in exchange networks: A comment on 'network exchange theory'. *ASR, 55,* 297-300.

Yandell, B. S. (1997). *Practical data analysis for designed experiments.* New York: Chapman & Hall.

Yates, J. F. (Ed.). (1992). *Risk taking behavior.* New York: Wiley.

Young, R. (1959). Observations on adoption studies reported in June, 1958, issue. *Rural Sociology, 24,* 272-274.

Zaltman, G., Kotler P., & Kaufman, I. (Eds.). (1972). *Creating social change.* New York: Holt Rinehart & Winston.

Zander, A. (1971). *Motives and goals in groups.* New York: Academic Press.

_____. (1977). *Groups at work.* San Francisco: Jossey-Bass.

Zetterberg, H. (1965). *On theory and verification in sociology* (3rd ed.). New York: Bedminster.

Znaniecki, F. (1967). *Social actions.* New York: Russell & Russell.

Zollschan, G. K., & Hansen, D. A. (1969). On motivation: Toward socially pertinent foundations. In *Explorations in sociology and counseling.* D. A. Hansen, ed. Boston: Houghton Mifflin.

Zollschan, G. K., & Hirsch, W. (Eds.). (1964). *Explorations in social change.* London: Routledge & Kegan Paul.

Zollschan, G. K. & Overington, M. A. (1976). Motivational ascription. In *Social change: Explorations, diagnoses and conjectures.* G. K. Zollschan & W. Hirsch, eds. New York: Wiley.

Index of Authors for Part Two
(Cross referenced to Index for Part One, and referenced to Notes for Part Two)

Abd-Ella M. M., 120
Adams, G. R., 260n
Ahrens, N., 139
Ajzen, I., 87, 261n
Anthias, F., 93, 95
Alexander, S. J., 260n
Allport, F. H., 257n, 265n
Althusser, L., 259n
Bandura, A., 257n
Bales, R. F., 87, 262n
Barlett, P. F., 125, 220, 227, 263n
Barnlund, D. C., 258n
Bierstedt, R., 260n
Beal, G. M., 94, 120
Beers, H. W., 101
Bennett, J. W., 101, 125
Berardo, F., 123, 127
Bergson-Larsson, M., 125
Bharadwaj, L. K., 119, 131
Bianchi, S. M., 124
Blalock, H. M., Jr., 140, 257n
Blau, P. M., 87, 125
Blood, R. O., Jr., 101, 123, 128, 221, 257n-258n
Blumer, H., 87, 125
Bohlen, J. M., 94, 120
Bokemeier, J. L., 125, 227, 258n
Bott, E., 258n
Boulding, K., 125
Bozeman, B., 258n
Brewster, D. E., 125, 263n
Broderick, C. B., 126, 258n
Broom, L. A., 94
Brough, O. L., 223
Brown, E. J., 119
Buckley, W., 87, 94. 126
Burr, W. R., 123, 258n

Burt, M. R., 178
Bush, A. J., 125, 195
Buttel, F. H., 258n
Campbell, B. K., 258n
Campbell, C., 93, 95
Cancian, F., 121
Carlson, J. E., 120, 124
Cell, C. P., 130
Centers, R., 123
Ceretto, M., 262n
Chamala, S., 227
Christensen, R., 258n
Claridge, C. L., 227
Cochrane, W. W., 227
Cohen, B. P., 149-150, 265n
Cohen, J., 115, 136-137, 259n
Cohen, P., 136-137, 259n
Coleman, J. S., 87, 152
Collins, B. E., 259n
Collins, R., 101, 260n
Cook, K. S., 266n
Copp, J. H., 119
Cottrell, L., 94
Coughenour, C. M., 125, 137
Cowan, P. A., 128, 259n
Cowles, M. L., 128
DeWitt, M. R., 105, 126-127
Dillman, D. A., 120
Di Tomaso, N., 259n
Donovan, J., 124
Dorner, P., 120, 131, 223
Duncan, R., B., 128
Duncan, O. D., 140
Dunn, T., 259n
Durkheim, E., 88, 93, 99
DuVall, E., 128
Edwards, A. L., 265n

Elder, G. H., Jr., 128
Emerson, R. M., 259n
Fararo, T. J., 152
Farrington, K., 126
Ferber, R., 101, 259n
Festinger, L. A., 88, 94
Fiedler, F. E., 141
Fishbein, M., 88, 261n
Fliegel, F. C., 119, 121
Flora, C. B., 259n
Flora, J. L., 259n
Foss, G. E., 126
French, J. R. P., Jr., 88, 105-106, 164, 173, 176, 259n
Gasson, R., 125, 259n
Gatlin, R., 101
Gillespie, D., 123
Gillespie, G. W., Jr., 258n
Giddens, A., 264n
Goffman, E., 94
Goldman, E., 124
Goreham, G. A., 263n
Gray, I., 259n
Gray, P. G., 137
Gross, N. C., 119
Guerero, S., 119
Gullotta, T. P., 260n
Hage, J., 88, 93, 128, 150-152, 219-220
Hall, R. H., 260n
Hamilton, H., 119
Haney, W. G., 101, 125
Hannan, D. F., 101 223
Harding, S., 101, 260n
Hareven, T. K., 128
Hartsock, N., 123
Hassard, J., 260n
Hays, W. L., 138
Hechter, M., 260n
Heider, F., 88, 94
Hetherington, M., 128
Hill, R., 101, 123, 128, 259n-260n
Hiller, D. V., 124
Hobbes, T., 88, 260n, 266n

Hochschild, A., 124
Hoffman, D. K., 260n
Hoiberg, 120
Homans, G. C., 88, 125
Huber, J., 260n
Iannello, K. P., 123, 260n
Jaeger, C. M., 137
James, W., 89, 125
Jensen, J., 125
Johnson, D. E., 130
Johnston, C., 124
Kanter, R. M., 260n
Katsiaouni, L. A., 101, 223
Katz, E., 119
Kelly, M. P., 93, 95
Kemper, T. D., 260n
Kenkel, W. F., 260n
Kennedy, J. J., 195
Keppel, G., 261n
Kirkpatrick, E. L., 128
Klein, D., 259n
Knop, E., 227
Knop, S., 227
Knowles, J. B., 101
Kohl, S. B., 261n
Komarovsky, M., 124, 261n
Larson O. G., 258n
Lawrence, P. R., 128
Leistritz, F. L., 263n
Levin, M. L., 119
Lewin, K., 89, 128, 228, 261n, 263n
Linn, J. G., 130
Lionberger, H. F., 123
Lippitt, R., 89, 228, 261n, 263n
Liska, A., 261n
Lorenz, K., 261n
Lorsch, J. W., 128
Lyson, T. A., 223, 261n
McDonald, G. W., 124
MacDonald, M. G., 262n
Maman, M., 261n
Marquardt, M., 131
Martin, P. Y., 262n-263n
Marx, K., 89, 93, 99

Mead, G. H., *89*, 93-94, 99, 125
Meeker, B. F., 128, 151, 261n-262n
Menzel, H., 137
Merton, R. K., *89*, 93-94, 152
Michener, H. A. 178
Mills, C. W., 93
Monroe, P., 227
Moore, K. M., 262n
Morgan, G., 260n
Moreno, J. L., 262n
Morrison, D. E., 227
Mouzelis, N., 93, 262n
Murstein, B., 262n
Nowak, P. J. 121
Nye, F. I., 123, 127
Office of Technological Assessment, 262n
O'Hara, P., 125
O'Keefe, G. F. Jr., 262n
Orkin, M., 263n
Osmond, M. W., 262n-263n
Pampel, F., Jr., 121, 123
Parsons, T., *89*, 93, 99
   AGIL, 125
   Equilibrium theory, 93-94
   Functionalist school, 101, 116
   pattern variables, 151, 173
   258n-259n, 263n, 275n, 268n
Pelz, E. B., 263n
Pennock, J. L., 137
Philliber, W. W., 124
Phillips, E., 259n
Popper, K. R., *89*, 263n
Posner, M. I., 263n
Powers, C. H., 219-220
Pym, D., 260n
Rainwater, L., 124
Rasmussen, W. D., 263n
Rathge, R. W., 263n
Raven, B. H., *89*, 105-106, 123, 164, 173, 176, 259n
Reinhardt, N., 263n
Reise, I. L., 123
Rickson, S. T., 101, 125
Rocheleau, D. E., 227
Rodrigues, A., 123
Rogers, E. M., 94, 116, 119-123, 137, 140, 223
Rogers, L. E., 121-123
Rosenfeld, R. A., 125, 227
Russell, B., 266n
Ryan, B., 119
Sachs, C. E., 125, 264n
Saville, D. J., 264n
Sawer, B. J., 125, 223
Scanzoni, J., 101, 123-124, 264n
Scheffe, H. A., 264n
Scott, J., 93
Selig, A. L., 264n
Sewell, W. H., Jr., 264n
Sill, M. L., 119
Simmel, G., 93, 99
Skvoretz, J., 152
Slocum, W. L., 120, 223, 264n
Smith, J., 126, 258n
Spain, D., 124
Sperber, I., 93
Sprecher, S., 265
Strange, M., 227
Summers, G, F., 223
Szinovacz, M. E., 101, 124, 264n
Tait, J. L., 258n
Tate, T. H., 261n
Tannenbaum, A. S., 265n
Tong, R., 124
Tough, R., 128
Tukey, 258n
Turner, J. H., 265n
U. S. Dept. of Agriculture, 265n
van Es, J. C., 121, 123
Vogeler, I., 125
Walker, H. A., 149-150, 265n
Warren, R. D., 120
Weber, M., *90*, 93, 99
Weitzel-O'Neill, P. A., 261n-262n
Whatmore, S., 101, 125, 265n
White, R. K., *90*, 228, 261n, 263n
Wilcox, R. R., 265n

Wilkening, E. A.,
 innovativeness in farming,
 94, 113
 ...*and family factors,* 119, 128,
 130-131
 ...*and the wife's role,* 101, 120,
 125, 139, 223, 227
Wilkinson, M. L., 126, 258n
Wilson, T. P., *90,* 265n
Winer, B. J., 195

Wolfe, D. M., 101, 123, 128, 221,
 257n-258n
Wollstonecraft, M., 124
Wood, G. R., 264n
Woodward, J., 151
Wrong, D., 260n, 265n-266n
Yamagishi, T., 266n
Yandell, B. S., 266n
Young, R., 152
Zedeck, S., 261n

Index of Topics for Part Two
(Includes references to Notes for Part Two)

Actor(s), 95-96, 99, 178, 258n
   (Bokemeier), 264n (Sewell)
   cognitions of, 125, 128, 140, 152,
     154-155, 201
   transitions of, 110, 158-160, 164,
     168-169
   See also Social entity
Attitude(s), *as cognitions,* 153, 156
   and system change, 167-168, 170
     176-177
   husband's, 199, 203
Assertive wife, *See* Dimensions...
Aware(ness), 153, 155, 157, 182-183
Beliefs, 163, 167-168, 170, 176-177,
   197, 257n (Bandura)
Causal analysis, 110, 123, 176, 221
   and type of change, 160, 163, 201
   See also Multiple causal analysis
Cognition(s), 109-110, 125, 154-155,
   157, 192
Cognitive contingency theory of
   social action, 109-110, 178
   See also Social action, *theory of*
Cognitive inconsistency theory of
   social change, 109, 182-183
   See also Social change, *theory of*
Cognitive (response) sequence, 109-
   110, 112, 152-154, 170, 176
Collaborative wife, *See* Dimensions...
Commitment(s), occupational (plan to
   continue farming), 113-114, 134
   in design of the analysis, 192-193,
     195-198, 200-201, 203-207, 210
   ...findings of the study, 211-212,
     216-218, 224-226
   in the predictive model, 153-156,
     159-160, 172, 182-183, 187
   role..., 164, 168, 179, 189

Conditions, 110, 221, 228
   in design of the analysis, 192,
     201-202, 204
   in predictive model, 152, 154, 176
   See also Resources
Consultative wife, *See* Dimensions...
Context, 104-106, 109, 114, 121n
   (Nowak), 127-128, 138-140
   in design of the analysis, 192,
     195, 197-198, 200, 202-03
   ...findings of the study, 214,
     218-222, 225-227
   in predictive model, 153-155,
     162-163, 169, 172, 188
Contextual variables, 140, 143, 145,
   148-150, 173, 180, 195, 215
Contingent..., 109, 153-154, 192,
   176, 226
Contingency, *model,* 141 (Fiedler),
   262n (Osmond), 287n (Fiedler)
   theory, 109, 128, 152 (Hage), 176
   See also Cognitive contingency...
Controls, 94, 110, 221
   in design of the analysis, 192,
     201-202
   in predictive model, 152, 154, 176
   See also Directives
Decision-sharing, 94-95, 261n
   (Lewin, Lyson), 263n (Pelz)
   in design of the analysis, 192,
     194-195, 202-204
   ...findings of the study, 221,
     223-224, 226-227
   indicator of family type, 101-102,
     114, 135, 138, 141, 146-147, 149
   in the predictive model, 156, 165,
     169, 171-175, 184, 188
   See also Family type(s)

Dimensions of wife's farm role, 115
  assertive, 184, 188, 199-201, 205, 207 *...findings of the study,* 215-216, 218-220, 226
  collaborative, 185, 199-200, 206-207 *...findings of the study,* 213, 215-216, 218-219
  consultative, 184, 199-201, 205, 207 *...findings,* 216, 218-219
  supportive, 171-172, 185, 187-188, 199-201, 203, 205-206 *...findings,* 214-216, 218-219
  See also Wife's farm role
Directives, 97, 110, 135
  in design of analysis, 193, 196-197
  in the predictive model, 153-155, 157-158, 161-163
  See also Controls
Discomfort, 110-111, 178-179, 210
Discomfort reduction, 158, 210
Domains of social action formation, 96-97, 140
  ...cultural, 167-168, 184, 186
  ...economic, 167-168, 171, 185-186, 196, 203
  ...personal/political, 167, 171, 184, 196-197
  ...social, 168, 203
  in design of the analysis, 193, 195-199, 203, 205 *...findings,* 209-210, 218, 221, 224-226
  in predictive model, 154-156, 158, 162, 164, 167-180, 184-187
Entity, See Social entity
Family (life) cycle, 102, 106, 111, 132-133, 139, 143-150, 158, 198, 260n (Hill), 264n (Scanzoni)
Family type(s), *and decision-sharing,* 101-102, 106, 138-139, 141, 262n-263n (Osmond)
  in design of the analysis, 192, 196, 198, 201, 203-205 *...findings,* 212-213, 215-219, 225
  in predictive model, 171, 173, 187

Farm roles, See Wife's farm role
Goal(s), 96-97, 99-100, 108, 126n (Wilkenson), 128, 197, 263n (Pelz), 265n (Tannenbaum)
  in the predictive model, 153, 157, 163, 168-170, 176-177, 183, 188
Higher-order interactive effects, 140-141, 257n (Blalock)
  in design of analysis, 192, 194-204 *...findings,* 210-211, 215-222
  in the predictive model, 157, 162-163, 171, 173, 180
  See also Interactive analysis
Hypotheses, 95, 102, 117, 123, 136, 140-141
  in design of the analysis, 195, 201, 203-208 *...findings,* 216-217, 219, 221, 224
  in the predictive model, 162, 173, 182-183, 188, 190
Ideas (sources of new, including wife), 100, 108, 111, 115, 119-120, 131, 140
  in design of the analysis, 199-201, 205-207,
  ...findings, 210, 214, 225-226
  in the predictive model, 153, 156, 163-170, 172, 174-177, 183-185
Inconsistency,
  See Cognitive inconsistency...
Inconsistency reduction, 158
Influence, 97, 100, 112, 124, 151
  in the predictive model, 153-154, 158-161, 164, 166, 176, 178
  See also Wife's influence
Information, 97, 106, 111, 146-147 198, 214, 221, 259n (French), 262n (O'Keefe)
  in the predictive model, 154, 156, 158, 160-161, 165-170, 177, 179, 184, 186
Innovation, 112, 119-123, 194
Innovativeness in farming, 94, 121-122, 214

Interaction, *See* Social interaction,
Interactive analysis, 97, *113-117*,
 120, 125, 135-138, 143, 149-150
 model of interactive effects, 135,
  150-155, 158, 164-166, 171,
  176, 182, 189-190, 192, 226, 228
 model of multiple effects, 135, 141,
  150-152, 155, 157, *165-171,*
  173, 176, 182, 189-190, 192, 226
 in predictive model, 152, 161-162,
  178-180, 182, 184, 188, 194,
  ...*findings,* 209, 214, 226, 228
 See Higher-order interactive effects
Interests, 105, 128, 168, 185
 formation of, 153, 163, 170,
  176-177
Intentions, 153, 170, 177-179
Interpretation, 95, 155, 167
Means, 97, 106, 110, 144, 221
 in the predictive model, 153-154,
  156, 160, 167, 178-179, 183
Model of interactive effects,
 See Interactive analysis, *model of...*
Model of multiple effects,
 See Interactive analysis, *model of...*
Motivation(s), 110, 127, 139, 197,
 in the predictive model, 153, 170,
  176-178, 181
Multiple causal analysis, 163, 165,
 169, 171, 179-181, 202
Need, 103, 132, 156, 170, 184, 188
 for income, 138, 140, 167-169,
  197-198, 205, 216
Need priorities, 95-97, 193, 205, 209
 in the predictive model, 153-155,
  160-161, 169, 176-178
Nontraditional families,
 See Traditional/Nontraditional...
 See also Family type(s)
Obligations, 103, 105, 113
 in the predictive model, 153, 163,
  168-170, 177-178, 183, 191
Orientations, *(action / object),* 135,
 155, 198, 209

Path analysis, 116, 140
Path model(s), *135,* 151-152, *164,*
 182, *188, 202*
Pattern variable(s),
 in design of analysis, 194, 196,
  202, 204   ...*finding,* 226
 in the predictive model, 162,
  172-173, 176, 179-180, 189
Patterns of change, 110, 113, 168,
 178, 260n (Hill)
Patterns of interactive effect, 117, 135
 in design of analysis, 192, 196,
  201-203   ...*findings,* 214, 216,
  221, 224, 226
 in predictive model, 151, 154, 157
  165, 171-172, 182-183, 187-190
 See Higher-order interactive effects
 See also Interactive analysis
Patterns of wife influence, 95, 102,
 109, 114-116, 120, 131
 in design of the analysis, 204, 208
 ...*findings,* 217-218, 220-221,
  224, 226
 in predictive model, 156, 159, 173
 See also Hypotheses
Perception(s), 101 (Wilkening), 108,
 178 (Michener), 259n (Ferber)
 of resources, 152, 154, 157, 161,
  163, 196, 198
 *of the wife's farm role and role
  changes,* 109-110, 115, 134,
  139, 143-144, 146-147, 199
Personal formation... change... and
 transfor mation, 152, 178,
 180-181, 257n (Bandura)
Phases of (family) transition,
 See Transition, *phases of (family)*
Power, *in social relations,* 97, 101,
 126 (Farrington), 128 (Blood)
 achieved (process-oriented),
  105-106, 164-165
 ascribed (structurally determined),
  105, 164
 cits., 257n-260n, 262n, 265n-266n

Power dimensions, 100, 105-106,
    164-165, 173 (French), 176-180
  expert, 106, 177-179, 185
  informational, 106, 176-177, 179
  legitimate, 105, 176-177, 179
  referent, 106, 176-177, 179-181
  reward, 105, 176-177, 179-181
  volitional (coercion, persuasion),
    105-106, 164-165, 176-179
Power sharing, 105-108, 113, 116,
    123-125, 191-192, 203, 209, 222
  theory of, 95, 100, 107-108, 209
Power sharing in transition,
  theory of, 107-109, 112, 116, 120,
    123, 138
  in design of the analysis, 184, 191,
    201-203, 208-209
  ...findings, 218, 222, 224-225, 228
  See also Hypotheses
Power-shift(s), 176-180, 185, 189,
    192, 194, 202-203 *...finding,* 224
Predictive model,
  considerations in building, 113,
    129, 157, 173, 181-182, 194, 199
  the model, 184-188
  predictive formulas, 200-201
Recognition, 152, 157, 161, 163,
    170, 184
Reliability, 121, 137, 161, 193
Resource(s), 97, 107-108, 110-112,
    115, 120, 124-126, 128, 135, 140
  in design of analysis, 193, 196-198
  ...findings, 221-222, 225, 228
  in predictive model, 152-155,
    157, 159, 161-163, 166,
    178-179, 186-187
  See also Conditions
Responsibilities, *model,* 163, 170, 177
Responsibility(ies), wife's, for an
  essential farm task, 104, 113-115,
    131, 139, 146-147
  in design of analysis, 196, 198, 205
  in predictive model, 156, 168, 182
  See also Dimensions...,*collaborative*

Reward disappointment, 127
Risk (financial), 168, 185-186,
  in design of analysis, 192, 195,
    197-198, 200, 204-207
  ...findings, 212, 214-216, 218,
    224-226
Risks and risk factors in farming, 127,
    209, 214, 227, 263n (Rathge)
Role, *See* Wife's farm role
Role changes, 109, 114-115, 138, 140
  in design of analysis, 192-193,
    196, 202 *...findings,* 215, 222,
    224-225
  in predictive model, 164, 188
  See also Wife's farm role
Role context(s), 138-140, 143, 169,
    188, 198, 202-203
  ...findings, 221-222, 225
Role interaction assessment(s), 140,
    195, 199, 202-203, 222
Role sharing, 100-101, 105, 108-109,
    113, 116, 124-125, 127, 193
Scope conditions, 149-150, 197,
    265n (Walker)
  See also Context
Sensitivity, 153-155, 258n (Campbell)
Sensitivity thresholds, 154, 161-162,
    171, 181
Social access, 97, 153-154, 156, 160,
    178, 199, 203 *...finding,* 221
  See also Dimensions...,*supportive*
Social action, 96-97, 112, 116, 176,
    265n (Turner)
  theory of, 95, 109-112, 116, 120,
    129, 135,
  in design of analysis, 194-195,
    201-202, 205, 209
  ...findings, 210, 224-226
  in predictive model, 151-154,
    176, 178, 181, 184
Social action formation, 95, 101,
    107, 125, 129, 140
  in design of analysis, 195, 199,
    203, 205, 209-210 (cont.)

Social action formation (cont.),
 in design of analysis (cont.),
 ...findings, 218, 221-222,
 224-225, 228
 in predictive model, 153, 158,
 166-167, 184
 See also Social action, theory of
Social change, 93-94, 99, 101, 107,
 116, 125-126, 259n (DiTomaso),
 261n (Komarovski, Lewin)
 in design of analysis, 201
 ...finding, 228
 in predictive model, 152, 158,
 160-161, 163, 165-167, 169-173,
 176, 180, 184
 theory of, 95, 109-113, 116, 120
 in design of analysis, 194-195,
 201-203, 209 ...finding, 226
 in predictive model, 151, 158,
 166, 181-184
(Social) entity, 96, 154-155, 159,
 167, 181, 220
 See also Actor(s)
(Social) environment, 109, 214, 227
 changing, 126-127, 157, 185,
 188, 201, 209
(Social) interaction, 99, 101, 199,
 260n (Hill), 265n (Wilson)
 See also Role interaction assessment
Social order, 93-94, 99-100, 228
(Social) position, 127, 161, 164, 166
(Social) process(es), 93-95, 116,
 125 (Boulding), 125-126,
 128 (G. Elder), 257n (Bandura),
 259n (Cowan), 260n (Hall)
 in design of analysis, 196-197
 ...findings, 215, 222, 228
 in predictive model, 153, 157, 163,
 169, 183
Social structure, 93-95, 125-126, 155
 163, 210, 214-215, 228,
 260n (Hall), 264n (Sewell)
Social system transformation,
 See Transformation of system

Supportive wife, See Dimensions...
Theory of power sharing,
 See Power sharing, theory of
Theory of power sharing in transition,
 See Power sharing in transition,
 theory of
Theory of social action,
 See Social action, theory of
Theory of social change
 See Social change, theory of
Three-way interactions (statistical),
 See Higher-order interactive effects
Tolerance, 111, 155, 178-179
 thresholds of, 178-179
Traditional/Nontraditional families,
 101, 113-115, 138, 146, 171
 nontraditional (egalitarian)
 families, 104-106, 173, 175, 207
 traditional families, 105, 108, 131n
 (Wilkening), 159, 164, 187, 206
 in design of analysis, 192, 202-205
 ...findings, 210, 212-213,
 217-218, 220-221, 224-225
 See also Family type(s)
Transformation of system, 107, 110,
 113, 203, 209
 in predictive model, 158, 166,
 169-170, 172, 176, 181-182
 See also Transitional phases...
Transitional phases of family transformation, 102, 107, 113, 158-160,
 169-170, 177
 in design of analysis, 196, 203, 205
 disrupted traditional, 115,
 167-168, 172, 178, 182-187, 206
 emerging nontraditional, 109,
 115, 167-169, 172, 182-184,
 186-187, 207, 213
 stabilized nontraditional, 221
Uncertainty, 110-111, 155, 158,
 178-179, 210
Uncertainty reduction, 155, 158, 210
Validity, 121-122, 157, 193,
 258n (Burr)

Value(s), 153, 155, 168, 170,
  176-177, 179, 183, 187
  in design of analysis, 197-198
  cits., 126 (Wilkinson),
  131 (Wilkening), 220 (Barlett)
Wife's farm role,
  in farm decisions, 103-106, 110,
  112-115, 120, 125-127, 131,
  background analysis, 134--135,
  138, 144-146, 148-150
  in farm work (essential tasks, e.g.,
  record keeping), 104, 106,
  110-114, 126, 131
  background analysis, 134-135,
  138-139, 144-148, 150
  in predictive model, 156

Wife's farm role (cont.),
  See also Decision-sharing
  See also Responsibility, wife's,
    for an essential farm task
  See also Dimensions of wife's... role
Wife's influence, 95, 102-110, 112-
  116, 120, 127-129, 146, 149
  in design of analysis, 192, 200,
  202-208
  ...findings of study, 218, 220-222,
  224-227
  in predictive model, 156, 159,
  164-165, 169, 171-173, 179,
  182-185, 188
  See also Patterns of wife influence
  See also Influence

* * *

About the Author

M. Ross DeWitt is the pseudonym of a social scientist who began studying farm families in the mid 1950s, and constructed interlocking theories in 1960-1961 to explain the seemingly contradictory findings of those early analyses.

Practical pursuits interrupted this work until 1975, when DeWitt re-enrolled in the Sociology Ph. D. program at the University of Wisconsin, submitted the theories for review, and obtained data from a 1979 farm study to continue this research.

Family responsibilities again interrupted the work, but in 1997, after working with a methodologist to streamline the analysis, DeWitt re-enrolled and submitted: *Two patterns of wife influence on farm innovation, a study of power sharing in transition.*

The theories, and more recently the research, have been accepted in partial fulfillment of Ph. D. requirements at the University of Wisconsin-Madison. Together, they provide a methodology for studying elements of social action formation and origins of social change.

DeWitt may be contacted for consultation on specific research applications at:
dewitt.hemingway@worldnet.att.net

* * *